There Is No More Haiti

There Is No More Haiti

Between Life and Death in Port-au-Prince

GREG BECKETT

University of California Press

University of California Press, one of the most distinguished university presses in the United States, enriches lives around the world by advancing scholarship in the humanities, social sciences, and natural sciences. Its activities are supported by the UC Press Foundation and by philanthropic contributions from individuals and institutions. For more information, visit www.ucpress.edu.

University of California Press
Oakland, California

© 2019 by Greg Beckett

Library of Congress Cataloging-in-Publication Data

Names: Beckett, Greg, 1975– author.
Title: There is no more Haiti : between life and death in Port-au-Prince / Greg Beckett.
Description: Oakland, California : University of California Press, [2019] | Includes bibliographical references and index. |
Identifiers: LCCN 2018040135 (print) | LCCN 2018044010 (ebook) | ISBN 9780520971738 (epub and ePDF) | ISBN 9780520300248 (cloth : alk.paper)
Subjects: LCSH: Haiti—Social conditions—21st century. | Haiti—History—1986– | Haiti—Economic conditions—21st century.
Classification: LCC HN212.5 (ebook) | LCC HN212.5 .B434 2019 (print) | DDC 306.097294—dc23
LC record available at https://lccn.loc.gov/2018040135

Manufactured in the United States of America
26 25 24 23 22 21 20 19
10 9 8 7 6 5 4 3 2 1

Contents

Photographs

Acknowledgments

This book would not have been possible without the generosity of friends and colleagues in Haiti. To each of them, I owe a debt I may never be able to repay, but I hope this book begins to make good on that debt. I hope, too, that for those no longer with us, this book serves as a testament that they were here and that their spirit remains with us, always.

The research on which this book is based benefited from the support of the Social Sciences and Humanities Research Council of Canada and of the Department of Anthropology and the Center for Latin American Studies at the University of Chicago. The Society of Fellows at the University of Chicago provided an intellectual home for me during an important part of the research and writing. A Faculty Development Grant from Bowdoin College offered generous support for a year of writing during which this manuscript was completed. Portions of chapter 3 appeared previously in "Master of the Wood: Moral Authority and Political Imaginaries in Haiti" (*PoLAR: The Political and Legal Anthropology Review*, 2004), and portions of chapter 5 appeared previously in "A Dog's Life: Reflections on the Humanitarian Situation in Haiti" (*American Anthropologist*, 2017).

Over the years, my thinking about crisis and Haiti has been shaped by many conversations with friends and fellow scholars in Haiti, the United States, and Canada. I thank all of you for sharing your ideas with me. I would like to give special thanks to Yarimar Bonilla, who provided intellectual support at every step along the way. Her own scholarship in the Caribbean continues to inspire me. I would also like to thank the many teachers and advisors who have pushed me to think more deeply about the world, especially John Comaroff, Stephan Palmié, and Michel-Rolph Trouillot. At the University of Chicago, I benefited from an amazing group of people who were always willing to give patient and supportive feedback.

Our many conversations helped shape my thinking immeasurably. I would like to thank in particular Andrew Dilts, Ben Eastman, Reha Kadakal, and Michael Ralph. I have also benefited from the influence and support of fellow scholars of Haiti. A special thank you to Fabienne Doucet, Chelsey Kivland, Millery Polnyé, Mark Schuller, and Pierre Minn. Pierre patiently read and commented on the entire manuscript, and the end result is much the better for it.

Thank you to Deborah Thomas and Brad Weiss, both of whom provided nuanced, thoughtful, and critical readings of the manuscript. Their comments and suggestions helped make this a stronger book. Thanks also to Chris Nelson for being such a supportive writing partner and to my many friends in Write Club who cheered me along as I completed the manuscript. This book would not have been possible without the support of friends and family. I would like to thank in particular my parents, for always being there, Cameron Brohman and Luke Mattar, for years of amazing conversations about Haiti and so much more, and Derek Bessey, who helped me find a way when I felt most stuck. Many thanks as well to my editor Kate Marshall and to everyone at University of California Press who helped shepherd this book from a hazy idea to a finished product.

Finally, I owe the greatest debt to my partner Michelle, who has lived with this project as long as I have. She has been my guiding star, and she helped me to see both the forest and the trees. Her love and encouragement, her persistence and presence, and her critical mind and sharp editorial eye have meant more to me than she may ever know.

Introduction

This is a story. A story about how crisis feels, about what it is like to live your life in the midst of forces that seem destined to destroy you. But it's not the story that I set out to write. You might say that the story found me, that I am a part of this story that takes shape somewhere in the gap between hope and despair. And like all stories, it has to start somewhere.

Perhaps it is a long story, spanning centuries. A story full of war and revolution, the rise and fall of kings and countries, the end of empires and the birth of new nations. A story of a new world, of slavery and sugar, of the massive demographic displacement of the Middle Passage. It is an epic story of freedom and rebellion, but also a tragic one of debt and dependency. It is a story of people living and working on their own land, of families growing food and tending crops and making their way in the world. And yet it is also a story of a global economy so vast in scale and scope that it can only be rendered in abstract terms as the momentous struggle between capital and labor. It is a story of the transformation of the environment, the shaping of the landscape, the cutting down of trees and the planting of sugarcane or coffee or other crops destined to be consumed by people on the other side of the world. A story that ends in deforestation and soil erosion as the hills turn to stone and the dirt runs away, to be chased later by the peasants who once farmed those same eroding hills. A story of a city that grew into a monster, a city full of people fleeing what the experts call the crisis of the countryside, a city full of people desperately trying to make a living. There are many places along the way where we could begin, and there are many ways to tell such stories. This story starts here, but it could just as easily have begun somewhere else.

I went to Haiti for the first time in the summer of 2002. Before that, I studied Haitian history and culture for years. When I was in school in the 1990s,

I learned about the history of the Caribbean and about the crucial place the region holds in world history. When I learned about the Haitian Revolution, which was an event of world-shattering consequence, I remember thinking: How have I never heard about this before? Haiti was in the news often during those years, as the first democratic elections brought Jean-Bertrand Aristide to power, and then as a military coup quickly sent him into exile. Everyone was talking about what they called the "democratic transition." But no one spoke of the country's past. No one said that it was the second independent republic in the Americas and the first one to be founded by former slaves. Later I came to understand why I had not heard of the Haitian Revolution. I came to understand how the revolution had challenged the very categories and concepts of Western society, so much so that it was impossible for many people to believe that slaves had proclaimed their own freedom. I came to understand how the revolution had been "unthinkable" as it occurred and how it was later "silenced" in the historical record.[1]

Before I went to Haiti, I moved to Chicago to study anthropology. There, I learned to think about globalization and the world economy from a Caribbean point of view, from a standpoint that made a place like Haiti central to the sweeping arc of world history. I read Haitian history with an eye to the present. I read about the revolution and its aftermath, about the rise of the peasantry and the urban merchant elite, about how the U.S. military occupation of Haiti from 1915 to 1934 set the stage for the economic and political crises that followed. I read about the terror and violence of the Duvalier dictatorship, about the democratic transition and the military coups that came with it, and about the many international interventions that some Haitians call a "second occupation." I read about the many crises facing the country, about what the international community referred to as "the Haitian crisis," as if the country were inextricably defined by that word. Later, after I went to Haiti, I came to see that the country was not as exceptional—not as *odd*—as so many people seemed to say it was. It was an ordinary place, a place where "the majority of Haitians live quite ordinary lives. They eat what is for them—and for many others—quite ordinary food. They die quite ordinary deaths from quite ordinary accidents, quite ordinary tortures, quite ordinary diseases. Accidents so ordinary that they could be prevented. Tortures so ordinary that the international press does not even mention them. Diseases so ordinary that they are easily treated almost anywhere else."[2] And I came to see how the "Haitian crisis" was ordinary too, that Haiti was a place filled with ordinary crises—crises so ordinary they could easily be prevented.

And so I began to study crisis. I hadn't planned on it. You might say that crisis found me, that I was drawn into its story. I began to see how the big crises that the experts talked about were not exceptional events, nor were they located in abstract places like the economy or the state. Rather, I began to see how crisis was a very personal thing, an intimate fact of life, that it was something that happened to people, that it was ever present and everywhere. I came to see just how *ordinary* crisis could be, how it could come to reside in your body, your house, your neighborhood, in your daily routines and habits. How it could become a way of being in the world. I came to understand how people talked about crisis and how, in talking about it, they folded it into their everyday lives as something that they lived with and sometimes died from.[3]

But before all of that, two things happened. The first thing that happened is that I met a forest. The second thing that happened is that I met a man named Manuel.

AN ARRIVAL OF SORTS

I have sometimes felt that doing ethnographic fieldwork is a bit like finding yourself in someone else's dream. The dream has its own logic and carries you along in ways you cannot imagine and might not expect. Anthropologists often joke that their research projects chose them, rather than the other way around. It certainly can happen that way when you are open to the possibility of being invited into other peoples' lives.

Before I left for my first trip in 2002, I had been researching the history of anthropology in Haiti. During the U.S. occupation of 1915–34, more and more people began to travel to and write about the country. I found myself reading a series of letters written between two of the first American anthropologists to work in Haiti, Melville Herskovits and Katherine Dunham. Herskovits had broken new ground on the study of African diasporic cultures by challenging the assumption that the populations brought to the New World as slaves had lost their cultural heritage. Slavery and colonial rule had destroyed much, to be sure, but there remained hidden continuities or "survivals" that, in turn, had helped form the foundation of the new creole or syncretic cultures, languages, and religions that emerged on the margins of the slave plantation system. Herskovits saw Haiti as an important part of that story, since slaves had won their freedom much earlier than anywhere else in the region, a fact that he thought meant Haitian peasants had retained a deeper level of continuity with their African ancestors.[4]

Herskovits was a mentor to Katherine Dunham, who went to Haiti to study the role of dance in Vodou ritual. The letters between them record a falling-out of sorts, as Dunham decided to undergo an initiation rite and become a Vodou practitioner, something that Herskovits insisted would result in an inevitable loss of her objectivity as a researcher. Dunham persisted, and she later became a Vodou *mambo* (priestess) and a figure of national importance in Haiti. Dunham did not, however, continue on as an anthropologist. Instead, she became a world-famous dancer and choreographer. She traveled the world but always returned to Haiti, where she eventually made her home and where she was later given honorary citizenship. The letters of Dunham and Herskovits were still on my mind when I went to Haiti, and it is perhaps for that reason that I mentioned reading them during a conversation with some colleagues only days after I arrived in the capital city. One of my colleagues said that I had to meet a friend of hers. We met a few days later and, as it happened, he was part of a small group of people who were working with Dunham, who was retired and living in the United States then, to transform her Haitian home into a botanic garden. They took me to see her estate and they introduced me to the property, which they simply called "the forest."[5]

I felt right away there was a compelling story to be told about the forest, even though the depth and complexity of that story would be clear to me only later. From that first visit to the forest I fell under its spell, and under the spell of the men and women who were working hard to turn the forest into a botanic garden. At the time, there was no comparable place in Haiti and the country was facing staggering levels of deforestation and soil erosion. I listened as those involved in the garden project told me about the extent of the environmental crisis and how they imagined the garden as a "gift to Haiti" and as a site for what they called the "rebirth of the country." It was a lot to expect from a small, forested estate of only a couple dozen acres. And yet it was a compelling vision of the future, unabashedly utopian in its striving for a restoration of the countryside and a resolution to the country's myriad crises. It helped that the forest was rather thick and lush and that it sat atop an underground aquifer that brought fresh water bubbling to the surface in small concrete basins that had been built on the property. It helped too that the forest was located in the middle of a large slum and that, when looked at from above, it appeared as a little bit of nature surrounded by the concrete anarchy of Port-au-Prince.

And so I decided to stay in the city and to study the forest and the botanic garden project, to study the history of the environmental crisis and the corresponding urban crisis, the latter propelled by the former as peasants fled their denuded fields and migrated to the growing slums in the city, in search of jobs in the tourist sector or in the newly built factories that made t-shirts and bras and other things for export to North America. As I learned more, the story grew into something else and I was pulled in new directions as I followed its various threads. The forest was taken over by an armed gang and the neighborhood around the property became part of a national political drama. A coup in 2004 flipped the script and revealed how the environmental and urban crises were deeply entwined with the crisis of the state. Along the way, I met many people whose lives intersected in one way or another with the forest and with Dunham, and with the gangs and the garden project. The story threatened to become too big, too complex. The more I tried to gather together all its parts—to tell *the* story of crisis in Haiti—the more I felt that I was losing sight of something. I could either see the trees or the forest, the part or the whole, but not both. An older colleague of mine, who had worked in Haiti for several decades, gently reminded me of the value of humility when he told me that I would never be able to understand it all. Over time, I came to realize that the story I most wanted to tell, the story I had been tracking the whole time, was not a story about a forest or about "the Haitian crisis." It was a story about people who lived and worked in or around the forest. It was a human story, a story about how crisis feels to those who live with it every day.

Looking back, this idea was there all along, but it has taken me a long time to come to terms with the weight of it.

MATTERS OF LIFE AND DEATH

I met Manuel about the same time that I met the forest. We became fast friends after a chance meeting in a crowded downtown market. After a long conversation about Haitian art, we realized that we had a mutual friend back in the United States. We laughed at the unexpected connection. Later our chance meeting would come to seem, to me, perfectly ordinary. After all, Manuel was widely known throughout the city. As a guide and fixer, he made it his business to know people, and especially to meet foreigners staying in the country. I was less surprised when I later learned that Manuel also knew about the forest and that he was good friends with some of the people working to turn it into a botanic garden.

Manuel was a slender man in his forties, although he looked much younger. Through him I came to know a tight network of middle-aged men who worked in the informal sector as guides, artists, and drivers. These men had come of age together during the brief tourist boom in the late 1970s and early '80s. Most of them had come to Port-au-Prince from the countryside, hoping to find work in the factories and hotels. Like Manuel, these other men had all been quite successful, making good money and becoming well respected around the city. Now, decades after the boom and bust of tourism, they helped each other get by, sharing clients, information, and even money. It was a difficult way to make a living, but they had, each of them, learned to live with the quite ordinary facts of unemployment, poverty, political violence, and instability. And I, in turn, learned from Manuel how to navigate the city of Port-au-Prince and the complexities of Haitian society.

One hot afternoon in August 2002, I was drinking beer with Manuel. We were sitting on the veranda of an aging gingerbread house that had been turned into one of Haiti's most famous hotels. A ceiling fan above us gently moved the air, but not enough to cut through the heat. Still, Manuel was energetic and upbeat, as usual. We talked about the hardships he faced daily and the many crises in his country. He knew that I was interested in the forest. I had become a convert to the botanic garden project, and I was telling him how important I thought the forest was and how urgent it was to address the ecological crisis in Haiti. He nodded along, smiling patiently at me.

"Yes," he said. "It's very bad." He took a drink from his beer and looked at me. He leaned in close to me and said, "But I have to tell you something." He leaned even closer and whispered a few words that have haunted me ever since.

"Haiti is dead," he said. "There is no more Haiti."

Haiti is dead. There is no more Haiti.[6] The words struck me and I asked him what he meant. He shrugged, smiled, drank some more of his beer, and turned the conversation to other topics. I can't say I remember what we talked about after that. My mind was still focused on his comment. In the days that followed, I would ask others about Manuel's statement. When I asked people from the Haitian elite, they scoffed at the idea and invariably replied in the same way: "A country never dies!" I felt that Manuel's comment somehow offended their sense of national pride. Yet when I asked anyone else, and especially when I asked people who, like Manuel, had to live day by day in the city, working hard just to make it, they all said a version of the same thing: "Yes, of course," they said. "We all know this is true." True or not, I wondered what it could possibly mean.

Manuel was born in Port-au-Prince, and while he maintained contact with relatives in his family's village in the countryside, he felt that the city was his real home. Living in the city, he had witnessed firsthand an ever-deepening crisis unfolding over decades. He came of age during a time when waves of new migrants flooded the city, all fleeing the collapse of the peasant economy and all hoping, mostly in vain, to make a living in the fledgling tourist sector and the garment factories. He had lived through the terror of the Duvalier dictatorship and had survived several years in prison. He had been tortured and still carried the scars on his legs and torso. He had found a livelihood as a guide to tourists, and when there were no more tourists he worked as a fixer, taking journalists around the city as they wrote about the fall of the dictatorship, about the violence that ensued, and about the seemingly endless democratic transition. Manuel had lived through economic booms and busts, though certainly more busts than booms. He had stood in the streets protesting military coups and had voted in the country's first free and fair elections. He had lived through an international embargo, when he had nothing to eat, and through an international military intervention that had promised to restore democracy. He had come through crisis after crisis, and now he was taking stock of what had happened to him, of what was lost and what remained.

Manuel did not live to see the worst of things, to see the city that he loved reduced to rubble and dust. He lived in a world that existed before the devastating earthquake that struck the country on January 12, 2010, and he died in that world too. On the day of his funeral, the streets of the city were blocked by anti-government protesters, themselves on their way to the National Palace, where they were soon met by gunfire and tear gas from the police. I remember thinking at the time that in Haiti, even the dead find little peace.

Manuel's words have stayed with me since that summer day in 2002, and I realized, only much later, that I have been trying to come to terms with what he said, with what he meant, ever since. Some might think that Manuel was giving voice to a fatal resignation, but that seems at odds with how he lived his life. No one who knew him would characterize him as someone who had given up. He worked hard; he was a loving father and husband; he was a well-respected person who had many friends; he laughed and joked and smiled. He lived what he felt was a good life, despite the obvious challenges that he, and so many others like him, faced every day. Yet, if he was not saying that he had given up hope or that he felt resigned to the harsh dictates of fate, what was he saying? Part of the answer lies in acknowledging that Manuel's comment that "Haiti is dead" was deeply personal. He was talking about his own life experience and, especially, about his relation to the world around him. But his comment was not *only* a personal one. If it had been, others would have responded to it as such: his friends might have said that he was entitled to his feelings, that his statement was true for him, that it told us something about his state of mind. But that was not the case, and to treat his words as idiosyncratic would be to ignore the startling frequency of such expressions, and the underlying sentiments they carry, in Port-au-Prince. I heard many others say the same thing, or, if they didn't say it, they seemed to agree with it when they heard others say it. His comment was thus both an expression of his own experience and a widely shared structure of feeling.

I heard such comments most frequently when talking to men who shared a common experience with Manuel, men in their forties or fifties who had come of age in the city during a time of unending crisis.[7] Much of this book is an attempt to capture their experience, an experience very much shaped by their gender and their age. When they describe their situation as a never-ending crisis or as the end of the world, these men are recounting the end of a particular world—that of the political generation that emerged during the democratic transition. These men had sought refuge from crisis by migrating to the city and seeking out opportunities to make their own lives within informal artistic or service sectors in which they maintained some degree of control over their work. These men lived through one of the region's most notorious dictatorships, watched the dictatorship fall, and took part in the popular movements that followed. They had believed, strongly, in the millenarian dream of hope, of the promise of a sweeping transformation of Haitian society, which had propelled Jean-Bertrand Aristide to victory in the first democratic elections. Some of these men had achieved a level of social mobility and success, becoming key players in the city's tourist and art markets. The city had brought them into contact with foreigners and with quick cash. It had brought them prestige and respect. Yet these men were also struggling to come to terms with something profound. They knew they could no longer go back to the countryside. They felt that the vision of a good life tied to the peasant family homestead was no longer viable, that land ownership and farming were things of the past. Many had come to the city as migrants, but they had come to see themselves as urban residents. The space of the city reminded them every day of the precariousness of urban life. They lived in slums and shantytowns, they moved through the margins of official city life, they were part of the vast informal world of the global economy, working all day but rarely getting paid. Whatever successes they had had in the past were just that: in the past. They remembered fondly the days when there were tourists, when their pockets were filled with cash. But they knew, too, that those days were gone, even when acting as if they might one day return. They lived in a present that was cut off from the futures they had once dreamed of, from the futures they had once hoped to inhabit. Men like Manuel knew that in Haiti the future was already filled with more crisis, more disaster, and more intervention. This book is an attempt to recount how crisis felt as it happened to them.

Shortly before he died, Manuel told me that he thought that crisis would last forever in Haiti. He said that to me in January 2004, just before President Aristide was removed from power for the second time, just before another wave of terror and violence engulfed the city, before another military intervention and the disasters that followed. When he died, I thought back to his comment about the death of Haiti. It was hard not to project the intimate fact of his own death backward in time, hard not to see his earlier comment as a prescient warning of what came later. I thought that perhaps Manuel had said Haiti was dead because he felt that the world around him, his world, no longer had any place for him in it. Perhaps, for him, it was as if Haiti itself were gone—or whatever version of Haiti he associated with a good life, a life worth living, a life he wanted to live, was no longer available to him. In retrospect, I thought he might have been telling me that he no longer felt it was possible to be the kind of person he had been and wanted to be.

Manuel said that Haiti is dead, there is no more Haiti. It is easy to think that he was talking about the end, about his own experience with a looming death, an all-encompassing finitude. Yet so much depends on how we listen to Manuel, and on what the idea of death and the idea of Haiti meant *to him.* Death can be understood as an end, as the end of experience for a person. But it doesn't have to be that way. In the Vodou cosmology and in much of Haitian culture (Manuel was a Vodou practitioner), death is a transformation of the self, not the end of the self. At death, the body goes away but the invisible elements of the self, the parts of what we might call the soul, go through a series of ritual changes. Part of the soul returns to Bondye, the supreme being who created the universe, but the essence of the person goes to a place under the water and then, later, when the surviving members of the family call the soul back, it goes to rest forever in Ginen, the mythical home of the *lwa* (spirits; pronounced "loa"). In Ginen, the dead are reborn as spirits and death is but a moment in a vast cosmological cycle. It is not the end of the world but rather a part of the world's remaking.[8]

This book is, then, a meditation on life and death, on living and dying in Haiti. It is my attempt to think with Manuel and the many others who shared their lives and stories with me, to think about what it means to struggle, to strive, and to try to live in a world that feels like it has already ended. While it is a sad story, filled with terrible things that happened to people, it is not a tragic story. Life goes on, even after death. Indeed, I would insist—and I think Manuel would insist too—that we should not see the stories that make up this book as expressions of fatalistic resignation, that we should not hear them as proof that Haiti is doomed. Stories matter, and how we tell them matters too, and for that reason I want to make clear that

I resist the dominant trope of tragedy in stories about Haiti. Why does this matter, the difference between a sad story and a tragic one? It matters because in tragedy the end is always preordained. The essence of tragedy is that we can never escape our fate, try as we might. The saddest part of the story told here is the realization that things could have been otherwise, should have been otherwise, that what happened did not have to happen and does not have to happen again. And so, even though there is sadness and despair in what follows, there is also hope—fleeting, perhaps. No sweeping transformations, no revolution. But a persistent dream, a dream that those who have died will be remembered, that those who are hungry will be fed, that those who are homeless will be cared for, that the world can be remade again. It is a dream in which the future can be imagined as good and just. A dream that the future remains open, that the end has not yet come, not just yet. That even if death has come for some of us, for some it has not. In the time that remains, we can hope. And we can live.

WRITING CRISIS

In writing about crisis, my aim is to give an account of what anthropologist Michael Jackson calls "life as lived." Jackson, who has been a leading figure in the application of existentialist and phenomenological approaches to anthropology, urges us to focus on the intimacies of lived experience and the many ways that people encounter the world. Phenomenological approaches have gained considerable ground in anthropology, where they merge well with the discipline's commitment to what Clifford Geertz, himself inspired by phenomenology, called "thick description." What unites the various kinds of phenomenological approaches in anthropology is a concern to dwell in the lived experience of others as they encounter the world, to pay attention to "the indeterminate and ambiguous character of everyday life," and to give priority "to embodied, intersubjective, temporally informed engagements in the world."[9]

To do that requires what Ruth Behar calls a "vulnerable" ethnography, one that is radically open to how people live in the world. Ethnography, she says, has an emancipatory potential because it can make other ways of living present for us—present in ways that are richly nuanced, in ways that are, to use the metaphors most commonly adopted by anthropologists, thick, deep, and intimate.[10] Ethnographic intimacy shares something in common with the best literary fiction and nonfiction; each of these genres seeks to move beyond mere description to something more like empathy and imaginative solidarity. Yet the power of ethnography comes from more than empathic writing. It comes, too, from the anthropological commitment to understanding other ways of living *on their own terms*. To do that takes time. Ethnography is slow, patient, curious, and strange. It helps us question our most taken-for-granted assumptions and embrace other ways of knowing. At its best, ethnography makes us vulnerable by exposing us to a world of difference.

I have chosen to write this book as a series of stories because I think that intimate ethnography accomplishes two things. First, it helps us understand the lived experience of others in all its complexity and ambiguity. Second, it helps us get away from the common understanding of crisis as a discrete event, to be reported only in the news, and to focus instead on how crisis can be an everyday experience.[11] My aim in writing about crisis is to make present for readers how people think and talk about something profound that has happened to them. To do that, I have tried to listen to what people say about themselves and about the world, to treat these people not as data for my own theories, but rather as theorists of their own experiences. It would be too simple to say that the stories told here speak for themselves. But in putting them together, in writing about how crisis feels, I hope to show how these stories are both intimately personal and irreducibly social, private and public, individual and collective. In them, we glimpse what Raymond Williams called a "structure of feeling"—that is, the "affective elements of consciousness and relationships: not feeling against thought, but thought as felt and feeling as thought."[12]

This book is based on over a decade's worth of research, done primarily in Port-au-Prince but also in other parts of Haiti and in the United States and Canada. Over that time, my thinking on the material presented here has changed dramatically, in part because the world described here has also changed, perhaps irrevocably. When I first went to Haiti to begin the research that would result in this book, it seemed to me that the city of Port-au-Prince brought together the many crises facing the country. The environmental crisis in the countryside had brought hundreds of thousands of migrants to the capital and had shaped the very space of the city, as people built their own homes and their own neighborhoods in the abandoned zones and marginal spaces left by an urban elite that retreated, ever more, to gated communities in the hills above. And so the crisis of the countryside gave birth, in a way, to the urban crisis, to the problems of slums and a lack of services, to the anarchic urbanism that began to take shape in the city as the state, too, retreated from public life, opting instead to govern through its persistent absence. City and country were bound together, as they always are, but they were expressions of the even deeper problems of poverty and dictatorship.[13]

Looking back now, the decades-long democratic transition and the popular movements that have arisen have all been responses to this constellation of crises. The dream of democracy that animated those movements was a kind of radical hope, a hope for what was once called "another Haiti" *(yon lòt Ayiti)*. A hope that the violence and death of the past would give way to new life, to a world reborn, a future world in which the many crises shaking the country would be resolved. A future in which people would be able to farm, grow food, eat, and be fed. A world in which there would be electricity and water and houses. A world in which the people would have a voice, a world free of the threat of coups. A future in which Haiti would not be the poorest country in the Western Hemisphere, in which there would be jobs, in which people would be able to live and not merely survive. A future world in which people would not die "stupid deaths" or be crushed by structural violence. Where people would not have to make a choice "between death and death."[14]

Those dreams are still dreams for some, but for many of the people whose stories I tell here, the future that once seemed possible now seems largely closed. Looking back on the past couple of decades, looking back after the disasters that have killed so many and destroyed so much, it has become harder and harder for them to imagine anything but future disaster, a disastrous future full of more crises, more suffering, more death. How does it feel when the future seems impossible? Where does hope go when disaster swallows the horizon of possibility?

When I began to work on this book, I had to confront the problem of how to write about crisis in Haiti. There has been so much written and said about the country that it has become commonplace to hear people talk about "the Haitian crisis" as if it were an objective fact, as if it were intrinsic to the country, as if you could account for it by simply pointing to the litany of economic, political, or developmental indicators and assessments. Political scientists call Haiti a weak or failed state. Economists say it is underdeveloped and that it needs to be more tightly integrated into the global economy. Some say the crisis is due wholly to international interference, while others blame Haitians themselves. A few even boldly assert that the crisis is due to a pathological culture and mentality, that the Haitian people are themselves to blame for anything and everything that has happened to them.[15] My goal here is to change the very terms of the question. Others have sought to give an account of the Haitian crisis. My goal here is to give a *Haitian* account of crisis.

The concept of crisis has a long history, but in the most general terms it is used to name a decisive turning point, a disruption in the normal order of things. Experts of various kinds regularly use the concept to name things that require our urgent attention or perhaps even some kind of intervention—economic collapse, political upheaval, disaster, humanitarian emergency. Common to all these uses is the tendency to treat crisis as an objective condition that can be named and described in the dispassionate terms of social scientific jargon. When we use the word *crisis* this way, we forget that it comes to us from the ancient Greek medical tradition—that is, from a context in which the stakes were immediate and life-threatening for someone. Recalling this deep history of the term is a good way to remind us that, as the philosopher Jürgen Habermas noted, there would be no thing called *crisis* if there were not people experiencing it. In medicine, the crisis is the turning point in the course of a disease after which the patient either lives or dies. The doctor, as expert, sees the crisis in abstract terms, as an abnormality that has blocked the normal functions of a human body. The patient, by contrast, feels the illness in a direct way—as something that is happening to him or her. As Habermas puts it, "the crisis cannot be separated from the viewpoint of the one who is undergoing it—the patient experiences his powerlessness *vis-à-vis* the objectivity of the illness only because he is a subject condemned to passivity and temporarily deprived of the possibility of being a subject in full possession of his powers."[16]

Yet people are never as powerless as this quote might suggest. Even in the midst of terrible circumstances, people strive to act in ways they find meaningful. They also strive to make sense of the world around them and to understand, in critically insightful ways, what exactly has happened and is happening to them.[17] As Karen Richman shows in her richly nuanced ethnography of Haitian migrants, sickness and death can become occasions for profound statements about the experience of crisis and about the ways in which the exploitation and alienation of a global capitalist system can take shape in the intimacies of everyday life. Richman describes one Haitian migrant, Ti Chini, who on his deathbed proclaimed, "The nation of Haiti will never be right. It will never be right." As Richman recounts it, Ti Chini came to understand the illness that would kill him, and the broader global forces that had propelled him from his village in Haiti to a life as a migrant worker in the United States, as an evil force that had invaded his body, as "a vast, sorcerous system that turns poor Haitian neighbors against one another" and that routinely exposes the most vulnerable among us to harm and possible death.[18]

How, then, to write about crisis? How to capture the way that it feels to those who live with it every day? My approach in this book has been to take up a distinction made by Kirin Narayan between situations and stories. Situations are like plots. They can be described in general terms and are the contexts in which people act. In the chapters that follow, the constellation of crises described above would be the situation in which people find them-selves. Stories, however, are narratives that seek to capture the emotional experiences people have as they live their lives in those contexts.[19] To that end, I have written the book not as a description of crisis in objective terms but rather as a series of stories within stories, stories told to me by people as they struggled to make sense of what is happening to them. In telling those stories, I have chosen to foreground moments of dialogue and debate—conversations—in which I am sometimes a participant and some-times merely an observer, though often both. By retelling these conversa-tions, I hope to give the people with whom I worked a direct voice, to let them speak for and about themselves in words of their own choosing. Writing these interactions as exchanges also highlights how I came to record and recount this story: it was told to me.

Stories matter, to the people who tell them and to the people who listen to them. People everywhere put their experiences into some kind of form, and they do so by thinking, by reflecting, and above all by talking about their experiences. Narrative is key to how we make sense of our lives. We use stories to "arrange and transform our experiences," to give an account of what happened and why, to tell people about ourselves, and to make our most intimate and personal experiences into accounts that are publicly sharable, into stories that we can exchange with others as we try to make our way in the world. Stories are always social and often political. They can also be therapeutic, a way of restoring meaning to the world around us, a way of talking and telling about what has happened so that we remain subjects—authors—of our own stories.[20]

The most common form of storytelling is ordinary conversation, which, as Elinor Ochs and Lisa Capps put it, "is the most likely medium for airing unresolved life events."[21] In this sense, conversation is not just a mode of presentation used in this book; it was also the primary method I used while conducting research. Anthropology is something like a study of the ordi-nary. When anthropologists carry out research, they usually spend most of their time accompanying people as they go about the ordinary business of their lives—waiting, talking, eating, working, and all the other things that people do everywhere around the world. As I did these things too, I often felt that my presence afforded people an occasion to talk not just to me but also to others in ways that allowed them to work out their own ideas, to explore and give shape to their thoughts and feelings, to articulate their own theories about what was happening in Haiti.

This book is a record of the many conversations, stories, accounts, and theories that I heard. It is a collection of stories, stitched together by me in a deliberate way. My hope is that in bringing them together I have accomplished more than mere addition. I was able to move across borders, both literal and figurative, in ways that few others could. I traversed social divisions and national borders as well as the subtler demarcations of neighborhoods, social relationships, and political affiliations. While I make no claims to totality here, I do feel that a larger whole emerges as these various stories are brought together. That larger whole, though, is inherently incomplete. In writing this book, I was pulled in two directions. On one hand, I had an impulse to tell an overarching story that would tie all the events together coherently. On the other hand, the very aspects of the world being described here resisted such narrative closure. In the end, I have tried to capture the complexities and contradictions of the experiences recounted here, to stay close to the feeling of uncertainty in the moment. At the same time, I have used two narrative devices to organize the book that give it a measure of coherence not always visible in the moments being recounted. First, while I have organized the book roughly chronologically, I also move forward and backward in time to better capture the differences between the uncertainty of an event as it happened and the retrospective significance of the event as it was folded into other events, into longer narratives, and into a person's life story. In so doing, I hope to show my own and others' later evaluations and explanations as well as our shifting experience of the temporal order of things. Second, I have organized the chapters thematically in such a way that each chapter discusses a specific set of issues and experiences. At the same time, I have arranged the chapters so that they move from an abstract experience of loss, which some describe as the death of the ideal peasant homestead, to the much more concrete experience of alienation from one's place in the world that came with the inability to feel secure in one's body or home during moments of intense violence and terror, and finally to accounts of what it was like to live through the destruction of one's world and to dwell in the aftermath of disaster.

PLAN OF THE BOOK

Each chapter tells a different story, but they all explore how national and global political and economic forces take shape in people's daily lives. Chapter 1 ("The Forest and the City") explores the environmental and urban crises through the story of a forest in the middle of a seaside slum. The forest was once a colonial estate, and then a private residence, and, from the 1990s to the early years of the twenty-first century, the site of a proposed botanic garden. The garden was imagined as a symbol for the rebirth of the country, but the property was taken over by squatters and an armed gang, and the garden project was eventually caught up in a national political crisis as people began to debate the limits of inclusion and exclusion and the very possibility of democracy in Haiti. The story of the forest is thus also an account of how crisis shapes the spaces in which people live and, in the process, shapes their experiences and expectations too.

Chapter 2 ("Looking for Life") explores how working men seek to build meaningful lives in the midst of the informal economy of Port-au-Prince. The chapter follows a group of urban men as they *chache lavi*, or "look for life"—that is, as they struggle to make a living by working as artisans, guides, and taxi drivers. Most of these men migrated to the city years ago, and as with so many other urban migrants, their attempt to look for life in the city was a response to the crisis of the countryside, as they fled the collapse of the rural peasant economy. Now, in the city, they must confront a whole new world of crisis. In order to get by, they have sought to build networks of support and solidarity that extend throughout the city. But such networks are fragile and rely on the constant reproduction of relations of respect and reputation. This chapter explores how these men think about crisis and how they talk about what it feels like to be caught up in the increasingly impossible project of looking for life in Port-au-Prince.

Chapter 3 ("Making Disorder") tells the story of the making of a political crisis that sent President Jean-Bertrand Aristide into exile for the second time and that ushered in an unconstitutional provisional government and an international military intervention, all during the bicentennial year of Haitian independence in 2004. Returning to the botanic garden project, the gangs and squatters, and the urban migrants discussed in the preceding two chapters, I explore how these various groups used the Haitian concept of disorder *(dezòd)* to make sense of the political crisis that precipitated the coup. The chapter moves across both social classes and social spaces to follow how people talked about the political crisis in the period leading up to the coup. By putting vastly different accounts of disorder together, I show how the coup came to seem inevitable even before it happened, and how the political crisis gave way to a prevailing sense of the impossibility of a vision of democracy long associated with the figure of President Aristide.

Chapter 4 ("Between Life and Death") explores the aftermath of the coup, as Port-au-Prince was engulfed in a wave of violence that pitted gangs, the national police, and United Nations peacekeepers against one another. Drawing on extensive interviews with people around the city, I show how residents talked about the everyday violence of the provisional period using the metaphor of the blackout *(blakawout)*—a term that means not only loss of electricity but also a more pervasive loss of power, a loss of power that was felt to be at once individual (the inability to do anything) and collective (the loss of political power of Aristide's party and his supporters). The metaphor of the blackout is an especially apt one for urban men, for whom power outages in the city are both anticipated and expected features of everyday life and, at the same time, sudden and shocking occurrences when they happen. As men talked about "living in a blackout," they also found a way to give voice to the experience of a kind of political violence that was pervasive but often intangible, that was at once intimate and general, that was felt in their bodies and in the houses, streets, and neighborhoods where they lived and worked. Amid the violence of the provisional period, I show how these men tried to make sense of the uncertainty that swirled around them and how they struggled to navigate the fine line between living and dying.

Chapter 5 ("Aftermath") weaves together several stories of disaster and displacement, placing the 2010 earthquake that destroyed over a third of Port-au-Prince into the broader context of recurring natural hazards such as hurricanes and floods that, combined with the long history of social vulnerability, regularly produce catastrophic disasters in Haiti. Drawing on research before and after the earthquake, this chapter explores the social and emotional dimensions of disasters as they unfold over time and across space. I focus, in particular, on how disasters, as both sudden ruptures and anticipated events, lead to various kinds of displacement, as people are pushed out of their villages and their homes. Returning to the themes of environmental and urban crises discussed in earlier chapters, I reframe the 2010 earthquake not as a singular event but rather as part of a long process of displacement. In so doing, my aim is to capture what it feels like to live in the aftermath of a disaster that has not really ended and what it feels like to face a future in which the only certainty seems to be that there will be yet more disaster.

Some of the people who shared their stories and their lives with me are no longer with us. Others are alive and still struggling to make a living. In both cases, I have used pseudonyms for everyone except public figures in order to ensure anonymity and protect people's privacy.[22] Although Port-au-Prince is a large city, the social worlds people inhabit in it are quite intimate, and at times I have had to alter some details of the stories told here so as to further ensure confidentiality and to protect people's identities. I have also left out some details of people's lives when they asked me to do so. Like all accounts, the one presented here is partial. I make no claim to speak for all Haitians.

On a personal note, it has been difficult at times to carry the weight of these stories with me, even though I know full well that my own difficulties pale in comparison to those suffered by so many others. Still, years ago, amid the violence and terror that followed the coup in 2004, I felt my spirit break. I felt as though I could not go on, that I should not go on, that it didn't make any sense to be asking people to tell me about their lives when they were so caught up in trying to survive, to get by, to find a way to make it through difficult, oppressive, and damaging circumstances. I shared these feelings with my friend Paul, who has lived in Port-au-Prince all his life. He told me not to worry so much. "It's important," he told me. "You can tell people what has happened here." I hope that I have been able, in some small way, to do just that.

1. The Forest and the City

On the southwestern edge of Port-au-Prince there is a small forest, nestled into the bottom of a mountain. The forest is surrounded by a city. If you look down from the mountains behind the city, you will see a thick green patch in the middle of gray concrete houses and tin roofs. If you squint your eyes, you might even think there is a hole in the city. The forest was here before the city that grew up around it. Its trees have stood for centuries. It was here before Haiti was Haiti. As Giambattista Vico suggested long ago, the forest was *first*.[1]

Like all forests, this one has a story to tell. Many stories, in fact. There are ancient rocks in the forest, powerful objects worshipped by the Taino Indians, the indigenous inhabitants of Hispaniola who were killed by Spanish colonists in the sixteenth century, after Columbus ran one of his ships aground on the northern coast of the island. The forest has many names, but the most common one is Habitation Leclerc, or Leclerc's plantation. The name comes from Napoleon Bonaparte's brother-in-law, General Charles Leclerc, who led a military expedition to the French colony of Saint Domingue in 1802 so that he might end the Haitian Revolution, arrest or kill the rebels, and restore slavery. Leclerc lived at the estate for only a short time. He died of yellow fever shortly after arriving in the colony, and the French forces went on to historic defeat, losing the revolutionary war and their most important overseas colony. The association of the forest with Leclerc has made it a popular place. Every Haitian knows the story of the revolution, and in that story Leclerc is one of the great villains. Like other famous French plantations, Habitation Leclerc still carries the weight of this history. People say there is buried treasure hidden throughout the forest, and every so often someone calls forth a magical beast to divine the location of the treasure.[2] But few ever find it.

For over a century, urban elites sought refuge from the summer heat in the forest. Older residents fondly recall weekend trips there to ride horses, hike, and have picnics. The harmonious images conjured up by stories of wooded areas, bubbling springs, and cool breezes on mountain trails belie the darker aspects of the forest's history. As you hear more and more stories about the forest, you become aware that there are really two stories. There is the story of genocide, slavery, and colonialism—a story that left buried treasure, haunting ghosts, and French place-names, a story of a landscape and a country saturated with violence. And then there is the story of the timeless forest, of pristine nature, of a Haitian arcadia.[3]

If you go to the forest you will see both of these versions. The stately trees will give you a sense of the firstness of forests, of a timeless moral order. But among the trees, you will see the ruins and remnants of human history. These two images will blur together. And the more you look, the more it will appear that the city, the people, the presence of human activity interrupts your idea of a forest. Leo Marx used the image of the "machine in the garden" to describe the sudden and shocking interruption of the industrial world into the imagined prelapsarian ideal of the American pastoral. Just as a train whistle in the distance disrupted Thoreau's peace at Walden Pond, the world of human activity pierces the space of the forest like "an alien world encroaching from without."[4] And you will come to see that here, in this place, the forest is not just a remnant from a time before the city but an active part of the city, just as the city is a part of the forest. And you will begin to wonder how you ever thought the forest and the city were separate.[5]

ECOLOGY IN A TIME OF CRISIS

I first heard about the forest in the summer of 2002, when a friend told me about a small community organization in Martissant called the Société Coopérative pour l'Environnement (SCPE). The SCPE, I was told, had been working for over a decade to protect the forest and to convert a portion of it into a botanic garden. Intrigued, I arranged to meet Luc, one of the founders of the organization. Luc was a slim man in his mid-fifties from a well-known mulatto family that, in Haitian terms, would be considered part of the petite bourgeoisie. A lawyer by training, he now held a mid-level position in a government ministry. "Nothing too political," he said. "I stay out of all of that."

We met for dinner at a restaurant in downtown Port-au-Prince. As we ate plates of chicken covered in tomatoes and cashews, he asked me what I knew about the environmental crisis in Haiti. I told him I had read that Haiti was one of the most deforested countries in the world and that it suffered from terrible rates of soil erosion, that it was one of the most transformed environments in the world.[6] I said I had learned that the environmental crisis had led to the collapse of the peasant economy, which in turn had sent hundreds of thousands of peasants to the city or overseas in search of work. He nodded along thoughtfully. I felt like I was at an audition. When I stopped, Luc looked at me. "Yes, yes," he said. "What you say is correct. You've done your homework!" He held up his index finger as he paused. "But what if I told you we could change all of that?"

He smiled as he let the question hang in the air. Then he snapped his fingers. "Like that," he said, "Haiti would be a different place, no?"

He dipped some bread in his cashew sauce and ate it.

"How?" I finally asked.

Luc smiled again as he chewed. "Yes. How? That is the question."

I spent the rest of the evening listening to Luc talk about the forest. I was captivated. To hear him tell it, the forest was a synecdoche for Haiti itself. Although it was a relatively small piece of land (about twenty hectares), Luc talked about the project as if saving the forest would save the entire country. "It will be a rebirth of Haiti," he said. "When we turn it into a botanic garden, we will have seed banks and nurseries, we will have agronomists and ecologists and botanists. We will run reforestation campaigns." I had my doubts that one project could do all of that, but his optimism was contagious. "My country is an agrarian nation. If we don't solve the environmental crisis," he said, "then that's it. We're finished."

I asked if I could see the forest and meet the people trying to save it. He smiled. "Of course," he said. "You must go. I'll tell them you are coming."

The next day, I drove to the forest with my friend Alexis, who worked as a private taxi driver. We drove west, along the large boulevard by the bay, then turned up the mountain slopes that led to Martissant. We drove through open-air markets that spilled into the road. Alexis threaded the car through an impossibly small gap between a bus and a food stall, somehow hitting neither. The car creaked and groaned. I looked out the front window and saw that the intersection ahead had almost completely eroded away. Where there should be a road there was only a giant sinkhole, big enough for a small car to fall into. Alexis slowly eased around the hole, driving mostly on the sidewalk. People and dogs scattered out of the way. One of the tires seemed to catch the lip of the hole and spin out, but then Alexis had the car back on firm ground. He turned and drove downhill, back in the direction from which we had come. I thought he was giving up, and was

The road to the forest. Photo by author.

about to ask him where we were going when he turned again and started to circle back up, winding through other streets that were less congested, heading slowly back up the mountain.

There were newer houses, small concrete boxes, lining the sides of the streets. Alexis took us around another curve and then across another eroded road. We passed the skeletal remains of a car that had been set on fire. "What happened here?" I asked.

"They block the roads with burning cars," he said, as if that was answer enough.

And then the houses and crowds disappeared and there was suddenly nothing on the side of the road. I looked down and could see the forest's thick canopy, its tall trees. Two large pigs sat in a muddy hole on the edge of the road. We drove around the forest, and then the road leveled out, the trees rose up above us, casting a shadow on the street.

"This is it," Alexis said.

The road, Rue Martissant 23, cut the forest in two. On one side of the road was a stone wall, now crumbling and falling apart, that wound around the largest section of the forest. On the other side was a shorter wall and iron gates. Alexis drove up to the gates. Several men approached us. I explained that I was here to see the forest, that Luc had sent me to meet Maxo. They opened the gates and we drove inside.

Alexis parked the car in the shade of a tree as two men led me down a small slope toward a stone patio. A short, stocky man in his forties stood on the patio, talking on a cell phone. He turned when we arrived and introduced himself as Maxo, the forest's caretaker. He held out two laminated identity cards that hung on a lanyard around his neck. One was for the SCPE, the other just said "security."

We sat in the shade, on plastic lawn chairs, and Maxo began to talk.

"I was born here," he said. "In Martissant. I have lived here my whole life." He pointed toward the road. "My family used to live just over there. We would come here when I was a kid. I remember this was all trees. There were very few houses here. Up until the 1970s we had lots of trees in Haiti. We had forests. We had birds. Right here." The two men who had opened the gate, and who were now seated on a concrete bench near us, nodded and murmured their agreement. Maxo continued: "Now, there is nothing. Nothing. The problem is political. After 1986 [the end of the dictatorship] we had insecurity. We had lots of crisis. Haitians have always been poor. But then, the people lost a lot and they started cutting trees. We are an agrarian country. We cannot live without trees. But when we have a crisis, what can they do? People come to the city from the countryside. They lose the connection. It starts with bad politics. Then bad economics. Poverty. Misery. You understand? When people need money so much, they cut trees to make charcoal. It's just like that. When people really, really need money, when they are too poor, they forget what a tree means."

"What does a tree mean?" I asked.

Maxo gestured to the trees around us and said, "Okay. For example, we are sitting under an almond tree *[zanmann]*.[7] The almond tree has a lot of significance. It has a medicinal value for blood pressure. It is a cure for [high] blood pressure. And the fruit, of course, is very, very good for you. Every tree in Haiti has medicine. There is medicine in every tree. This is science, yes. But Haitians, we know all of this. And look at what a mango does. It refreshes you. It gives you sweet fruit. But we can sell mangos! That is export. Why would we cut this export, cut the mango? There was a time when Haiti sold a lot of mangos. Now, we cut them to make charcoal."

Maxo sat silent for a moment. Then he gestured toward the road and the sprawl of Martissant. "Look! What is happening in our country? In Haiti today, we do not respect the environment. We do not protect the environment. Haiti must change." He shook his head and looked down at the ground. "Haiti is in a hole *[twou]*."

In Kreyòl, *twou* has several connotations, ranging from a pothole to a bodily orifice to a deficit. But it can also simply mean a void, a kind of empty space. Maxo seemed to be drawing on all of these meanings. A steep economic decline and deep poverty had put the country in the hole, but the environmental crisis was also marked by a startling absence, an absence of trees and soil due to deforestation and erosion. That sense of absence gave the sheer presence of the forest in which we sat a special resonance for Maxo and the other members of the SCPE.

"In thirty, forty years our forests have disappeared," he said. "This forest," he pointed to the trees all around us, "this forest here. I will fight for it. You, me, all of us, we must fight for it. It is here now because of us. Every day we defend it against bad people who want to steal the trees. We guard the forest. This is the last war *[lagè]* in my country."

I was struck by Maxo's phrasing, but as I listened to him describe how he came to join the SCPE, it began to make sense. The environmental movement in Haiti is quite recent, although the problems it confronts are not. But it became possible to speak openly about ecological issues only after the fall of the Duvalier dictatorship. As an important early report put it, it was only after 1986 that *"la parole écologique,"* or ecological discourse, was "freed."[8] Before that, the thirty-year-long dictatorship had violently suppressed any discussion of the environmental crisis. The dictatorship had also played an active role in deforestation, using its paramilitary forces to arrest those who cut trees without permits while at the same time granting (or illegally selling) tree permits to large lumber, firewood, and charcoal vendors. In the wake of the dictatorship, the environmental movement emerged alongside the broader democratic movement and was shaped by the liberation theology of Jean-Bertrand Aristide. To talk about ecology at all was to talk about politics and economics, about freedom and social transformation.[9] The SCPE, like the Haitian environmental movement more broadly, was thus characterized by a strange mixture of conservative and revolutionary impulses. The SCPE sought to restore a past tradition and recuperate a lost world by saving the forest from falling into the "hole," but it also wanted to transform the country through a radical rebirth. Maxo's claim that this was "the last war" gave expression to both of these impulses.

This sense of struggle has been with the SCPE from the beginning. Maxo was a founding member of the group and one of its most prominent leaders. Luc first approached him in the late 1980s. Their families were well acquainted, and Maxo's father had worked with Luc's father in the past. Among other things, Luc's father had been a vocal critic of the lack of centralized urban planning and development in Port-au-Prince. For decades, Luc and his father had advocated for the protection of an important watershed in Martissant, the same watershed that surfaced in the forest as a series of freshwater springs. When Luc approached Maxo about his concerns, they decided to form a new organization to protect the area.

The SCPE was one of a number of grassroots organizations that blossomed in the early years of Haiti's democratic transition. Collectively known as "popular organizations" (*òganizasyon popilè* or OPs), these new groups were based on traditional peasant organizations and cooperative work groups that formed the foundation of the popular uprising against the Duvalier regime. By the 1990s, popular organizations were everywhere. Often ephemeral, and almost always small in size, OPs used preexisting social networks as a basis for new forms of political affiliation and mobilization.[10]

"From Luc," Maxo told me, "I learned about the environment. And then I met a man from the Ministry [of the Environment] and he told me we had to protect the environment. They came from the ministry here, to Martissant, and they spoke to us. They told us if people cut trees there will be no future for Haiti. It will be impossible for people here."

It was this sense of possibility and impossibility that gave the forest such symbolic resonance for the SCPE. They saw the forest as a kind of miracle, as one of the last areas of old-growth coastal forest left in the country. Thinking of the forest this way made it easy to see protecting it as a last stand, and this in turn gave the forest a significance that far outweighed its material importance by any economic or ecological calculation. For Maxo, the forest was an emblem for the Haitian crisis writ large. It was here, precisely here, that "the last war" would be fought. And for him, the forest became a double emblem, signifying both the possibility of a future in which the environmental crisis would be reversed and the country reborn and, at the same time, the possibility of another, darker future, in which it would be impossible to live.

The SCPE had been created in a time of great hope, during the years of the democratic transition. Much of that hope had been bound up with the figure of Aristide and his Lavalas movement. "At that time," Maxo told me, "we had a lot of hope that things would change." Things did change, but for the worse. Aristide was ousted in a coup in 1991 and the country was plunged into a new crisis as a brutal military junta cracked down on the popular movement. Aristide went into exile, and many of his supporters were killed or arrested. Some, like Maxo, went into hiding and waited for a call to arms from Aristide or other leaders. "We waited," he told me, "we waited. But nothing. We should have fought. Aristide, the international community, they said we need a political solution." Maxo shook his head. "You can't have a political solution to war."

When Aristide returned to power three years later, after an international military intervention, things were different in Martissant. Maxo, for one, had lost faith in the Lavalas movement and in the government, and he and other members of the SCPE began, increasingly, to think of the Haitian state as an adversary rather than an ally. By the time I met him, the hope that had spurred Maxo and Luc to create the SCPE had given way to disappointment and disillusionment. "The environment is the biggest crisis for Haiti," Maxo said. "If Aristide's Lavalas had been a real revolution, Haiti would be a different country now. Aristide—he was just talk. If we had democracy here we would be living in a new Haiti today. There is no political consciousness of the environment here. The people have consciousness, but not the state."

At that moment, as if on cue, we were interrupted by the sound of a helicopter flying overhead. We all looked up but could not see it through the trees. The other men sitting on the patio began to chuckle. I asked who they thought was in the helicopter (a rare sight and sound in Port-au-Prince). One of the men shouted out, "It's Aristide!" Maxo broke into a wide grin.

"Really?" I asked, unsure if they were joking.

"Yes, of course," he said.

"Where's he going?"

Maxo looked me in the eyes and said, "He's looking at the forest."

I laughed nervously, again not sure if he was joking.

Maxo was no longer smiling. He nodded his head. "Yes. He likes to look at the forest." He held up an index finger, commanding my attention. "Aristide loves the forest. But he doesn't protect it."

THE CITY THAT EXPLODED

"Look at this," Luc said as we drove slowly through a crowded street market. He gestured out the window to the throngs of people selling food, batteries, sunglasses, expired medication, and just about everything else you could imagine. We were driving down one of Martissant's main streets. It had once been a wide, two-lane paved road but was now a narrow, rutted strip. Most of the road had become an open-air market. Drivers traveling in opposite directions had to slowly negotiate the right-of-way and ease their cars or buses past each other. Luc, who held a government post that came with a government vehicle, was driving fast, forcing people, dogs, and cars out of his way. The government tag on his license plate, and the hulking presence of his SUV, gave him the de facto right-of-way.

"This place has been abandoned," he said.

We were talking about what he called the "slumification" *(bidonvilizasyon)* of Port-au-Prince. Luc had grown up in Martissant, and his family had lived in the area for three generations. Now he was building a new house in a small, gated community in the hills above the city. "I don't want to leave," he told me, as he honked the horn twice and swerved the car, barely avoiding a man pulling a wooden cart loaded with bags of charcoal. "But what choice do I have? For me, for my family? We are no longer safe here."[11]

I asked him why he felt unsafe. He once again gestured to the street and the crowd outside the window. "Look. You see the roads! We had roads here. Now, we have no roads. You see all this," he added, indicating the market stalls. "It wasn't here before. This used to be a good neighborhood. A good neighborhood. You can still see some of the old houses, but most of them are gone. It's sad what has happened here." He told me that street markets had been illegal under the dictatorship. That under the regime the streets had been clear and well cared for. There had not been piles of garbage on every corner, as there was now.

"Before," he continued, "the government would arrest these people. They wouldn't be here, in the streets, in this neighborhood." We passed a large squatter settlement, with houses in various stages of construction. A group of men were mixing concrete, as housing blocks dried in the sun. Others were welding rebar or tin sheeting. The houses were stacked on top of each other like a layered fan, running from the edge of the street up the mountain slopes. We came to the end of the road and turned again. Luc stopped the car at an impromptu roadblock. Two men sat on either side of the street holding a thin piece of wood across the road with a sign on it asking for "donations." Luc muttered under his breath and honked a few times. He rolled down his window and waved his hand dismissively at the men. The barrier was moved so that we could pass. "They do this all the time," Luc told me. "They sweep the street a bit and then they want money. But they are the cause of all this. Haiti is broken *[kraze]*. The city has exploded *[eklate]*."

Luc pulled his car into a gravel driveway and honked. A drowsy security guard came out of a small hut and opened the gates. We drove up a curvy laneway, parked, and walked down a stone path to a large patio. Luc introduced me to Gabriel, an elderly mulatto man in his eighties. Gabriel stood, towering over me, and shook my hand. "Sit," he said, more a command than a request. He looked at me and smiled. "So, you're the anthropologist."

I nodded and started to introduce myself, but Gabriel just smiled again. It was clear Luc had already told him about me. "You want to know about Martissant," he said. I nodded again. He nodded back. "Very well."

Gabriel called into the house and a young woman quickly emerged. He asked her to bring coffee. She returned a few minutes later and set down a platter on a small iron table. Gabriel lit a cigarette and offered one to me. I declined. Josephine, the young domestic servant, poured coffee into small cups and dumped a large spoonful of sugar into each one. She returned to the house. Gabriel handed me a cup and we all drank, he quickly, finishing his coffee in two gulps. He laughed and smacked his knee as I blew on my coffee and sipped it. "Maybe you prefer American coffee?" he said, mimicking a comically large cup with his hands. I laughed too and downed the remaining coffee. And then Gabriel began to tell me his story.

"In Haiti," he said, "we have what is called the problem of the city. The urban crisis. When you look at Port-au-Prince, what do you see? It is a port town. A capital city. But it is also a slum *[bidonvil]*. Everywhere you look, you see people building houses, people in the streets. All along the mountains here," he said, pointing to the slopes behind his house, "you see people. You don't see trees, you don't see soil. Do you know that joke?" he asked me.

"What joke?"

"What are the only two exports of Haiti?" he asked.

I thought for a moment and said, "Coffee and sugar?"

Gabriel laughed. "No," he said, shaking his head. "People and soil."

Luc and Gabriel both laughed, partly at the earnestness of my answer, at my misunderstanding, but partly at the joke too.

"People leave," Gabriel continued. "They get in boats or they swim. To get out of here. They leave because they cannot live. They say there is no place left for the living in Haiti. But when they leave, the land loves Haitians so much, it follows them out to sea. You can see it from the sky, when you fly overhead. The sea, our sea, is the most beautiful blue. But around Haiti, it is brown, it is mud."

"This is why we fight to keep the forest," Luc said. "We must have reforestation so that we can keep the soil."

Gabriel nodded his agreement. "Yes, I agree absolutely. Today, Haiti faces a profound crisis. In the countryside, there is the rural crisis. In Port-au-Prince, there is the political crisis. They are the same thing. They meet here, in the city. It is a simple story." Gabriel went on to recount the last century of Haitian history, linking together the repeated political crises with the problem of economic stagnation and decline.[12] A key turning point for him was the 1915 invasion of Haiti by the United States. The U.S. military occupied Haiti for nineteen years, and during that time they reorganized the local economy, restructured the government, and opened the country up to global trade. The U.S. administration rewrote Haiti's constitution, removing a prohibition on the foreign ownership of land and paving the way for the penetration of foreign capital and imported goods. Rural cultivators initially responded with an armed struggle against the U.S. Marines, but they were defeated. Afterward, rural life in Haiti was significantly transformed. In the decades after the occupation, Haitian peasants went from being producers of their own food to being consumers of imported goods. As Gabriel's joke suggested, the main commodities peasant families now make are mobile migrant laborers.[13]

"People came to the city from the countryside," Gabriel continued. "That started with the American occupation. And the Americans also brought cars and bulldozers. One hundred years ago, Martissant was the countryside. But now it is the city. People came in the 1930s and the 1950s. All the time. But the city exploded in the 1970s."

This was a common refrain among long-term residents in Martissant like Luc and Gabriel. For them, the problem of the city became a full-blown urban crisis in the final decade of the Duvalier regime, when Jean-Claude Duvalier, backed by the international community, imposed a series of structural adjustment policies on the country. Those policies are widely regarded as the final death knell of the rural economy. Hundreds of thousands of migrants arrived in Port-au-Prince looking for jobs in newly built factories and industrial parks.[14] Most of those who arrived ended up living in squatter settlements in the large slums of Cité Soleil and La Saline. By the 1980s, as those slums expanded, migrants began settling in other parts of the city. Martissant's empty mountain slopes and flat, muddy expanses along the coast made it a new frontier for migrants to settle.

"These people came here," Gabriel said, "and they just took land. They built houses. They took the streets. But they are not city people. They do not understand. They are country people [moun andeyò], they are common people [moun pèp]. They do not understand the city. They think it is theirs. These people come here and they have nothing. No jobs. No houses. But they want everything."

Gabriel was right about the volume of people. Rural-to-urban migration overwhelmed the city in a short span of time. In the early 1980s, there were an estimated seven hundred thousand people living in Port-au-Prince. By the mid-1990s the city's population had doubled, and by the mid–2000s it had doubled again. Current estimates put the greater metropolitan area of Port-au-Prince at nearly three million. There has been little investment in housing or infrastructure to match this population growth. Most houses and even whole neighborhoods are "informal," which is to say they are built by individuals, with no oversight, regulation, or planning from the municipal or national government. Gabriel and Luc were part of a generation of urban intellectuals, all from elite families, who persistently called for the establishment of regulatory bodies that would address the urban crisis. Gabriel, in particular, thought there should be a civilian panel of experts who could advise the government on zoning issues, building codes, waste management and drainage, and the protection of watershed systems. But both Luc and Gabriel (and many other urban intellectuals) cast the problem of the city in terms of an invasion of *moun andeyò*. In so doing, they drew on a long-standing sense of the social distinction between the country and the city, a distinction that has historically been reinforced by the spatial distance between the urban and rural populations. The massive wave of migration to the city collapsed that spatial barrier and now threatened to collapse the social barriers of difference and distinction too. While Gabriel repeatedly insisted that the urban crisis was created by the economic and political problems of the Duvalier regime, he also insisted that it had been exacerbated by the populist politics of the democratic era.[15] I asked him why.

"Aristide is a political beast," he said. "He does not respect the law, and now we have the political crisis. Me, I was never a Duvalierist. Never!" He swiped his hand through the air as if to underline the word. "But what is this? What has happened to my country? Aristide. Lavalas. All these people. They think democracy means they can take everything!"

This, too, was a common refrain among Aristide's critics. This view was most famously expressed by Aubelin Jolicoeur, a well-known journalist and former Duvalierist minister who said of the 1990 elections, "The people made a choice that is at the root of all our problems. Aristide was elected by 67 percent of the vote, maybe 70 percent. But that is an erroneous way of seeing democracy and perhaps a terrible error because people who cannot read cannot possibly make a valid choice."[16] Unlike Jolicoeur, Gabriel and Luc had actually been active supporters of Aristide in the 1990s, and they still counted themselves as supporters of the popular movement. But they had grown increasingly critical of Aristide's government and his supporters and they accused him of encouraging the illegal seizure of private and public land by squatters in order to appease his urban base.

"We have to stop the slumification of the city," Gabriel said. "In the city, we have a political crisis, an economic crisis, and yes, also an environmental crisis. All together. We need planning. We can't have this anarchy. It's like your forest," he said, pointing to Luc.

I asked him what he meant.

"The forest is like the countryside, yes?" Gabriel said. "But it is not *in* the countryside! You understand? The forest is in the city. If you want to save the forest, you need planning. You need to evict *[degèpi]* these people. You need to protect Morne l'Hôpital. You see, that forest is not just a forest."

For Gabriel, and for many other urban intellectuals, the SCPE's project to save the forest in Martissant was, at its core, a project to save the city. Protecting the forest was, in his view, really an act of urban planning. Saving trees from being cut down would do little, he thought, unless there was a concerted effort to remove the squatters from the forest and the surrounding area, especially from the mountain slopes above it. "What is the environmental crisis?" Gabriel asked. "It is a disaster. We have lots of disaster here in Haiti. Why? This is a mountainous country and a tropical country. When the rain comes and there are no trees, no soil, we get floods. When it rains in the mountains, by the time the water gets down here. . . . People, things, neighborhoods. Washed away [bote]. If we had trees on the hills instead of houses, this would not happen. Instead, we have deadly floods [lavalas]."

The double sense of *lavalas* was deliberate—he meant both the dangerous floods from the rainy seasons and the political movement associated with Aristide. His comment thus intentionally blurred the line between natural disasters and political crises. But while the political critique was an important aspect for Gabriel, he really was concerned with flooding. Gabriel had been a vocal supporter, though not a member, of the SCPE since its inception. While he was happy that the SCPE was so dedicated to reforestation and conservation, the issue that most concerned him was water. And yet, despite this difference, he still saw the protection of the forest as both an urgent necessity and a kind of last battle. The city lacked the necessary infrastructure of drainage, which caused not only flooding but also widespread pollution in the water system. Gabriel estimated that, if properly managed, the freshwater aquifer that sits under the forest could supply clean drinking water to a quarter or even a third of the urban population. And because it sits in an important watershed, the forest was a critical part of the natural drainage system around the city. As more and more trees have been cut down on the mountainside and more and more houses built, the erosion and flooding has worsened each year. If the forest were cut too, the already deadly floods would become catastrophic for those living at the bottom of the hills.

After we left Gabriel's house, Luc took me for another drive through Martissant. He told me the names of all the families that lived in the larger houses, those whom he felt were the "real" residents of the neighborhood. Then he took me to his own house, a modestly sized, beautiful stone house that was not far from the forest. Behind his house there was a lush, well-cultivated garden. A stone path wound through the garden and ended at a shallow basin, where a small spring bubbled up from the ground, just like in the forest. Luc pointed to a steep hill at the edge of his property. The slope was covered with thick vegetation, but I thought I could see a few concrete houses between the branches. He told me he owned the land all the way to the top of the hill, but that there were squatters living up there now. "They've been living there for years, but what can I do? When they start to build with concrete, you know they will never leave. There is nothing we can do now to stop this." When I asked about calling the police or pursuing a land claim in court, Luc said, "That is not possible. The courts do nothing. The courts, the police, the government—they're all corrupt."

Gabriel and Luc were engaged in a struggle over the ideal form of the city—what it should look like, who should live in it, and how it should be governed. In a similar way, Maxo and the SCPE (which included Luc, who was a key founder of the organization) were fighting to define the ideal form of the forest. In both cases, the city and the forest were both real locations and also symbols standing in for the nation as a whole. This slippage between the local and the national, between the particular and the general, was not accidental. It was an effect of the historical entwinement of conservation and planning with the practices and politics of the democratic era in Haiti. Any overt talk about the environmental and urban crises had been suppressed under the dictatorship, along with so much more. After the fall of the regime it was suddenly possible to talk about the crisis. The transition from dictatorship to democracy was felt, at least at first, as a moment of radical possibility. At that time, everyone was dreaming of "another Haiti" *(yon lòt Ayiti)* and imagining a total transformation of Haitian society. But as the democratic transition dragged on, the radical hope of the early years gave way to frustration and disappointment. In the wake of that disillusionment, democratic politics and democratic practices (at least of the kind associated with Aristide and his Lavalas movement) were themselves deemed part of the problem. In this wider context, the struggles to define the forest and the city were, at root, struggles to define crisis itself, to diagnose the problem and prescribe solutions and to decide on the proper course of action.

But, as I would soon learn, this was only the beginning of the story.

MEETING THE FOREST

"It's a miracle," Cameron said as we climbed a crumbling stone path and looked down into the dense patch of trees below, "that this place exists at all. There's no other place like it in Haiti. We need to save it."

It was early in the morning on a hot August day in the summer of 2002. A few women were still setting up their marketing stations on the sidewalk, laying out small bunches of fruit and vegetables for sale. Farther down the street a woman was cooking on a small charcoal stove. But the city's streets were mostly empty. Soon, the dust and heat and traffic would take over. Cameron was leading me on a tour of the forest. We had set out just after sunrise, hiking up a steep mountainside ringed with new squatter settlements. I had been to the forest many times before, but always by car, driving through the congested streets of Martissant. Cameron wanted me to see it "the way it was meant to be seen." And so we walked up the mountain, out of town, then back down the other side.

Cameron was the director of the Katherine Dunham Botanic Garden Foundation (KDBGF), an organization he helped create in the late 1980s to manage and protect the portions of the forest owned by the American dancer and anthropologist Katherine Dunham.[17] The Katherine Dunham Botanic Garden existed largely in name only, although in 1993 it had been formally listed with Botanic Gardens Conservation International (BGCI), a network of gardens that promotes a global strategy for plant conservation. At that time, the KDBGF had a development plan and a fund-raising operation that was well underway. The affiliation with BGCI helped raise international attention for the project, and at the end of 1993 two European botanists came to catalog plant species on the property. "That was during the de facto regime," Cameron told me. "Everything was fucked up then. There were daily raids in Martissant. People were being shot. One day, some guys with guns showed up and kicked everyone out of the forest. The junta said we were hiding a terrorist training camp in the forest." One of the caretakers who worked at the garden was brutally killed and his dismembered body was left in the street outside the property. The botanists, fearing for their own lives, left the country. In the face of the bad press, the fund-raising campaign died off. Cameron, though, had refused to give up. When I met him in 2002, he was still working hard to make the dream of the garden into a reality.

Cameron was a charismatic Canadian who had lived in Haiti off and on since the 1980s. He had originally been hired by Dunham to track down several antique statues that had been stolen from her estate during the various military coups that took place after the fall of the dictatorship. After a few weeks, Cameron's investigation ended abruptly when several high-ranking officers in the Haitian army told him to stop looking for the antiques. "I thought that was it," he told me. "But then Dunham asked me to come meet the forest. That was the word she used—meet." Cameron continued his story as we headed down into the forest. It dawned on me that we were now acting out just the sort of "meeting" he was recounting. He folded back the broad leaves of a plantain tree and led me through a small grove and into a clearing inside the forest.

"It was obvious this place was a forest." Photo by author.

"Back then," Cameron said, "Haiti was changing a lot. Everyone knew it. This was before Aristide's election, before the coup. But we all knew something big was coming. Duvalier was out. Democracy was in. Dunham brought me here. I lived in her guest room. She wanted to find a use for the estate, and she asked me to think about what to do with the property. When she asked me what she should do with the property, it didn't take long. I mean, it was obvious this place was a forest." Above us was the thick green canopy. Rays of light shone down on us. The air was thick and humid and I could no longer hear the sounds of the streets outside. The dust and noise of Port-au-Prince were gone. A curly-tailed lizard ran out of a bush and darted between my feet.

I have to admit, Cameron's words captured my imagination, and as we stood there, quietly looking around at the trees, I felt the obviousness he was talking about. I knew well the history of the property. I knew that it had been a French plantation during the colonial era, that it was still a private estate, and that it had once even been a hotel. I had been inside the buildings, touched their walls, felt the stone and concrete, the material presence of people. And yet, hiking into the forest, listening to Cameron talk about it, I felt even my own awareness of the human presence, the historicity of the place, drift away, replaced by a mythic sense of a primordial forest, an untouched bit of nature resting in the middle of a crowded city. I felt like we had walked back in time.

I knew this was exactly how Cameron wanted me to feel. Over the years, he had taken dozens of people on such walks. Arriving at the forest this way, while listening to Cameron's narrative of the place, had a deep emotional effect on me, as I suspect it had on countless others before, Cameron included. He had an easy charm, and when he spoke of the forest he was able to conjure up an authentic sense of myth and enchantment. I understood why he had spent years working here, and why he cared about the place so much. And yet, the walk to the forest was not just an emotional experience; it was also a *claim*—a claim that was central to the botanic garden project.

At the core of the garden project was the claim that Habitation Leclerc was irreducibly a space of nature, a sylvan landscape that had always been there. This was, in a sense, true. But there was a deeper claim, too, an assertion that the forest was a kind of primordial landscape that needed to be protected from forces that threatened to destroy it. The idea that "the forests were *first*" is a powerful one in the modern cultural imagination.[18] To paraphrase Claude Lévi-Strauss, we might say that forests are good to think with. They evoke a range of ideas about time, order, nature, and wilderness, and they do so in relation to other kinds of spaces, including farms and cultivated land, which symbolize the human control of nature, and especially cities, which symbolize civilization. Rome, it is said, began first as a forest and later became a grand imperial city. This transformation was made possible by the material and symbolic boundaries between the forest and the city.[19] In the case of Habitation Leclerc, the forest was first because it predated Haiti itself. It even predated the French colonial era (despite the lingering presence of the name of its former owner). For Cameron, as for the others involved in the botanic garden project, the forest was a sacred place that existed outside of the historical time of colonialism, outside of the legal categories of property law, and outside of the political space of the city. It existed in the mythic time of nature.[20]

As we continued our walk, Cameron told me that the forest really belonged to Mèt Gran Bwa, the Master of the Wood, one of the Vodou spirits *(lwa)* who lived in the forest. "The only reason this place still exists," he said, "is because everyone knows it is sacred. You've seen Haiti. Have you ever seen a place like this?" I shook my head. We kept walking down a dirt path toward a stand of particularly large trees. "People have been cutting trees down everywhere in this country. It is one of the most deforested places on earth. People climb mountains to find trees to cut down, to burn to make charcoal. So how come no one cuts these trees down?"

We stopped at a mapou tree. The mapou, also known as the kapok or silk-cotton tree, is indigenous to South and Central America and the Caribbean, although it is now found throughout the tropical world. Mapou trees are known as what botanists call emergent trees. They reach up to sixty meters in height, providing canopy space for birds to nest and larger animals to live and hunt. They also have deep roots that raise the water table, which means that freshwater springs are frequently found near them. In Haiti, the mapou is a sacred tree, and it is often referred to as a home *(kay)* for the lwa. Cameron gently touched the trunk of the mapou and looked up. "These are what protect the forest," he said. "It would be unthinkable to cut these down."

I had heard similar remarks, in almost the same terms, many times before. I had found that if I asked people what happens when you cut down trees, they responded with accounts of the environmental problems that come with deforestation. They told me about soil erosion and the tragic trade-off of the long-term value of trees for the short-term gains of making and selling charcoal or firewood. Their answers seemed to confirm Maxo's assertion that there was already a public consciousness of the environmental crisis among Haitians, even if there was no political will to address it. Yet, when I asked people what happens when you cut down the home of the lwa, they responded with an immediate sense of shock. For example, when I put the question this way to Serge, a young man who sometimes did work for the KDBGF, he waved his hands at me and said, "No, no, that's not possible! If we do that, we die, we are finished."

This double sense of the importance of trees was key to the conservation project. On one hand, there was the ecological value of trees, water, and the natural world. On the other hand, there was a deeper spiritual value to them, one that gave the forest not only a deep history but also a timeless, mythic aspect. The KDBGF deliberately sought to draw on both of these registers, merging global conservation with the Vodou cosmology. Cameron called this "culturally salient resource management."

"You can tell people not to cut down trees all you want," Cameron said, as we continued on our walk. "But they are still going to do it because they *have* to. No one here wants to cut down trees, except the big families that run the logging and charcoal and cement businesses. What are peasants going to do? The economy is gone. They can't live on dirt, so they cut trees. Charcoal is the country's leading cash crop. So, they're stuck, getting the one-off economic value of trees. But trees aren't mere commodities! Some things are beyond market prices. What about the medicinal value of trees and plants? The value of a fruit tree?" For Cameron, rural Haitians were stuck in a vicious circle, caught between a declining rural economy and the demands of everyday life. Maxo had said something similar when he noted the bitter irony that Haitians cut down trees in order to survive, knowing full well that in doing so they were committing themselves, their families, and their ancestors and gods to a certain death. "It is crazy!" he had said. "They do it to live, but we all die!"

We walked along another path and came to a clearing, in which there was a low brick building and a large paved circle. The circle was partially ringed with short stone walls, each painted with an image representing one of the lwa. In the center of the circle was a tall slender pole that reached at least as high as the surrounding palm trees. It was an old Vodou temple *(ounfò)*. Inside the building there were two rooms, one with an altar. The tall pole was the center post *(poto mitan)* around which people danced. "This was a great temple, years ago," Cameron said. "The roof blew off this place during Hurricane Mitch, but the pole's still standing." Cameron encouraged me to look around as he sat down on a small ledge. As I was looking at the paintings in the altar room, Vincent approached from behind, tapped me on the shoulder, and said hello.

Vincent worked as a groundskeeper at Habitation Leclerc. He joined me as I walked around the temple and then said he had something to show me. We took a short path back to Dunham's house. Behind it, near an empty pool, there was a small garden. "Here," he said. "This is my garden." Vincent stood proudly beside the potted plants, telling me the names and qualities of each of them. He did gardening on Dunham's property, but he was also studying to become an herbalist, or "leaf doctor" *(doktè fèy)*. He made extra money selling some of his plants at a nearby market. I asked him how he had come to be involved with the garden project.

"I was born here," he said. "My father lived right here, beside the forest. Katherine [Dunham] is my godmother *[marenn]*. I was born in her arms. I

have known her all my life. And I have known this forest all my life too."
He smiled as he spoke and I could sense his fondness for Dunham and for
the forest. After that first meeting, I soon came to know Vincent quite well,
spending days on end walking through the forest with him as he told me
about the various plants and their uses. He had an easygoing manner and a
kindness that radiated from him, despite the fact that he suffered from a
chronic illness that left his body frail and that often reduced him to coughing fits so strong they would sap him of energy for hours at a time. Through
Vincent I met Laurent, who was just a teenager when we first met. Their
fathers had been neighbors and good friends. Now Vincent paid Laurent to
help him with his gardening duties. Laurent would often accompany us on
walks through the forest, teaching me about the lwa and their associations
with the natural landscape. Laurent was an apprentice of Gesner, a well-
known Vodou priest *(oungan)* in Martissant, and he hoped one day to take
over his temple when Gesner retired.

These types of connections played a key role in the project to save the forest.
Both the KDBGF and the SCPE were organizations anchored by thick relations
of affiliation and alliance. In some cases, these relationships were familial. For
example, Maxo's sister Daphne worked as a housekeeper at Dunham's estate,
just as their mother Yolande had done for decades before her. And Maxo's
brother, who was a member of an elite antigang unit with the national police,
helped provide security and support for the SCPE. Most of these relationships
were mediated by the figure of Dunham, who had been a sustained presence in
the neighborhood for sixty years. She was a godmother to several residents in
the area, many of whom, like Vincent, had a strong connection to the forest
project. Gabriel, who was closer in age to Dunham, had been a lifelong friend of
hers. Luc was her neighbor and friend too. Other supporters of the project had
worked for Dunham, or danced with her troupe, or had been trained by her in
the past. (Dunham had helped found a national folkloric dance troupe in Haiti.)
These connections gave to the KDBGF and SCPE a strength that was out of
proportion with their small size. They also helped ground the claim of Cameron
and others that the forest was, above all, a sacred place. In the Vodou cosmology,
the lwa are the ancestors who have become gods. If the forest was filled with
spirits, it was only because the descendants of those ancestors still lived in the
forest and still remembered the dead.

The image of a sacred forest gave the project a particular kind of authority and legitimacy—a moral force grounded in the twin appeals to the natural order of things (ecology) and the cosmological order of the gods (Vodou).
The sacred forest was mythic, above and beyond the realm of human affairs
but beset on all sides by the craven politics of the city. The forest, as Cameron

saw it, was under threat from the degradations of a pernicious kind of democratic politics, the same kind of degrading politics that Gabriel associated with Aristide and the Lavalas movement. "All Haitian governments have relied on misery as a tool," Cameron told me. "It keeps the system going. Aristide is no different. Misery is the key to power." And the city was a space of misery, a space of power. Cameron imagined the forest as the antithesis in a dialectic that would ultimately remake the country. But in order to bring about that transformation, the forest had to become a garden.

THE BIRTH OF THE GARDEN

The modern idea of environmental conservation came from the historical experience of the effects of colonial expansion. Those effects were most immediately visible in Europe's island colonies, where the environmental damage of colonial extraction and exploitation gave birth to a new moral imperative to restore the natural world, to remake Eden in the tropics. As Richard Grove notes, "while the early oceanic island colonies provided the setting for well-documented episodes of rapid ecological deterioration, they also witnessed some of the first deliberate attempts to counteract the process artificially."[21] Colonial conservationists turned to the medicinal gardens of early modern Europe for inspiration. Those early modern gardens gave symbolic expression to the Christian, impulse to tame a wild nature and to regather the various species that had been scattered around the world after the Fall.[22] The colonial gardens that arose on the island holdings of European empires were similarly imagined as spaces of both conquest and recuperation.

The Caribbean islands were Europe's oldest and longest-held overseas colonies.[23] Like the rest of the New World, they were significantly transformed by the "Columbian Exchange"—the massive transfer of plant and animal species and human populations from other parts of the world to the Americas. In the Caribbean, this transformation was nearly total, as a "colonized environment" replaced the indigenous pre-Columbian one.[24] This sense that the Caribbean is defined by a geography of discontinuity has given local environmental movements a particular shape. They tend to be broadly critical of capitalist development, and they tend to frame ecological questions in terms of the history of colonialism and the politics of empire. For this reason, many environmentalists working in Haiti have focused less on the conservation or protection of a "pure" or indigenous nature and more on issues of economic development and political change. Gerald Murray, for example, has been critical of what he calls the "protectionist" response to environmental problems in Haiti. For Murray, protection and conservation are flawed approaches because there is "not that much untouched natural forest left either to protect or manage."[25] Instead, Murray and others have argued that the Haitian environmental crisis is really an issue of economic development. Cameron was not convinced of the development approach. "I've heard all that stuff before," he told me. "They say there is nothing to save. They told me that saving forests is for the Amazon not Haiti! That's what development experts say. But that's not what Haitians say."

It was Cameron who came up with the idea to turn the forest into a botanic garden. "Back in the late 1980s," Cameron said, "when Dunham first hired me, she asked me to think about the forest. That's what she said. 'Think about it.' And to do that, she told me I had to get initiated. So, I did the *kanzo* [Vodou initiation rite] with Gesner." From Gesner, Cameron learned about the sacred value of trees, about the relationship between the lwa and the natural landscape, and about the obligations those who serve the lwa have to take care of the trees, water, and mountains. "That really brought home for me that we needed to not just protect the forest but to really *care* for it. And so here I was, living in Dunham's house, living in the forest. And the more I thought about it, it just seemed obvious to me," he said. "Everyone in Martissant wanted to protect the forest. I knew we had to stop it from being cut down. But I also knew that we could do something *more*. I thought, 'this could be the start of something bigger.'"

Cameron had long been interested in environmental issues, and he had experience working with development organizations in Cuba and Haiti. As he saw it, the development approach had largely failed. Instead, there has been a steady increase in rates of deforestation and soil erosion since the 1970s. Much of the land nominally protected by the law has gone unprotected in practice, and there is evidence of active tree poaching throughout the country. By most estimates, only about 1 percent of the country's land is forested (down from 10 percent in the 1970s and 30 percent in the 1940s).[26] Beginning in the 1970s and '80s, international development agencies launched a series of reforestation campaigns, planting millions of trees throughout the country.[27] In 1983, the Duvalier government, under pressure from foreign development agencies, created two new national parks, La Visite and Pic Macaya, both in remote mountain regions. Both parks have seen extensive logging, despite legal restrictions.

"They planted all those trees, for decades," Cameron said. "But where are they now? Gone. You need to do something else, something more radical. Something deeper. Something that speaks to the people. The problem is politics here. The people want this, but the people in power, that is a different story. How else can you explain the fact that the country with the most devastated environment in the region does not have a national space for conservation? Everywhere else you look, there are botanic gardens, there are national protected areas. Haiti is the only country in the region that doesn't have a botanic garden."[28]

"What about the national parks?" I asked him.

He said the government lacked the money or the will to protect them. He said the trees were being actively cut down by charcoal traders and loggers. He said this was nothing new: "Look, it is clear that the government is not capable of protecting the environment. Under Aristide and Préval, the democratic governments, there was an interest in protecting the environment, but no means. Under the dictatorship, the military governments, the junta, there was an active assault on the environment. So, we had to bypass the state." Cameron, like Maxo, Luc, and others, had come to see the Haitian state as an obstacle to saving the forest. He continued: "I started talking to botanists and conservationists working in other parts of the world. I told them about the problems here, and about the forest. You know what they said? They all said to make it a botanic garden. I took the idea to Dunham and she liked it. She knew about gardens. She knew what a garden would mean to a place like Haiti. She wanted the garden to be her gift to the Haitian people."

Cameron began work on the garden project in 1989. He made connections with regional and global centers for botanical research and conservation, including institutions in the neighboring Dominican Republic as well as in the United States and England. With support from researchers at Kew Gardens, the Missouri Botanical Gardens, and BGCI, Cameron got researchers to prepare a catalog of plant species found on the property and a development plan. Both were completed in 1993, and the Katherine Dunham Botanic Garden was formally listed with BGCI.

The plan was ambitious. It envisioned the garden as a "resource center for botanic science, biodiversity conservation, horticulture, environmental education and natural culture in Haiti."[29] Faced with what they saw as a mounting environmental catastrophe, the KDBGF imagined the proposed garden to be a decisive intervention. As they noted in the development plan, "few countries are more seriously threatened by environmental crisis than Haiti. This and the reliance of Haiti's economy on mixed agriculture and horticulture make the development of a botanic garden a vital and urgent necessity."[30] And yet, a decade after the initial development plan, the garden project remained largely unrealized.

In the summer of 2002, I spent a week going through the KDBGF's archives, reading through their development plan and about a decade of correspondence. Most days, after reading through the archival material,

I would join Cameron for dinner. One evening, I was fixated on the budget for the project, which was rather modest, even considering that costs would have escalated since the budget was first proposed in 1993. "I just don't get it," I said. "There's so much development money coming into Haiti. The country lives on aid! Why hasn't anyone funded this?"

Cameron leaned forward, put his elbows on the table, and looked at me. I felt that I had offended him with my question. I could tell he was frustrated. After a tense moment, he picked up his glass, took a drink, and smiled. "That's an excellent question." He paused, still smiling. "You know, you can raise millions of dollars like that," he said, snapping his fingers. "If you want to build churches or bring missionaries to Haiti. *Millions.* But no one would put up money for the garden."

I already knew how hard Cameron had worked over the previous decade to make the project a reality. I knew he had appealed to scores of scientists, philanthropists, journalists, and politicians in Haiti and the Dominican Republic as well as in Canada, the United States, and England. I hadn't meant to imply that he had failed at an easy task, and I started to apologize. He waved his hand and laughed. "Look," he told me, leaning in again. "There is an absolute consensus about the extremity of the situation here. Everyone knows what is going on. Everyone knows how bad it is. And we know what to do about it." He paused and sat back. "There's just no political will. And without that, how can you get funding?"

I asked him why there was no political will. "The international community is afraid of Haiti," he said. "They have donor fatigue. They know it's an unstable place. And they don't know what to make of Aristide. So, everyone is worried about sinking money into a project here." Cameron felt there was little he could do about this issue. He was proud of the fact that the garden project had the support of some of the world's leading scientific institutions working on biodiversity and conservation. But he had also spent years trying to convince foreign agencies to fund the project, with no success. "They just wouldn't go for it," he said. "I don't know what to do about that." He shrugged. "But that is only part of the problem. The other problem is that there is no political will for a botanic garden in Haiti itself. There is a lot of concern about the environment, and a lot of interest in reforestation, in soil erosion, and so on. But we needed to convince people of the value of a botanic garden. And to do that, we had to think ourselves about the value of a garden, the value of a garden *in Haiti.* We had to rethink the idea of a garden."

We had to rethink the idea of a garden. To do that, Cameron worked with the SCPE to develop a series of educational and media campaigns. The aim of the campaigns was to explain to local residents what botanic gardens do and why such an institution mattered in a place like Haiti. They came up with two related ideas that they began to use when talking about the project. The first was that Habitation Leclerc would become a "national garden" *(jaden nasyonal)*. They used this term to suggest that the garden would be a national project, not just a local one. The second idea they developed was that the garden would become a "national lakou" *(lakou nasyonal)*. In Haiti, the term *lakou* refers to the extended homestead of the peasantry. It invokes not only a social space but also a set of thick, intimate relationships, since the lakou is a space shared by close family members. This new idea of the garden as jaden and lakou fit well with a long-standing discourse in which the peasantry and rural life more broadly provide the symbolic core of Haitian cultural identity. By linking the garden project to rural peasant life, the KDBGF and SCPE were able to rebrand the project. It was no longer just a project for the restoration of the natural world (like the earlier colonial botanic gardens). Now it was imagined as a particularly *Haitian* project of redemption and regeneration.

A NATIONAL LAKOU

Almost everyone who arrives in Haiti by airplane comments on the curious experience of seeing the island from thirty thousand feet above. While some foreigners are surprised to learn that Haiti and the Dominican Republic share the island of Hispaniola, almost everyone who lands in Port-au-Prince recounts the uncanny feeling of seeing the border between the two countries rendered in stark relief. Jared Diamond, in his characteristically hyperbolic prose, describes it this way: "The border looks like a sharp line with bends, cut arbitrarily across the island by a knife, and abruptly dividing a darker and greener landscape east of the line (the Dominican side) from a paler and browner landscape west of the line (the Haitian side). On the ground, one can stand on the border at many places, face east, and look into pine forest, then turn around, face west, and see nothing except fields almost devoid of trees."[31]

Diamond's language is telling here, and it repeats a widely held sentiment that the Haitian landscape has been wounded—*cut by a knife.* The deforested fields and mountainsides become scars, bearing the traces of a past violence. Haitians express a similar idea in somewhat different terms. They point to the deforested and eroded hillsides and say that the mountains' "bones" *(zo)* are showing. This is because many of the mountainsides have not only been deforested, they have also been mined so thoroughly that all you can see are limestone quarries or rock outcroppings. In local and foreign media, Haiti has likewise been described as "an eroding nation" and as a "ruined landscape" full of "treeless forests."[32] Consider how Charles, a member of the SCPE, described a proposed ecotourism project in the mountains above Port-au-Prince: "I heard some people talking about ecotourism, about tours to those windblown rock formations in the high mountains." He laughed and shook his head. "I remember, ten years ago, when those same rocks were underground, under the dirt! The devastation has been that fast, that total. Ecotourism? I don't know. Then again, some people like to visit graveyards."

These images render Haiti as a landscape of loss. The limestone hollows, the treeless forests, the scars in the dirt all point to an eerie absence. For many Haitian environmentalists, that absence signifies the death of the nation itself. This is because Haiti has historically been an agrarian country. While the majority of Haitians now live in urban areas, there is still a strong sense of identification with the agrarian past. Most urban residents have family ties to the countryside, but beyond such connections of kinship there are deeper symbolic connections between the land and national identity. Thus, when Haitians talk about vanishing land or about the environmental crisis, they tend to mean two things—the loss of natural resources, like forests and trees, and the loss of a *world*.

This sense of a lost world is best captured by the persistent talk of the "death of the lakou."[33] Most development experts have focused on saving trees and, thus, on a narrow version of the environmental crisis. But in seeking to turn the forest into a national lakou, the KDBGF and the SCPE found an idea with wide resonance in Haiti. Saving trees makes sense to many people, especially to peasants who farm. But saving the lakou makes a different kind of sense, an immediate sense, to all Haitians. To understand why, it is important to understand what the lakou is and what it means, for the story of the birth of the lakou is, in good measure, the story of the birth of Haiti, or at least the story of the emergence of the Haitian peasantry from the ashes of the colonial slave-plantation.

Much has been written about peasant social life in Haiti, more than I will recount here.[34] But let me offer a brief sketch. The central feature of rural social life is the extended family compound. Each household within the compound is an autonomous unit, and its members are defined by coresidence and shared cooking. But each individual household is part of the larger social and economic unit, and this unit is called the lakou. The term *lakou* has a wide range of meanings, although in the simplest terms it means "courtyard." In practice, the term names both the spatial formation of the extended family compound and the social relationships that hold among coresidents. Such compounds range in size, but they typically include several households organized under the authority of a central "head," usually an elderly male relative. The compound also includes shared cooking areas and a garden and may also include a family cemetery. It is the site of ritual services to commemorate the Vodou lwa, and it is a key site for the economic life of the family. The lakou also includes a plot of land collectively owned and used by all members. When children are born, their incorporation into the family and the lakou is marked by the burial of the placenta at the base of a fruit tree in the family yard, a rite that signifies group membership by literally merging the child's substance with the material ground that anchors social life.[35]

The lakou has a deep history, one that extends back to the provision grounds of the slave plantation. Located on marginal land not used for cultivation by planters, provision grounds consisted of chunks of land given over to slaves for them to grow their own food. These garden plots were useful to planters, who wanted to find cheap ways to keep their labor force alive. But they soon became crucial sites for slaves themselves, who did more than grow their own food—they also sold or traded the surplus, a practice that gave rise to a thriving internal market between and across plantations. In the process, slaves also remade themselves as socially recognizable people. As Orlando Patterson reminds us, slavery is characterized by social death and natal alienation.[36] Social death removes all legal rights of personhood from slaves, while natal alienation removes all rights of kinship, including the right of a woman to keep her child. In the Caribbean colonies, social death and natal alienation were taken to an extreme. Slave traders and planters divided up their slaves across cultural, linguistic, and familial lines, so that slaves arriving in places like Saint Domingue would be stripped of all aspects of personhood. Nevertheless, in the midst of this oppressive system, slaves found ways to build new social relationships, collectively giving birth to new cultural formations, new languages, and new religions. Richard Price calls this the "miracle of creolization," and much of this miracle took shape on those same provision grounds. In the act of growing their own food, slaves transcended their legal category as property and became agents. When slaves bought and sold on their own markets, their personhood was again recognized by others. As Sidney Mintz notes, "it was on such lands that the slaves acquired or perfected their horticultural skills, developed their own standardized agricultural practices, learned the characteristics of Caribbean soils, mastered the cultivation of new crops, and otherwise prepared themselves for their reconstitution as peasantries."[37] And for those new peasants who emerged after the revolution, the provision grounds remained an important space. They became, after the end of the plantation system, the shared family land of the lakou, giving land a material and symbolic significance that "far exceeds any obvious economic considerations."[38]

This is why the lakou stands for so much. It symbolizes social relations of kinship and connection across time, uniting residents with ancestors and with future generations. It is also a material resource available for family members. To have access to the lakou is to be a member of the family. But the lakou is not just the space in which family life takes place—it is also the name for the community that shares the land. The lakou is thus both a spatial form and a social group. As the latter, it names the most meaningful relations of belonging and affect at the center of Haitian culture. To belong to the lakou is to be a part of an intimate moral community. All those who are not part of the lakou are outsiders. As Drexel Woodson puts it, the lakou "figure[s] prominently in local conceptions of public and private space, and in the differentiation of persons, relationships and forms of conduct."[39]

The idea of a national lakou was thus a powerful one. It tapped into a deep sense of cultural nationalism and it gave the project a specifically Haitian character. Few Haitians have a frame of reference for understanding global conservation or the issues of biodiversity. Yet, as Maxo and the SCPE frequently noted, there was a widely shared sense of the environmental crisis among Haitians. Turning to local concepts to talk about that crisis made sense on many levels. It also gave the project a new kind of politics, one based on both redemption and inclusion. By referring to the garden as a national lakou, the KDBGF was able to claim that they would intervene in the cultural catastrophe of the death of the lakou, which for Haitians signified not only the loss of trees or soil but the loss of a whole way of life. At the same time, calling it a *national* lakou aligned the garden project with the revolutionary populism of the democratic movement in a way that the earlier efforts of resource conservation had never been able to do. Could a national lakou at Habitation Leclerc give visible, concrete shape to the imagined community of the nation? This was certainly the intended implication of the new campaign. As a national lakou, the garden project would be something more than a restoration of the old peasant traditions—it would also bring about a revolutionary change that would unite the nation as a new moral community, a group defined precisely by their shared stake in a national garden.

The garden project had always positioned itself as different from other conservation efforts. It had, for example, positioned itself as a radical alternative to the development model of reforestation or agroforestry. Development campaigns had failed because their vision had been too narrow, seeking only to manage the crisis. By contrast, the garden project had a messianic quality. It was a redemptive project, one that promised to remake a lost world. Thus, the idea of a national lakou gave the project a specific relation to time and crisis. In the face of the catastrophic death of the lakou, the garden would be a revolutionary leap out of the present and into a future where the nation itself could be reborn. It was, in a sense, everything the democratic era had promised but not delivered.

"We are saving trees, yes," Maxo once told me. "But that is not all. This place is our garden, our lakou. This is for all Haitians. For Haiti." During that same conversation, Vincent added that what made this project different was that the forest was cared for by an entire community. In essence, he was saying that the forest was already a lakou, but one that would now be opened up to the entire country. "We live here," Vincent said. "This is our home."

Maxo nodded his agreement. "We must save it," he said. "And we must save the countryside, the land, the peasantry. The lakou, yes! Haiti is an agrarian nation. The lakou is our past. But it is also our future."

THE SITUATION OF CRISIS

"Crisis is the only word to describe the conditions facing the Katherine Dunham Botanic Garden."[40] So began a March 2002 memorandum circulated by the KDBGF to their members, the members of the SCPE, several journalists, ministers in the Haitian government, and officials from several international development organizations working in Haiti. The memo, called "Situation Report," was a significant turning point in the garden project. While the KDBGF and SCPE had always framed the project in the language of crisis, their main points of reference had been the environmental and urban crises. By 2002, things had changed. In the Situation Report, and in the "rescue phase" launched with the report, they began to frame the crisis as a political one.

I first read the report in the spring of 2003, when the rescue phase was well underway. It was already clear at that time that the situation at Habitation Leclerc had worsened significantly. The garden project had been imagined as a project of redemption, steeped in an ecology of care and a sense of the moral order of the natural and cosmological worlds. But by the time the Situation Report was written, the project had become mired in crisis. Large portions of the forest had effectively been taken over by a squatter community and by an armed group that variously called itself the Red Army (Lame Wouj) and the Popular Organization for the Liberation of Haiti (OPLA, Òganizasyon Popilè pou Libète Ayisyen). Under the banner of the Red Army, the group operated as a gang. Like other gangs around the city, the Red Army was a criminal entrepreneurial group that used violence to enforce its control over the various legal and illegal economies in its zone of operation. But as the OPLA, the group was also a neighborhood organization that provided a range of services to those within their zone. These services included protection but also the provision of basic public goods such as water, electricity, and housing. Taken together, the Red Army/OPLA was an example of what Chelsey Kivland calls a "street sovereign"—that is, a group that combines elements of gangs, grassroots social movements, and governmental organizations. In Port-au-Prince, such groups have come to fill the void left by the Haitian state over the past few decades.[41]

The Red Army was an active presence in the neighborhood in the 1990s, but in the early 2000s they began to exert their control in new, often violent, ways. They killed several nearby residents, burned numerous houses, and displaced rival gangs from a large section of territory. By the time of the Situation Report, they were actively using the forest as a base of operations. In April 2003, I went with Cameron as he gave a tour to an American journalist and self-described "war photographer." Maxo and the SCPE had been working hard to keep cordial relations with the squatters and the gangs, and they had established a détente of sorts.

Despite the relative calm of the standoff, the KDBGF was adamant that the situation with the Red Army had significantly transformed the garden project. According to the Situation Report, the forest had been seized by an illegitimate group that now threatened to destroy it. The report began by reiterating the mythic version of the forest as a sacred space and noted the importance of the watershed and the springs. It described the presence of mapou trees on the property as evidence of an "ancient agreement between water and trees" and it called the forest as a whole a "unique remnant of Caribbean coastal forest." But after this brief description the report changed in tone, casting the forest as a natural space that was being "held hostage by vicious criminals who terrorize the community and prevent the two million citizens of Port-au-Prince, Haiti, from using and enjoying their only botanic garden." It referred to property owners who lived near the area as "citizens" but to other groups living in and near the forest as "illegal squatters," "criminals," and "murderous thugs." The oppositions were clear, and rather stark—nature and city, citizen and criminal, life and death. Finally, the report cast the standoff as a national political issue, asserting that local residents were still waiting for the national police to do their job and remove the gang. In the absence of such actions by the police and the government, the report warned that local residents were willing to take matters into their own hands. Local residents, the report stated, "would prefer the Haitian police rectify the gang problem but have also informed us that they will clear the property of the gangs if necessary. This would be a fight between machetes and M-16s—a bloody catastrophe." That is, if urgent action was not soon taken, residents would rise up against the gang, and be killed in the process.

Even before the Situation Report was circulated, the SCPE had shifted their day-to-day work from gardening to policing. They had acquired several handguns (the market in small weapons is rather large in Haiti) and were paying a few local residents to patrol the area as a private security force. They had also made repeated appeals to the police, but with little success. "When we call the police—nothing," Maxo told me. "If they come, maybe they take someone away. And then he [the mayor] goes to the jail to see them and like that," he opened both of his hands, "they are released." Maxo shook his head. "What can we do?"

Maxo was convinced that the Red Army had deep political connections. This was a common sentiment around the city, as more and more critics were accusing Aristide of aligning with and even arming political gangs called *chimè* (ghosts, or chimeras). In Martissant this was hardly a matter of speculation, since the Red Army had frequently declared themselves to be "with Aristide" *(nan Titid)*. Of course, just because they claimed political connections does not mean they actually had them. There was, for example, a performative element to such claims, since it allowed the Red Army to position themselves as the defenders of the people and as a legitimate community organization doing the work of democratization. But as Maxo noted, when the police did arrest gang members, those same members often reappeared in the area a few days later, and the most prominent leader of the Red Army, a man named Abel, frequently boasted of his close ties to the local mayor.

For their part, the SCPE and KDBGF cultivated their own connections to the government and the police. Maxo's brother worked for the antigang unit in the national police. When he talked about calling the police, he really meant calling his brother. The police were reluctant to engage in official policing actions at the forest, but everyone in the area knew about Maxo's brother, and the familial connection to a feared force gave him some measure of protection. Cameron, Luc, and others had also worked for years to pressure government officials to do something about the situation, although they had not had much success. By 2002, they had begun to appeal to international agencies instead, in hopes that well-publicized accounts of gang violence would influence the international community to press the Haitian government into action. Locally, the SCPE had been paying residents for information for years, including members of the squatter community living in the forest. Maxo had managed to build enough trust among some of the squatters that they would tip him off about gang activities, especially when those activities involved cutting down trees.

As the rescue phase wore on, Cameron grew increasingly frustrated and disillusioned. He had worked on the project for almost fifteen years, and the vision of a national botanic garden seemed farther away than ever before. He was especially distraught by the fact that the gang had started poaching trees. "We pay informants, we pay the police. But it never ends. And we don't have the money to keep doing this," he told me in the spring of 2003. And yet, one of the curious benefits of the situation was that the police had come to see protecting the forest as a lucrative side project. The lure of bribes at least made them more willing to show up. "But then again, they probably get paid off by the gang too," Cameron added.

"A vicious circle," I said.

Cameron grew quiet for a moment and then let out a long sigh. "Yeah. Vicious is right. Disorder is big business in Haiti. Everyone gains, and everyone loses."

Another quiet moment passed.

"You know," Cameron said, "when we started this we wanted it to be a model of conservation for the whole country. Now, we're just trying to save it. And the only way to do that is to guard trees with guns."

Cameron laughed and shook his head, as if realizing the absurdity of what he had just said. "We're sitting on the edge of an ecological apocalypse here," he said, "and what is happening? Gangs are cutting down trees, killing people, setting houses on fire. And the government does nothing. Nothing. And the squatters, they're stuck too. Stuck in the middle. They have nowhere else to go, so of course they're going to side with the gangs. No one else is doing anything for them. We had a plan to move them, to help them. But now, I just don't see how this thing is going to end."

A few days after my conversation with Cameron, I met with Luc to talk about the rescue phase. Luc had been instrumental in some of the behind-the-scenes planning of the report, and it was he who had first suggested arming members of the SCPE. He was still adamant that the current situation in the forest was a symbol of the urban crisis. The squatters and the gang were just further evidence to him of how the unchecked democratic politics of Aristide had begot violence and disorder. "It's a money issue and a policing issue," he told me. "In Haiti, it's the same thing. But we can't do anything with the forest until we get the gangs and the squatters out. These people come from Cité Soleil or they come from elsewhere in the city and they think they can just take, take, take. Take what they want." Luc's account cast the situation in the forest in terms of a political crisis in which hordes of invading others—the people, the demos—threatened the rule of law.

Luc's critique of democracy sounded pretty antidemocratic to me, but it was rooted in a particular urban middle-class and elite experience of the city. Luc clearly saw the presence of "these people" as a disruption to the proper order of things, in all senses of that phrase. And yet Luc was an ardent political activist and an advocate for democracy. It is just that he embraced a minimalist view of democracy that gave leadership roles to experts and that upheld a strong commitment to the rule of law. He supported democracy when it meant a formal change in the governing institutions, but he did not necessarily support it if it meant a substantive change in social relations.

As the rescue phase wore on, the KDBGF began to adopt a similar perspective. This was a major change, since the project had initially aligned itself with the radical hope promised by Aristide's Lavalas movement. In the first years of the project, the KDBGF had included a resettlement program for squatters in their planning efforts and their budget. They had also planned to compensate those who would be removed from the property. The KDBGF had always recognized the pressing need for land among the urban poor, and they had hoped to bring these squatter groups into the project directly and to mediate between the interests of long-term residents, who were concerned about their own properties and about their safety, and the squatters living in and near the forest. Throughout the first decade of the project, the KDBGF predicted that the main source of conflict between the garden's supporters and the squatters would not be land at all, since they could always pay squatters to relocate; rather, they thought it would be water. They knew the garden would need a lot of water and that public access to water was likely to be a key issue in the community. As part of their educational and promotional efforts, they had tried to present the case for the garden to all residents, including squatters, by suggesting that the garden would protect the spring, thereby guaranteeing fresh water for everyone.

Water is, however, a deeply political issue in Haiti. For the urban poor, access to water has been a key concern for decades. During the Duvalier dictatorship, water management was a lucrative way for public officials to make money. Those charged with the management of public standpipes or the delivery of water could easily monetize this public good by stealing the water and selling it on the black market or by charging, illegally, for access to standpipes.[42] In the 1990s, the democratic governments of Aristide and René Préval built new standpipes and reopened or repaired existing ones in an attempt to democratize access to water. One of those new standpipes was in a squatter settlement along the road that borders the forest. Long-term residents in Martissant saw the standpipe as a clear sign that the government would never remove the squatters. For their part, the squatters asserted that they had a "right" *(dwa)* to live there. Squatters throughout Martissant, and Port-au-Prince more broadly, do not see themselves as unlawfully taking private property. Many of them live on state land, or on private land that is not actively being used. Under Haitian law, squatters can gain legal title to such land after a certain period of residence. This makes the issues of removal and of service provision deeply political. When the government does not forcibly remove squatters and when it supplies them with public services, it is at least tacitly consenting to their right of residence.

The politics around squatter settlements, informal housing, and service provision is a common one in cities across the global South. Although they are often socially and political excluded, squatters become a political community in part through their collective violation of the law.[43] In Haiti, squatters have an ambiguous relationship to the law. On one hand, they live precariously on the margins of the law. On the other hand, they are rather literally in the center of social and political life—in the streets and slums of the capital city. This is because the Haitian state has, for decades, directly encouraged rural-to-urban migration as a short-term response to the collapse of the rural economy and as part of an economic shift to cheap, flexible labor in export-producing zones. Urban migrants have also been key constituencies for various political parties, and nearly all governments since the 1940s have rewarded their urban base with either formal public housing or informal access to state land and services.[44] In addition, squatting on public land has a long history in Haiti, and many current landowners have gained legal title through informal expropriation. In Port-au-Prince, land seizures, squatters' rights, and access to services became highly charged issues after the end of the dictatorship. During the democratic transition, many urban residents began to not only claim more access to public services and public space but to do so precisely in the terms of a democratic politics of inclusion. The sense that Aristide's government was unable or unwilling to intervene was not mere perception. In 1995, the mayor of Port-au-Prince, Evans Paul, who was a member of Aristide's Fanmi Lavalas party, noted that the government was simply incapable of preventing land seizures or removing squatters. As Paul saw it, the central problem was that the new government had to act democratically and so could not use violence or terror to repress the people (the main tactics used in the past to relocate squatters). By contrast, he noted, the people were under no similar obligation to act democratically.⁴⁵ His comments were widely taken to mean that the Aristide government would look the other way when its supporters took land.

There was an added layer to this at Habitation Leclerc. The description of the forest as a national lakou had allowed the squatters and the gang to make a claim of legitimate occupation and ownership by positioning themselves as members of the lakou. A few leaders from the squatter community began to hold Vodou rites in the forest, and some of them even claimed that Dunham, still the legal title holder of the property at the time, was dead and that they were the inheritors of the property. This might explain why some of the squatters were also eager to work with Maxo and the SCPE to prevent tree poaching, since they too had a vested interest in the long-term conservation of the forest. When I talked to squatters living in the forest, I was surprised to find just how much their own claims to the property mirrored those made by the KDBGF and SCPE. Not only did they appeal to the law and to the lwa, but they also repeatedly referred to the forest as a national lakou—a sign that the KDBGF's campaign had been highly successful, albeit perhaps not with the intended audience. As one squatter put it: "This is our lakou. Us, the people, we live here. It is our right." In making this claim, the squatters also made a broader one, suggesting that as members of the nation—as what Aristide's Lavalas movement called simply "the people" (pèp la)—they had a legitimate claim to live on the property.

Faced with this challenge, the KDBGF and SCPE had begun to shift their language from the cultural and moral register of the lakou and of gardens to the political and legal register of policing and rights. As they shifted the framing of the project from conservation to security, they also shifted their focus. By the time of the Situation Report, members of both groups had begun to cast the project in terms of a seizure of private property and public goods by an illegitimate and illegal group of people. While they were concerned with the continued presence of squatters in and around the garden, the KDBGF was most concerned with the Red Army, since the gang represented the clearest and most direct challenge to the project. But they also used the presence of the Red Army to effectively criminalize all other groups occupying the forest and, at least to some degree, to delegitimize democratic practices as a whole.

For their part, the Red Army and the OPLA returned fire by calling the KDBGF and the SCPE invaders and illegitimate outsiders. They did this not only through their claims of affiliation with Aristide and state and municipal governments but also through a series of campaigns in which they declared themselves to be protectors of the forest, saving it from foreigners.

Graffiti on the ruins of a building. Photo by author.

As part of these campaigns, the OPLA periodically spray-painted walls in and around the forest, marking it as part of their zone. Some of that graffiti proclaimed "death to foreigners" *(blan moun mouri)*. Of course, they had repeatedly made real threats against Cameron and others, so there was a literal claim to the signs. But the messages also parlayed the wider symbolic opposition between national sovereignty and foreign invasion into an apt metaphor for their own view of the struggle to control the forest. Along these same lines, Abel claimed that he had been hired by Dunham to manage the forest and that he also worked for the municipal water authority and was in charge of the local standpipes. When faced with these claims, Cameron scoffed. "Abel is just fucking crazy," he said. "He doesn't work for water management. He works for people who want to *steal* the water!"

In the end, the rescue phase fundamentally transformed the garden project, changing the very terms in which it was understood as well as the practices pursued by all those involved. Even as they remained committed to addressing the environmental crisis in Haiti, the KDBGF and SCPE became embroiled in an irreducibly political crisis. The political crisis, in turn, brought a shift of focus from conservation to security. As their dream of a botanic garden faded from view and they were left merely guarding trees with guns, they began to drift from a politics of hope, which saw the garden as essential to the rebirth of the country, to something else—a politics of disillusionment that saw in the future nothing else but more confrontation, more crisis, and more catastrophe.[46]

THE CRISIS TOURS

One night in April 2003, I had dinner with Cameron. I could tell he was upset. The rescue phase had dragged on for well over a year with little progress. He had brought journalists to the forest to report on the situation, had held a press conference about the garden project, and had spoken repeatedly to government ministers and to officials from international organizations. No one seemed willing to support the project, especially now that the Red Army had taken control of most of the property. "We have to do something," he said. "Something new."

When I met up with Cameron the next day, his mood had changed markedly. For over a year he had been frustrated. He had contemplated walking away from the garden project altogether. But now he seemed energized and full of hope. I hadn't seen him this upbeat since he first took me to meet the forest a year ago. We headed over to the forest to meet Maxo.

The meeting was short but decisive. Cameron and Maxo decided to take advantage of the détente with the gangs and the squatters to do something new. The Red Army still had de facto control over a large chunk of the property, but they were currently trying to persuade whoever would listen that they were not a gang and that they were in fact protecting the forest. For the moment, at least, the gang seemed content with making peace as they pursued their own legal claims. For their part, the SCPE had been using the time to try to convince the squatters to side with the garden project by assuring them that they would be compensated for their eventual relocation. Yet while the standoff meant an end to violence, it also meant that the project was stuck in a permanent state of limbo. No one would finance it as long as the gang and squatters remained on the property. The police would not relocate squatters without proof that the project had the financial capability to prevent them from returning. And the government seemed to be either unable or unwilling to do much of anything. The longer the situation went unresolved, the greater a case the squatters would have to challenge Dunham's legal title. "Things must change," Cameron said.

The plan was simple enough. Cameron and Maxo had decided the best approach would be to just start acting as if the garden was operational. Instead of being stuck in an endless waiting period as the standoff dragged on, they would start to run programming at the garden. They spent the next week contacting friends throughout the city. Their idea was to build on the kind of tours they had been running already. Before, they had brought people to meet the forest. Now they wanted to bring people to see what they called "the situation."

For years, Cameron and Maxo had garnered support for the garden project by bringing people to walk through the area and directly experience the place. Maxo saw such tours as a way to produce in participants a "new political and social consciousness of the environment." Cameron, too, saw them as a kind of consciousness-raising, and he was deeply committed to the idea that a direct experience with the forest would spur people to action. "People need to see this," he had said repeatedly. And he was right. I had heard him speak with many people about the project. Most voiced support for it, but few did more than that. I had also accompanied him numerous times as he took people to meet the forest, just as he had once taken me to meet it. Those who saw the forest this way tended to become more directly involved, often donating time or money to the project. Now, with the project caught up in a tense dispute with gangs and squatters, Cameron felt that bringing people to see the forest was more important than ever. But given the prevailing situation, the tours were now meant to produce something different in participants. Instead of coming to see the forest as a purely natural space to be saved from destructive forces outside of it, visitors would see firsthand the stark realities of the penetration of those forces into the forest. Instead of harmonious nature, they would see social conflict. Instead of order, disorder. Indeed, one might say that during the rescue phase these "crisis tours" served to produce a direct, intimate, and immediate experience of crisis itself.

The most ambitious of these tours was also the last of its kind. Frustrated with the lack of support for the project, the SCPE and KDBGF decided to start running educational field trips to the forest. The plan was to have students in ecology classes visit for the day. Cameron saw this as a way to show a new audience how a botanic garden would serve as a public good in the city, and he hoped that by making it about an educational experience, it would be seen as a nonpolitical act by the gangs and the squatters.

I met Cameron early in the morning on the day of the first, and last, such field trip. He was excited and eager to get started. We had a quick breakfast of coffee with bread and bananas and then we left. He had already arranged for two drivers with pickup trucks to handle transportation for the day. We walked to where the drivers, Kenny and Gedulin—both cousins of members of the SCPE—were waiting for us. Then we all drove to a private junior high school that catered to professional middle-class families.

We met Raymond, who was a historian by training but currently taught courses on ecology and environmental studies. Raymond seemed excited to meet us. He had been approached by Luc and Gabriel, both of whom knew Raymond's family, about building connections between the school and the botanic garden. He proudly showed us around his classroom and described his curriculum to us. Cameron then gave Raymond a brief account of the history of the garden project and ending by proposing that the garden could serve as a kind of "living classroom" in which students could get hands-on experience to bolster their studies of ecology, agronomy, and botany. Raymond was visibly excited and everyone was in high spirits. He told us that few of his students had ever been outside of Port-au-Prince. They had no real connection to nature or the environment, and they had few opportunities to learn about it outside of the classroom. He said that the botanic garden would be an ideal educational experience and that he was already imagining teaching entire courses at the garden, in which students might earn credit for ecological research, training in resource management, and volunteering in reforestation campaigns.

A buzzer rang, signaling the end of classes. Students filed in and out of rooms. The group of ten environmental studies students arrived, and Raymond led them to the trucks. Sitting in the backs of the trucks, we drove off toward Martissant. I watched the students as we drove through the city. They laughed nervously as the trucks navigated the rugged, rutted streets. As we climbed up a steep, severely eroded road, one of the trucks almost got a rear tire stuck in a large hole. The smiles and giggles were replaced by tense expressions as the students held on tightly to the side panels. As we rounded a long curve and approached the forest, a few students nudged each other and pointed to the burnt cars, the crumbling stone wall, and the pro-gang graffiti.

And then we arrived. Maxo and Vincent were waiting for us. They opened the gates and we drove inside. Kenny and Gedulin parked under the shade of

A hole in the perimeter wall around Habitation Leclerc.
Photo by author.

some trees and we all hopped out of the trucks. After brief introductions, Maxo and Vincent led the group on a tour of Dunham's house. Cameron and Raymond followed behind the group, chatting excitedly about possible future programs and joint ventures between the school and the garden. The students looked mildly bored as they listened to Vincent talk about Katherine Dunham and her role in Martissant. But their expressions soon changed as we left the house and walked along a narrow stone path into the forest behind it. The students listened raptly as Maxo told them about the SCPE's efforts to protect the forest and about the importance of the underground spring and the mapou trees. Raymond began to join in the conversation, making connections between the trees and plants around us and the students' coursework. As the tour progressed, we walked back toward Dunham's house and toward the trucks. As we walked out through the gate, Widson and Begory, two men from the SCPE, joined us, walking along either side of the group. We crossed the road that cuts the forest into two distinct segments, stepped through a large hole in the perimeter wall, and entered the gang-controlled section of the forest.

Maxo and Vincent led the group along an overgrown path. We passed the crumbling ruins of a building, covered in graffiti. I could sense a shift in the mood. Cameron seemed on high alert. He kept looking around and was no longer paying attention to the tour. I could no longer see Widson and Begory, but I suspected they were still with us, following and watching our group from inside the tree line. A few young children in torn clothes ran up to the students. They tagged alongside the group, laughing and gently teasing the students about their uniforms. Maxo led us over a small bridge, and we stopped to look down at the concrete basins below, filled with stagnant water. He started to explain the importance of protecting the watershed, telling them how deforestation and mining along the mountain slopes behind us was destroying the water system. As he spoke, an older woman named Celeste joined us.

Celeste was well known throughout the neighborhood, where she lived and worked as a prominent goat trader. When I had first met her the previous year, she told me she used to be a dancer at Habitation Leclerc, a claim that both Cameron and Dunham denied. I would later learn that her son was one of the leaders of the Red Army and that Celeste herself was involved in the property dispute.[47] In 2003, though, Celeste was something of an ally of the garden project. She knew many of the squatters living on the property and facilitated negotiations with them. She was also a *mambo*, a Vodou priestess, and it was common to find her at the basins, cleaning trash and debris out of the water.

As we stood looking at the basin, Celeste seemed to naturally take over the tour. She told us that her patron spirit Simbi, a Vodou lwa who lives in water, had appeared to her in a dream the night before and told her to come to the spring. She then proceeded to tell the students about the symbolic and sacred aspects of water, about the importance of conserving and protecting these sacred springs, and about her obligation (*devwa*) to purify and cleanse the springs as part of her ritual service (*sèvi*) owed to the lwa. "Only the lwa give us water," she said. As she spoke, a few of the students began to wander off, curious about the buildings they could see scattered among the trees. The younger children who had joined us from the squatter settlement climbed atop a nearby structure and looked down on the students with amusement. Celeste continued talking, addressing her comments more to Maxo and Cameron now. She said that natural resources like trees and springs were "gifts" from the lwa that were meant to be used by those who "fed" the lwa in return. While I had heard much the same account of the sacredness of the natural world from those involved in the garden project, the implication carried by Celeste's impromptu lecture was that the forest belonged to those who served the spirits, and not necessarily to those who held legal title.

As Celeste was talking, Maxo pulled Cameron aside. They spoke quietly for a moment and then returned to the group. "Maxo thinks we should leave," Cameron said. Before I could ask why, he was off gathering the students who had strayed. Raymond followed him, looking confused and concerned. Widson and Begory emerged from the trees and flanked the group of students as Maxo began to lead us back toward the wall, the road, and the trucks waiting at Dunham's house. I hung back, trailing behind the group, and chatted with two young boys from the squatter camp. Then I noticed that Maxo and Cameron had stopped up ahead and were talking to Abel, the leader of the OPLA and the Red Army.

I reached into my bag and pulled out a camera. I raised it to my chest, zoomed out, and started taking pictures as I walked toward them. Maxo and Abel were talking to each other, both gesturing aggressively. I couldn't yet hear what they were saying, but I could see that Maxo held a cell phone in his hand and was pointing at it. Widson and Begory stood on either side of them, their hands behind their backs. I realized I wasn't sure if they were armed or not. As I neared them, the conversation erupted into a heated argument. I heard Maxo tell Abel that this was Dunham's property and that she had the legal title. He pointed again at his phone and then handed it to Abel, telling him to talk to Dunham's lawyer. Abel took the phone and had a brief conversation in which he insisted that we were trespassing, that he had been hired to protect the property. He also stressed that he worked for the government. After repeating this a couple of times, he tossed the phone back to Maxo. I took a couple more pictures, with the camera still at chest level.

"You shouldn't do that," a voice beside me said.

I turned to see Secundo, another leader of the OPLA and Red Army, standing behind me. He spoke in English, which surprised me. He pointed to my camera and then shook his finger in front of my face. I put the camera in my bag and walked quickly toward the rest of the group. Secundo followed closely behind me. I could feel the heat of his body near mine. I heard yelling and looked up to see Maxo and Abel staring at each other. Abel was waving his hands around, pointing at Maxo and then at the rest of the group. "Thieves!" he said. "You're all thieves! [Nou se vòlè! Nou se zenglendo!]."

Maxo's face tightened in anger. He started to yell back at Abel, then marched off. Widson and Begory stood their ground as Cameron and Raymond ushered the students out of the forest. They stepped back through the hole in the wall and crossed the road. Maxo waited in the middle of the road for all of us to cross. As I stepped into the road I looked back. Abel was still calling us all thieves. Secundo stood silently beside him on the path, a small smile on his face. He had a hand under his shirt, at his waist. Was he holding a gun or just pretending? I couldn't tell. Widson and Begory walked backwards toward the road, their hands out in front of their bodies, palms up.

We crossed the road. Abel followed, still calling us thieves. Kenny and Gedulin already had the students loaded and the trucks running. "Get in," Cameron said. I climbed into the back of the truck with him. Raymond was in the front with Kenny, on the phone with someone. Widson and Begory shut and locked the gates and then joined us. Abel waved angrily at the trucks, shouting for us to leave "his area" *(zòn m)*.

"Where's Maxo? Where's Vincent?" I asked.

"They've gone to get reinforcements," Cameron said.

CROSSING THE THRESHOLD

We drove off. Behind us, Abel stood in the road, still yelling. Kenny and Gedulin drove faster than usual, too fast for the eroded streets. I held on to the side of the truck but could do little to hold steady. We jostled around in the back, leaning into one another for support. We came careening down the hill of Rue Crepsac, turned sharply, and then hit the smooth pavement of Boulevard Jean-Jacques Dessalines. Kenny and Gedulin downshifted as we entered the mid-morning traffic. The students began to chat a bit, now that we were out of Martissant and amid the everyday scene of buses, taxis, and street markets. We dropped Raymond and the students back at their school, then headed downtown. Once there, we all dispersed. Widson and Begory wanted to stay out of Martissant for a while. Cameron went to talk to the foundation's lawyer and to make some calls. We made a plan to meet up later.

The next day, Cameron sent a report to the Haitian Minister of Foreign Affairs in which he detailed the purpose of the students' visit, reasserted the foundation's claim of legal ownership of the property, and described the confrontation with Abel. In the report, Cameron reiterated that the KDBGF had been created to manage and protect "this rare remnant of Caribbean forest in perpetuity so that it can be made available to the students of

Port-au-Prince." He then added that "during our tour of Leclerc one of the gang leaders, Abel DuPres, who is illegally occupying the forest, exited the buildings in the forest and proceeded to harass, intimidate, and physically threaten the group. We were forced to cut short the field trip and return to Miss Dunham's residence across the road. Mr. DuPres continued to harass the group with specious and erroneous claims that he works for Miss Dunham and physical threats. We left the property altogether."[48]

The field trip had been meant to build connections between the KDBGF and the private educational sector, but it ended up breaking more alliances than it forged. The fallout from the trip was swift and decisive. Raymond was upset with Cameron and Maxo. The school administration was likewise angry at both the KDBGF and Raymond for putting their students in danger. And the parents of the students who had attended the tour were livid with everyone and warned Raymond against any further contact with the KDBGF. The Haitian government gave no response to Cameron's report, but foreign agencies and possible donors soon heard of the encounter and made it clear they would not give further support to the garden project until the security situation was resolved. News of the confrontation spread across the city, as various accounts were reported in newspapers and on the radio. Facing public pressure from a number of supporters, Cameron held a press conference to assuage their fears. At the conference, he questioned why the police and the government were refusing to enforce the law and he publicly called for Abel's arrest. This, in turn, ended the détente between the Red Army and the KDBGF and SCPE. Word quickly spread through Martissant that Abel had promised to kill Maxo or Cameron if they returned to the area. In the following weeks, members of the Red Army set fire to a portion of Dunham's house, destroying both her own personal documents and much of the KDBGF's archives. The forest, and much of Martissant, was effectively under gang control and would remain so for several years.

The final "crisis tour" was a watershed moment. In its wake, the KDBGF and SCPE joined the ranks of a growing opposition to Aristide's government. The opposition had been staging demonstrations and marches for months and would soon begin to call for Aristide to step down. Some supporters of the project, like Luc and Gabriel, had already been vocal critics of Aristide for years. "Haiti is at a crossroads," Luc had told me back in 2002. "Aristide must go. That is the only way forward."

In February 2004, Aristide was forced out of the country in a coup d'état. In the aftermath of his departure, the city was engulfed in violence. The Red Army went on a rampage in Martissant, fighting with rival gangs and with the national police. Habitation Leclerc became the headquarters of a kidnapping ring. Shortly after the coup, Cameron told me: "With Aristide gone there is a power vacuum. This is going to get so much worse before it gets better." I asked him what would happen to the forest. He was cautiously optimistic. "The gangs will continue to fight, but they won't destroy the forest. They need it as cover. But the only real chance we have to save it is if there's another UN intervention." Within a few months, a UN stabilization and peacekeeping mission arrived.

THE VIEW FROM THE GROUND

There is a picture of the forest that the KDBGF and SCPE used in their promotional material. It is an aerial photograph of Martissant, taken from a helicopter. The forest is centered in the frame, appearing as a dense patch of green vegetation surrounded by a sea of concrete houses and roads. The aerial photo, as they called it, perfectly captured the idea of the forest as a space of nature beset on all sides by the disorder and degradation of the city. But like any top-down view, the photograph offered only a "thin simplification," an easy abstraction that allowed the viewer to see the situation through a series of binary oppositions: nature/culture, forest/city, order/chaos, care/violence, and sacred/profane.[49] And this is precisely how those involved in the project talked about the crisis at the forest.

The view from the ground, however, was different. When walking through the forest, it was impossible to see it as a timeless space of nature. The evidence of history was everywhere, a patina of historical accretions made up of ruins, stones, walls, paths, and roads.[50] The idea of the forest as a purely moral order, cast against the disorder of the democratic era and the crass politics of the city, was similarly hard to maintain on the ground. There, on the road, in the street markets, on the paths, and among the squatters, the separation of forest and city, of nature and politics, was impossible to sustain. Everything was blurry. There were no clear edges, no sharp lines. The walls were permeable—we had walked right through them. Walking through the forest was like constantly crossing boundaries, stepping over one threshold after another. Instead of two distinct spaces, two different realms, the forest and the city coalesced into a liminal space conjured up by the collapse of borders.

The view from above tells us much about the ideas behind the garden project. We might even read it as an exemplar of the separation of the realm of nature and the realm of the city that underlies so much of the political paradigm of the West. There is even a curious inversion of that opposition, whereby the city as polis is no longer imagined as the space of reason and democracy but instead becomes a disorderly space that threatens to destroy the world, while the forest, once conceived of as wild and untamed nature, becomes a sacred space in which a new moral community dwells. This is all broadly true, and the leaders of the garden project would likely agree with such an analysis. Indeed, at many times they mobilized just these sorts of oppositions to justify their position. The view from the ground, however, shows something else. It shows how the experience and expectation of crisis can come to shape everyday life. It shows how crisis becomes ordinary as it settles into the routines and habits of residents, into their language and thoughts and feelings, into the materiality of their everyday lives. Crisis infuses everything, it spreads, it proliferates, it becomes a normal feature of daily life. It makes the exceptional ordinary.

The story of the forest does not end here. The story continues, and the forest still stands. The gangs and squatters are gone, and so too is the idea of a botanic garden and a national lakou. Instead, the forest has become a national park and a monument to those who died during the 2010 earthquake. Things change. Everything becomes something else. What remains is crisis.

2. Looking for Life

The migrant leaves a village in the south, traveling by bus along dirt roads. The bus is too full. Chickens on the roof try to peck through bags of rice stacked so high they look as though they might fall off at any moment. The migrant comes to the city from the countryside. There is no work in the village. The land is overcrowded and eroded. They say there is work in the city, that the government has built houses and factories, that you can make good money. The migrant leaves a village in the south and arrives in the city, doubly free—free to work and free from any other means of living.[1]

The city is confusing at first. There are nameless streets and streets with two names, or three or four names, names that change with the age of the speaker. Streets that end abruptly in markets. Streets that change direction. One-way streets with two-way traffic, and two-way streets with one-way traffic. Cars stop at streetlights that never light up, the drivers nevertheless aware of some other, less visible system of turn-taking. The migrant soon learns there are two ways of seeing the city. There is the city that the planners see, that the government and the elite see. It has angles and grids. It is made of concrete and wood. It is laid out in orderly shapes, interrupted periodically by the chaotic rush of people. But there is another city too. A city made of people—of relationships that reach out across roads, that move in and out of buildings. A vast web of interconnected people, a living, breathing city.[2]

The migrant arrives in the city and seeks out a sibling, a distant cousin, or a friend. Those others who have come before, who have come to look for life. They live together on the edge of town, in a rented house made of corrugated metal. When it rains the house floods. Sometimes they sleep in shifts. They are hungry. In the village there was always food, even when there was nothing else. The migrant goes out each day, looking for work.

Always there are the long stretches of time that take up days on end, time in which there is no work, or work but no money, or money but not enough.

Everything is for sale in the city. Markets pop up and disappear, people haul baskets and buckets of goods. Everything is sold in the smallest units. And, alongside the tiny fractions of food, the slivers of soap, the lone matches, the single tablets of medicine, there are giant bundles of things, larger than the migrant has ever seen. Stacks of charcoal towering over the women who sell them, their faces and hands stained with the black dust that wafts off the coals. Everything is for sale in the city, in the city full of people with no money.

The migrant works in what the experts call the informal economy. The migrant lives in what they call informal housing. Slums. *Bidonvil.* The migrant hears these words and comes to use them too. But the migrant has other words for the city. The city is home. The migrant is a city person now. And the migrant does not work in the informal sector, no. The migrant moves through the city, talking to people. Selling things or buying them. Or sitting and waiting. Or driving. Maybe even making something. Always, the migrant moves through the city, looking for life. They say that this is how capitalism began, just like this. With peasants pulled off the land and down the dusty roads, pulled to the factories and the slums and the monstrous cities. That's how they say it began. And it goes on. Like those other peasants, in other places, the migrant comes to the city looking to make money. Money is how people live. And if they don't have any, what then?

Each day more migrants arrive. Some stay only for the day and leave again, or they stay for two days, until they sell all the onions or rice or charcoal they have brought with them. Some stay longer, searching for a place to sleep, a place to live. They find distant relatives in the slums. They call upon a cousin or a cousin's cousin, or someone from their home village. Some stay in the city. Some return to the village. Some take small boats across the big sea, hoping to make it to Florida or the Bahamas. Some just disappear.

The city remains, always changing. The migrant left the countryside, left the village, left the crisis behind. The migrant came to the city and found crisis too, of a different kind.

WAITING WITH ALEXIS

Spring 2003.   Alexis's car was parked in the shade of a tall palm tree. It had been there for days. I asked if he was driving today. He shook his head no as he waved a hand at the hotel behind us. He had already been to the lobby that morning, looking for guests who might want to hire him.

"There is no one here," he said.

We sat in plastic lawn chairs near the hotel gate. Behind us was a stone wall that ran the perimeter of the property. Beyond the wall the city was waking up. Bus drivers blurted their horns, making a distinctive gobble sound that cut through the din of traffic and the sounds of the morning markets. Inside the hotel wall, in the shade of the trees, it was quiet and calm. A few workers picked up leaves and debris from the lawn. A couple of guinea hens pecked away at the ground. The smell of fresh bread drifted over from the kitchen. Above us, the palm trees swayed gently.

Alexis was born in the southern town of Les Cayes. He came to the city in 1972, when he was fourteen years old. "I had nine years of school," he told me. "That's all. Then I came to Port-au-Prince to look for a living." Most migrants come to the city to make money to send home. Many of them imagine they will one day return to the countryside and buy some land, maybe become a farmer. Alexis had no plans to return to the countryside and rarely went back to his home village. I once asked him why.

"If I go back, I must be crying," he told me. "All my people are dead there."

Most urban migrants have large extended families in the countryside. For the families who remain in the villages, urban migrants are a crucial source of money and goods. Alexis had once sent money back, but over the years his brothers and his sister had joined him in Port-au-Prince, and his parents and extended kin had died or relocated elsewhere. He had a distant relative in the Dominican Republic, but they had not spoken in years and Alexis was not sure where he was or if he was still alive. He considered the city his home now.

Alexis came to Port-au-Prince just after Jean-Claude Duvalier took over from his father, the infamous dictator François Duvalier. Over the next decade, the Duvalier regime pushed through a series of economic reforms and structural adjustment programs designed to spur growth in offshore textile production and tourism. It was supposed to be a great "economic revolution." Hundreds of thousands of people left their villages and came to the city looking for jobs. The slums on the edges of the city swelled quickly. Alexis remembers it as a time of plenty. "When I came to the city, there was *Jean-Claudisme*," he said. "There were lots of tourists. They were everywhere. *Blan* everywhere. French Canadians would come by plane and stay for a week or two. Americans would come by ship and stay for the day. At the time, we had too many tourists. We didn't have enough places for them to sleep!" He raised his hands in the air, as if he was surprised at how different things had been then. "People slept in the streets, in the big boulevards. They would sing and dance and party all night in the streets. It was easy to find work. If you showed someone around for the day, you could make a dollar or two. If you tried hard, you could make a lot of money."

When he first arrived, Alexis worked informally as a guide, taking tourists on day trips around the city. He taught himself English. He made a name for himself and he made good money. A wealthy fixer who provided services to several downtown hotels hired him as part of a crew of drivers. Later, when he had made enough money, he bought his own car and went into business for himself. "My pockets were bursting!" he once told me, thinking about that time.

The tourist boom disappeared almost overnight. The big cruise ships stopped coming in the early 1980s, amid rumors that Haiti was the origin point of HIV/AIDS.[3] The end of tourism dispelled any sense that the regime's economic revolution had worked. Haiti was growing poorer every year. Thousands were fleeing the country, risking their lives on the treacherous Caribbean Sea, hoping to reach south Florida. And then came the protests against the dictatorship, and the inevitable military crackdown. Finally, there was the popular uprising against the regime, followed by the much-heralded democratic era. Alexis always grew wistful when he recalled that time.

"We had a lot of hope," he told me. "Hope that Haiti would change. We danced in the streets and sang songs. The day Aristide was elected, the people came out into the streets, they painted the entire city. It was beautiful."

But the democratic transition never seemed to happen, and Alexis thought the country was stuck in a protracted crisis punctuated only by periodic foreign interventions.

"We have a lot of crisis," he said. "But with crisis you have blan." In Kreyòl, *blan* means both "foreigner" and "white."

Tourists were replaced by journalists, and then by aid workers, and later by humanitarians. At the time we talked, Alexis was still driving foreigners around, and he still thought of himself as working in the tourist sector, only his clients now wanted to see different things. The new visitors, however, didn't pay like the old tourists did. They haggled about prices, they wanted the same prices as locals.

"Today, these blan think things are cheap in Haiti, because we are a poor country," Alexis said. "But things are very, very expensive here. In Haiti, life is expensive."

With fewer visitors, work was scarce. Alexis spent most days waiting at a hotel where he parked his car. Sitting in the shade. Joking or talking politics with a few other guides who also worked the hotel. I had been hanging out with Alexis for weeks, collecting life histories from him and his friends. I wanted to know how people like Alexis lived with crisis on a daily basis. How they thought about crisis, what they did each day when there was nothing to do. I wanted to understand why Wilson, a fifty-year-old painter, still packed up his canvases and walked up the mountain to an old tourist spot every morning, even though there were hardly any customers anymore. Or why Toto and Jean, two guides and fixers, sat outside an old gift shop every day, waiting for a journalist, or perhaps an intrepid humanitarian worker, to come by looking for a guide. Or why Wilfred, who owned the gift shop, kept it open at all when, as far as I could tell, he hadn't sold anything from it in years. Everyone seemed to be waiting for something to happen. I asked Alexis to explain it to me.

"It is like that," he shrugged. "We are all looking for life. When you look for life [*chache lavi*] you wait."

And I waited too. The days took on a rhythm, of sorts. But they also bled into each other. I was having trouble telling them apart. Anthropology is sometimes described as "deep hanging out," but I have to admit I was getting bored.

I asked Alexis if he got bored too.

He gave me a sly smile. "We wait, we wait," he said. "You understand?"

I sat quietly for a moment, not sure that I did. Then Alexis got a dreamy look in his eye. He leaned back and smiled. "I'll find something else to do."

I wasn't sure if he was talking to me.

"The blan who come now, they all have their own drivers."

Alexis looked up at the sky, lost in thought. "I have to do something else." He was still for a long moment, then he closed his eyes and said: "One day, I'll open a restaurant. A small place. I'll cook good food. I'll call it Caribbean Restaurant. Or maybe Chez Alexis."

We sat quietly. Waiting. I listened as a woodpecker tapped away above us.

LOOKING FOR LIFE AT THE ARTIST GIFT SHOP

"Sometimes, when you look for life [*chache lavi*], you die," Wilfred said. He shrugged. "It is like that here. It's not easy to live, you understand?" He shrugged again and wiped his hands together twice, the way people do to emphasize a point they can't quite express. As if to say, that's it, that's all there is. Jean and Toto, who were sitting with us, nodded their agreement. A cool breeze drifted in from the bay, a momentary respite on an otherwise hot afternoon.

We were talking about the difficulties of making a living. It was spring-time, in 2003, before the coup, before things got really bad. I had left Martissant in April, after the Red Army had taken over the neighborhood. I had moved to a guesthouse close to downtown. I started spending my days with some friends who worked in the informal sector as guides, drivers, dealers, or hustlers. I waited with them as they waited for work. Sitting, talking, and hanging out at hotel bars, street corners, shops, and shady spots on the side of the road, they spoke of crisis, but not in the way that experts did. For them, crisis was not a sudden interruption in their daily lives. Crisis *was* daily life. It was everywhere, all the time. Ever present. And to live with crisis, they had to "look for life."[4]

We were sitting on a concrete stoop in front of Wilfred's store, the Artist Gift Shop, in a small one-room building at the far end of a main commercial street near the downtown core. It was crammed full of paintings and small handmade objects, mostly wood carvings in the shape of animals, although there were also a few *ason*, decorated gourd rattles used in Vodou rites. These were the sort of things you could find in any craft shop throughout Port-au-Prince. The sort of things vendors sold outside hotels or at tourist spots. The sort of things tourists used to buy, when tourists used to come to Haiti. I rarely saw Wilfred inside his shop. The concrete walls and tin roof made it too hot to stay inside for any length of time. And I never saw any-one come to his shop to buy from him. But Wilfred was proud of the fact that he had made everything in the shop himself. And if you asked around, it seemed that everyone in the city knew him and his work. You could still find his paintings and carvings decorating hotel lobbies and elite homes. These days, he didn't paint much anymore. While he still thought of him-self as an artist, he made his living as a fixer. If you needed information, if you needed to find someone or to get into a neighborhood, or if you needed more illicit services, Wilfred could get it for you. Most of his clients were foreigners—journalists, aid workers, and the odd tourist who still turned up. But he was also a broker between the great social chasm of class, provid-ing wealthy urbanites with access to all the goods and services on offer in the city's slums.

Wilfred was born in Port-au-Prince in 1950. If there is a middle class in Haiti, he once belonged to it. As a teenager, he apprenticed with a famous artist. He quickly earned the respect that came with mastering a commer-cially successful style known for its brightly colored depictions of peasant life.[5] In the 1970s he made enough money to open his own shop. By the end of the decade, he had international clients regularly buying his work. "When people came to Haiti," he said, "they came here. They knew me. Everyone

Ason made by Wilfred. Photo by author.

knew me." But by the mid-1980s few people came anymore. Wilfred thought about leaving Haiti, but around that time his wife got sick. "I had to stay," he said. "I had to take care of her." So, he kept his shop going.

"In those days, no one wanted paintings anymore. It was all flags," he told me, referring to the sequined and beaded flags used by Vodou practitioners. "Some people would come and they would buy a lot, a lot of flags. So, I sold flags."

He did not, however, make flags. Instead, Wilfred positioned himself as a broker. He spoke English, knew dozens of artists around the city, and had contacts at all the major hotels. Whenever foreigners came and asked about buying flags or art, Wilfred's contacts would tip him off. For the *ti blan* (little whites, a term that invoked race, class, and foreignness), those who were not really going to spend a lot of money, Wilfred would show up at hotels with flags or other work to sell. For the *gwo blan* (big whites), the wealthy foreigners and art collectors, he would arrange day trips to artists' homes. When sales were made, the money always went through Wilfred. He set his own rates and took the first cut before dispersing the remaining cash to the artists and to any others who played a role in the sale. Discussions of rates, wages, or prices rarely happened openly, and never in front of clients. The only exception was payment for driving, which was usually negotiated separately and paid directly to the driver—typically Alexis, whom Wilfred always recommended to his clients. The system ran on trust and credit. Tourists and other foreigners rarely paid at the point of purchase. Some buyers didn't settle accounts until the end of their trip. At that point, everyone relied on Wilfred to get the best prices possible. He, in turn, had to rely on his clients paying the prices he quoted, or at least reasonable prices after some negotiating. This system gave Wilfred a great deal of autonomy in setting prices. It also gave him opportunities to make a bit of surplus off the top. For example, foreigners typically paid in U.S. dollars, but Wilfred paid artists and others in Haitian gourdes. He could usually make a little extra off the exchange rate before he even started distributing the money. When I asked Wilfred how these payments worked, he stressed to me that he always gave fair rates. "I give good money," he said. "I have to give everyone good money. They know who I am."

He was right. Everyone seemed to know Wilfred. More importantly, they seemed to trust him. Perhaps this is why his gift shop had become a regular hangout for many of his friends and acquaintances. It was not just a convenient place to spend the day waiting for something to happen. It was also the proximity to Wilfred himself that was so key, since he was a central node in a wide network of relations of affiliation that spread throughout the city. And Wilfred could command enough respect and prestige in that network that people came to him with possible deals and clients. For the men who gathered at the gift shop, men like Alexis, Jean, or Toto, the shop was a space of possibility, where things might happen—even if it looked to the casual observer that nothing much was happening there at all.

The men I met at the gift shop all had similar stories. Most had come to Port-au-Prince in the 1970s, as Alexis had done. And they had come of age in the brief boom of tourism and factory jobs. Only Wilfred had been born in the city, which may account for the depth and breadth of his connections around the capital. All the men were vocal supporters of Aristide and his Lavalas movement, and they had all suffered under the dictatorship. Some had been jailed. Some had been tortured. They remembered the Duvalier dictatorship as a time of both economic opportunity and crushing political oppression. It was not lost on them that the relative political freedom of the democratic era had come with equally crushing economic misery.

One morning, Wilson, the painter who dutifully walked up the mountain each day to wait for tourists, suggested that things had been better under Duvalier. It was an increasingly common sentiment in the city, a kind of nostalgia for stability that erased the terror of the regime. Alexis and Wilfred were quick to remind him of just how terrible things had been.

"Do you remember what happened," Wilfred asked Wilson, pointing down the street. "There. Do you remember?"

Wilson nodded.

"The *makout* [paramilitary] came with a 'communist.' They pulled me out of my shop. They made us all come into the street and watch. They killed him and left the body right there." Wilfred pointed again, as if he could still see the body and the blood in the road.

Wilson sat silent, his body tense.

Alexis joined in. He said that he remembered the tourists. And that he remembered all the money. "Our pockets were full!" he said. Wilson cracked a smile and nodded, clearly relieved that someone was agreeing with him.

"But with Duvalier we still had hunger," Alexis said. "We still had misery. And you can't eat if you are dead."

Both the dictatorship and the democratic era loomed large in everyday life. It never took long for conversations at the gift shop to turn to the political crisis or to the economic crisis. As I sat with them and listened, it was easy to see why. These men, all roughly in their forties or fifties, had lived through one crisis after another. Indeed, if there was one thing they had come to expect in life, it was crisis. Even the sense that the dictatorship had been a time of stability was an illusion, since most of them had left their villages and their families and come to the city precisely because of the steep decline in peasant livelihoods and the economic crisis of the countryside. As urban migrants, they had also directly experienced the urban crisis, settling in the worst slums of the city on their initial arrival and only later making enough money to relocate to better neighborhoods. They had come to the city to look for life, and they had found it—but they were also acutely aware that it was fleeting, provisional, always threatening to slip away or to turn into its opposite. As Wilfred had said, when you look for life, sometimes you find death.

Looking for life begins with the imperative to make a living outside of the home.[6] Rural migrants look for work outside of the village so that they can send money back, so that they can keep the lakou going. It is, above all, a way of responding to the deep crisis of social reproduction that peasants and environmentalists alike call the death of the lakou. Looking for life is risky because it means dwelling in the informal world of wageless work, squatter settlements, black markets, and debt. For the men who gather at the gift shop, looking for life carries with it both the possibility of finding life, or food, or money, or prestige, and also the possibility of not finding those things. To live in such a world requires great skill and flexibility, but it also requires good relations—networks of trust, credit, mutual assistance, and solidarity. That was, in good measure, why they all gathered at the shop. It was a way for them to come together, and the concrete walls and tin roof gave a hard materiality to the otherwise intangible social infrastructure of those networks.

In a pioneering work of urban ethnography in Haiti, Michel Laguerre argues that migrants often settle into urban residence patterns that replicate the spatial form and social arrangement of rural homesteads.[7] These "urban lakous" reproduce the underlying logic of the rural extended-family homestead and transpose it to the new spatial order of the city. Residents of the sprawling slums and popular quarters tend to cluster in small groups, united by bonds of kinship or friendship. Shared service at local Vodou temples, ritual god-parenthood, and other practices help anchor those social relationships in space, giving people a sense of belonging to their neighborhoods and zones *(zòn)* that replicates, at least in part, the relationships they left behind in their home villages. But urban migrants do not simply transpose rural traditions to urban settings—they actively remake them. For example, the men who gathered at the gift shop had spent decades looking for life in the city. In the process, they had taken on a new sensibility and a new disposition to work and personhood. They lived in different neighborhoods, but all lived in areas that would be called slums or popular quarters. They had deep connections to family and friends in those zones (as the urban lakou model suggests), but they also depended on the dispersed networks of affiliation and support they had built throughout the city. The kind of work they did required contacts and connections everywhere, and this in turn had given them not only a set of work relationships but also a profound sense of identity bound up with the city itself. In a very real sense, their social relationships were not just a means of surviving in the informal economy—they were also shaped by that economy. The city was not a proxy home for them. They saw themselves as urbanites, and their sense of personhood and identity was tightly bound up with their ability to navigate both the vagaries of the informal economy and the ad hoc and unplanned space of the city itself.[8]

The distinction between country people *(moun andeyò)* and city people *(moun lavil)* is one of the great chasms of social life in Haiti.[9] By becoming urban residents, the men who gathered at Wilfred's shop ceased to see themselves as country people or as peasants. As Alexis noted, he had no connections to his home village anymore. For others, those connections were ignored or "forgotten."[10] These men showed no nostalgia for peasant life. They did not dream of returning to their family villages or owning land. Some spoke with open derision about rural life. Richard, a drug dealer and pimp who worked out of several downtown hotels, was especially known for ridiculing the peasantry. When I asked him if he ever thought of returning to his family's village in the north, he scoffed at me. "No way!" he said, shaking his head. "I'll never go back. That's the past, man." He smiled slyly and laughed. "Scrapping all day in the dirt. Who wants to be a fucking peasant!" Others were less severe in their judgment, but no less clear that peasant life was not a viable or attractive future for them. They had come to fully embrace urban life and to find the challenges and opportunities of the informal sector to be rewarding and meaningful in their own right. This was partly due to the fact that they had attained some level of prestige during the tourist boom. They enjoyed the social position that this prestige made possible, and they also enjoyed their increased access to money and material goods. Looking for life had, for them, become a way of opening up new possibilities for living and working in the midst of an ever-present crisis.

While it might open up possibilities, looking for life was also felt to be a constant struggle. And things were getting harder and harder all the time. Fewer and fewer foreigners bought art, and the flag market was dwindling too. The few big-ticket buyers who still came to Haiti preferred the high-end galleries in Pétion-Ville, where the most famous artists sold their work. Most foreigners these days were younger. They were missionaries, aid workers, or adventure travelers, and they saw art objects primarily as trinkets and souvenirs. They balked at the prices Wilfred charged and preferred to buy the knock-off paintings sold by any of the dozens of street vendors who competed with each other. Each vendor sold the same paintings—copies of copies churned out in bulk at a couple of factories down by the wharf.

A manager from one of the factories had once offered Wilfred a job. Years later, when he told me about the offer, Wilfred seemed to still be offended. I asked him why he hadn't taken it.

"I would *never* work there," he said, shaking his head. "No! Never."

His reaction was not very surprising. After all, the wages in those workshops were extremely low and the conditions were terrible, with no air conditioning, long hours, and abusive bosses. But there was more to his refusal than just bad conditions. Wilfred's response reminded me of a time I asked Alexis why he didn't drive his car as a *publique,* a public taxi. Alexis had shaken his hands at me and told me he would never do that. To drive a public taxi, he had said, he would need to get permits, work regular routes, and charge regular rates. There were unions, government agencies, and political factions to contend with, too. I understood the challenges, but I was struck by the fact that both men eschewed the possibility of regular, formal work and wages, opting instead to continue the daily grind of looking for life. They were both acutely aware of the hardship that looking for life entailed. And yet they were deeply committed. Looking for life in the world they had been thrown into, they had found a way to make it a world they could meaningfully inhabit. In so doing, they had come to think of what they did all day—working, waiting, sitting around, hustling—not as a way to get by, but rather as a way to make a living.[11]

MAKING SOMETHING HAPPEN

January 2004. I was sitting with Alexis under the palm tree again. It was early morning. Jean and Toto were sitting with us, talking about the barricades and the shootings, the protests against the government. Toto said that in his neighborhood people were getting ready for a coup. Jean shook his said. "No, no, no! We are done with coups! We need a *strong* state." He clenched his hands into fists and flexed his arms. "We need to be strong against these guys!"

Jean, Toto, and Alexis were all supporters of President Aristide and his Fanmi Lavalas party. They lived in the lower-class neighborhoods and slums that were the base of Aristide's support in the city. For years, Aristide's government had been paralyzed by the international community, which had blocked foreign aid and backed a coalition of political parties that called themselves the Democratic Convergence. Aristide's supporters were calling on him to stand tough against the opposition. Some supporters were taking up arms and attacking the anti-government protesters. But without broad support from the international community, and without foreign aid, there was little that Aristide's government could do. The national police force was small, poorly trained, ill equipped, and internally split, with some factions of the police working with the anti-government groups. There were rumors that the former army, disbanded by Aristide a decade earlier, was training armed groups in the Dominican Republic. Everyone was braced for a battle, or for another coup.

At least the instability was bringing journalists. Daphne, a young woman who worked the front desk of a downtown hotel, had tipped Alexis off about a couple of American reporters expected to arrive tomorrow. They had already asked about drivers, and Alexis was banking on booking them for the duration of their stay. With the protests escalating every day, they might be here for a week, maybe longer. They would need fixers too, to get them into the popular neighborhoods, to bring them to community leaders, to make sure they stayed safe. Jean and Toto had already put the word out that they might be bringing journalists around. They planned to spend today making the rounds, checking in with their contacts in Martissant, Bel Air, Cité Soleil, and other neighborhoods. They would have to get permission in advance from neighborhood leaders before they could bring journalists into the zones. And they would need to find out where the protests and barricades were going to be next. Journalists always want photographs of burning tires and crowds in the streets. Alexis would take them around to the neighborhoods that afternoon. First he wanted to bring his car to his mechanic, to get it ready for work.

When the morning traffic died down, we all got up and put the chairs away. We got in Alexis's car, a late-model sedan that was starting to show its age. The car hung low to the ground and, despite frequent washing, always looked dusty. Alexis had covered the backseat with blankets, to hide the torn seat covers and absorb some of the bumps. But the car had always handled well, and as he liked to remind me often, people hire *drivers*, not cars.

Alexis turned the key and nothing happened. He turned it again. Jean feigned anger and teased Alexis. "I thought you said this was a good car?!" Alexis waved his hand at Jean. "It's a good car, it's a good car! Don't worry." He tried the ignition again. Again nothing. He leaned back in his seat for a moment, then popped the hood and got out of the car. We all looked at each other. Jean and Toto grew worried. They were counting on Alexis booking the American journalists. For that, he needed to have his car in working order.

"What's happening?" Toto said.

Alexis still had his head under the hood. He said nothing.

"What's happening?" We got out of the car.

Alexis closed the hood. His lips were tight, his body tense. He waved for us to get out of the car.

"It's dead," he said.

"The car?" Jean asked.

Alexis shook his head. "The battery."

We all stood there for a moment, looking at the car.

"Okay," Alexis said. "Okay. Not a problem." He nodded his head a few times. "We'll push."

We all moved to the back of the car as Alexis got inside and shifted into neutral. We pushed the car down the gravel path to the hotel gates. Once outside the gates, Alexis pulled the parking brake on. We quickly made a new plan. Alexis and I would take the car to the mechanic while Jean and Toto would go to Martissant to meet Josué, a Vodou priest who had a temple in the neighborhood. Josué had deep connections everywhere in the city, and he would be able to help guarantee their safety when they went to Bel Air and Cité Soleil later.

Alexis and I got back in the car. He released the brake, stepped on the clutch, and put the car into second gear. Jean and Toto kept pushing until we reached the crest of a hill. The car started to slowly roll down the street. Alexis let the car go for a bit, gaining some speed. He took his foot off the clutch for about a second, then quickly pressed it down again. The engine started. He turned to me and gave me a small smile. "It's no problem," he said.

A gentle breeze wafted in through the window as Alexis drove the car through traffic. "You see," he said to me, "it's a good car."

"A good driver," I replied.

Alexis smiled. He was rightly proud of his skills as a driver. They had brought him fame and many clients over the years. But his car was clearly reaching its limits. I remember thinking, as we drove through the streets, that the car was an apt metaphor for this thing called looking for life. It was idle for hours on end, sometimes even for days. Waiting for something to happen. Then, when things lined up, the car was there, ready to go. Except it wasn't always ready, just like it wasn't always easy to make things happen. Sometimes you have to fake it. Sometimes you have to pop the clutch. When you push start a car, you roll it downhill to send mechanical energy to the alternator, which in turn sends energy to the battery, recharging it and allowing it to start. So much of looking for life had this same quality; you had to have a solid network of relationships, you had to have help in order to make things work.

The problem with popping the clutch is that it only gets you so far. As soon as you turn the car off, the battery will die again, and you will need to push start the car again. That's not such a big deal for Alexis when he is driving himself around, but foreign clients don't like cars that won't start. In order to book the journalists coming in, and to keep them as clients for the duration of their stay, Alexis would need to get his car in working order. The dilemma, of course, was that he didn't have the cash to buy a new battery. This was a constant problem for Alexis. As a driver, his car was essential to his livelihood, but it was an older model that required regular maintenance. Alexis had good relationships with a network of mechanics around the city. There was, I had come to learn, an entire sector of the economy in Port-au-Prince dedicated to auto repair and maintenance—a sector that paralleled but was largely distinct from the official car dealerships and repair centers that the elite frequented. Drivers like Alexis got their tires patched or retreaded, not replaced. They knew how to do basic repairs themselves, even if those repairs were always quick fixes, like patching car windows with cardboard or using metal rebar to replace a window crank. And drivers like Alexis did not buy new batteries.

Alexis turned down an alley and we entered a maze of narrow streets, another world hidden behind the official storefronts. He stopped at an iron gate with a painted sign that read, rather ominously, "Alpha and Omega Auto." He honked a couple of times and someone came out to talk to him. Alexis explained the situation. Then he turned the car off, got out, and opened the hood. He returned to the car.

"We're going to rent *[lwe]* a battery," he said.

"How much?" I asked.

"Five dollars American."

I gave Alexis the money. I didn't want to wait for him to ask. I knew he didn't have it.

"Can they charge the old one?" I asked him.

"Yes, yes. They'll charge it too. We'll come back for it."

The mechanic took the old battery out and put in the rental. Alexis got back in the car. It started easily. He smiled and nodded. "Okay," he said. "Now we can go."

MAKING RELATIONS

December 2003.   We were sitting in front of the Artist Gift Shop again, eating fried plantain that we got from Mirlande, a street-food vendor who worked down the road. We bought food from her often. Wilfred and Alexis knew her well, and most days we would wander down the street to chat with her. She was upset today. There had been burning barricades in the streets earlier, set up as part of an anti-government protest. The acrid smell of burnt rubber still hung in the air. Protests always meant there were fewer people on the streets. It was bad for business.

I asked Wilfred if the political crisis made it harder to look for life.

"Yes," he said. "Yes. When you have a political crisis, you have disorder. It is not easy."

He ate another plantain fritter. "How can I explain it to you?" he said. "Today, we have a political crisis, you see?"

I nodded.

"But, we have crisis *every* day. The political crisis. The economic crisis. It's all the same. In Haiti, this is called insecurity *[ensekirite]*."

"What do you do when you have ensekirite?" I asked.

Wilfred looked at me. "It's the same thing," he said. "You must look for life."

I finished my last fritter and folded up the paper plate.

Wilfred pointed down the street at Mirlande. "It is like this," he said. "We are sitting here, at my shop. If we get hungry, what do we do?" He paused, looking at me. I had thought his question was rhetorical.

"We eat," I said.

He grinned. "Yes! If we get hungry we eat."

"Haitians are always hungry," Alexis added.

"Of course," Wilfred said. "We have hunger [grangou]. But today, we have food." Wilfred pointed at my folded plate. "If I want to eat fritters, I always go to Mirlande. Maybe if I don't have money she would still give them to me. Every day we see Mirlande. Every day we say hello, we talk. You see? In Haiti, to look for life you must make relations [fè pratik]."

Webs of affiliation are essential to life in the city. Everyone I knew was part of a set of overlapping networks that connected them to family, friends, and associates. Those networks extended across neighborhoods and even beyond the city, back to home villages or across the sea to transnational migrants. In Port-au-Prince, social relations are the foundation of the informal economy and people are, in a very real sense, a kind of "infrastructure" or "platform for reproducing life in the city."[12] Wilfred, Alexis, and others spoke of such relationships all the time. When they did so, they tended to use terms like affairs (afè), relations (relasyon), or rapport (rapò). This time, however, Wilfred used the phrase fè pratik, which refers to a specific kind of relationship—the recurring relations of buying and selling that take place in Haitian markets. A literal translation is "making habit" or "making a practice of," as in "we make a habit of buying fritters from Mirlande." Wilfred certainly meant it in that way, as his example above shows. But in Haiti, making relations is more than that. It is a thick ethical concept that brings together a related set of ideas about personhood, action, and time.

Everywhere you go in Haiti, you find markets. These markets are small in scale, but taken together they make up what is probably, as Sidney Mintz suggests, the only national institution in the country.[13] The internal market system brings together peasant producers, small traders, commercial intermediaries and speculators, the state customhouses and tax officers, and, of course, consumers. The market system has allowed the urban elite and the state to parasitically profit from the peasantry, but it has also allowed Haitian producers to have a semblance of autonomy and control over the most immediate aspects of their lives.[14] Pratik relations help contribute to that sense of control, because they allow buyers and sellers to navigate the vagaries of the market, such as the absence of credit, fluctuations in price, and scarcity of goods. As Sidney Mintz puts it, "under such circumstances, *pratik* relationships stabilize sequences of dyadic economic transactions."[15] How, though, does pratik work?

When people talk about these relations, they say you can "have pratik" *(gen pratik)* and that you can "make pratik" *(fè pratik)*. To have pratik is to have a recurring commercial relationship with someone, either as a buyer or a seller. To make pratik is to engage in such relationships. A simple kind of pratik is the one Wilfred described with Mirlande—being a repeat customer and buying a certain product (fritters) from the same person, rather than from their competitors. Pratik entails an expectation that, barring some disagreement, commercial transactions will be repeated in the future. There is often the added sense that these relations are reciprocal. In most cases, reciprocity in a market relationship does not mean that the buyer and seller simply reverse roles. Rather, it means that the seller promises to give a "good price" *(bon pri)* to the buyer in exchange for repeat business. Once established, pratik relations can anchor systems of money lending, as sellers agree to give their regular customers goods on credit with the expectation that they will be good for the money. Pratik relations are thus not only recurring and reciprocal—they are also binding, carrying with them a social and moral force that ties people together in relations of obligation and responsibility over time.[16]

Pratik relations make certain kinds of trade possible, but it would be a mistake to characterize them solely as market relations. They often emerge out of other relations of affiliation that unite people across space and time, such as godparent and godsibling relationships or extended kinship relations. Even when people are not related in any way, pratik relations are often referred to in kin terms. In Port-au-Prince, those making pratik were often called "cousin" *(kouzin)*, even when, as was usually the case, the partners did not share any blood relatives. These terms symbolize the fact that commercial ties have integrative functions that bind people together in ways that are both economic and, more importantly, deeply social. The model for this is the lakou and the extended family, where relations of production emerge out of kinship relations. In markets, which bring together strangers from all over the country, people engage in pratik in order to establish social relations of affinity that, in turn, become the foundation for stable, recurring, and trustworthy economic exchanges.[17]

Making relations plays a similar role in the informal economy of the city. To fè pratik is to build networks that extend across space and time, networks that can turn strangers into friends, fictive kin, and reliable trading partners. In some cases, pratik relations are based on close friend-ships, like that between Wilfred and Alexis. In other cases, the relations are thinner, but still useful. They might involve only periodic exchanges or one-sided relationships in which one party cannot afford to reciprocate. Each connection, however idle or one-sided, helps build overlapping webs of affinity that can be called upon when business opportunities arise or when someone needs help and support. Pratik relations can provide people with access to credit or with goods advanced without payment, both of which are crucial to the maintenance of urban households.

For the men who gathered at Wilfred's shop, these networks extended to almost every area of the city. The spatial extension of their networks allowed them to move from neighborhood to neighborhood with confi-dence, safe in the knowledge that they knew people in each zone who could vouch for them or who could connect them to clients or vendors. Pratik relations also allowed them to extend their interactions and exchanges not just over space but also over time, as each recurring exchange provides a foundation for trust and expectations of future interactions. Pratik gives a systematicity to the informal economy that is difficult to see from the out-side. It is an invisible infrastructure made up of the collective weight of small social interactions, a web of social relationships that can be mobilized for economic or other ends.[18] It is also "a kind of mentality and way of liv-ing in the world."[19]

In Wilfred's example, buying fritters from Mirlande was never just about fritters; it was also about the habitual reproduction of relations of exchange and mutual support. Each time we went down the street to get fritters, or even just to talk with her—to joke about the day, share informa-tion about protests, or assess the current political situation—was an acknowledgment that we were bound together, that we owed something to each other, and that we could be counted on to help one another.

"If I am hungry," Wilfred said, "I want to eat. I look around. I look for food. But I don't forget [pa bliye] Mirlande."

"What does that mean?" I asked.

"I remember [sonje] her. She remembers me."

This sense of remembering others brings us to the heart of what it means to make relations in the city—personhood. Wilfred and others often referred to particular people in their networks as friends (zanmi) and to the networks in general as "my people" (moun pa m). These terms contrast sharply with the prevalence of strangers (etranje) in the city. For Wilfred, Alexis, and others, it was dangerous to go to areas where you had no friends or family. As guides, drivers, and fixers, their jobs required them to travel to almost every part of the city, and in order to do that they needed to have people they could count on, people they could trust. Being known meant having good relations. That, in turn, meant being remembered by others.

In Haiti, to be a person *(moun)* is to be located socially and spatially in a set of relations of mutual interdependence.[20] The ideal form of this is the lakou, which is both the space of the family and the name for the extended family group that dwells on the homestead. Amid the collapse of the peasant economy, migrants flooded into Port-au-Prince, making new homes in the city's slums. Neighborhoods replaced lakous. The streets and zone became the locus of home and family life. But life in the city requires connections beyond the zone, just as the peasant homestead requires markets outside of the lakous. To be a person in the city, then, is to be located in networks of association and affinity. And for that, you have to have people.[21]

Being a person and having people are two sides of the same coin. In order to be recognized and remembered by those in your network, you must also show that you recognize and remember them in return. Personhood is an eminently social thing, in which selfhood presupposes and entails mutual recognition from others. When Wilfred talked about remembering Mirlande, he was talking about an ethical disposition according to which he was obligated to her in some way. He could buy fritters from someone else, but he visited her stall regularly. He did this often, despite the fact that he rarely had the extra cash to buy street food at all. But when he could afford it—or, more to the point, when I was with him and had cash—he made sure to buy from her. When I asked him why, he answered in terms of responsibility *(reskonsab)*. Pratik relations are thus part of a wider ethical framework of moral personhood, in which people are evaluated on the basis of their conduct toward others. A good person is one who behaves in a proper manner, who has a good comportment *(bon kondwit, bon konpòtman)*, or who acts well *(fè byen)*. Acting well, in turn, means fulfilling your obligations *(fè devwa ou)*.[22]

Pratik relations are reciprocal, but they are rarely equal. Wilfred, for example, had no expectation that Mirlande would buy something from his shop. While he sometimes got food on credit, he always paid her back quickly. The relationship seemed, to me at least, to be mostly one-sided. Yet Mirlande had family in Cité Soleil, where Wilfred did a lot of business. The exchange, then, was neither direct nor immediate. It was more like a promise—a future wager that, for the small price of the occasional fritter, Wilfred would have people in Cité Soleil who could vouch for him and with whom he could do business *(fè afè)*. Responsibility is, then, a way of talking about the hierarchical aspects of social relationships. Those who have more money or who have a higher social position have a greater responsibility to take care of their friends and family. When migrants return from working overseas, for example, they are expected to go see their family members and close friends individually, distributing small gifts *(ti kado)* of cash or goods. Social relationships of this sort are necessary to daily survival, but they can also be quite demanding, especially since not being able to fulfill one's obligations has grave consequences for one's public standing as a good person.[23] Having good relations with others and having a large network of people is a central part of looking for life in the city. But the more successful you are at making relations, the more obligations you accumulate.

The men who gathered at the gift shop all had large networks, in part because they had been working in the city for decades and in part because they had gained positions of prestige in the informal economy. They were all well known, and they knew people all over the city with whom they had good relations. Being known afforded them a particular kind of mobility, one that was indispensable to their work as drivers, guides, and fixers. Alexis, for example, knew mechanics who could help repair his car, but he also knew families in many parts of the city who had small children who would watch his parked car and even clean it while he waited for fares. And he knew people who worked at major hotels in the city. They would tip him off whenever potential clients (tourists, journalists, or aid workers) arrived. Of course, money changed hands in many of these exchanges. But in the informal economy, cash is always in short supply. What really made these relationships hold together was repetition of small acts of social interaction. Visiting friends, talking, joking, drinking or eating together—all of these are ways of making relations. The same can be said for the days on end spent hanging out at the gift shop or at hotels. Simply being with other people, waiting with them through long periods of inactivity, passing the time together—these were all key ways in which men like Wilfred and Alexis reproduced relations of interdependence. And when something suddenly seemed like it might happen, these relations could be easily converted into relations of production, as when Alexis heard about the possibility of foreign clients arriving at a nearby hotel.

In the informal economy, the relation between work and money, activity and value, was not always clear. You could spend days sitting around waiting for some business. But if you spent this time waiting with your people, talking and socializing with your friends, then, when opportunities arose, you could convert your networks into business relationships, and, in the process, convert your activity into money. Making relations, then, was not just about being a good person and fulfilling one's obligations. It was also the condition of possibility of looking for life. It allowed people to transform potentiality—the rumor of clients, a tip, a business connection—into durable forms of value like cash and social prestige. And cash and prestige could be shared with others, thereby allowing a person to make good on their obligations and, in the process, reproduce themselves as social persons.

THE CITY AT NIGHT

Spring 2003. I was waiting for Manuel at a downtown park. As I sat there, I watched the marketers pack up their wares and depart. The sun sets early and fast in the spring, and everyone moved briskly on their way in the fleeting twilight. As I waited, *tap-taps* (small public buses) full of people drove their final routes. There were only a few cars on the roads, and soon there would be hardly any. The noise and bustle of the city's streets was replaced by an eerie silence. Street dogs roused in the dwindling light and began scavenging, sniffing out scraps of food in trash piles and gutters.

Manuel wanted to show me the parallel economies of the city at night, with its black markets and illicit services. It was a world in which so many people, Manuel included, dwelt. But it wasn't a world that just anyone could enter. You had to have connections. You had to have people.

Manuel arrived, with a grin on his face. I was relieved to see him, and he knew it.

"How are you?" I asked.

"*Anfòm, anfòm,*" he said. "I'm good, I'm good." He raised his shoulders up and made fists with his hands as he said it.

We sat and chatted for a bit as the sun went down. There had been rolling brownouts and blackouts recently, and tonight the city was blanketed in darkness. Nearby, a couple of parked cars turned their lights on, creating a yellow pool on the street corner. One of the drivers turned up his radio and lit a cigarette. A couple of young women approached him. They stood together in the pale light, laughing and joking. Soon, there were competing songs filling the air from other radios, or from bands warming up at nearby bars. Manuel did a little dance to the music, clearly enjoying himself. He pointed to the young women, still standing in front of the car.

"*Bouzen,*" he said. Prostitutes.

"And the driver?" I asked.

Manuel shrugged. "*Jandam.*" Policeman.

"They like the prostitutes," he added. Then he raised a finger in front of his lips, as if telling a secret. "We have lots of policemen at night. But they are not policemen, you see?"

We started walking, heading into the shadows. We left the park and the familiar sights of downtown. Manuel led the way through a maze of side streets. They seemed to get narrower as we walked. Candles and paraffin lamps flickered in windows, casting a red glow on the street. We had entered a kind of intimate public space, away from the businesses and the formal facades of the main streets. Doors and windows were open. Families were cooking and eating dinner. Kids joked and played, or crowded around the lamps to read or do homework. Groups of men huddled around radios, listening to news reports or dance music.

Manuel waved and called hello as we passed by the houses. He seemed to know everyone, and they knew him. "This is my neighborhood," he said. "These are my people."

"Here," said Manuel, pointing to the left. We turned into an alley. I stumbled over the rutted street, barely able to see in the dark. Manuel held on to my arm and we continued until the alley ended in front of a two-story concrete house. Two women sat at a small wooden table outside the house, mixing something in a large bucket. Inside, a young man sat on a couch. Behind him were stacks of electronic equipment—radios, televisions, and VCRs—sitting idle on wooden shelves. When he saw us, the man stood up.

"What's happening?" he asked. "What do you need?"

He walked toward us. His face lit up when he recognized Manuel. They greeted each other and Manuel explained that we were just hanging out, that he was showing me how people make a living in the city at night. The man smiled and pulled me inside.

"I'm Junior," the man said. "Welcome to my house."

I introduced myself. Junior sat down beside me, looking me up and down with bemusement. He asked me what I was doing in Haiti. I told him that I was an anthropologist, that I was interested in crisis. I told him I had been studying the forest at Habitation Leclerc and that now I was trying to understand what it means to look for life in Port-au-Prince.

"Forest?" he asked. "Where?"

"In Martissant," I said. I started to describe the forest and the garden project. When I asked him about the environmental crisis in Haiti, he laughed.

"Crisis!" he said. "Yes, we have that here." He shrugged. "Fuck that," he added, in English. He held out his hand. "Look," he said. "You want some?" He had three tiny rocks of crack cocaine in his palm.

I shook my head no.

Junior looked at Manuel. "Who is he?" he asked.

"A friend," Manuel said.

"A friend?" Junior repeated. He stared at me for what felt like minutes. "Okay," he said, breaking the silence. "Okay."

He stood up and walked over to a shelf. He returned with a large plastic container and three small plastic cups. He poured us each a drink of *kleren,* a common rum made in people's homes. He gave Manuel and me each a cup and raised his glass.

"Friends," he said again. We drank. The rum burned my throat. He poured us another glass. We drank again. It burned again. I could already feel my head getting cloudy.

Manuel and Junior started talking business, which had been slow recently because of the political crisis. Manuel said that disorder was always bad for business, because people buried their money instead of spending it. As the night wore on, Junior starting telling me about his livelihood.

"In Haiti," he said, "there is big trade *[gwo biznis]* and little trade *[ti biznis].* We do ti biznis."

Junior's little trade was a family affair. The two women in front of his house were his mother, Roseline, and his sister, Lovelie. They were in charge of making crack rocks from the small batches of cocaine that he got on credit from his "chief" *(chèf).* Roseline told me it was a simple formula—they mixed the cocaine powder with baking soda and water, then boiled the paste until it hardened into rocks. They broke the rocks up into tiny units, like the ones Junior had offered me. Cocaine and marijuana are easy to find in the city, their everyday presence contrasting with their marked foreignness. Everyone knows they come from elsewhere, and the most common Kreyòl terms for these substances are English borrowings—*kokayin* and *marigwana.* I asked Junior what crack was called in Haiti.

"*Viza,*" he said.

"*Viza?*" I asked. "Like papers *[papye]?*"

He nodded.

Manuel said they called it that because it lets you get out of Haiti for a while. You can get out of your head. You can get away.

"Yes, but my visas are better than papers," Junior said.

"Why?" I asked.

"Because you can get them!" He laughed.

As we spoke, Junior would stop to make occasional sales. His clients were all men, and most of them seemed to be in their thirties or older. They would buy a couple of rocks and some marijuana, and then go up the stairs beside Junior's house. There, they rolled joints of weed and crack and smoked while sitting in plastic chairs on an open patio on top of the neighboring building. A few men stumbled back down to buy more before returning to the patio again. Eventually, someone would come back asking for more after they had run out of money. Junior turned them away brusquely. They shuffled down the alley and disappeared into the night.

"I do ti biznis," Junior said. "It is not much." He gestured around the room at his younger siblings. He said that he had taken over the business from his father, who had been murdered a few years ago. Neighbors had found his mutilated body in the street one morning. I asked Junior what had happened. He shrugged.

"People are made to die," he said. *Moun fèt pou mouri.* I thought of Wilfred's comment, that when you look for life, sometimes you die.

When he died, Junior's father owed money to his suppliers, so Junior took over his job as neighborhood dealer. There wasn't much else for the family to do, and drugs brought in a regular income for the household. Roseline, who periodically joined our conversation, said that her youngest son was doing well in school and that they needed to keep the business going so they could pay his school fees.

I asked if they worried about violence or about the fact that selling drugs was illegal.

Junior laughed at the question.

"Violence?" he said. "Not really. We are strong!"

"And the law? The police?" I asked.

"Not really," he said. "The state, the law, the army, the police. Gangs. We have all that. We also have guns *[zam]*. If you have guns, you are okay. If you have people you are okay. But if you have the law? What is that?"

Junior poured more kleren. "You see, I only do ti biznis. It is not much. In Haiti, we have ti biznis and gwo biznis."

"Who does the big trade?" I asked.

Junior looked at me, smiling. He said nothing.

"The police?" I asked.

He nodded.

"The army?"

He nodded again.

"The government?"

He nodded.

"Now you understand," he said.

Junior leaned back in his chair and closed his eyes. He seemed to be done with our conversation. I looked at Manuel to see if we should leave, but he was out of his chair and dancing to a *konpa* song drifting over from a nearby radio. After a few minutes, Junior sat up and started talking again.

He told me about the gwo biznis, the big trade, in drugs. He said that "big gangs" from South America would drop shipments out of planes in rural areas. Then, Haitian gangs would collect the drops and send them on to the United States.[24] Portions of these shipments stayed in the country and fed the small but growing internal market. Like other commodities, cocaine and marijuana were sold in large quantities to the big dealers, who then broke them up into smaller and smaller units for sale along a marketing chain. Most of the little dealers got their drugs on credit. The difference between what they owed their chèfs and what they could make left some room, however small, for profit. Junior said the key to making money with drugs was having good connections.

I heard loud voices from outside the house. We all turned to look out the open door. Roseline and Lovelie were talking to a heavyset man.

"Where's the blan?" the man said.

"In there," Roseline said, pointing at me.

The man looked at us. He raised a large flashlight and shined it in my eyes. I squinted. I saw red spots.

"Hey blan," the man said. "What are you doing here?"

I tried to stand up, but I could barely see. He still had the light aimed at my eyes. I put a hand up to block it. The man held up a badge of some kind, but I couldn't read it. I told him my name. Fear and panic ran through my body, like an electric shock.

The man asked me what I was doing in the neighborhood.

"I'm with Manuel," I said. I started to explain what we were doing, but the idea that I was doing research suddenly sounded very strange. The light was still in my eyes. He lowered it at last. When I could see again, I recognized him as the driver of the car from the park, the one who was hanging out with the prostitutes. I could see the badge now, prominently around his neck. He was from the National Police.

"This is my neighborhood," he said. He spoke in English.

I nodded, unsure what else to say.

"Do you know who I am?" the man asked.

I shook my head.

The man looked at Roseline, then at Junior. "Who am I?" he asked.

"Bòs," they both said.

"Bòs," the man repeated. Boss. I wasn't sure if it was a name or a title.

The man looked at me. He stepped closer. "Do you know who I am?" he asked again.

"Bòs," I said quietly, unsure of the rules of this particular encounter.

The man grinned and nodded.

"Good," he said. "Now you know who I am."

Bòs turned away, apparently done with me. He chatted with Roseline for a few minutes, flung a few sexual innuendoes at Lovelie, then walked up the stairs to the patio. I heard him talking to the men upstairs, calling them drug addicts, saying he should arrest them, making sure they all knew who he was. Manuel grabbed my arm and whispered that it was time to go. I tried to thank Junior for his time, but Manuel ushered me down the alley and out into the street. We walked quickly in the dark for a few minutes, until we were back on a main street. I asked Manuel about Bòs.

"He's a makout," said Manuel. I was surprised. The makout were the paramilitary forces used by the Duvalier regime. But they had been abolished decades ago, and many members of the makout had been killed when the dictatorship fell.

"You mean he *was* a makout?" I asked. "Under Duvalier."

"He was a makout, yes. He is a makout again."

We walked down the darkened street. A few clouds drifted in front of the moon. I could hear music in the distance, coming from the few bars that were still open. I thought about what Manuel had said. The Haitian National Police had been created in 1995 after the Haitian government disbanded the army. I had often been told that members of the army and of paramilitary groups had joined the national police. Manuel, for one, liked to joke that the makout and the army had simply changed uniforms.

"Why did he want me to know who he was?" I asked.

"Bòs is a chèf," Manuel said. "If you do ti biznis in this zone, you have to know him."

"Do you work with him?" I asked.

Manuel shrugged. We walked in silence for a few minutes. I was tired, and he seemed frustrated with my questions. We kept walking. A dog barked nearby.

I thought back to a conversation from a few months ago. Manuel and I had been sitting on a patio, enjoying a quiet evening, drinking beer after a dinner of rice and beans. He had grown nostalgic, telling me stories of the boom years in the late 1970s and early '80s, a time when he had been quite famous, when international art dealers had sought him out for his connections to local artists. We drank and laughed as he told me stories of ridiculous amounts of money paid for paintings and flags. He told me about lavish parties. People dancing in the streets. And then, without any warning, his tone shifted and he told me that one day the makout had shown up and taken him away. He spent months in Fort Dimanche, the dreaded Port-au-Prince prison where the makout had interrogated and tortured people. As he told me the story, he lifted up his shirt to show me a series of scars across his back. He lifted a pant leg. More scars. And then he had switched again, back to telling stories, back to laughing.

When the Duvalier regime fell, groups of vigilantes had hunted down the makout. It was called the *dechoukaj*, the uprooting. The term comes from the peasantry, from the idea that before you can plant new crops you must first uproot the old ones. The first years of the democratic era had been full of such imagery, of the idea of a radical cleansing, a clearing away of dictatorship and the old centers of power. François Duvalier's tomb had been razed, as had other symbols of the regime. The makout, when caught, had been "necklaced"—publicly killed by having burning tires placed around their heads. Fort Dimanche had been closed and turned into a monument. Still, many Duvalierists had remained in positions of power. Apparently, many makout had as well.[25]

I asked Manuel what it was like to have to work with people who had tortured you in the past. He didn't answer. We kept walking. The street started to slope upward. I could feel the worn stones, slippery under my boots.

Finally he said, "Makout or police. It's the same thing. In Haiti, you always have chèfs."

A car approached us from behind, its headlights bathing us and throwing our shadows up the street. I hadn't realized how quiet things had gotten until I heard the car's engine. We stepped to the side of the street. The car pulled over behind us and flashed its headlights. Once. Twice. I squinted and raised a hand to block the light. I couldn't see much, but I could tell it wasn't a police car. It was an older model, a worn-out car. Probably a taxi.

A man opened the rear door and hopped out. "Manuel, what's happening?" he said, grinning. "It's me, Richard!"

Richard was a guide and fixer, like Manuel. He worked out of a downtown hotel during the day, but he specialized in illicit goods like drugs and prostitutes. The other guides didn't like him very much, although he would often show up at Wilfred's shop or at other gathering places. Manuel had the closest connection to Richard, probably because Manuel also dabbled in dealing drugs. But everyone tolerated Richard because he had good connections with the police and the gangs. He was from an elite family, and his father had once been well connected but had fallen out of favor after the end of the dictatorship.

Richard waved us over to the car. "Get in," he said. He had a pistol sticking out of his pants, obvious enough that it was meant to be seen. He caught me looking at it.

"*Zam m,*" he said. My arms. My gun.

I looked inside the car. There was a man driving whom I didn't recognize. He had a gun on his lap too. There was a young woman in the backseat. Richard laughed, probably at my reticence. He offered us a ride again. He said he was out making some deliveries and that he would drive us home. I looked at Manuel. He tapped me on the arm and said, "Let's go. I'm tired."

Richard took the front passenger seat and we climbed into the back, joining the young woman. Once in the car, I could see she was even younger than I had first thought. Maybe a teenager. I said hello but she didn't say anything. She turned and looked out the window at the empty street.

We drove for a while, in the opposite direction from where Manuel or I lived. We drove up a steep road to Pétion-Ville, a suburb set in the hills over Port-au-Prince. Richard talked to me as we moved through the dark streets. He spoke in English, as he often did.

"This city is dead," he said. "Look at this place! There's nothing." He turned in his seat to look at me. "You ever been to New York?"

I said that I had.

"That's a fucking city, man!"

Richard had lived in New York for most of his life, until he got deported from the United States. He often spoke quite frankly about his disdain for Haiti. He seemed to feel stuck here. Like it was a form of punishment. Like he was doing time.

The driver turned onto a curvy street then pulled into a laneway. There was a large metal door blocking the way. On either side of the door were brick walls with broken glass sticking up from the top. I couldn't see the house behind the walls, but I could see a satellite dish atop a tall pole.

"Wait here," Richard said. I didn't know if he was talking to me or the driver. Switching to Kreyòl, he spoke to the young woman, telling her to get out of the car. She opened the door and joined him on the side of the road. The two of them approached the large metal door. Richard knocked on it. It opened slightly and he spoke to someone on the other side. The door opened more and Richard led the young woman inside. He returned alone a minute later and got in the car.

"Okay," he said. "Let's go."

We drove back down the hill and into the city. Manuel drifted off to sleep, his forehead resting on the car window. Richard asked me what we were doing out in the city at night. He laughed when I told him about our evening.

"Bòs likes to think he's a big man," he said, again in English. Richard turned around in his seat to look back at me. "He likes his neighborhood.

His fucking crack dealers. I don't have a neighborhood, man. I'm every-where. This is *my* fucking city."

A FARE FIGHT

April 2003. I was sitting inside the bar of a hotel with Manuel. We had been walking to Wilfred's shop when the sky had darkened. Everyone in the street began to scatter, seeking shelter. The rainy season was here. We made it to the bar just before the clouds opened up and a torrential rain began to fall. We ordered drinks and sat down to watch the rain. A small van came down the road, going too fast for the slick streets. Manuel made a disapproving sound and shook his head. "That driver is crazy!" The streets filled with water. A slurry of mud and garbage ran down the sloped streets, down to the center of the city, and out to the bay.

About an hour later, the rain stopped, as suddenly as it had begun. The low afternoon sun came back out. The air was still and humid. We finished our drinks and left, walking carefully up the slick road to Wilfred's shop. We passed a large drainage canal that was full of a slow-moving sludge. Plastic food containers swirled on top of brown eddies. I held my nose as we walked, trying to block out the stench. There was a man on his stomach, reaching into the canal with an iron rod, probing the morass. Water was still flowing into the canal and I imagined him falling in, being washed away in a sea of waste and excrement. Manuel shook his head.

"What's he looking for?" I asked.

A shrug. "He's looking for life, like all of us."

We kept walking. I looked back a few times, to make sure he was still there. Before we turned a corner, I looked back once more. He was standing up, pulling something over the edge of the canal.

People were coming back out into the street. Some of them swept water out of doorways and into the gutters. Cars and buses were starting up again. There were still a few more hours in the day. As we approached the gift shop, I could see Alexis and Frantz, another taxi driver, talking excitedly to Wilfred. I pointed to the group of men. "What's happening with them?"

"They're having an argument," Manuel said.

We walked faster, eager to find out what they were talking about.

Frantz saw us approaching and waved to Manuel, shouting, "Come, come!"

"What's up?" Manuel asked.

"Tell them!" Frantz said. He was visibly upset, his face red with anger, his hands clenched into fists. Wilfred was trying to calm him down. It seemed like he and Alexis were as unsure of the situation as we were. Frantz told Manuel to tell us about "his clients" *(kliyan m)* from the hotel.

"The aid workers?" Manuel asked.

Frantz nodded. He spoke quickly to Manuel. I couldn't follow everything he said.

"Tell them! Tell them!" Frantz said, pointing at Wilfred and Alexis.

Manuel told us that a few aid workers had arrived at a downtown hotel frequented by Frantz earlier this week. Manuel had been at the hotel restaurant with some other clients when he overheard them asking the hotel staff about hiring a driver or a guide during their stay. Manuel had approached them later that day and said he knew a driver with a good car. The aid workers were in town for about a week, apparently on vacation before starting on a new development project in the north of the country. They wanted to take a few day trips to the beach at Jacmel, and maybe see a few sites around the city. Manuel had agreed to take them to a Vodou ceremony and to see some art, and they had made plans with Frantz to handle the driving. It promised to be a big score, potentially hundreds of dollars.

"So, what happened?" Manuel asked. "You didn't go to Jacmel today?"

Frantz shook his head. "No!" He seemed calmer now that he had Manuel here to help explain things. He said that he had arranged to drive the aid workers to Jacmel for the day. They were going to meet up with a guide he knew there, to see the town and to meet some artists who made papier-mâché masks. Then he was going to take them to a hotel where they could eat and swim at a private beach. But when he arrived to pick them up, they were just getting into another taxi and preparing to leave. Frantz had approached the other driver, a man named David. The two of them had argued briefly. Threats were made. The hotel staff had asked Frantz to leave, and the aid workers had told him they were hiring David for the week instead of him.

Frantz was angry with the aid workers, whom he continually referred to as "bad whites" or "bad foreigners" *(move blan)*. And he was furious with David, whom he kept calling a thief *(vòlè)*. After hearing his story, everyone began to talk at once, saying that David was a bad person *(move moun)*, agreeing that he was a thief, and even suggesting that he used sorcery for his own material gain. With the group clearly on his side, Frantz's anger subsided. As we continued to talk about the situation, he began to boast about his own proficiency as a driver and about how he had better contacts than David. Frantz said that he knew everyone in Jacmel, that he would have gotten better prices on everything. He said that he had been driving foreigners around Haiti since before David was even born.

"He has no respect for you," Wilfred said, his low voice introducing a calming influence on the heated discussion. Everyone agreed, and the tone and topic of the conversation switched from anger about the economic loss to gloomier accounts of how young people didn't have any respect anymore. Frantz had stood to make more money off the aid workers than many households earn in a month. The loss of the potential income was devastating for him, and for Manuel, who would surely be cut out of the deal as well, since David had his own network of guides and fixers with whom he worked. Yet the inability to convert potential work into actual work, activity into money, was a regular and expected problem for these men. Foreigners were known to be bad customers, demanding impossibly low prices and constantly renegotiating the terms of various deals. Aid workers, in particular, came and went quickly, so there was no expectation of future relationships, as there had been decades ago with tourists and art dealers, and as there sometimes still was with journalists who returned to the country frequently. As I listened to the conversation, I came to realize that Frantz and the others did not see this as a case of competition winning out; rather, they saw it as an ethical breach, since David had violated what these men took to be the shared norms regulating the informal economy of the city.

Having framed the incident in moral terms, the men began to talk about what they might do in response. Although he was deeply offended by the theft of his clients and by the loss of such a substantial fare, there was little Frantz could do. The hotel allowed a set number of drivers to operate on their property, but they did not manage the fares and they had a strict policy against open conflict or fighting. Frantz had been told to leave by the hotel staff after he had confronted David, and he would now likely have to apologize in order to ensure he could continue to work at the hotel. Beyond the hotel itself, there was no agency or institution to which he could appeal for remediation, since both he and David were self-employed drivers. There were, of course, informal standards that governed where, when, and how drivers worked, but David's actions seemed to indicate that he did not feel bound by those informal rules. David had stolen Frantz's clients and, in so doing, had also disrespected Frantz by violating the hierarchies of age, experience, and connections that regulate much of the informal sector.

THE FORGOTTEN ONES

Spring 2003. We were sitting at Wilfred's shop again, with Jean, Toto, and Manuel. It was a few days after the argument between Frantz and David, but the incident was still a frequent topic of conversation. Wilfred had approached David in an attempt to broker a deal, but he had been rebuffed. This had prompted speculation among the group about David's motives and character. Frantz had said repeatedly that David got his money through nefarious means, probably from sorcery. When Toto suggested this again, Manuel scoffed at the idea.

"David has a boss," Manuel said. "He's a gangster. He's a *chimè*." The chimè, or "ghosts," were gangs said to be linked to the Aristide government, gangs like the Red Army in Martissant. I wondered why a gangster would bother being a taxi driver, since they are usually involved in more lucrative, and less legal, trades. Toto said he had heard that David's "people" were connected to a prominent downtown gang, and that his cousin had ties to the drug trade there. It seemed to be a more satisfying explanation than sorcery, although it was just as strong a moral condemnation of David's character. Talk turned to his flashy clothes, his cell phone—a rare item in Haiti in those days—and his new car. It seemed unimaginable that someone half their age could have access to so much cash. I would later learn that the hotel owner had recently hired David as his personal driver, which meant he had a recurring source of cash coming in weekly.

I told the group that I had met the clients. They were missionaries, not aid workers, on their first trip to Haiti. When I had asked them about the situation, they didn't think much of it. David had approached them with a better car and a better price, and, in their minds, he had simply offered a more competitive bid. They had said to me, "In America, the customer is always right."

Wilfred gave me a knowing smile. "But Grégoire, we are not in America!" Everyone nodded. I nodded too.

Wilfred went on to give his assessment of the situation. He said David had acted poorly, since he had known that Frantz had made prior arrangements with the foreigners. David should never have offered a lower price, and that even if the blan had approached him, the proper thing to do would have been to refuse to take them as clients. The others nodded their agreement.

I suggested again that the missionaries might not have understood what was happening, that they had their own cultural norms about hiring drivers and guides. "They come to Haiti, and they don't know Frantz or Manuel, or you," I said.

Wilfred raised his index finger in the air. "Yes!" he said. "They don't know him. They don't know me. That is the problem!"

I said I didn't understand. Jean took a turn explaining it to me. He said that for decades, whenever people came to Haiti, they would come to

Wilfred's shop. Everyone came to buy his art. He was known everywhere. In the 1970s and '80s, the tourists and art collectors had been "good blan" *(bon blan)*, they had come often and always returned to buy more art, to hire the same guides, to use the same drivers.

"So, they would fè pratik?" I said.

"Exactly!" Jean answered emphatically. He continued, saying that while there were fewer and fewer foreigners in Haiti, this was only part of the problem. The bigger problem, as he saw it, was that the foreigners who came now did not build any relationships with people in Haiti. They came and went, they hired different people all the time, or they bought fake paintings that were churned out en masse in large workshops and sold on every street corner. "Now, when blan come to Haiti, they forget us," Jean said. He pointed behind us at Wilfred's shop. "No one comes here. No one buys from him. They don't know him." Being forgotten in this way made it almost impossible to make relations, and without good relations, without being able to count on people, it was very difficult to look for life.

Jean felt that foreigners *ought* to know who Wilfred was. His comments suggested that foreigners coming to Haiti did not enter into a blank social field. When they came to the city, they entered a world built around over-lapping sets of obligations and responsibilities, a world made up of the small, repeated interactions that defined the informal economy, a world built up over decades. Foreigners had an obligation to be bon blan, even if they were unaware of these obligations or what they might entail. Jean, Wilfred, and the others all had reputations in the city. They were, or at least had once been, quite famous. People *knew* who they were and acted accordingly toward them. These men expected the weight of their reputations, earned over time through hard work and good relations, to carry over into each new interaction and give them a certain prestige and social standing with both potential clients and potential competitors. When such expecta-tions were not met, they saw it as a profound insult. Bad customers or competitors who forgot about them were acting improperly, either by shirking their responsibilities or by refusing to recognize the underlying norms of the informal economy.

What Jean was describing is a kind of moral injury. To be a person in Haiti is to be part of an extensive web of social connections held together by relations of obligation, responsibility, and mutual interdependence. For the men at Wilfred's shop, those connections were built up over time by repeated instances of recognition and acknowledgment, such as pratik rela-tions. Having such connections helped them survive in the informal econ-omy by giving them a position in a social network. It gave them a place, a name, an extended sense of self. At times, these relationships seemed to me to be improvisational, and these men seemed to be constantly acting as if they had stronger connections to and claims on people than they really did. As I spent time with them—hanging out, waiting, or traveling around the city trying to make something happen, to make a living—they seemed overly conscious of their actions. Like those moments of heightened awareness before an action becomes automatic, habitual. I had once asked Manuel about this fleeting quality of social networks. He told me they were more solid than they appeared, that his relationships across the city were like "roots" *(rasin)*. "When you have roots," he told me, "you can rely on people" *[konte sou moun]*. But still, sometimes you have to ask *[mande]* them to be responsible too!"

Being responsible to others and being able to rely on others were two sides of the same coin, two parts of a dialectic of recognition. Moral personhood was judged, in good part, on the outcome of that dialectical relationship. If a person remembered others and acted well toward them, he or she was considered a person of high moral standing. Those who forgot others or shirked their responsibilities were said to be bad people. Sometimes they were suspected or accused of sorcery or illegal activities, as in the case of David. Or they might be shamed into behaving differently. Yet the moral consequences of forgetting others did not end with shame or accusations of impropriety—they extended also to the forgotten ones. To be forgotten was to go unrecognized as a social person. It was to be cast out of the thick web of relations that made it possible to be a person at all.

The fallout from the fare fight lasted for days. Frantz eventually returned to the hotel, but he held out little hope that he would be able to compete with David for clients in the future. For his part, David seemed resolutely unapologetic about the whole affair. Everyone at the gift shop took this as a sign that Frantz should stay away from him and avoid future confrontations, in case he did, in fact, have gang connections or protection from a powerful boss. About a week after the incident, I met Alexis at another hotel. He was sitting in the shade on a plastic lawn chair. His car was parked in the large laneway, next to a few others. He was still waiting for work, although he had heard from the hotel staff that some guests were arriving in a few days. I asked Alexis if he had heard about what had happened to Frantz. He said he had, that Wilfred had told him. I asked him what he thought about it.

"We have a lot of problems," he said.

"Drivers?" I asked. "Guides?"

"Yes," he nodded, then sat quietly for a moment. "But everyone too. Everyone. In Haiti today, people don't have any respect [*respè*]."

I asked him what he meant.

He told me that David had been in the wrong, but that he wasn't really a bad person. Alexis rejected the idea that David was a gangster or even that he was intentionally violating the norms and expectations shared among private drivers. For Alexis, the problem was different. It was that the younger generations simply didn't know any better. They didn't know that what they were doing, how they were acting, was wrong. Alexis's assessment was not so much an apology for bad behavior as it was a commentary on the collapse of the institutions and practices that had previously anchored social life in the city. He agreed that David had shown a lack of respect for Frantz, but Alexis felt that this was the result of a broader problem—that people no longer had any respect at all.

Respè is a complicated term in Haiti. Its closest English equivalent is "respect," but in Kreyòl it names a wide semantic field that includes ideas of prestige *(prestij)*, honor *(lonè)*, character *(karaktè)*, and dignity *(diyite)*.[26] When people talk about other people in moral terms, they often talk about whether or not a person gives respect to others and whether or not a person is respected by others. There is a dialectical relationship at play in the giving and getting of respè, such that those who have respect for others are themselves well respected in turn. Respè, in this sense, is a corollary to responsibility and good relationships. Someone who fulfills their obligations to others in their network and who is responsible to their people will also be regarded as having a high moral standing. Someone who forgets their people or shirks their responsibilities will be said to have no respect. If you don't give respect, you don't get it. Respè, and the prestige and honor associated with it, are all earned by repeated demonstrations of good conduct and good character. Respè accrues over time, and while there is a reciprocal element to the giving and getting of respè, it is also hierarchical. Those with more respè are not only admired, they are also deferred to in social situations; they are called upon by many people to be responsible for them, to enter into relations of interdependency and support. Generation, gender, class, and color all factor into the hierarchies of respè, and in Port-au-Prince older men, in particular, have expectations about the amount of respect they are owed by younger men as well as by their peers.[27]

The topic of respè comes up often in discussions of people's conduct and character, either in positive evaluations of a person or in criticisms of a person's actions. Wilfred's assertion that David had no respect for Frantz was an example of the latter. In that case, the criticism of David did little to change the situation, but in other cases such public judgments might influence people to change their behavior—to act "responsibly," to remember their friends and family, and to show respect to those who thought they were owed it. These kinds of publicly declared negative evaluations are a key part of the everyday ethics of interpersonal relationships in Port-au-Prince.[28] Respè, much like one's livelihood, is never a settled issue. There are people who command a lot of respect from others, but they are still open to criticism should they fail to meet their obligations. Respè is thus not something you can truly ever "have." You can give it and get it, and you can earn a lot of it over time, but it is never an isolated attribute of an individual person. It is socially mediated in a double sense: it emerges out of repeated social interactions, such as fulfilling one's responsibilities to others, and it requires reciprocal recognition from the moral public of one's peers and associates.

When Alexis said that people didn't have any respè anymore, he was no longer participating in the moral evaluation of David's conduct. Instead, he cast the whole affair in broader terms, using it as a starting point for a criticism of what he saw as a prevailing condition in Haitian society. He was no longer talking about the moral or economic loss that Frantz had suffered, or even about his own precarious livelihood as a driver. To talk in those terms was still to talk in the language of respè, as if it were something that he or Frantz should be given, something they were owed but were not receiving. To talk in that way would make sense in the general terms of reference that anchor respè and moral personhood. But to say that people in general no longer had respect was to say something different. Instead, Alexis was describing the breakdown of a whole world and a way of life.[29]

Like so many others, Alexis had come to the city to look for life. And he, unlike many others, had found it. He had found a way to make a decent living, despite the difficulties of the informal economy. Those who lived in this informal world knew crisis intimately. How could they not? It was what brought them to the city. It confronted them every day. It shaped their lives, their jobs, their houses, their roads. And yet they had found a way to live with crisis that was both morally good and socially meaningful to them. They had found a way to live as *persons*. But the more I sat with Alexis and Wilfred and the other men who gathered at the gift shop and listened to them talk about their lives, the more I came to realize that beyond the urban crisis and the economic crisis and the political crisis was the everyday challenge of just surviving. And beyond that was something much worse—the existential problem of not being able to be a person.

THE HIGH COST OF LIVING

Winter 2003. I was sitting with Wilfred and Toto outside the gift shop when Alexis arrived. He was angry. He had just come from the gas station, where there had been long lines. He said that everyone there had been worried that the cost of gas, which was already at a record high, would go up again tomorrow. There were fears of gas shortages too, as rumors spread throughout the city that the elite were buying up all the gas, stockpiling it for their generators.

Prices had been going up for months. Food, gas, cooking oil, and rent were rapidly becoming unaffordable. People called this inflationary economy *lavi chè*, the expensive life.[30] Everyone was tightening their belts, trying to scrimp and save. In the street markets, goods were turning up in smaller and smaller units—a cup of cooking oil, a sliver of soap. In the big supermarkets, the shelves were bare. Even those with money couldn't afford to buy anything. Or maybe they had already bought it all. Maybe the rumors were true and people were preparing for another coup.

I asked how lavi chè was different from the ordinary poverty they called *mizè*.

"It's like this," Toto said. "If I don't work, I don't have money." He looked at me, to make sure I was following what he was saying.

I nodded.

"And, if I don't have money, I can't eat."

I nodded again.

"Okay," he said. "But, when we have lavi chè, things are more difficult. If I have money or if I don't have money, I can't eat." He rubbed his hands together in the air. "It's like that. If I am hungry, if I have hunger *[grangou]*, still I can't eat. When you have lavi chè, you can't eat. You can't live. You can't do anything."

The expensive life marked a significant change for them, one they discussed in comparative terms. They could remember the prices of various goods, the exchange rate between the Haitian gourde and the American dollar, and the market price for wages and services under each government. And they knew, too, what money had looked like in different moments, under Duvalier, after Duvalier, and then during the democratic era. Denominations. Units of goods. Rates of exchange. Prices. Wages. They had an intimate knowledge of them all, the symbolic and material forms of life in Port-au-Prince.

As we were talking, Alexis pulled a few coins from his pocket. He held one up between his thumb and forefinger. It was a five-gourde coin. "What can you buy with it?"

"Not much," I said. It was the price of a short bus ride. Or maybe two sachets of purified water that young kids sold on the street corners.

"Under Duvalier," Alexis said, "you could buy more." He listed a range of goods and their corresponding prices. What had cost five gourdes in the 1970s, he said, now cost 100 gourdes. This was partly because the Duvalier regime had fixed the prices of many household goods. In the democratic era, however, there had been intense international pressure to liberalize the economy. Haiti had become a net importer of food, and foreign food had flooded the local market. Despite what the experts had said, this had led to a steep rise in prices and a dependence on foreign food aid.[31]

Alexis held the coin up again. "Of course," he said, "with Duvalier, we were poor too. We didn't even have five gourdes." The others laughed with him. They often referred to the dictatorship as a period of economic stability, but they also stressed that they had no nostalgia for that time. Alexis had long maintained that while it had been bad under Duvalier, things were worse now.

"Today," Alexis said, "we have 250 gourdes, 500 gourdes," referring to some of the common denominations of paper money. "I never knew about these." He said that years ago, under the dictatorship, he had never even known that such bills existed. He had never seen a 250- or 500-gourde note. "But today," he told me, "everyone has them." He looked at Wilfred and Toto. They smiled and shook their heads, agreeing that these had once been unheard-of sums of money. "Now, they are like your dollars," he pointed at me, referring to the U.S. one-dollar note.

In Port-au-Prince, U.S. currency is a common medium of exchange, and for men like Alexis it is the preferred one. This is because the value of the American dollar is stable, which means you can wait until the exchange rate is better before converting U.S. dollars into gourdes. Even when it is not in circulation, the U.S. dollar exerts a strong influence on the Haitian economy. For much of the twentieth century, the Haitian gourde was pegged to it. The old exchange rate of 5 HTG to 1 USD, set in 1912, still casts a long shadow in the local economy. Prices are often given in "Haitian dollars," an imaginary currency with no material form that is based on the old rate of exchange.[32] One Haitian dollar is equivalent to five gourdes. If you are quoted a price in Haitian dollars, you have to quickly calculate by fives. Twelve Haitian dollars is 60 gourdes. Four Haitian dollars is 20 gourdes. And so on. Of course, the other side of this old relationship had long ago changed. The gourde was floated in 1989, and since then it has seen significant devaluation. In 2003, the prevailing rate of exchange was about 25 HTG to 1 USD. As the discussion of lavi chè suggests, this was considerably higher than it had been in previous years. It would soon go up even more, doubling over the next few years.[33]

Talk of money carries the weight of this history. People remember the old exchange rate, and it continues to shape their sense of the value of things in everyday interactions. Giving prices in Haitian dollars is, at least in part, a way of recalibrating commodity exchanges. For foreigners, it can be confusing. If you are not adept at doing quick calculations in your head, you might even get short-changed by a trading partner. But the use of this imaginary money tells us something about how people establish enduring economic relations even in the face of widespread informality and crisis. The U.S. dollar is held up as the paradigm of security, its value guaranteed by the strength of the American economy. The gourde, by contrast, is known to be unstable, its value constantly shifting. The immateriality of the Haitian dollar gives people a stable way of measuring things. It is a shared form of conversion and calculation that doesn't fluctuate in the same way the gourde does. Or at least it feels like it doesn't fluctuate, until one has to convert a price into a means of payment—which usually means into gourdes. Still, the Haitian dollar, just like the history of prices and of forms of exchange, shows how money has a social history and how economic calculations are grounded in social and cultural ideas of the proper value of things.[34]

The men at the gift shop all work in the informal economy, which means that they participate in what Michael Denning calls *wageless life*—a mode of living and working that takes place almost wholly outside of the formal economic system.[35] They work and are paid in money, but their labor and their wages are irregular and often invisible, at least from the point of view of formal economic institutions. They live by means of money, but cash payments for their services do not easily fit any standard definition of a wage. Nevertheless, these men have a strong sense of what their labor *ought* to be worth. When they negotiate prices with clients, they do so with a deep appreciation of the value of their labor-power, judged in part by their skills and in part by their access to extensive networks of people—their good relations, their respect across various neighborhoods and groups in the city. What they are worth, in this economic sense, is grounded in their social standing as persons. Yet their ability to demand adequate payment for their services has been called into question by challenges from competitors, like David, and from what Alexis described as a collapse of the social conditions of respè. Without respè, what were they worth? To make matters worse, the value of their labor was declining at the same time that the price of goods was increasing. This inflationary economy left them unable to eat—literally and figuratively—because even when they had money, they could not afford the things they were once able to buy.

It was impressive to listen to these men talk about inflation, currency devaluation, and purchasing power. They never used those terms, but they had a detailed understanding of the economic issues they faced on a daily basis. Why shouldn't they? They had been living with a pervasive economic crisis their entire lives. They had come to the city to escape the crisis of the countryside, but they came in full knowledge that they would still have to look for life to survive. And looking for life was, above all, a way of surviving in the precarious world of the informal economy.[36] I was struck, though, by their sense that something significant had changed, that the problem of lavi chè was a new kind of problem. It wasn't a lack of money. That was always an issue for them, and besides, they had more money than most Haitians. The problem seemed to be that money itself was no longer able to accomplish what it once had. As Toto said, even if you had money, you still couldn't buy food.

It had been a difficult year for all the men at the gift shop. By the end of 2003, amid a mounting political crisis and growing inflation, they continually told me they were no longer able to live *(m pa ka viv)*. I thought about Toto's remark. I thought of Alexis's complaint that nobody had any respè anymore. I thought of Wilfred's comment that "sometimes when you look for life, you die." All of these comments, and the countless others that they regularly made, seemed to point to the breakdown of a way of life. Crisis was nothing new to them—they had known it their whole lives. But lavi chè, the expensive life, seemed to name something different for them. It wasn't that they couldn't find work, or that they didn't have any money. It was that the norms and routines of social life no longer seemed to hold. The expectations of deference that came with respè did not prevent people like David from poaching clients. The expectations of the value of their labor did not translate into good prices from their clients. And the expectations of the value of things, the cost of living, were blown out of all proportion by rapid inflation.[37]

When Toto said that money was no longer able to buy things, he also said he was no longer able to do anything *(m pa fè anyen)*. This inability to do things, this inability to act, to convert your actions into stable forms of value like money or respè, was the result of a loss of context—the dissolution of the broader social frameworks that had once grounded the men's experiences and expectations.[38] A few days later, sitting at the shop again, I asked Wilfred if prices were still going up in the markets. He said yes, they were. He said things were even more expensive. "But," he said, "my life is not worth very much" *(lavi m se pa vo anpil).* "I don't have money," he said. "If I don't have anything, I can't do anything."

When you look for life, sometimes you die. But sometimes you don't. Sometimes you get stuck somewhere between living and dying.

FOREVER CRISIS

January 2004. I was sitting with Alexis and Wilfred. It was still early but the air was hot and dusty. I could smell burning charcoal from the food stalls down the street. It mixed with the aroma of fresh bread that occasionally wafted over from a nearby bakery. A crowded tap-tap drove past us, heading toward the morning traffic jams it would soon encounter downtown. We were all in a somber mood. There had been more political protests yesterday. Pro- and anti-government groups had clashed with each other. There had been barricades and shootings. People were worried there might be a coup.

I asked them what they thought was going to happen.

Wilfred shrugged. "I don't know."

We sat quietly for a while, watching people go about their morning routines. After a few minutes, he looked at me and said, "I don't know what life will bring for me."

The political crisis was making it harder to look for life. It was dangerous to travel around the city. Prices were skyrocketing. People were stockpiling things, preparing for the worst. Each day, more and more journalists came to the city to cover the violence. More and more potential clients arrived all the time. Alexis and Wilfred knew some of them, and they were making money. But at great risk. It was hard to get good information, and it was harder still to get access to the slums. Gangs controlled whole neighborhoods. The other day, protesters had set two cars on fire to block a street. Alexis was worried about his own car. He had it parked at the hotel, where it was safe. But when he was out with clients, anything could happen.

"What will happen?" Wilfred said. The question hung in the air. "I don't know," he said, finally. "I don't have much hope."

We sat in silence for a moment. I watched as two men worked across the street. They were lying on their stomachs, pulling mud and waste out of a large sinkhole in the road. Their arms disappeared into the hole, came back out holding thick globs of sewage. Each handful of muck made a wet slap on the ground.

"Yes," Alexis said. "In Haiti, we don't have hope." He smiled slightly. "But we have *a lot* of crisis."

We talked endlessly about crisis in those days. What else was there to talk about? One day, while walking with Manuel, I asked him how he lived with the constant sense of uncertainty.

"Today we have crisis," he said, waving his arm around us, as if to indicate our surroundings. "And tomorrow we'll have crisis. It's like that here. Crisis—it will be here forever. Forever."

I couldn't make myself understand. Manuel was not the only one who spoke in such terms. But the terms didn't make any sense to me. I thought that crisis was supposed to be fleeting—an event, a moment. A rupture. Something sudden. It came and then it went, and things were normal again. Or they were different. Either way, something happened. Manuel seemed to be talking about crisis as a permanent condition. It was *forever*. But crisis wasn't supposed to last. It wasn't supposed to be forever.

I kept asking Manuel to explain it to me, to explain the idea of a crisis that did not end. He seemed unbothered by the temporal ambiguity. For him, a crisis was always like a shock *(sezisman)*, a term Haitians use to talk about a sudden event or situation.[39] Even though shocks were sudden and unexpected, Manuel said he expected a shock every day. He asked me to think about the difference between being hungry one day and being hungry every day. Or about the difference between not working one day and not working every day. He tried a few other examples, too, all of them very close to his experience (and far from my own). They hinged on two related ideas. First, his examples highlighted a temporal dimension of "forever crisis," according to which acute events that were usually considered shocking or disruptive were encountered as routine, recurring aspects of daily life. Second, his examples all showed that he had come to expect crisis. He was braced for it. He knew it was coming, even if he never knew exactly what would happen or when.

How could he have known what would happen? How could any of us have known? How could I have known that in less than a month Manuel would be dead? And that just a few weeks after that, Aristide would be gone? That Aristide's departure would bring unprecedented violence to the city? That so many more people would be injured, arrested, or killed? How could any of us have known the other disasters to come? The ones that would level the city, that would bring disease, that would ruin the country in new, unimaginable ways?

3. Making Disorder

"I still haven't told you everything," the dead man said. But it was hard for me to hear him now. I wanted to tell him that he had been right, that I understood what he had said before. And I said that I was worried about what was happening, what was coming. "I know," he said. "I know what it feels like to wait, to wait for it to happen, to wait for the blow to strike, to wait for the end to come." He told me not to worry. He said, *"Bondye pa yon Bondye dezòd, men se yon Bondye lapè."* It was from the Bible. I had to look it up. "For God is a God not of disorder but of peace" (1 Cor. 14:33). How could that be, I wondered? If God is good, why is there so much disorder in the world?

"You will understand later," he said. "After."

After what?

"After it happens," he said.

I wanted to ask what he meant, but the dead man was gone. I looked for him in the darkened streets, in the shadows and the alleyways. I called out to him but there was only silence.

Has it always been like this? Always waiting for something to happen. Always waiting for something that has already happened. What a tragic situation; waiting for the inevitable, the reversal of fortune, the turn of the screw, the cruel hand of fate. Waiting for the plot to finally reveal itself after working so hard, secretly, behind the scenes. Realizing too late that all your actions have been in vain, that there was nothing you could have done, that things were always going to turn out this way.

They say that this is a crisis country, a basket case of a country, a shithole country. That it is a weak state, always teetering on the edge. Ungovernable.[1] They say these things because there is too much disorder here. Does that mean that God has forsaken this place? It is true, there is too much disorder here. The country has fallen into disorder. There are people living with it everywhere. But disorder doesn't just happen. Disorder is made.

DE MIL KAT

December 31, 2003.   I took a public taxi to a hotel across town. As we made our way through the afternoon traffic, we passed a gleaming white office building. It was the headquarters of Téléco, the state-run telecommunications company.[2] Téléco had long been a topic of debate. The elite and the international community had been pressuring the Haitian government to privatize several public companies since the 1990s, and the telephone company had been repeatedly held up as an example of incompetence and corruption. These days, the rumor was that the chimè were all employed by Téléco and that the government used such jobs, and even the utility trucks, some claimed, to funnel money to the gangs. My driver pointed out the window at a series of banners that had been hung along the front and side of the building.

"*De Mil Kat,*" he said. Two thousand and four. The bicentennial. Two hundred years since the declaration of Haitian independence.

I asked him if he was going to celebrate tomorrow. The driver shook his head.

"No," he said. "*M pa fè politik.*" I don't do politics.

His sentence stuck in my head. I had heard it a lot recently, as people criticized Aristide for politicizing the celebrations. Some members of the opposition had refused to take part in the festivities altogether. It seemed the political crisis had taken hold not only of the present but of the past, too. Then again, in Haiti, history has always been political. In the nineteenth century, political parties vied for control of the state, each armed with its own version of the country's past.[3] And when it came to politics, the revolution was always the most important part of that past, as political leaders aligned themselves with figures from the revolutionary period. In the twentieth century, history and ethnology became the twin pillars of a cultural nationalism that, in turn, grounded the political project of *noirisme*—black power. It was noirisme that finally challenged the racism and exclusion of the lighter-skinned elite, although it did little to change the fundamental structures of power and exclusion. Duvalier had turned noirisme into a totalitarian political ideology, but it had its roots in a reevaluation of the contribution of Africa to Haitian culture—and thus in the political reevaluation of legitimacy as residing not in "the most competent," which was the elite's familiar claim, but in "the most representative," which entailed a new formulation of popular sovereignty.[4] With Aristide, the revolution and noir-isme were mixed with liberation theology and Aristide's own brand of mil-lenarianism. To these were added references to the peasant uprising against the U.S. occupation in 1915 and to the doctrine of universal human rights. Aristide's speeches were littered with references to the past, sometimes overt, sometimes covert. He spoke in Kreyòl (no other president had done so before him) and drew on a rich oral tradition that used parables, idioms, and stories to craft a new mode of political speech. Indirect and allegorical, una-bashedly theological, Aristide's speech could seem strange, even unintelligi-ble, to foreigners. But in Haiti, everyone got the point.[5]

As we drove on, we passed a billboard with an image of Toussaint Louverture, one of the great revolutionary heroes, beside a picture of President Aristide. Across the top the sign read: "Two men, two centuries, one vision." Haitian politics is always conducted in the shadow of the revo-lution, and politicians make frequent references to revolutionary heroes and to the country's founding fathers.[6] François Duvalier, for example, had declared himself to be the symbolic heir to Jean-Jacques Dessalines, who had defeated the French, won the revolutionary war, and declared independence. It was a double claim that positioned him both as an authoritarian leader ready to use violence against his enemies and as the legitimate defender of the nation, charged with ensuring its independence from foreign rule. (The metaphoric use of Dessalines thus immediately got the point across that Duvalier's enemies were enemies of the nation and that they would be dealt a swift death.) Aristide had chosen Toussaint Louverture, presenting himself as Louverture's political descendant and suggesting that he, Aristide, would finish the revolution Toussaint had begun.[7]

Toussaint Louverture is probably the most famous of Haiti's revolution-ary figures, in part because he is also the most universalizable. There have been far more histories written about him than about the other leading figures of the period, and most accounts of the Haitian Revolution focus on his leadership. Of course, as many Haitian nationalists will tell you, Toussaint remained loyal to the French right up until General Leclerc arrested him and exiled him from the colony. It was Jean-Jacques Dessalines, not Louverture, who turned the revolution into a war of independence and who presided over the birth of the country. Perhaps, though, it is best to see these figures as two poles that mark out the symbolic field of Haitian national politics. According to that schema, Toussaint was a moderate leader who negotiated with the international community and who initiated self-rule in the colony. He imagined a future that eschewed a return to slavery but that kept Saint Domingue within the French empire. He is an epic figure who went from being an enslaved coach driver to top military and civilian leader in the colony, but he is also a tragic figure who fatefully misjudged the French, realizing only when it was too late that they intended to arrest him, to kill the remaining revolutionaries, and to restore slavery in the colony. By contrast, Dessalines was the brutal but effective military leader who took command of the revolutionary forces after Toussaint's downfall. As the leader of the newly named Indigenous Army, Dessalines led the revolutionaries to victory, defeating the French in a series of decisive battles. He knew that freedom would come only through violence, and after declaring independence on January 1, 1804, Dessalines made his officers swear a blood oath to defend the nation from any foreign invasion. Later he ordered the massacre of the remaining white planters in the colony, an act that has since made him a pariah to foreigners. As Dany Laferrière has noted, Dessalines is regarded as a "monster," but for Haitians he is *their* monster—the only one who brought freedom and independence.[8] And yet he, too, is a tragic figure. Just two years after independence, Dessalines was assassinated by some of his closest generals and his death launched a civil war that lasted more than a decade.

As we drove past the billboard, I recalled a conversation I once had with a British expat who had lived in Haiti for decades. We had found ourselves walking together, part of a small group on a tour of colonial-era buildings in the seaside town of Jacmel. As we chatted about the history of coffee exports, she said to me that the problem with Haiti was that it had gained independence too soon. The country would have been better off, she said, if Toussaint had remained in charge of the colony and if the colony had remained a part of France. It is a common view among expats in Haiti, one that reads the history of the country as a tragedy. When I mentioned this conversation to a Haitian friend, a historian and a devout nationalist, he brushed the comment away with his hand and said, "She is wrong. She thinks this because she is not Haitian. Westerners like Toussaint because he did not kill the French." He looked at me and paused, then said, "But this is not Toussaint's country. This is Dessalines' country!"

WAITING FOR THE COUP

December 31, 2003.   The sky was clear. I leaned on the veranda railing and looked out at the city. Most nights, Port-au-Prince was a city of shadows, the darkness held back only by the moon or the faint, flickering glow of paraffin lamps and candles. Tonight, the city was shining.

I turned to Manuel and said, "I've never seen so many lights!"

He smiled and leaned close and said, "They've been saving gas for months."

Behind us, a band was playing. People were dancing. The government had been storing gas for months, preparing for the bicentennial celebrations. There would be no blackouts in the city that night. I stood quietly next to Manuel for a few minutes, listening to the band. I watched as more and more people arrived, and I wondered how they could possibly fit inside the hotel. Manuel tapped my arm. I turned to him and smiled. "You have to dance, Grégoire!" he said, pointing to the crowded room inside. "Tonight, we all dance!"

He tugged my arm and pulled me toward the crowd. A woman walked past us and handed us glasses of champagne. We drank it quickly and joined the other dancers, bodies pressed together. The heat and weight of the room. I felt the drums and the bass in my chest and under my feet. And then it was midnight and the sky exploded in fireworks.

January 1, 2004, the Bicentennial of Independence. The morning of the bicentennial, I sat at a hotel bar drinking coffee and eating scrambled eggs, watching a television that hung in the corner, waiting for the speeches and celebrations to come. Aristide was in the coastal city of Gonaïves, where Jean-Jacques Dessalines had read the Act of Independence two hundred years ago. Gonaïves was a "hot" city. Gangs once loyal to Aristide had broken ranks with him. A gang leader had been killed in September, his mutilated body left in the streets. People said Aristide had ordered his death, and now the gangs were threatening to kill him when he came to their city. Everyone in the capital was on edge, waiting to see what would happen. Waiting for the coup. Wondering if there would be an attack during the speeches, or if someone would attack the capital while the president was away. Neither happened, of course. The coup came two months later, when the gangs in Gonaïves, led by ex-army officers, paramilitary leaders, and former members of the national police, rebranded themselves as a revolutionary army and began to march on Port-au-Prince.

That morning, as I drank coffee and listened to the speeches, two South African soldiers came into the bar and sat beside me. They were in Haiti as part of the security detail for President Thabo Mbeki, who was here for the bicentennial celebrations—he was the only foreign head of state to come—and was currently sitting on the dais with Aristide in Gonaïves. He would give a speech in which he compared the Haitian Revolution to the struggle against Apartheid in South Africa, saying that the two events were both great moments in the history of human rights.

I gestured to the television and asked the soldiers why they were still in the capital.

"We're guarding the airport," one of them said.

His tone made it clear that was all the explanation I would get. I returned my attention to my coffee and the television. Aristide was speaking now. He was talking about the revolution, about its historical significance and what it meant in the present. He also spoke of the many problems that Haiti faced today and of the way the international community had failed Haiti. He called on France to pay reparations, citing a figure close to $22 billion, as a means of making restitution. It was not the first time he had made such a demand. The previous year, the Haitian government had begun preparing a legal brief seeking reparations from France for an indemnity that Haiti had been forced to pay its former colonial master as compensation for the property lost during the revolution.[9] Reparations had become a cornerstone of the bicentennial celebrations, and there were banners hanging over the streets of the capital with the slogan "Reparations + Restitution = 2004." Aristide's critics accused him of politicizing the bicentennial, and many of them had refused to participate in it. For their part, the French government was not impressed with the talk of reparations. They sent a commission to Haiti to investigate the issue. The commission authored a report that denied any legal or moral case for reparations, although the report did manage to revive the old colonial argument that it was, in fact, Haiti that was indebted to France, since the latter had brought the French language and thus also, presumably, civilization itself. As pressure mounted against Aristide in the months after the bicentennial, France was the first foreign government to call for him to step down. And after the coup, a provisional government installed by the international community, under the behest of France, Canada, and the United States, quickly dismissed the legal case for reparations.[10]

"What's all this about then?" one of the South African soldiers said. I turned to look at him. He pointed with his chin at the television.

"The speeches?" I asked.

He nodded. I started to tell him about the bicentennial celebrations and the revolution. He brushed that aside with a dismissive hand gesture. He told me he knew about all of that. He asked me why I was watching it, why I cared about it. I told him that the Haitian Revolution was an important event, not just for Haiti but for everyone. He seemed less than convinced.

"When was this? Two hundred years ago?"

"Two hundred years. Yeah," I said.

"Too long." He shook his head. "Too long ago! Who cares about that now?"

I tried to respond. I wanted to say that I cared, that more people *should* care, but he kept going.

"In South Africa," he said, "it has been ten years. Ten years since the end of Apartheid, yeah?"

I nodded. "Yes, I—"

"Ten years. You see? We still remember. *I still remember.* What it was like to live with that. We all know what we fought against. But this—it was so long ago, who remembers that now?"

His friend, who had remained silent all this time, stood up abruptly and pointed at his watch. "Time to go," he said. They tossed some cash on the bar and left.

Michel-Rolph Trouillot has famously argued that the Haitian Revolution was "unthinkable" as it happened, since it challenged the very concepts and categories that anchored the Western world.[11] How could slaves proclaim their own freedom when they were not deemed subjects at all? In the two centuries since independence, the revolution has remained largely unthinkable, as the event itself has been silenced or trivialized and as Haiti has been politically and economically marginalized. Now, at the bicentennial, it seemed like the revolution was being silenced yet again. Only one foreign head of state came for the celebrations, and most of the foreign correspondents in the country seemed more interested in the current political crisis than in the historical significance of the revolution. The South African soldier's suggestion that the revolution was simply too long ago to matter now seemed like another version of silencing—the denial of the retrospective significance of the event. But maybe there was something to his claim, even if he was not quite right. Maybe the bicentennial could never be what it claimed to be. The commemoration was part of a claim for reparations and reconciliation, but without any formal political recognition from the international community, to which such claims were partly addressed, the bicentennial celebration was bound to fall on deaf ears. The full extent of this silencing became clear two months later, when Aristide was forced out of power and out of the country—kidnapped and sent into exile just as Toussaint Louverture had been. Only this time, there was no Dessalines and no Indigenous Army, no war of independence. There was only the coup, followed by an international military intervention.

The night of the bicentennial, I had dinner with Manuel at the hotel. There were conflicting reports in the news. Some people were saying the gangs had fired at Mbeki's helicopter, but the South Africans were denying it. Different radio stations were reporting vastly different accounts. Anti-government stations said Aristide had never made it to Gonaïves, that there had been no speeches, that he had been chased out by gunfire from the gangs. In the capital, there had been protests against the government. There had been shootings. The police had fired tear gas on the crowds. Aristide supporters had clashed with the protesters, with one group chanting *Aba Aristide* (Down with Aristide) and the other responding *Titid Pou Senk An* (Aristide for Five Years).

We ate and talked about the bicentennial and the protests. I asked Manuel why this was happening. Why was the opposition refusing to allow Aristide to finish his term, refusing even to commemorate the revolutionary founding of the country? He said the political opposition did not want to let Aristide have the bicentennial. He said they were accusing Aristide of making it political, but they were the ones making it political. They had refused to participate in any of the commemorative events. Many prominent bands, artists, and intellectuals had joined the political opposition in a boycott of the bicentennial. History was political. Claiming the revolution was a way for Aristide to perform his own legitimacy, and the opposition wanted to cast him as illegitimate, as a dictator. There was even some curious graffiti scrawled on walls in the city that read "Aristig." I had thought it was a misspelling when I first saw it, but later I realized it was a pithy critique, a play on the president's name and on the Kreyòl word for tiger, *tig*. Why a tiger? Because François Duvalier had called himself the tiger and had called Dessalines a tiger. In one simple word, a neologism written in paint on the wall, there was a whole chain of associations—Aristide was a tiger like Duvalier, Aristide was a monster like Dessalines.

I had heard several members of the opposition make these comparisons directly. They had also been vocal in their assertions that Aristide was politicizing the bicentennial. They said he was paying people to work on the bicentennial programs, which was at least partly true, since the government was employing crews to beautify the city and to prepare and staff the events. They accused him of using these government jobs as a way to bribe and pay his supporters, so as to ensure their continued loyalty. For the opposition, the bicentennial was just another example of Aristide's authoritarian tactics. And yet I couldn't help but think that their own refusal to participate in the celebrations was a symbol, too, a symbol that they were willing to sacrifice the country's very independence in order to remove a political rival.

"They're trying to make a coup," Manuel said, "but they don't have the force." I asked him what he meant. He said that the opposition and the elite wanted Aristide out but that they didn't have the popular support to get him out.

"They have to pay people to protest," he said. "They make disorder [*fè dezòd*] so they can say 'Aba Aristide.'"

A burst of loud laughter came from a nearby table, where a group of American journalists were getting drunk and swapping war stories. Manuel finished his beer, ordered another one for both of us. The beers arrived. The waitress set them on the table and cleared our empty plates.

Manuel told me about *dezòd*. The word meant disorder, but not just disorder. It could mean political disorder, or even anarchy. It could also mean division, panic, disturbance, or terror. But as Manuel described it, disorder wasn't something that just happened, like a natural disaster. It was something *made*, something done by people. And in Haiti, he said, it was always a key part of politics.

There was another round of loud laughter from the drunken journalists. One of them was telling a story about hiding in a bathtub during a firefight. I thought about other meanings of disorder. There was the medical usage, in which a disorder was a malfunction, something that disrupted the proper order of things. But that sense didn't capture the agency involved in the making of disorder. The Old French usage did, though, as did the Medieval Latin usage. In both of those languages, *disorder* meant "disordain." It meant to undo the work of ordaining something. To undo what had been arranged. To remove from the church. To make the sacred profane.

The journalists were still laughing loudly. One of them was telling a story of how he had exchanged recordings of gunfire with another journalist earlier that afternoon. He was saying that the improved sound quality had made his radio report about the bicentennial really come alive. "You can hear every shot, just like being there," he said. "Pop, pop, pop!"

THAT WHICH YOU SEE, IT'S NOT THAT

Sunday, January 4, Martissant.   On a bright, clear morning, I returned to the forest. It was the first week of January, 2004, just a few days after the bicentennial. I had not been back since the Red Army had taken over the area the previous spring. But in recent months, a tenuous truce had taken shape between the gang and the SCPE and KDBGF. Maxo and other members of the SCPE had returned to Martissant (they had been in hiding elsewhere in the city for months), and they had begun once again to patrol portions of the forest and to broker relations with the squatter community. Cameron was optimistic that a turning point was coming, and that they would soon be able to move forward with the botanic garden project.

I had heard from Maxo and Vincent that some of the squatters had started to get involved in conservation efforts. They seemed eager to work with the SCPE and to position themselves as stewards of the forest. Through Vincent, I had been invited to attend a cleansing rite at Habitation Leclerc conducted by Celeste, the woman who had appeared at the spring to talk to the environmental studies students during the aborted tour last April. Excited to return to the forest, I eagerly accepted. I met Vincent at his house. We were joined by Laurent, but not Maxo. I asked if he was coming too.

"Not today," Vincent said. "Don't worry. We're good."

And with that, we walked down the road, stepped through a hole in the wall, and entered the forest.

We walked along a recently cleared stone path toward the empty concrete basins where Source Leclerc once bubbled up from the ground. Celeste was waiting for us when we arrived at the spring. She was dressed all in white and was accompanied by her son, whom she called "Papa Oungan," and three women who served as *ounsi,* or ritual assistants. They too were all dressed in white. A man sat on a metal lawn chair, silent as he watched us. A few women and teens from the squatter camp wandered over to join the group. Celeste announced that we were gathered at the spring to call on the lwa and the ancestors to "guarantee" *(garanti)* the spring and the forest.

Cleansing rituals are part of the annual rites of service *(sèvi)* conducted to honor the ancestors and the lwa. Unlike other Vodou rites, these do not involve sacrifice, dancing, or possession, nor do they take place in a temple *(ounfò)* or require the ritual authority of an oungan or mambo. Rather, they are often led by the head of the lakou, and they play an important role in the ritual reproduction of good relations between a family or resident group and the lwa who inhabit the landscape. Along with first yams festivals, purification rites, and ceremonies held in honor of the dead, cleansing rites are family matters, and their main purpose is to ensure the cosmological reproduction of natural resources like land, water, and trees.[12]

As ceremonies go, the one held by Celeste was short and simple. Celeste's son drew out several *vèvè* (signs representing specific lwa) in cornmeal around a concrete basin. He then placed a lace cloth on the ground and made a small altar, on which he set an offering of eggs and flour, apples, and white rum, along with two white candles. He also left an offering of eggs in the basin. After that, Celeste led the group through a serious of prayers and songs. The focus of the rite was Danbala, a lwa who lives in forests, but the group also honored Katherine Dunham—whom they referred to as the "head" or master *[mèt]* of the estate—and Ayizan Velekete, a kind of

Cleansing rite in the forest. Photo by author.

Earth-Mother associated with the worship of elderly female ancestors or *grann* (literally "grandmothers").[13]

When the ceremony was over, the man who had been sitting in the chair stood up and left, accompanied by Celeste's son. The teens from the squatter camp dispersed slowly, chatting and hanging around. I sat down with Celeste and Vincent and we talked briefly about the cleansing rite. She stressed the importance of such rites, telling me that without anyone to serve the lwa the spring would remain dry and the forest would fall down. I knew from previous interactions with her that Celeste was deeply invested in her own spiritual claims on the forest, but I was intrigued by how she used the cleansing rite to align herself not only with the lwa who dwelt in the forest and the spring but also with Katherine Dunham. I asked why they had sung in honor of Dunham.

"She is our grann," Celeste said, as she gestured toward the squatter community. "She is our ancestor *[ras]*."

"And she owns the estate?" I asked. "She lives here?"

Celeste nodded. "Yes! She lives here," she said, pointing to the ground. "She lives here," she repeated, this time pointing to the trees. "She lives here because Danbala lives here. And we live here too."[14] She stood up and waved her arm. "Come," she said. Vincent and I followed Celeste to the squatter camp. She took us on a brief tour, introducing us to several residents. Her son was there, but he did not talk to us. She told me her son had been living there for several years and that he was the leader of a popular organization that protected the forest. (He was also a member of the Red Army.) I asked Celeste and some of the squatters about the botanic garden project. They were all aware of it, and Celeste was especially supportive of it. "Yes," she said excitedly. "This is a garden. You see? And we should be able to live here too!"

As Vincent and I prepared to leave, a young man named Tidjo approached us. He told us he had lived in the squatter camp for years. He walked with us as we headed toward the broken wall and the street outside the forest. Tidjo asked me what I was doing at Habitation Leclerc. I said Celeste had invited me to the cleansing rite. He shrugged, as if to suggest I had answered the wrong question.

"In Haiti today," he said, "we have a big problem."

I asked him what he meant. He told me that the country was on the verge of a war *(lagè)*. He said that there were two kinds of people in Haiti, the rich and the poor. The rich people where making dezòd because they wanted to kill all of the poor people.

"The *boujwa* [elite] like to eat," he said, putting a hand to his mouth to mime the ingestion of food. "They are fat, they eat so much. Well, we are hungry too."[15]

I asked him who he meant by "we."

"We, yes," he said pointing to himself and then gesturing to the camp behind us. "We are the people *[pèp la]*. We are with Aristide."

Monday, January 5, Downtown.   The next morning, Luc called me and suggested we meet for lunch. I agreed to meet him at a restaurant downtown. When I arrived, I saw that Maxo was with him. They were both agitated. As soon as I sat down, they began to ask me questions. They wanted to know what had happened yesterday, they wanted me to tell them everything about the cleansing rite—who was there, what they did, who had arranged it. I was confused at first, having been under the impression that Maxo had known about it. I told him as much, and he shook his head vigorously. "No!" he said.

I told them about the events of the previous day. They listened as I spoke, nodding along. I suspected they already knew most of the details. Somewhere during my story, we ordered lunch—plates of *poul nan sòs*, stewed chicken in tomato sauce, with white rice on the side. When I was finished talking, they were both quiet for a few moments. We ate, and I waited for their response. Maxo seemed visibly angry but remained silent.

Finally, Luc spoke. "In Haiti," he told me, "we have a proverb. *Tout sa ou wè, se pa sa.*" He leaned over his plate and looked at me. He said it again: "Tout sa ou wè, se pa sa."

I had not heard the proverb before. I repeated it back to him and asked what it meant. The phrase is idiomatic, but a rough English translation would be "That which you see, it's not that." The essence of the proverb is that things are other than what they seem. But Luc stressed a deeper meaning. For him, the lesson of the proverb was not just that there are different points of view. Rather, it was about a particular relationship between appearance and essence, between the way things seem to be and the way they really are. The proverb was about deception. I thought I knew what I had seen at the forest—but did I really know what had happened?

At that point, Luc and Maxo began to tell me a different story about yesterday's events. Their account differed from my own in nearly every detail. They said that Celeste was not a mambo, that her son was a member of the Red Army, and that the other participants had all been members of the squatter community and the gang. They said that Celeste had no ritual authority to conduct a ceremony at the spring, and that the real mambo in the area was Lourdes, who ran one of the most respected and revered Vodou temples in Martissant. Lourdes and her late husband Gesner had long been affiliated with Dunham and Habitation Leclerc, and Luc told me that they— not Celeste—were responsible for serving the lwa at the forest.

"In Vodou," Luc said, "you always have two sides. One for the tourists and one real one." He meant that the ritual had been staged, that it had been a fake. A performance. And I had played a role in the staging, serving as the audience. Luc continued, reminding me of the history of Habitation Leclerc and of the botanic garden project. He reminded me that the gang and the squatters were illegally living on the property.

"These people are thieves," Maxo said.

I ate the rest of my chicken and listened. I felt like I was playing the part of the audience again, for another performance. I settled into the role. I asked them why they didn't go to the police, or the courts. They said that it was a money issue and a policing issue. They couldn't afford to pay the police to come to the area, and the police were politically aligned with the state. They said that the courts were controlled by the state too. I had heard it all before. We had had the same conversation dozens of times. They knew it and I knew it, but the conversation played itself out as if it were scripted, like its own kind of ritual.

There was something new, though, in the way they talked about the situation. For as long as I had known them, Luc and Maxo had presented the standoff at Habitation Leclerc as a struggle between two different sides—a series of legitimate organizations with the capacity and authority to protect the forest (the KDBGF, the SCPE, and their international affiliates) and an illegitimate and disorderly mass of people that actively threatened to destroy the forest (the gang and the squatters). But as we talked more about the cleansing rite and what it might mean for the struggle over the forest, Luc and Maxo began to make a more pointed critique of the state and of Aristide's government. They had once been supporters of Aristide, but over the years they had grown disenchanted with him, and also with his political party and its base of supporters in the slums. For years, they had complained that the government was simply not doing enough to stop the spread of gangs and the growth of squatter settlements. They had said the government was too weak to address the urban and environmental crises. But as the conversation drifted from the events of the previous day to a wider explanation of the political crisis, it became clear that they now saw Aristide and his government as being directly responsible for the rise of gangs and squatters, in the forest and elsewhere.

"The gangs have a problem," Luc said. "There are demonstrations all the time. We are standing up against the government. They know if Aristide goes, they will go too."

"Aristide has the mayors," Maxo said. "The mayors tell the gangs what to do."

It was like the old *chèf de section*, the rural section chiefs, used by the Duvalier dictatorship to extend the control of the state into the most banal parts of everyday life.[16] Section chiefs controlled the movement of people in and out of rural areas, they controlled the licenses for marketing and other economic activities, and they worked with paramilitary groups to enforce the property claims of big landowners. According to Maxo, the same structure of appointed government officials and paramilitary groups had taken shape under Aristide.

"They call themselves *chimè*," he said. The term is related to the French word for chimera. In Haiti, it means monster or ghost.[17] "But they're all gangs," he added. "The chimè, the Red Army, the government. They're all the same."

"So, Abel and the others work for Aristide?" I asked.

Maxo nodded. "He's an assassin *[asasen]*. He kills for them. Aristide pays the gangs to make all this dezòd."

"Why?" I asked.

"In Haiti," Maxo said, "disorder is big business."

"And," Luc added, "to do business you have to do politics *[fè politik]*." He brushed the back of one hand in the palm of the other. "They're the same thing."

"Everywhere you look, you see that in Haiti we have lots of disorder," Maxo said. "Lots of disorder. But who makes it?" He paused, waiting for me to answer.

I shrugged. "Gangs?"

Maxo nodded. "And who pays the gangs?"

"You're saying Aristide pays them," I said.

"*Leta,*" Maxo said. The state.

"Now you understand," Luc said, leaning back in his chair.

DEMONSTRATIONS

Wednesday, January 7, Sogebank.   I was standing in line at the bank when I heard it. It sounded like an explosion in the distance. A few muffled bangs followed. Two security guards came rushing into the bank, closing the doors behind them. More sounds from outside. Chanting, drums, yelling. Was that gunfire? The sounds of a crowd grew louder. And then it was quiet again.

We waited inside the bank. Just waited. Standing still, holding our breath. And then the guards cautiously opened the doors and stepped outside. They held their shotguns up, ready, and walked out into the morning sunlight, closing the doors behind them. We remained still for a moment, and then everything went back to normal. A teller called for the next person in line. She moved up to the counter and did her banking. People just went on as if nothing had happened.

I got out of line and left the bank. I passed the guards on the front stoop, still holding their guns up. I walked around them and hurried down the street, eager to be out of their line of fire. I could hear crowds chanting again, but they sounded far away this time. I saw smoke rising in the distance. I walked down the street, passed shuttered shops and cars with smashed windows. Stacks of burning tires blocked a nearby intersection. The smell of burning rubber. My eyes watered. The streets were empty.

Thursday, January 8, Champ de Mars.   When I got to Champ de Mars, the downtown public plaza, the demonstrations were over. The crowds were gone. Police officers in riot gear stood near a tall fence ringing the National Palace. Smoke and tear gas still hung in the air, but it no longer hurt to breathe. As I crossed the plaza, I saw a young man walking quickly toward me. I waved and said hello, but he didn't respond. He looked directly at me. When he was just a few feet away, he held out a book in his hands. He opened the front cover to reveal a faded black-and-white photograph of François Duvalier, dressed in a suit and bowtie. I stopped walking, confused. The man looked at me and smiled, then shut the book, turned abruptly and walked away. I wanted to ask him who he was, why he had shown me the photograph, but he turned a corner and disappeared.

Friday, January 9, Walking in the Street. I hurried down the street to Wilfred's shop. The city was closed, the streets were empty. It was the second day of a general strike called by the opposition. Banks, gas stations, schools, and most businesses were closed. There were still some brave market women in the streets, but for the most part everyone had stayed home. Anti-government protesters were making their way toward the National Palace. I heard chanting, yelling, and sporadic gunfire. I saw smoke rising from the barricades and smelled tires burning. The air felt thick, filled with electricity. Beside me, a few other people walked quickly, with their heads down. We offered none of the customary pleasantries people normally exchange as they pass others on the street. It was like we were racing to get home before a storm.

A few blocks from Wilfred's shop, a white pickup truck came speeding down the street. The truck's back bed was full of men with guns, dressed all in black, their faces covered by balaclavas. A man beside me hissed under his breath. I looked at him and said, "Police?" He shook his head and said, "Chimè." The truck turned a corner and disappeared. Like a ghost.

Sunday, January 11, Lunch with Luc. I was having lunch with Luc at a French restaurant in Pétion-Ville, where earlier that morning one of the largest anti-government protests had begun at Place Saint Pierre, the central public square. The geography of the city read like a map of the social and political divisions in the country. Pétion-Ville was a suburb on the hill, perched above Port-au-Prince. It had long been home to the country's elite families, although in recent years many of them had relocated even higher up the mountain, where small gated communities hid, clustered among the trees, guarded by private security forces. The opposition, led by high-profile elite businessmen, would start their marches here, above the city, and then wind their way down one of the main roads, moving through middle-class neighborhoods and hillside slums, down to the flat plains of the city itself, and then through the larger slums, the zones where Aristide's base lived, all the way to the National Palace. These marches had become an almost daily occurrence. And so, too, had the inevitable clashes with Aristide's supporters. It seemed that every day ended the same—with violence.

Luc was talking about the protests, telling me all the reasons he thought Aristide had to go. We had been having the same conversation for months. I didn't want to have it again. I looked up from the table as a large group entered the restaurant, brimming with excitement. A woman from the group raised her arm above her head and gave a big wave, then walked over to our table. "Luc!" she said loudly, as she bumped into the table. I steadied it with both hands to keep things from spilling.

"Rachelle!" Luc said. "How are you?" He stood up and gave her a kiss on the cheek.

"I've just come from a demonstration!" She was giddy, almost shaking.

"For which side?" I asked, playing dumb.

Rachelle looked down at me over the top of her glasses. She paused for an uncomfortable amount of time. Then she touched one hand to her bare forearm. The gesture was a common one among the elite, a subtle way of indicating one's skin color, and therefore one's class position and social standing.[18] As she touched her arm she said, in a matter of fact tone, "Which do you think?"

But I already knew the answer. I had known the answer before I had even asked. Like Luc, Rachelle was light-skinned and her family was from the country's traditional elite. She was marching against the government. She was marching against Aristide. I let her question hang in the air. I doubt she expected an answer anyway. I leaned back in my chair as she and Luc talked some more.

Monday, January 12, at Gabriel's House. Gabriel was already sitting in the garden behind his house when Luc and I arrived. He lit a cigarette and waved for us to sit down. We joined him as his maid served coffee and bread.

"So," he said, "tell me what happened at the forest."

Gabriel had heard about Celeste and her son conducting a cleansing rite at Habitation Leclerc. Still, he seemed eager to hear me tell the story. I went through it again, and then listened, again, as Luc and Gabriel explained to me that I had not seen what I thought I had seen, that something else had been going on. Gabriel lit another cigarette and asked me if I knew what had really happened.

I told him I thought that the ceremony had been a kind of property claim made by the squatters and the gang, a claim in which they had positioned themselves as having both ritual and legal authority over the property.[19] He nodded in agreement. But then he held a finger in the air and looked at me.

"Yes, of course," he said. "And also, something else."

"What?"

"They are nervous!" he said. "You see? They know what is coming." He continued, telling me that all over the city Aristide's supporters were getting anxious. He said they knew that when Aristide went, they would be arrested. As Gabriel saw it, the gang and the squatters were trying to position themselves so they could survive after the coup.

"And the police," he said. "They're worried too!" He seemed excited by this. During the demonstrations yesterday, the riot police, known as CIMO (Corps d'Intervention et de Maintien de l'Ordre), had moved to protect the anti-government protesters from Aristide's supporters. There were already rumors circulating that CIMO officers, whom Gabriel considered to be both better trained and politically neutral, had recognized off-duty police officers among pro-government demonstrators. "This is a sign," he said. He told me that if the police turned on Aristide, the government would fall.

I asked him why he thought Aristide had to go. Shouldn't he finish his term? Wouldn't it be better to seek change through democratic means?

Gabriel laughed. "Haiti is not a democracy! Aristide is not a president; he's a dictator! We can't fight a dictator with elections."

"This is not a democratic moment," Luc added. "It is a *revolutionary* moment."

"Exactly!" Gabriel said. "And besides, Aristide, Lavalas, all of them. They're not politicians. They are uneducated. These people are not responsible. They are not competent. They're corrupt. All of them." He stood up, walked over to the edge of his garden, and removed a small insect from one of his ferns.

MAKING DISORDER

January 6, Talking with Alexis. Alexis was standing outside his house when I arrived. I waved hello and asked how he was. He didn't answer, just gestured for me to come inside. It had taken years for Alexis and his wife, Nadège, to save enough money to build this house. They continued to add to it whenever they could. A few years ago, they added a fence to mark off their small plot. This year, Alexis wanted to repair the roof, which had recently started to leak.

Alexis and Nadège had been married for over twenty years. Their children were all grown and gone. One was overseas, working in construction in the Bahamas. Nadège had worked at a factory on the edge of town until she was laid off a few years ago. Now she ran a small business out of the house, mending clothes on an old treadle sewing machine. She greeted me with a warm smile, stood up from her machine, and brought over a small wooden chair. "Sit, sit!" she said.

Alexis had not been to the Artist Gift Shop in several days. I knew from Wilfred that he was struggling to get by. There was no business, and the political situation had everyone on edge. The opposition had called for a general strike at the end of the week. Everyone needed cash to buy things in advance, before the stores closed.

"A *ti kado*," I said as I handed him a small envelope filled with U.S. dollars and Haitian gourdes. I knew he needed cash, and I knew he wouldn't ask. He reached out a hand and took it but didn't look inside. He put it in his pocket and gave a small nod of thanks. Then he sat down and we began to talk.

Alexis was angry. Very angry. We talked about the political crisis and the protests against the government. He said the crisis was being manufactured by the elite in order to remove Aristide from power. The traditional elite knew they could not win elections, so they had to find another way to gain power. He saw it as a coup by other means.

"It's the boujwa," he said. "They don't like him so they pay people to make disorder *[fè dezòd]*. But if they kill him, there will be blood in the streets."

"Eh, eh!" Nadège added from the other side of the room. She looked up from her sewing machine and raised a hand in the air. "No, no! *Titid pou senk an!*" Aristide for five years. It was the current slogan of his supporters. Every time I heard it or saw it scrawled on the walls across the city, I was struck by just how odd it was that people had to protest for a democratically elected president to finish his full term of office. It was a long way off from the utopian dreams of the first decade of the democratic transition, when people like Alexis and Nadège had dared to dream of what they had then called *yon lòt Ayiti*—another Haiti. Now they seemed to be losing hope in democracy.

"It's because of them," Nadège continued. "We have lavi chè. We can't eat. We can't live because of them. They hit *[frape]* us but we won't break *[kraze]*."

Nadège was usually in good spirits. She often teased me or cracked jokes when I visited. But in recent months, she had become angry. Like so many others, she and Alexis were resentful of the political crisis. They had fought for decades for democracy in their country. And they had won—twice. Or so they had thought. Now the elite and the international community were conspiring to destabilize the country and to remove Aristide. A month ago, I had refused to believe that a coup was coming. Now it seemed inevitable. I shared some of their anger, or at least I could understand where it came from. Their anger seemed to me to be what the anthropologist Jason Throop calls a "moral mood," an emotion laden with value that anchors "people's ethical reflections in their efforts to make sense out of their current political situation."[20] Who wouldn't be angry? Or anxious? Or resentful? I wanted to understand the political crisis. I wanted to understand what Alexis meant when he said that people were making disorder. But to understand what crisis means you have to understand what it feels like when it happens to you.

"They say we have democracy in Haiti," Nadège said. "But we don't have real democracy. We have disorder. Lots of disorder."

"Aristide gave us too much democracy," Alexis said. "Yes, we have democracy, but we do not have a leader. We need a strong leader. A strong state." He meant a state that could withstand coups and that could act independently of foreign influence.

I asked what he meant by too much democracy.

Alexis sighed. "The boujwa make all of this disorder and then they say Aristide is bad, there is no state. They make disorder and they say *we* make it. They pay people to come into the streets and say, 'Down with Aristide.' That is not right."

"The elite do not know God," Nadège said. "They only know money and power. They fight the people, they fight Aristide, but democracy is not for them. They only care about money. They make disorder because it is profitable."

Alexis nodded his head in agreement. Then he stood up, put his chair against the wall, and said, "Okay, it's late. Let's go." He had to pick up his car from the shop where it was getting minor repairs. The cash I had brought him would allow him to cover those costs as well as the exceedingly high cost of gasoline. Then he had to pick up Wilfred and drive him to Boutilliers, an old lookout spot above the city where Wilson and other artists sold paintings and crafts. Wilson occasionally sold Wilfred's work there, and Wilfred wanted to collect any cash from the sales. The two of them had invited me along for the drive and I had readily accepted, thinking it would be nice to get out of the city. We said goodbye to Nadège and stepped out into the street.

We walked to Alpha and Omega Auto. Alexis went inside to talk to the mechanic and to pay his bill. I stayed on the street, chatting with a few young boys selling small sachets of water. I bought a few for our drive. When Alexis returned with his car, I got in the passenger seat and we left. On the way to the gift shop, we passed the city's main cemetery. Alexis had taken many tourists there in the past, when there had been tourists. "If you want to know about my country, look there," he said, pointing at the wall that surrounded the colonial-era burial ground. "Read the names on the big tombs. The names of the big families. It's still the same names today."

A few minutes later we were at the gift shop. Wilfred got in the car. I handed out the water sachets and we drank them. They had warmed in the sun but were still cool enough to be refreshing, clearing the dust of the city out of our throats. Alexis put the car in gear and we drove off. Soon we were climbing the hillside road with the city behind us. A cool breeze drifted through the open windows.

We talked about the protests and the upcoming general strike. Wilfred was angry too. He said that Aristide should finish his term, that the international community needed to recognize that it takes time to build democracy. "In Haiti," he said, "the government has always been a leta. You understand?" *Leta* was the Kreyòl word for the state, the government. But colloquially it also means "bully." The double sense of the word allowed people to speak openly but also critically of the government.

"We had a dictatorship for a long time," Wilfred said. "Now we have democracy. We go to vote. We vote. And then we have a coup. Okay. So, we get an intervention. The international community calls it that."

"Occupation!" Alexis said forcefully.

They were talking about the country's first democratic elections in 1990, which Aristide had won by an overwhelming majority. Seven months into his term, there had been a coup and a military junta seized power. Three years later the United States led a multinational intervention that restored Aristide to power. Aristide's supporters protested the intervention (and some broke ranks with him over it, saying he came back compromised). They also protested the fact that he was only allowed to serve the remainder of his term, rather than making up the three years he had spent in exile.[21]

"Yes, it was an occupation," Wilfred said, agreeing with Alexis. "But then," he held up a hand in the air. "Then we go to vote again. Again, we have democracy. And now?" He gestured out the window, to the city below.

"Now they say we can't have it. They make disorder and they say look! Aristide is a dictator!"

Like many of his supporters, Wilfred and Alexis seemed to be equating democracy with Aristide himself. But it was the figure of Aristide that was most important to them, not the man. He stood for the political inclusion of the *pèp la*, the people. It was the first time in the country's long history that the urban and rural poor had ever had a government responsive to their needs and interests. Aristide's election had ushered in a radical vision of politics that aimed to democratize not only the state but society too. It had proven to be too much. The established political and economic elite saw it as a kind of class warfare. In the 1990s, they had backed the military coup that had derailed the democratic transition and killed thousands of Aristide's supporters. Now they were playing a different game, trying to make Aristide himself seem like an obstacle to democracy.

Alexis shook his head. "And who are they?" he said. "They were with Duvalier! They are still with Duvalier! And they say we do not know democracy. They say the people are the problem!"

Wilfred nodded. "Yes, they are making a coup."

Alexis shook his head again. "A coup will be very bad for us."

"After the coup, we will have war," Wilfred said. He leaned back in his seat. I looked out the window. We all grew silent, feeling the gravity of the situation.

Then we rounded a curve and arrived at Boutilliers. Alexis parked the car at the side of the road and we walked toward the observatory. There had once been an expensive restaurant at the lookout. Diners could sit behind a wall of curved windows and look down at the city below. But the restaurant has been closed for decades, and the lookout felt like a ruin of a bygone era. Wilson was in front of the observatory with a few other artisans. Wilfred approached them, and he and Wilson went off to talk in private. Alexis found a shady spot to sit. I stepped down the cracked concrete stairs to the abandoned observatory terrace. A few coin-operated telescopes were mounted on the edge, but they didn't work. I leaned on the railing and watched a small cloud drift across the sky.

A few minutes later Alexis joined me. He pointed to a large house on the side of the mountain. "Look," he said. "You see this big house here?" I nodded. "And the wall there," he pointed at a low stone wall running along the house and down the hillside, marking out the boundaries of the property. "All that land for one family," he said. "And for what?" He was quiet for a moment, then he continued. "The boujwa have so much. They have everything. We have nothing."

EXPECTATIONS OF INTERVENTION

January 13, Talking with Cameron. The sky was dark blue, fading to black. The sea moved with an agitated rhythm, silvery white caps marking the tops of the waves. The city seemed quiet now, but it had been another tense day with demonstrations and barricades, smoke and fire. A group of men armed with sledgehammers had tied up guards and smashed radio antennas at a hillside transmission center. The opposition accused the government of sponsoring the attack, which took seven private stations, most of them critical of Aristide, off the air.

"Things are really heating up," I said.

"It's getting warmer," Cameron said. "It won't be long now."

Cameron thought it was time for Aristide to go. I had heard it many times before, from Cameron and from many others. I had even heard it from Katherine Dunham herself. She had said it over lunch one day the previous summer, after an event I had helped organize in her honor at the University of Chicago. Cameron and I had hoped that the event would bring renewed attention to the botanic garden project. But most of the participants had wanted to talk about Dunham's work as a dancer and choreographer, or they wanted to talk about Aristide and the political crisis. At lunch, after a morning of panels about Dunham's work and a presentation from Cameron about the garden project, we sat at a large wooden table talking about the future of the country, about what was happening, what might happen, what was going to happen in Haiti. And that's when Dunham had said, quite simply and with some sadness, "I think it's time for him to go."

I was shocked when she said it. Dunham had been a staunch supporter of Aristide. In 1992, when Aristide was living in exile, Dunham had gone on a hunger strike in protest of the coup. When Aristide returned to Haiti in 1994, Dunham had hoped to return herself and take part in the rebirth of the country. In the post-coup period, the botanic garden project, which would transform her home into a national garden, had grown increasingly important to her and had come to symbolize, for her, the broader politics of hope long associated with Aristide and his popular movement. A decade later everything was different. Dunham, Cameron, and many others, people who had once advocated for Aristide's return from exile, were now actively calling for his removal, even if that meant a coup and an international intervention.

"Another coup will tear the country apart," I said, pushing back.

"Sure," Cameron said, "it will be bad. Things have to get worse before they get better." I didn't think they did, or that they would. He knew we disagreed on this.

"I know how you feel," he said. "When I was working here in the 1980s, everything was just fucked up. After the dictatorship, the army was running things, and they were just killing everybody. I remember my friends telling me things were going to change soon. I didn't believe them. But they kept telling me. They said, 'We've got this priest.' And one day they took me to his church."

"Who? Aristide?"

"It's hard to explain." He was quiet for a moment. "There was so much going on. You had the army killing people, terrorizing people all day, all night. And you had this priest, this skinny guy. And everyone was starting to stand up to the tanks, to the guns. After the election, the whole city came alive. People were crying in the streets. Praying. Carrying pictures of him everywhere. I'd never seen anything like it." He paused. "After the dictatorship, no one thought it could ever get worse than that. And then came the fucking coup and we saw how bad it could get."

The de facto period was even more deadly than the Duvalier dictatorship had been. The military and paramilitary forces systematically targeted Aristide's supporters. At least four thousand people were killed, and three hundred thousand were internally displaced. Many more fled the country. The coup regime terrorized popular organizations, silenced radio stations, killed journalists, raped women and children, burned houses, and arrested and tortured those suspected of supporting Aristide. Years later, the de facto period still haunted the poor neighborhoods of Port-au-Prince. The scars, wounds, bullet holes, and burnt homes were visible reminders of the absences—of people disappeared or killed, of democratic hopes dashed, of a movement violently cut down.[22] The memory of the violence lingered, adding to the dread most people felt now, as the idea of another coup went from mere possibility to near certainty.

"During the coup, I was living in the forest. The army would shut the power off and come to Martissant at night. And just shoot people. It would be pitch black, but you could hear the shots. Hear the screams. Hear the trucks driving away."

"You think it will be any different this time?" I asked sharply.

He did. There was no army this time, so there wouldn't be the same kind of violence. The international community would step in and broker a transfer of power.

Cameron was partly right. The international community did step in and broker a transfer of power. But he was wrong about the coup being better this time. It would be just as bad. He was also right that there was no official army, since the army had been disbanded by Aristide after his return from exile. To his supporters, abolishing the army was an act of liberation, since the Haitian armed forces had only ever fought the Haitian people. But to Aristide's critics it was a sign that he was seeking to consolidate power by other means—by removing the one national institution that could challenge the presidency. To make matters worse, the disbanding had been done by executive order, in violation of the constitution, giving fodder to those who accused Aristide of governing by decree. Aristide had referred to the disbandment of the army as the end of the coup d'etat in Haiti, but it would soon become clear that coups could happen without armies, and besides, even if it was true that there was no army in Haiti, there were plenty of soldiers and officers around. Some had become police officers or gang leaders. Others were in hiding in the countryside or in the neighboring Dominican Republic. In the coming years, after the 2004 coup, several former military officers would launch a campaign to restore the army. They would even demand ten years' back pay.

Cameron knew all of this, of course. Or he knew as much as anyone could know at the time. So, too, did the many others calling for Aristide's removal. Some of them, like the opposition leaders, were directly fomenting armed insurrection. But for the most part, people were creating a narrative they found comforting and convincing, a narrative in which a coup against a democratically elected president could be justified, could even be the right thing to do, as long as it was not a *military* coup and, most importantly, as long as it was followed by an international intervention. For those opposed to Aristide, dezòd served to both delegitimize the government and to legitimize the coming coup and subsequent intervention. But just like coups, Haiti has had its share of interventions, and they've never worked out well.

"I know what you're thinking," Cameron said. "But things are that bad again now. You just have to look to see it. Aristide came back different. After the [1991] coup, everything changed. He started arming the gangs, he started killing journalists. It's like Duvalier all over again. The only hope now is for a UN mission. Without it, there will be a civil war."

January 18, Late Night with Georges. Georges invited me for dinner and drinks. I was wary of going out at night, but he assured me it was safe by telling me that everyone would be too busy preparing for tomorrow's demonstrations to cause any trouble at night. So I went.

Georges was part of the professional middle class. His family had lived in the city for several generations, working as lawyers, doctors, and teachers. They were not part of the elite by any means, but they were secure in their economic and social position. Georges had a professional job too, but his real passion was history, and I had come to rely on him for his detailed and expansive knowledge of the country's past.

Georges described himself as a nationalist. He was proud of his country and of the historical importance of the revolution. He was equally proud of the fact that this "little country," as he liked to call it, was so frequently a thorn in the side of the world's greatest superpower. And he hated the United States, a fact he enjoyed telling me repeatedly, often while acknowledging my Canadian citizenship and commenting that he had several good friends in Montreal. He was particularly fond of telling me how much he hated Bill Clinton for his role in the U.S.-led multinational force that restored Aristide to power in 1994. As Georges saw it, Clinton had presided over what he called "the second occupation" of Haiti, the first being the American occupation of 1915–34.

"The first time the Americans came," he told me, "we fought them." He was referring to the rural insurgency that fought the U.S. Marines for the first five years of the occupation. "The second time they came, we just *looked.* The result was the same. Now, it doesn't matter. They can invade us every week. We will beat them every time. We cannot win on the battlefield, but we will always win on the political field." He laughed as he said it. He hated the idea of more foreign interventions in his country, but he knew that another one was coming. Even if the territorial sovereignty of Haiti was routinely violated by foreign forces, the Haitian people were still able to "win" politically by refusing to become passive colonial subjects. As Georges saw it, Haitians were adept at waiting, at letting outsiders who thought they could come in and fix the country crash under the weight of their own hubris. Like many nationalists, Georges had an essentialist view of his country, one steeped in what Michael Herzfeld calls "cultural intimacy." As Herzfeld describes it, cultural intimacy is a "recognition of those aspects of a cultural identity that are considered a source of external embarrassment but that nevertheless provide insiders with their assurance of common sociality, the familiarity with the bases of power that may at one moment assure the disenfranchised a degree of creative irreverence and at the next moment reinforce the effectiveness of intimidation."[23] In Georges's case, it was a recognition of what he called "the Haitian mentality," a particular way of thinking and acting that made Haitian politics inscrutable to outsiders.

"When Americans look at Haiti," he told me, "they see a nation of monkeys. But we are an old people, with four hundred years of history, just like the United States. Even if the United States is a symbol of success, and Haiti is a symbol of failure, we are and will always be the second independent country in this hemisphere. Give us the respect and recognition we deserve, and things will go fine. Treat us like monkeys and we will jam everything up. We will make the U.S. lay eggs."

He held up a finger as he paused to take a drink. I knew better than to interrupt him when he was on a roll.

"Americans also think that a solution that works there can be exported everywhere." He swept his arms out as he said it. "This is not true! And also, Americans believe that we Haitians have a political sense of fair play and compromise. This, too, is not true. Due to our French and African origins, this is totally foreign to us."

Georges shifted the conversation to the present political crisis. Whenever we talked about contemporary politics in Haiti, he always began with these sorts of history lessons, as if he were presenting evidence in a case. As he started to talk about the demonstrations against the government, I thought I knew what he was going to say. I already knew he disliked Aristide and that he was a vocal supporter of the political opposition. But he was such a staunch nationalist that I couldn't help but think he would be against a coup, since a coup would almost certainly mean an international intervention. I don't think I hid my surprise when he said that the best thing that could happen now was the assassination of Aristide.

"He must go," Georges said. "Aristide must go! He should be killed. He will try to leave before the coup, but it will be too late."

I stopped writing and looked at him. I don't remember if I said anything.

"No, it's true," he said. "Listen, Grégoire, you have to think like a Haitian. In 1991 Aristide was removed by General Cédras." He paused and looked at me.

I nodded.

"But Cédras did not *kill* him. Why?"

I said I didn't know, that maybe he wanted to avoid an intervention for as long as possible.

Georges shook his head. "No," he said. "Cédras did not kill him because he [Cédras] is a Protestant. He thought like a Protestant. He thought like an *American*. Cédras believes he has to account for his actions, for his sins. This time, when Aristide goes, it will be at the hands of the Haitian people. They will act like Haitians. He will be killed and his body torn apart. His torn body will be paraded in the streets."

Later that night, Georges drove me home. There were no other cars on the streets. The city was dark. I looked out the window at the houses and walls caught in the car's headlights. There was anti-Aristide graffiti everywhere in Georges's neighborhood (just as other, poorer neighborhoods were full of pro-Aristide graffiti). We passed a wall covered in a spray-painted slogan, repeating along the length of the road. It read *Jije Aristide.* Judge Aristide. I read it out loud as we drove by it. Georges turned to me and nodded. "We will," he said.

January 20, with Luc and Gabriel.   I met with Luc and Gabriel after another tense day of demonstrations. The police had used tear gas to disperse the crowds, and the acrid smoke seemed to be clinging to the city. It was a relief to leave downtown and retreat to Gabriel's garden. Like so many other intellectuals and professionals in the country, Luc and Gabriel had been avid supporters of the democratic movement in the 1990s. Gabriel had never been fond of Aristide, but both men had championed his first election as a political milestone for the country. And like so many others of their social position, they had broken with Aristide and joined the civil society movement seeking his removal from power. I wanted to understand why.

"The democratic transition in Haiti has been very difficult," Luc said. "It is not an easy thing, to change from a dictatorship. We had Duvalier for twenty-nine years. And in 1987, we made a new constitution that said, 'No Duvalierists for ten years.' Okay. But then we had a problem. How do you change the state, the courts, the mayors, the section chiefs? The people said, '*Dechoukaj!*' You understand dechoukaj?" He made a fist and mimed pulling a weed from the ground.

"Like uprooting," I said.

He nodded. "Yes, it's like that. But the roots are deep. Very deep. And so, the people said, '*Lavalas!*' That's like a flood."

Gabriel scoffed at the mention of *lavalas,* a term that had not only come to stand for the popular movement but was also the name of Aristide's political party, Fanmi Lavalas. The term does not have an easy English translation, but it means "the family of the cleansing flood," with *flood* here referring both to the rainy season that comes before the planting of crops and to the Biblical flood of Genesis, the great deluge that washes away one world and begins another.

"We had elections and Aristide won," Luc continued. "It was a big win. And it looked like real change." He held a finger in the air and paused for a moment. "It *seemed* like real change." He looked at me as he stressed the word *seemed.* "We had politicians who were from the people. They were from the countryside. They were from the slums. They were from elsewhere. They were not from the political class. They took the bus to work.

They ate soup at restaurants downtown. They walked in the public square. They walked among the people."[24]

Gabriel made another noise, a sound of derision.

Luc looked at him and smiled. "But it's true!"

Gabriel swatted the air with his hand.

"It was like that," Luc went on. "But these people, Aristide, Lavalas, all of them. It is true they are not from the political class. They are not politicians. But what does that mean? It is also true that they are not *leaders*. They are uneducated. They are illiterate. They are not competent."[25]

"But Aristide is educated," I countered.

Luc nodded. "Yes, of course."

Gabriel said, "Aristide is a *nèg*. His family is from the south. He is educated only because of the church. He would be working in my garden if he was not president!"

Luc looked mildly uncomfortable. Gabriel's hatred of Aristide was palpable, and an already established fact, but Luc didn't seem to share his hatred or the deep-seated prejudice toward the man and his social class. And yet the two of them had common ground in their opposition to Aristide's government. It was just one of the many ironies of the political crisis. People from all places on the political spectrum, from left to right, nationalists and liberals, Duvalierists and champions of democracy alike, had come together, unified only in their total rejection of Aristide-the-man and his political project. Aristide's efforts to put "the people" in power, to appoint people from local areas to positions of authority, like mayors and section chiefs, had simply been too much for the established political class. Aristide's victory threatened to transform the political and social bases of power in Haiti, and so it was seen, perhaps rightly, as a direct attack on the traditional elite.

After an awkward moment, Luc continued. "With Aristide, we learned quickly. All of the new politicians, they were the same as the old ones. We had corruption right away. Aristide says everyone will sit at the table, everyone will eat. But he is a *gran manjè* [big eater] too! It's like the forest. To make the botanic garden, we have to bypass the state. If we don't, they'll take it."

This was becoming a familiar refrain among intellectuals and the professional classes, two groups that had once supported Aristide and the democratic movement but who had now joined the opposition. In their view, the state was irredeemably corrupt. Democracy and development could only come, they argued, from civil society and the market. Luc's insistence on the need to bypass the state was just another version of the neoliberal structural reforms that had, since the 1990s, weakened the Haitian government through privatization and debt and encouraged the explosive growth of non-governmental organizations (NGOs) in the country. Now the opposition was dressing itself up in the guise of a grassroots civil society movement in order to delegitimize not only Aristide's government but the very idea of state-led national development.[26]

For Luc, though, it was the only possible solution to the constellation of crises in Haiti. He was committed to a minimalist vision of democracy (unlike Gabriel, who longed for the return of something like Duvalierism), but he saw populism as a tyrannical form of democracy. For him, there really was no difference between Aristide's leftist populism and the Duvalier regime's conservative authoritarianism. I thought back to when Maxo had joked about how Aristide liked to look at the forest from his helicopter, and recalled how the proponents of the botanic garden project had come to see the poorest and most disenfranchised residents in the neighborhood, including the squatters living on and near the property, as obstacles to the project. According to that view, both the state and the people—the two emblems of democracy—had come to be seen as threats. The same logic was behind the demonstrations now, as the opposition painted Aristide and his supporters as antidemocratic forces.

"They want to take everything," Luc said, referring to the Lavalas movement. "Just like Duvalier. We call this Aristide's authoritarian drift. With Aristide, we do not have democracy. We have a dictatorship."[27]

Gabriel swatted at the air again. "Aristide is a monster!" he said, almost spitting.

I asked what they thought would happen next.

"Aristide must go," Luc said. "There is no other way."

"And if he goes?" I asked. "It will be a coup!"

"No," Luc said, waving a hand in the air. "Not a coup. An intervention."

Friday, January 23, a Party in the Hills. Robert invited me to a party at his aunt's house, high above the city. The night air was much cooler in the mountains. We drove up a steep dirt road that ended in a small gated community. A couple of private security guards opened a gate to let us pass. There were six or seven large homes beyond the gate.

Robert had grown up in the United States but had returned to Haiti in the 1980s. His family was wealthy enough to be able to socialize with the country's elite families, but his American education and business connections made him foreign enough to be considered an outsider among them. He was also considerably more liberal politically than many members of the elite. He liked to remind me, often, that paramilitaries had tried to kill him during the de facto period for speaking openly in praise of Aristide's return. "Luckily," he told me, "I got a phone call before they came to my house. By the time they showed up with their guns, I was gone man!"

The party was a small affair, but too loud for my taste. I spent the first hour looking at Robert's family's art collection. Every wall held beautiful paintings by some of the country's leading artists. I sipped my wine and tried to avoid the obvious topics of conversation, but everyone was talking about the political crisis. About the demonstrations. About the coming coup. The mood seemed celebratory, as if they were toasting the success of something that hadn't even happened yet.

Robert found me staring at a painting by Stevenson Magloire. The canvas was dark, broody, but still full of color and light and energy. Vodou symbols mixed with expressionistic figures. Robert pointed at it with his chin. "What do you think?"

"It's great," I said. "His work is great."

We stood in silence for a moment, looking at the painting. Then Robert spoke again, but his tone had changed, his mood shifted. "The fuckers killed him." Magloire had been stoned to death in 1994 by paramilitaries loyal to the military junta. "They used to kill people like that. Just on the street. Anytime. Anywhere. It's the same thing now." He turned to look at me. "You don't think so, but Aristide is just the same as those fuckers. The only difference is that he learned a lot when he was in exile. He learned about human rights." He said the last two words as if in quotes. "He learned how to use human rights. See, the army used to kill people with machine guns. Aristide, he's like a sniper. Very effective, but it doesn't attract as much bad press."

I didn't know how to respond.

"Aristide likes to talk about the rights of the majority. But what about the rights of the minority? We have human rights too."

I looked down at my glass. Drank some wine. Robert's mood shifted again, as if he had just remembered he was at a party. He slapped me on the back and smiled. "Don't worry so much!" he said. "Don't worry." He scanned the room, like he was already looking for someone else to talk to. He turned back to me. "We're trying to steer the ship from the sidelines. Aristide. Demonstrations. New elections. All of it. We're working it, man. But the news here, or in the U.S., the news will tell you that we are on the brink of a civil war. Or already in its midst. There's a script for Haiti already, and maybe some people benefit from that. They like to write about disorder. What the fuck else are they going to write about? Do you think some journalist is going to come here to write about the piles of garbage on the street?"

He waved to a woman across the room. He started to leave, then turned and said again, "Don't worry, man. We're working it." He left. Kissed the woman on the cheek. I could see them talking, laughing. I stepped outside, into the garden, and walked among the jasmine and hibiscus plants. I sat down in the dark, looked up at the stars, and thought about what Robert had said, that people were "working on it." That disorder was a script journalists followed. Something made, a story told about the country. And behind the disorder was an invisible order. People steering the ship from underneath, like a rudder.

A man joined me in the garden. He said Robert had told him I might need a place to live. He told me he was building some new houses in Port-au-Prince. "Very nice houses," he said. "Easy access to the airport, to downtown. Guards twenty-four hours a day." I told him I already had a place to live. He continued, unperturbed. His houses were almost finished, a gated community in the city. Each house would be finished to "European standards." They would have marble countertops, imported tile floors, all the amenities. I asked him how much. "Very reasonable prices," he said. "Only three thousand a month. American dollars." *Fuck*, I thought. They're already building houses for the occupation.

ON NOT KNOWING

January 9, Waiting with Alexis and Wilfred. I was sitting on the stoop in front of the Artist Gift Shop. Alexis had his car in storage again. He didn't want to risk taking it out on the streets. He was worried it might be stolen or damaged or set on fire. It was better, he said, to wait things out.

Waiting was just about the only thing there was to do. Even if he could afford to buy gas, the stations were all closed. A general strike called by a coalition of anti-Aristide groups had shut down most of the city. And food and gas shortages had sent prices skyrocketing. There were rolling blackouts daily. Those who could afford to do so were stockpiling gas and goods. Everyone was preparing for the worst.

I wanted to understand what was happening. Everything seemed uncertain. Every day there were conflicting versions of events. I was having a hard time believing anything anymore. I felt like I couldn't even believe the things I saw with my own eyes. I couldn't make things make sense.[28]

I asked Alexis and Wilfred if they felt the same way. They were both quiet for a moment. Alexis looked off in the distance. Wilfred looked up at me and shrugged. "What do you want to know?"

I said I wanted to understand the political situation.

"Ah," Wilfred said. "You would have to be Haitian."

Anthropology has always been predicated on the opposite claim—that one can gain an understanding of a different culture and a different way of life through a kind of cultural immersion. Was Wilfred saying that the anthropological aim of cross-cultural translation was impossible? Was he saying you had to be a certain kind of person in order to think and know in a certain kind of way?

I asked him what he meant.

"In Haiti," said Wilfred, "we have lots of problems. All the time." He gestured to the streets around us. "It is always like this."

"This person or that person," Alexis added, "they want to take power. They make dezòd. And we have a coup."

The two of them went on to explain to me that they had seen dezòd many times before. To fully understand what was happening now, they were telling me, required a shared history, a shared experience of the politics of disorder. Like most Haitians, they were experts in it. Their experience gave them a particular understanding. They expected disorder and disruption. They didn't see it as an exception to regular life. For them, disorder was quite ordinary; it was just the way that things worked. Dezòd was not the limit of power and its control over life; it was the means by which power operated.

Maybe they were right. Maybe the experience of dezòd was untranslatable. Maybe you couldn't share it. Maybe you just had to feel it, live it, as Wilfred and Alexis and so many others had done and were doing again.[29]

January 10, at the Gift Shop Again. Talking about politics again. Talking about disorder again. Toto says that everyone is scared, walking around saying, "*M pa fè politik.*"[30] I don't do politics. To say that you don't do politics was to distance yourself from political parties, to take a neutral stance, to say that you are not on either side of the political struggle. But it was also a commentary on politics itself, on the way that politics was playing out in Haiti. To say you didn't do politics was also to say that you didn't lie, that you didn't make disorder, that you didn't play the kind of political games people called *jwèt mò*—deadly games. That you didn't engage in *move kou*—subversion. That you were not doing *mannèv* or *taktik* or *manipilasyon*—maneuvers, tactics, manipulation.

Alexis says that people used to say they didn't do politics after the coup in 1991, when the army and the paramilitary would come looking for Aristide supporters. It was a way of keeping yourself alive, if they believed you.

"But today," Alexis tells me, "it is not enough to say, 'I don't do politics,' because now you don't know who people are." The others signaled their agreement. He continued: "You can't speak freely now. It is dangerous to talk about politics at all. You don't know. When you are in public, when there are lots of people, you don't know if they are with Aristide or not, so you can't say anything. If you don't know, you can't say."

Jean agreed. "You never know who is there," he said. "It is too dangerous to talk politics."

It was dangerous to do politics. It was dangerous to talk about politics. And yet, weren't we doing both at the gift shop? Perhaps it was a sign that Alexis and the others trusted me enough to still be able to talk politics with me. But more than that, our conversation seemed to be a sign of just how far dezòd had reached into everyday life. Dezòd was not just a topic of conversation; it had also come to shape the very ways in which we talked. And it had cast a long shadow over social relations. The men at the gift shop relied on their ability to move easily around the city and to make relations, but now they could no longer be certain who people really were. Were they with the government or against the government? Were they friend or foe? Would they lure you into a conversation about politics, only to inform on you later? Did they have ties to the gangs, the police, or other armed actors? These questions and others were always on people's minds. Dezòd might make you angry, but it also made you nervous. Anxious. Suspicious. Uncertain. And that was part of it too. When people make dezòd, they also make *laterè* and *panik*. Terror and panic.

And when you have dezòd, it is hard to know who to trust or what to believe. When you have dezòd, the pillars of security that anchor social life begin to shake and then collapse.[31]

January 7, Talking with Cameron.   Cameron was optimistic about the botanic garden project, even though the mood in Martissant was tense. "Everyone is waiting to see what's going to happen with the country," he said. "If Aristide falls, the gangs will fight for their lives."

I asked what that would mean for the forest.

"The gangs won't leave. They have nowhere to go. Someone's going to have to go in there and get them out." He said it would be hard on everyone, that the squatters and some of the residents were with the gangs because the gangs were the only ones that kept order in the area. "What choice do they have?" he said. The gangs had almost total power and control over the neighborhood. And they had a kind of legitimacy, too, since they were the closest thing to a government in the zone. They controlled housing and markets, they controlled access to services like water and electricity, and they provided security. They ran the area like their own garrison community.[32] As Cameron saw it, both the squatters and local residents in Martissant would welcome an intervention because it would free them from the gang. He saw their allegiance to the gang as mere strategy, something done under duress. "There's no alternative for them," he said. "It's a hard position to be in."

He paused for a moment. "Maxo thinks Vincent is working with the gangs."

I was surprised.

"He thinks he's been double dealing, working for both sides."

I asked Cameron what he thought. He told me several other SCPE members had been under pressure from the gangs. The gangs paid them off or scared them into giving information.

"Do you believe it?" I asked.

"Sure," he said. "He probably is working for them. Everyone wants to be aligned with whoever might win." I thought back to the cleansing rite and Celeste, to Vincent's claim that Maxo had helped arrange it and to Maxo's insistence that he had not known about it. I thought back to Luc's comment: Tout sa ou wè, se pa sa. That which you see, it's not that.

Dezòd was a deadly game, with allegiances and counter-allegiances. People wore masks. You could never tell whose side they were on. It was hard to be sure of anything anymore. The accusation against Vincent could easily be true, but it could just as easily be false. Amid the mounting political crisis, fear and fantasy had collided to form what Michael Taussig calls a "nervous system"—a world in which the exceptional has become the norm.[33]

January 15, Talking with Manuel.   There were anti-government protests again today. The daily demonstrations, barricades, and shootings were taking their toll on everybody, even those who stubbornly declared, "I don't do politics!" But what would it mean to not do politics, to not have a stake in a political crisis that would so clearly shape the future of the country? To me, it seemed that politics was everywhere, that the tenor and terror of the political situation had infused all social relationships. Disorder had become its own kind of mood.

I spent much of the day with Manuel. He was upbeat, as usual, even though I detected hints of anger and resentment below the surface of his smile. He had been working for much of the previous week with an American art collector. She had been coming to Haiti for decades and they were good friends. Manuel and a few other guides and drivers had been taking her around the city, as best they could, to meet new artists. He was flush with cash for the moment, and I imagined it felt good for him to still be treated as an expert fixer, to be treated with the respect and prestige he felt he was owed.

We sat at a table on a second-floor restaurant, drinking beer and looking down at the city streets, which were blessedly calm for the moment. In the middle of a conversation about Haitian art, his mood shifted and he grew quiet. I asked him what was wrong. He took a long, slow breath and then told me that a mutual friend of ours had publicly accused him of stealing money. There had been a heated argument. More accusations. They had both left on bad terms. Manuel's job often involved handling people's money. Clients would give him American dollars and he would get them exchanged for Haitian gourdes from street traders, who had better rates than the banks. Or clients would give him cash in advance and he would buy paintings or flags for them directly from the artists who made them. Like Wilfred, Manuel would sometimes get paid only at the end of long trips, and he would then have to disburse money to the other guides, artists, fixers, or drivers with whom he had worked. It was thus important to him that he was trusted to handle money responsibly. Being called a thief was a grave insult that could have severe consequences. At the same time, I knew the mutual friend quite well and could not easily imagine him making idle accusations. Caught between conflicting allegiances, I tried to suggest the whole thing might be a misunderstanding, that perhaps it would blow over in a day or two.

Manuel smiled and took a drink. "Maybe," he said. He leaned over the table, and in a hushed tone he said, "But do you know what he did?"

I shook my head. Manuel then told me a story. Our mutual friend worked for an important NGO. Manuel told me that a few years ago, someone else was supposed to get the job, but before they were hired they had been killed, their throat slit in the middle of the night. So instead, our mutual friend was hired. Manuel then leaned back in his chair and spread his arms out. "I don't know," he said. "I don't know who did it. If I didn't see it, I can't say."

He leaned forward again, his voice low. "There are people who say he [our mutual friend] did it. They say the two of them were always arguing." He grinned at me, his hands up in the air. "But if I didn't see it, I can't say."

January 13, More Demonstrations.   There were demonstrations again today. Masked men shot at the crowds. Who was under those ski masks? Were they Aristide supporters terrorizing the opposition, or anti-Aristide agents fomenting violence? Were they police dressed as chimè? And if not, whose side were the police on anyway? Aristide was accusing the opposition of trying to mount a coup, while the opposition was accusing Aristide of causing violence so that he could clamp down on the opposition. Maybe both versions were true. Disorder seemed to have taken on a life of its own.

But that wasn't quite true either. Disorder was not some intrinsic condition or essential feature of Haitian social life. Against a "metaphysics of disorder" that treats violence as a fixed reality, a permanent feature of Haitian culture, I reminded myself that disorder was the outcome of political action.[34] It was actively being made—made by people with intentions and reasons and goals. It was easy to focus on the masks, on the screens, on the fantasy of free-floating terror. After all, *dezòd* means disturbance, panic, and terror. But it also means division, and divisions are always social, always political. And it means *chen manje chen*—dog eat dog. *Kou pou kou*—blow for blow. And *jwèt mò*—deadly game. Dezòd is the mask behind which politics hides.

January 16, Coffee with Denis.   Denis liked to call himself a mediator. "I'm not a fixer," he once told me. "I don't fix things. I move between them." He laughed. "Eh? You know? I bring people together. I bring the knowledge to the people, like that." He clasped his hands in front of him. "The new and the old. Fusion!" We were speaking in English. He said Kreyòl was for lovers and servants, and French was for poetry and philosophy. "But we're talking politics, man. For that, you've got to have English." It was an odd point to make, since his job was translating American political concepts like local governance, decentralization, and civil society into terms that were meaningful to rural Haitian communities.

I had met Denis a year ago, when a mutual friend introduced us. He had offered to rent his house to me, and although I had not taken him up on his offer, we had met again several times. (His house, located in a central Port-au-Prince neighborhood, would be firebombed in 2005 and Denis would sell his property to a developer and move to a new house in a hillside suburb.) Denis liked to talk politics, and he seemed to take pleasure in explaining the peculiarities of Haitian politics to me. When our mutual friend told me that Denis was back in Port-au-Prince for a few days, I asked him to arrange a meeting. He agreed, and on Friday morning we sat in the garden behind Denis's house, drinking coffee and smoking Dominican cigars that tasted of café con leche and cinnamon. Our mutual friend commented on the creaminess of the cigar. Denis nodded. "These ones are great for the morning. Smooth, with a touch of sweetness." I drank my coffee and waited for Denis to begin. He liked to ease slowly into a conversation.

Denis and our mutual friend were both part of a civil society organization called Groupe des 184, started a year earlier by Andy Apaid and Charles Baker, both wealthy businessmen from elite families. Groupe des 184 had managed to secure broad support from the professional and managerial class in Haiti, and its membership now boasted many of the country's most prominent academics, intellectuals, writers, and artists—including many left intellectuals who had once backed Aristide and the Lavalas movement. Much like the political opposition—united under the banner of a multiparty group called the Convergence Démocratique—the civil society movement had as its core aim the removal of Aristide from power. It was Groupe des 184 that had been leading the recent demonstrations, and it was they who had called the general strike. In addition to their opposition to Aristide, Groupe des 184 was also advocating for what they called a "new social contract" and for a new approach to governance that sought to limit the role of the presidency and the state, decentralize Haiti's departments, and deregulate trade.[35]

When Denis finally turned the conversation from his garden and cigars to the political situation, he began to tell me about his current project. He had been on the road for months, traveling around the country. He was in the city for a few meetings with members of the civil society opposition, and then he would be heading north for a tour of several towns across the Artibonite, North, and Center departments. "We're bringing the new social contract directly to the people," he said. Denis had a contract funded by foreign grants (and paid for by international NGOs) to lead training workshops in civics programs in small towns in the north of Haiti. He was training mayors and community leaders in what he called "local self-government." As he put it, he was "giving them the knowledge they need to govern themselves. That's democracy, man!"

"We don't have democracy in Haiti," our mutual friend said pointedly.

Denis laughed. "Not yet."

"The Haitian people are not ready for democracy," our mutual friend said.

Denis laughed again. "That's why I'm here! You have to teach them."

I said I thought it was pretty clear what the people wanted. They wanted Aristide. It was our mutual friend's turn to laugh.

"You think Aristide is one thing," Denis said. "But he's not. He's a dictator. Just like Duvalier. And his gangs are like terrorists." He smoked on his cigar and gave me a wide smile. "But don't worry," he said. "Aristide will be gone in less than a month. One way or another."

It took a little longer than a month, but Denis was right. Aristide was gone by the end of February. As armed insurgents entered the city, I thought about Denis and our conversation in his garden. I thought about the towns he was visiting for his civil society training and how they were the same towns the rebels had taken in their march to the capital. I thought back to the rumors, told in hushed voices in Port-au-Prince, that the Haitian elite and the United States had been training and funding the rebels, and I wondered what Denis's workshops had really been about.

January 20, Our Man in Haiti. I had breakfast with Robert. We ate scrambled eggs with onions and tomatoes and fresh bread from a nearby bakery. I told him I was hearing a lot of rumors. People were saying that the United States was training, funding, and arming insurgents in the Dominican Republic, that they were behind the coming coup. It was clear enough that the United States wanted Aristide gone. The international community had been trying to broker a power-sharing deal between the government and the opposition for over three years, with little success. After all, how could you share power when the opposition's only platform was the removal of Aristide? Beyond that, the United States and international financial institutions had been withholding loans and aid from the Aristide government for years. The Haitian state is dependent on foreign aid, and the loss of the loans had made it nearly impossible for Aristide to accomplish anything as president.[36] And now there were rumors that a famous American spy had returned to Haiti.

"The spy" was an American agent who had worked in Haiti since the 1970s. He had a background in anthropology and agronomy and had worked with peasant groups under the Duvalier regime. People said he had "run things" in Haiti for decades, but that he had had to leave the country after he had become too well known. Now people were saying he was back.

I asked Robert if he had heard the same rumors. He laughed. "Yeah, I heard that," he said. Robert knew the spy. He seemed to know most of the Americans working in Haiti. It was a small country after all, and expats tended to run in small circles. I asked Robert if the rumors were true.

He shrugged. "He's been living in the Dominican Republic for years," he said. "He runs some kind of NGO there." Robert looked at me with a sly smile. He liked to talk this way, with vague statements full of implications. It was all winks and nods with him. He was always hinting, always suggesting that he was in the know, privy to a vast secret knowledge.

"What kind of NGO?" I asked.

He laughed again. "The kind of NGO that gets money from the State Department."

That included a lot of NGOs in Haiti. The U.S. State Department funded USAID, which dispersed much of its funding through contracts outsourced to third-party NGOs.

"It's like in that Graham Greene book," he said. "You know the one about Cuba?"

"*Our Man in Havana.*"

"Yeah." Robert laughed. "Yeah, that one. Where the guy keeps sending back all this intel, all these plans. But it's just—what?"

"Plans for a vacuum cleaner," I said. In the book, a vacuum cleaner salesman named James Wormold is recruited to spy for the British secret service. Wormold has no information to pass on, so he invents a fictitious world of secret agents and military installations in the mountains of Cuba. The fake world gets mixed up with the real world when a man with the same name as one of Wormold's imaginary agents is killed.

Robert laughed some more. "Yeah, yeah! A vacuum cleaner." He tore off a piece of bread and dipped it in his coffee. "Our friend is like that. He just feeds the U.S. whatever info they want. Whatever they want to hear. That's how he gets paid."

Sometimes the stories we tell end up being true. Everyone in Haiti knew something was going on. Someone was making moves behind the scenes. A deadly game, the game of dezòd and destabilization. On the surface of things, in the streets, on the radios, in rumor and idle talk, those hidden moves presented themselves as a series of conflicting stories. Aristide was a dictator. Or he was a democratically elected president. The elite were paying gangs to stage a coup. Or they were peaceful protesters marching against an authoritarian regime.

"They say he's in the Dominican Republic planning a coup," I said.

Robert leaned forward, his elbows on the table.

"You're thinking like an academic," he said. "You think if you look around long enough, you'll figure things out. But it's not like that here. Politics is about impressions. You're looking for the truth. If you mix the two, things get all fucked up."

PROVISIONAL ARRANGEMENTS

After

I left Haiti just before commercial flights to and from the country were canceled. I left just before the U.S. Embassy pulled out its nonessential staff. Before they suggested that all foreign nationals leave. Just before the Front pour la Libération et la Reconstruction National (FLRN), an armed group made up of ex-military personnel, paramilitaries, and gang members, began taking cities and towns across the north of the country, where they proceeded to raid police stations and round up Aristide supporters. I left before the FLRN prepared to enter the capital. Before Aristide left on a U.S. military plane, heading for exile yet again. I left before the coup.

Leaving was a luxury, and a strange relief. I knew that some of my friends would need to leave the city or go into hiding, and that there would be more violence after the coup. I knew that others would be happy, perhaps ecstatic, when the coup finally came. And I knew what would happen afterward—I could see the end of the story even as I watched it unfold from afar, as the news reports told stories of heroic rebels entering the city, of the removal of Aristide from the country, and of the formation of a new provisional government. A provisional government that would last two years, that would usher in a United Nations military intervention that would last much longer, that would unleash another terrible wave of violence and destruction in the country.

A few weeks after I left Haiti, I received a phone call from a friend. "I am sorry to tell you that Manuel is dead," he said. I didn't know what to say. I immediately assumed the worst, that he had been killed by gangs or paramilitaries. He had been an outspoken supporter of Aristide and the Lavalas movement, and he had been jailed and tortured before for his political activities. But his death was much more ordinary than that.

"What happened?" I said.

"He had tuberculosis," my friend said.

I had seen him only weeks ago. He hadn't seemed sick. He wasn't coughing. He had energy. I can still see him smiling, even though I never saw him again.

"He didn't tell anyone," my friend said. There was a short pause. The phone line hummed. "They say he had AIDS," he said, his voice quieter now.[37]

I asked about his family, about the funeral. I said I would try to send money soon. I asked how my friend was doing, what things were like in the city now.

"It's bad," he said. "The coup is coming."

Afterward, I thought about Manuel. About what he had said to me, years earlier—that Haiti was dead. I thought about his comment that there would be crisis in Haiti forever and that even though each new event, each new blow, was a shock, it was also expected, anticipated even. You could feel the blow coming before it struck. I had been braced for the coup, but I hadn't been braced for this. It felt so sudden, and yet it surely must have been slow and painful for Manuel. He must have known he was sick, especially in the end. He must have known he was going to die.

Ernst Bloch, the great philosopher of hope, once said that "death depicts the hardest counter-utopia." The experience of death is the experience of the end of possibility, of the possibility of impossibility. Hope thrives in moments of the not-yet, when we conceive of and strive for a world that does not yet exist but that might exist one day. In death, though, there is no not-yet. Only the already-happened, the finality of finitude. Bloch tells the story of a shipwrecked man swimming at sea. The man is "swimming in the waves and struggling and squirming for his life when he receives the message that this ocean in which he finds himself does not have a shore but that death is completely in the now in which the shipwrecked man finds himself."[38] As he swims in whatever forever he has left, the shipwrecked man lives his death before he dies.

Later

I was still in the midst of grief and loss when I heard the news. It came first in an early-morning email from Haiti with the subject line "it's happened!!!" The message was jubilant but brief, saying that Aristide had finally left the country. I searched the news for details. The reports said that Aristide had resigned and that, on the night of February 29, he had been escorted by U.S. Marines from his home in Tabarre to the airport. From there, he and his family had been flown on a U.S. military plane to the Central African Republic. Later, when he was able to make a statement, Aristide would say that he had not resigned but that he had been "kidnapped" and taken into exile. He even quoted Toussaint Louverture's famous statement, made as he was being arrested by the French and sent to die in a prison at Fort Jura, that "in overthrowing me, they have uprooted the trunk of the tree of the liberty of the blacks; it will grow back because its roots are many and deep."[39] The following day, the FLRN entered the capital. They were greeted by small crowds as Aristide loyalists hunkered down and prepared to fight. The rebels moved swiftly through the city. They took the police headquarters and the weapons located there, and then they occupied the Ministry of Women's Affairs. The ministry was new, having been created by Aristide. It had been housed in the former army headquarters, a move that many at the time had seen as loaded with symbolism, a virtual castration of the army. At the ministry, the rebels removed paintings that had been mounted for a show on Haitian art about the revolution. They brought the canvases into the street and lit them on fire.[40]

It made for good political theater, but not as good as what followed. The rebels refused to take the National Palace, an act for which they were later praised by the foreign press, the international community, and the provisional government that soon took power. By only taking the former army headquarters, the rebels had allowed the elected government to remain in power. With the president gone, control of the government fell to Boniface Alexandre, the chief justice of the Supreme Court. And thus, it seemed that the rebels had merely liberated the country from an authoritarian ruler and that they had left the state in the hands of a civilian government. It all seemed constitutional. Of course, it only *seemed* that way.

The new government promised to hold elections in the near future (it would take two years). The political opposition, the Convergence Démocratique, experienced a rapid divergence, as its elements became opponents again, now that their shared enemy was gone. The civil society opposition called an end to the demonstrations. The Organization of American States formed a Tripartite Council tasked with setting up a provisional government. The Tripartite Council then appointed what they called a Council of Sages, composed of seven members, all but one of whom were from the opposition. The council, in turn, named Gérard Latortue, a technocrat who had worked for the UN and had been living outside of Haiti for decades, as the new prime minister. At the end of March, Latortue traveled to Gonaïves, where he called for a moment of silence for slain gang leader Amiot Métayer and praised the rebels as "freedom fighters." In another piece of political theater, Latortue called on the gangs in Gonaïves to disarm and then watched as they turned in a handful of old guns to the authorities. It was a symbolic transfer of power from the rebels and gangs back to the provisional government. In August, the government held a trial in the middle of the night for Jodel Chamblain, one of the most prominent rebel leaders. Chamblain had been the head of a paramilitary death squad during the de facto period and had been convicted in absentia for the 1995 assassination of Antoine Izmery, a prominent Aristide supporter. The new trial acquitted Chamblain of the murder charges.[41] It was a sign of things to come, as the provisional government rolled back the gains made under Aristide to prosecute the 1991 coup leaders and paramilitaries. In October, Latortue closed the circle by laying a wreath commemorating the 198th anniversary of the death of Jean-Jacques Dessalines and accusing Aristide of arming and provoking his supporters even from exile. Latortue had succeeded in playing Dessalines to Aristide's Toussaint, and in so doing he wrapped the provisional government in the mantle of the legitimacy of the country's most important founding figure. The rebels had become freedom fighters, and the provisional government had become the defenders of the nation, the guarantors of freedom. Never mind that the same provisional government had welcomed a UN military intervention or that it had opened up a seemingly endless state of exception that, for many, would come to mark the end of Haitian independence. For the provisional government, the UN mission was only a temporary force. Latortue, almost immediately after being sworn in as prime minister, declared he would appoint a commission to oversee the return of the Haitian army.

What had really happened? Michel-Rolph Trouillot once described the aftermath of the Duvalier regime as "a badly dubbed movie where the words and gestures do not always match." When Jean-Claude Duvalier left the country on February 7, 1986, it appeared as if his downfall were the result of a popular uprising. To be sure, there was an uprising, but what happened after Duvalier's departure was anything but a revolution—it was a well-orchestrated transfer of power, a *"takeover of the state machinery by a group of apparently disparate individuals."*[42] The fall of Aristide was perhaps better dubbed and better scripted, but for all of its staging it felt like a rerun, reenacting elements of the end of the Duvalier regime and the 1991 coup, with elements of the U.S. occupation and the Haitian Revolution tossed in for good measure. All the elements of the story were in place, a story so often repeated that it has taken on the fixity of myth—the story that Haiti cannot govern itself. Behind the story of dezòd and the coup, behind the story of a state of exception and the UN intervention, there was something else—the slow but deliberate end of Haitian sovereignty. The end of the dream of democracy. If it all seemed like an event, a crisis, an emergency that demanded urgent action, all the better. But Lévi-Strauss's famous comment about myth is also true of politics: Repetition reveals a structure.[43]

4. Between Life and Death

After death, what happens? I asked. When you died, where did you go? The dead man laughed and said, "You mean after life, what happened?" He said that when he stopped living, his body fell to the ground and he was at last free from the struggles and miseries of life. "Haitians are born to suffer," he said. "But then we die."

I said that I missed him, that I wished he was still here.

"Do you know that joke? The one about the end of the world?" the dead man said.

I shook my head and said that I didn't know it.

He said, "One day, God came down to earth. He spoke to three people and he told each of them two things. Then he sent them back and he told them to tell others what he had told them.

"The first person was from France. He went home and said to everyone, 'I am sorry to say that I have two bad things to tell you. The first bad thing is that I have been chosen by God to bring you this message. I am sorry to have to tell you this. The second bad thing is that the world is ending and we are all going to die.'

"The second person was an American. He went home and said to everyone, 'I have good news and bad news. The good news is that I have been chosen by God to bring you this message. The bad news is that the world is ending and we are all going to die.'

"The third person was Haitian. The Haitian went home and said to everyone, 'I have good news! I have been chosen by God to bring you a message! All our suffering will soon be over!'"

The dead man laughed. "You see how we think about death here?"[1]

Then he told me not to worry. He told me what had happened after he died. There had been a separation, an ending and a new beginning. His body went into the ground, where it would dissolve back into the earth. His soul was now freed from its flesh, freed to go to its proper place. "The soul has three parts," he said. "There is the *ti bon anj,* the little angel. That was my conscience. That went to heaven. And there is the *mèt tèt,* the guardian lwa. For me, it was Danbala, he was the master of my head, and now that I am dead he went back to Ginen. And there is the *gwo bon anj,* the big angel. That was me. Whenever you saw me walking and talking, that was my gwo bon anj doing the walking and talking. That was my life, my blood, my breath. When I died, I went to live under the water, where it is cold and dark and wet. I waited there for a long time, until I was called back and sent to live in Ginen, with the lwa. Now, I live in the community of the dead."[2]

Death is not the end, it is a beginning. He told me to imagine a circle. From death came the spiritual forces that made the material world move. From death came the ancestors who became the lwa, the spirits who protect us, who guard us, the spirits whom we serve when we sing and dance, the spirits whom we feed so that they will take care of us. They died so we could live, just as we will die so others can live. But the dead man was worried that he would be forgotten. He said he hoped that those of us who are still here will remember him, that the dead needed the living, that one day, in the future, he would return to the world of the living. And he hoped that it would still be there.

THE TRANSMISSION OF DEATH

After the coup, many people died. I was in Chicago, trying desperately to stay in contact with friends and colleagues in Port-au-Prince. Those who could afford to do so left the country. Most stayed. Some went into hiding in safer neighborhoods or in the countryside. Some were killed, or shot, or robbed, or raped. Some disappeared forever. I read the news with dread. I searched the radio stations for signs of hope. Occasional emails brought reports of terror and violence. A friend stopped sending emails after one of the few remaining Internet cafes in the city was ransacked, the equipment stolen or smashed, the storefront set on fire.

The official story, told by the provisional government, the UN mission, and the international press, was that armed gangs had taken control of the city's slums and were waging a civil war against residents and the government.[3] It was a convenient story that legitimized the provisional government's suspension of the constitution, justified the UN intervention, and explained away the extrajudicial killings. But it was a fiction, or perhaps a fantasy. The coup had released a wave of repressive violence in Haiti. If there was a civil war going on, it was being waged by the same repressive elements that had always waged war on Haitian citizens—the army, the state, the elite, and the international community. I heard time and again from friends still in the city that this was the worst things had ever been, worse even than the de facto period, worse because the violence was dispersed, free-floating, everywhere. It came dressed in the uniforms of the national police, or UN peacekeepers, or the disbanded Haitian army. Or it came wearing a mask. It came at night or during the day. It came in the streets, in your neighborhood, in public. It came in your home, like a bullet through a wall. Like a grenade thrown through a window. It came like a tank. It came like fire. And it left death in its wake. My friends told me about dead bodies in doorways, in streets, in marketplaces. They told me about parts of bodies left as warnings. Of mutilated bodies that no one could identify. Of bodies that no one came to collect. That no one buried. That no one would mourn.[4]

Out of this talk of death and survival, another story began to emerge. It was the story of the criminalization of the Lavalas movement and the repression of whole neighborhoods. The rebels who had helped destabilize the country were still roaming free, some of them dressed in old uniforms and referring to themselves as a restored Haitian army. The national police, under the direction of the provisional government, made arbitrary arrests of Aristide's supporters. Uniformed police officers killed people. Masked men killed people. People disappeared. The provisional government and the international community blamed the violence on pro-Aristide gangs, but it was just another round of state-sponsored violence, a terror campaign that sought to eradicate the democratic movement and restore power to the old guard, the former Duvalierists, the military, and the elite.[5]

In the slums of Port-au-Prince, the police and the UN ran daily patrols, which often turned into raids. The white armored personal carriers would rumble into a street. Blue-helmeted soldiers would watch as the Haitian police shot and killed people without arrest. Or the UN would join in, adding their superior firepower to the attacks. To anyone who was reading beyond the headlines, beyond the official transcripts, it was clear what was happening. By the end of 2004, human rights investigators began to publish evidence of extrajudicial killings. They released witness testimonies, photographs, and forensic evidence to show the extent of the violence.[6] The details were shocking, but so too was the method of presentation. There were images of dead bodies, infected wounds from untreated gunshots, and corpses in the streets.[7] While these images were meant as proof of the violence, they invited even more uncertainty, as the Haitian government and its supporters began to share their own images, or the same images with different accounts of what had happened. One day in late 2004, I received an email that, without warning, contained several images of three headless bodies. The bodies were naked and had been placed on a concrete floor, but the photographs provided few details about the victims or the location of the corpses. The author of the email, who was a supporter of the provisional government, said the bodies had been police officers, killed and beheaded by gangs loyal to Aristide. The author said that Aristide's gangs were "terrorists" who had launched a war against the government, a war that, he claimed, they were calling "Operation Baghdad."[8] Later, others told me they had seen the same photographs. They said the bodies were not, in fact, police officers, that they were actually Aristide supporters who had been killed by the police. Still others said that the photographs were fake, that someone had stolen corpses from the morgue and removed their heads so that they could accuse the gangs of killing and beheading police officers.

The images and stories were meant as proof. They circulated as evidence. But as they spread, they only made things murkier. Who were the victims? Who were the perpetrators? Had these bodies been killed at all? Dead bodies, wounds, bullet holes, corpses. These are the remains of violence that governments and human rights experts use to document abuses and to determine, through forensic analysis, what really happened during times of war. In her masterful book *The Body in Pain*, Elaine Scarry reminds us of what we all know but often forget—that war is organized violence, that it is violence organized around the reciprocal injuring of bodies.[9] Why is killing so central to war? Because, Scarry tells us, the reality of the dead body is essential to the fiction of power. No other means of measuring the results of conflicts seems quite so material, quite so factual as death. And yet modern wars do not always claim their dead, hence the need for forensic analysis, for documentation, excavation, and reconstruction. These forms of representation have their own materiality—they can be handled, circulated, transmitted, shared. They create their own publics, communities formed around the transmission of death.

After the coup, many people died. And many others did not. But everyone was touched by violence. Violence came from all directions—from the police and the UN, from gangs and masked men, from men with guns. And violence begot more violence. It was contagious, it expanded to fill the world, to remake it in new and terrible ways. Everyone was caught between life and death.[10]

THE RED ZONE

One morning in the summer of 2005, a dead body turned up in the street in front of the entrance to the forest at Habitation Leclerc. There had been other acts of violence in the zone since the coup, but people talked about this unidentified body for weeks afterward. They took it as a sign that more violence was coming. Martissant had been classified as a "red zone" by MINUSTAH (the UN Stabilization Mission in Haiti), which meant many things. It meant that the UN and the Haitian government considered it a dangerous neighborhood; it meant that aid groups and NGOs could not work in the area without police and UN protection; it meant that gangs controlled much of the area; it meant daily patrols and raids; and it meant there was violence.

Martissant was one of several red zones. The other large slums had also been classified this way, as had the road to the airport, which had become the site of kidnappings, shootings, and roadblocks. Red zones were considered "no-go" zones, and the official position was that everyone should avoid going to them. But what if you lived in one? What then? For those unlucky enough to live in the red zones, the designation meant you were classified as a potential security threat. The UN and the national police ran aggressive operations in the red zones and considered anyone residing in them and anyone coming or going from them to be possible gang members. Alongside the patrols and the raids and the possibility of being killed, those in red zones had to live with other threats, including a lack of access to food and services and the ever-present possibility of kidnappings, robberies, or other acts of violence. Less than a year after the coup, people had started to refer to Port-au-Prince as one of the most dangerous cities in the world. By the summer of 2005, there were an average of ten to twelve reported kidnappings each day. And one of the main bases of operations for one of the leading kidnapping gangs was in the forest at Habitation Leclerc.

In the months after the coup, the Red Army had finally taken full control of the forest, but their dominance in the neighborhood was soon challenged by a rival gang from the nearby area of Gran' Ravine. By late 2004, the entire zone was engulfed in violence as gangs fought each other and the police. The Red Army was displaced and Abel disappeared. People said he had been killed. With the Red Army gone, a rival gang seized control of the forest and much of the surrounding area. The garden project was on indefinite hold. The members of the SCPE went into hiding. I was still in Chicago, having canceled a trip to Haiti after the granting agency declared Port-au-Prince too dangerous and refused to release the funds. I felt stuck as I watched the news, heard the stories, worried about my friends. We spoke as often as we could, exchanging whatever information we had at the time. One friend said repeatedly that Martissant was "under siege." It was an apt phrase.

When I returned to Haiti in 2006, I found that violence had come to shape whole communities and neighborhoods. It penetrated into every conversation, every interaction. A walk to the market might mean passing a corpse, or maybe just a decapitated head. Bodies lay in the streets, unclaimed for days as pigs or dogs ate them or they rotted in the sun. People were kidnapped on their way to work. Others disappeared. Families went to the morgue hoping for news of their missing relatives. Everyone I knew had been hurt or had a relative or close friend who had been injured, kidnapped, or killed. Violence proliferated beyond acts of bodily injury and harm; it proliferated too in talk about violence, in stories, accounts, reports, and rumors.[11] Conversations began with people recounting who had been robbed or killed, where, and how it had happened. Talk of dead bodies slipped casually into conversations, just as casually as the bodies themselves slipped into public spaces.

People spoke of violence, shock, and crisis. They told me about the red zones and said to avoid them. They also said that the entire city was like a red zone, that anyone could meet violence at any time. Violence was like a shock—a blow for which they were braced. But it was only the surface appearance of a deeper problem, the problem of trying to live in the midst of oppressive forces that threatened to kill you. That deeper problem they called *ensekirite,* or insecurity, a Kreyòl word that, as Erica James has shown, is used to name "the social vulnerability that accompanies the crisis of the Haitian state."[12] It is a robust term, used to talk about violence in all its forms—from political and criminal violence to structural and economic violence. Above all, it is the word people use to talk about how violence *feels.*

I remember a conversation with a friend who was in hiding in the city. He was telling me about life after the coup, about how the anticipation of sudden violence merged with the expectation of its more routine forms. He said everyone was living with ensekirite now. I had asked him what the term meant for him.

It was too dangerous to work. His work required travel around the city, and each time you left your street, he said, you took a risk, you took a chance that you might be robbed or killed. "When you have ensekirite, you can't eat, you can't work. You can't do anything," he said. "If you can't eat, if you don't find food, your whole family suffers. It is not a good time for Haiti. But, it is not a good time for *Haitians.* You see? Between suffering and starvation, you have violence. Because people have no money, no jobs. We have nothing. In Haiti, we have only misery [*mizè*]."

In her account of ensekirite during and after the de facto period, James describes the experience of ordinary crisis as the "routinization of rupture."[13] Social life is built on routines. The repetition of stable and recurring events shapes our expectations—we come to expect more of the same. What happens, then, when social life devolves into the opposite of routine? What happens when disruption becomes normal, when the unpredictable is expected, when rupture repeats so often that you no longer know anything else? Anthony Giddens calls this condition "ontological insecurity."[14] It is an existential condition in which crisis is "built into the regularity of social life" so that the extraordinary becomes ordinary.[15] It is hard to live with ontological insecurity, as my friend had said. But it was equally hard to know *how* to live with it, since ensekirite also destroys the contexts in which meaningful action takes place.[16]

When I returned to Haiti in 2006, I returned to a city in the grip of ensekirite. Unable to go to Martissant, I settled into the familiar routine of waiting—at hotel bars, on the street corner, in people's homes, and at the Artist Gift Shop. Waiting for something to happen, hoping that nothing would.

One day, while Alexis and I were walking, he touched my arm and told me to move quickly. We hurried down the street, around the corner, and down another street. "It is no good," he said, as we walked. "If you don't see anyone on the streets, leave fast. If you see too many people, leave fast."

His advice wasn't just meant for me. He was doing his best to follow it, too. That summer, he was all but out of work and was spending most days at the gift shop with a few close friends. I knew he was struggling to get by, but he also seemed relieved not to be out in the streets. Alexis was still looking for life, as he had always done, but it was getting harder and harder for him to make a living. He spent most days waiting in the shade of a tree, listening to news reports about kidnappings and demonstrations, about road blocks and street closures, and about which neighborhoods to avoid.

One hot afternoon, we sat together drinking warm beer. Thick black smoke rose up from the southern edge of the city. The air smelled of burning rubber. Alexis pointed to one of the plumes. "See the smoke," he said. "That's Martissant." The radio was full of stories about the violence there.

"Martissant is burning," I muttered.

Alexis nodded slightly. "Yes," he said. "The gangs are fighting each other. They burn each other's houses. They burn everything." And then, as if warding off a possible request to drive me there, he added, "*You* can't go there. *I* can't go there. If the cops see you there, they'll shoot you. If the gangs see you there, they'll shoot you." He shrugged. "It's the same thing."

A few days later, I was at the gift shop with Wilfred and Jean. They, too, said I could not go to Martissant.

"Listen, Grégoire," Wilfred said. "I am your friend." He put one hand on his chest and the other on my shoulder and looked me in the eyes. "If I tell you to go to Martissant and you get killed or kidnapped, I am wicked. No, I can't say that."

Jean looked away, down the street. His body seemed tense. He turned back and looked at me. "It's not safe to go anywhere," he said. "I could take you to Cité Soleil, and if we meet people that I know, we might be okay. But if not, we might be killed. It's dangerous to be where you don't know people."

I appreciated their concern for my safety, but they weren't just worried about me. They were also worried about their own safety. The constant threat of violence was taking its toll on them. I could sense it in their mood and tone, in their body language. Their livelihoods and their sense of self both depended on their ability to travel freely around the city, to cultivate networks of people, to be known and to be able to make relations. Now they couldn't do any of that.

"It is dangerous to go out, to go to work," Jean said. "People get robbed, killed. Two or three men with guns will stop a tap-tap and take all the money. All the jewelry. If you don't have anything for them, maybe they will beat you in the street."

I asked if it was like the dictatorship or the de facto period. They both said it was worse now, worse than it had been with the makout or the paramilitaries.

"Before," Wilfred said, "under the dictatorship, you were safe if you didn't do politics. Today, it doesn't matter. I say, 'I don't do politics.' But the gangs, these people, they're all crazy. They'll kill you anyway."

"Things in Haiti are very bad," Jean said. "This is the worst time. Now, I can't say anything. I don't know who is listening. I don't know who they are with." He smacked his hands together and then shrugged. "It's like that. Anyone can kill you."

NARRATING EVERYDAY VIOLENCE

People talked about the violence after the coup as if it were something new. Yet the blurred boundaries between criminal and political violence and between the explosive violence of fighting and the slower violence of a collapsed economy were nothing new. Haitians had been living with ensekirite for decades. But something felt different. The prevalence of armed groups, of gangs and unknown actors, gave the violence after the coup a different character. People expected the state to use violence against citizens, but they also expected the state to abide by certain rules. If you didn't do politics, you were supposed to be safe. Now it seemed that the rules had changed, that there were no rules anymore. It seemed that violence could cross all boundaries, all lines of class and social divisions. It could find you in the streets, at work, on the bus, and at home. It didn't matter who you were. Anything might happen. To anyone.[17]

As violence became an ever-present possibility, it also became, paradoxically, something ordinary. The more you expected violence, the less shocking it was when it happened to you or to someone you knew. Violence is dramatic and sudden, it bursts into one's life. But it also dwells in what Veena Das calls "the ordinary"—that is, the ongoing relationships and routines that make up the undramatic, uneventful stuff of everyday life.[18] In the ordinary space of life, violence might sharpen social distinctions of class and exclusion, especially when people seek to defend themselves from the possibility of violence by criminalizing others, building walls, and hiring private security guards. But violence might just as easily break social barriers, moving across them with ease, opening up a shared experience across lines of distinction. In Port-au-Prince after the coup, the breakdown of the institutions that controlled the means of force and violence allowed it to spread everywhere, as if it were contagious. The gangs, the police, and the UN were caught up in waves of reciprocal violence, but they were not able to contain it. Violence seeped out; it saturated social life; it shaped relationships, bodies, and neighborhoods; it structured time and space.[19]

More often than not, it appeared in stories.[20]

I held the grab handle tight, my knuckles white. Georges drove without stopping, taking the corners fast, hitting his horn to make people jump out of the way of the car. The traffic lights weren't working, but I doubted that he would have stopped for them if they had been. We had the windows rolled up, the doors locked. Paranoid style.

"I don't stop for anything," Georges said, with a slight smirk. Was he enjoying this?

"It's not just the red zones," he said, turning the wheel with determination. Georges said you couldn't stop anywhere in the city. If you stopped, someone might stick a gun in the window. If you were lucky, they would just take your car. Or they might take you, too, hold you for ransom somewhere. Somewhere like Habitation Leclerc, where an armed gang was keeping people. There had been more kidnappings earlier in the week. Everyone was talking about them, on the radio, in the newspapers, on the street corners.

We made it to lunch without incident. It was a moderately priced restaurant in a nice neighborhood. There were other people there, too, eating as if everything was normal. Just another day in the city. Serge was already there, waiting for us at our table.

Serge was an agronomist who worked in a southern province of the country. I had met him several years ago, through mutual friends. He was a conservationist who had spent decades trying to tackle the issues of deforestation and soil erosion in several African countries. He had left Haiti in the 1960s, under the dictatorship, but he had always planned to return. He said that all of the development projects he worked on elsewhere were a kind of training for his return to Haiti.

"I left under Duvalier," he once told me. "Under Duvalier it was not possible to *think*." And so he had gone to school in Europe. He studied and worked hard, built connections, and eventually became the head of a reforestation project in East Africa. He came back to Haiti a decade ago, when René Préval was first elected president. "Préval was an agronomist too," he said. "He knew about the crisis in the countryside. Aristide didn't know. He thought he could go like that," he said, waving a hand in the air, "and make the problem go away. He thought he could push land reform through, quickly. But no! In Haiti, land is the biggest problem. You can't just say 'land reform.'" Serge had told me that wealthy landowners had all hired paramilitaries to take back their land. They had killed peasant leaders and their families. Serge envisioned a restored peasantry and a massive redistribution of land, but he thought it would take decades to accomplish. "You have to move slowly in Haiti," he said.

As we ate lunch, we talked about his latest project, working with peasant groups to plant cooperative forests. Each member would contribute money or land. The work would be done in collective work groups *(konbit)* and the proceeds would go into a mutual assistance fund. The radical part of his plan was that he wanted them to grow cash crops—either fast-growing trees grown to be cut down (like bamboo, which could be used to make furniture) or eucalyptus, which could be used to make charcoal.[21] Many funders were reluctant to contribute to reforestation programs that were based around cutting trees down, but for Serge it was the only approach that had a chance of succeeding. Peasants were already cutting trees down. They would continue to do so as long as it was the only viable economic option for them. If they had trees that could be cut and sold and then replanted again, it would save fruit trees and larger trees from getting the ax.

After lunch, we lingered at the table, drinking beer. Our conversation felt surreal, like a shared dream in which we conjured up an image of a possible future world, a world that was green and vibrant, a world in which peasants had control over their lives and made a decent living. A world with trees.

Only then, at the end, did we slip into the customary pleasantries, asking after each other's families, asking after mutual friends.

"My niece was kidnapped two days ago," Serge said, suddenly.

I was shocked. Georges seemed to have known already. Serge told us what had happened. There wasn't much to the story. She had been living in the city recently, working for an NGO. She had been kidnapped on her way to work one day. Someone had called her family with a ransom demand. The family had approached the police, but they were not able to do anything. Serge had been working with her parents to raise the money. They would pay the ransom and then, he hoped, his niece would come home.

"It was last week," Suzanne said. "I was driving home on the Route de Delmas." Suzanne lived in upper Delmas, a residential and commercial neighborhood of Port-au-Prince. It was usually a safe area. "I stopped only for a moment at the side of the road. Someone was calling me on the phone. And then a man grabbed my arm through the window. It was open." She pointed beside her, as if to show where the car's window had been. "He grabbed my arm and stuck a gun inside the window. He was yelling at me to get out of the car. I refused. I yelled back at him and tried to pull my arm away. He was holding my wrist. Another man behind him started to open the car door and I don't know. I just put the car in gear and drove off. Fast. And well—"

She held up her left arm. The forearm was broken and now in a cast. She seemed mildly embarrassed by the whole thing. As if anticipating any comment that I might make, she continued. "I don't know if I was brave or lucky. Stupid, maybe. I found out later that my friend heard the whole thing. I was still holding the phone. I didn't realize until I got home." She finished her story with a small, almost nervous laugh.

Suzanne was an expat who had been living in Haiti for decades. She had first come as part of a medical aid mission during the dictatorship. As she liked to say, she "fell in love with the country." She returned many times, eventually returning for good just after the fall of the Duvalier regime. She found work with various development projects, and then as a translator. But her real dream was to restore tourism to the country. She had worked with several government administrations, with taxi unions and tour guides, and with artists and hotel owners. She had a wide network in the city and throughout much of the country. I had first met her several years earlier, when she had taken several tour groups to Martissant to see the forest. Now she was running Kreyòl language classes for aid workers and occasional day trips for UN staff and their families.

I was surprised when she showed up to breakfast with a broken arm. She told me the story without any prompting, before I could even ask if she was okay. Now, with the story out of the way, we settled into an easy rhythm, eating breakfast and chatting. I dipped some fresh bread into my coffee as I listened to her talk about her work.

We chatted some more, our mood upbeat. Then Suzanne touched her arm, as if remembering it was in a cast, remembering it was broken.

"I've never seen anything like this," she said.

"The violence?" I asked.

She nodded. "Never."

I thought about the violence that the poor had lived through under the dictatorship and during the first coup. I thought about the kind of violence that doesn't come from a gun or a masked person, that comes from a shattered economy, a precariously built city, a destroyed environment. But I didn't say anything. I knew what she meant. Her middle-class position, her skin color, and her foreign passport had kept her safe during those other moments, just as it had kept me safe. But Suzanne was no stranger to risk or danger. She worked alongside people who struggled to make a living. She worked hard to help build a tourist sector so that they could find work. She knew the stark realities of looking for life. And she knew what her friends and neighbors, her drivers and guides, had lived through. Despite all of that, or because of it, the violence now felt new, different. Different because it didn't announce itself in the old ways, it didn't come as you might expect. It was anonymous and public, it spread throughout the city, it touched everyone, regardless of social class or privilege or standing. Regardless, even, of nationality.

"The worst part is no one seems to care," Suzanne said.

I asked what she meant.

"The UN soldiers," she said. "They're all from Brazil or places like that, places with a lot of gangs and violence. They come to Haiti and think this is nothing. Of course, for them it isn't so unusual, maybe. But for us, here, in Haiti, it is unprecedented. So, they don't do anything. All those patrols and they just sit and watch. No one can do anything to stop the kidnappings, the carjackings, the shootings. Where they are from it might be normal, but in Haiti, this violence—it's a whole new world."

I looked down at my coffee. I thought she might be right. Something had been opened up after the coup, and I wasn't sure it could ever be closed again.

I met Gabriel at his new home in a gated community in the hills. There were security guards at the entrance to his private street and a high stone wall around his house. The wall had shards of broken glass embedded in the concrete along the top—a common local substitute for barbed wire.

As usual, I went to meet Gabriel with Luc. We sat in Gabriel's garden and talked about the political situation. Luc, who had moved out of Martissant a few years earlier, was cautiously optimistic about the standoff in the forest. He thought the UN would have the security situation under control soon, and that the botanic garden project would finally be able to proceed. Gabriel was less sure. He thought the UN mission would not go far enough to resolve the underlying issue in the country, which, as he saw it, was the prevalence of Lavalas and Aristide's supporters. For Gabriel, it was pro-Aristide gangs who were solely responsible for the violence, despite the rumors (later backed up by arrests and confessions) that the most prominent kidnapping rings were run by young men from the country's elite families. Gabriel hoped the situation would escalate so that the UN would treat it as a military operation and, in his words, "restore order" *[retabli lòd]* to the country.

For now, though, Gabriel was done with the city. He didn't go back to Port-au-Prince much, even though he still had his old house in Martissant. He had tried to sell or rent it, with no luck. "It was not possible. No one wants to live in a red zone," he said, slapping the back of one hand into the palm of the other. He shrugged, as if the story was over. "What can I do?"

There was more, though. After the conversation had moved on to other things, Gabriel suddenly brought it back to the house in Martissant. A relative of his had been living in it until late last year, when the house had been attacked by armed masked men. The intruders shot a private security guard and injured his relative. Both of them survived the attack, and the injured guard had managed to return fire and to fend off the attackers. The house had been empty since, although Gabriel said a neighbor recently told him someone had set fire to it.

"If I had been there," he said, "I might be dead. I had a good guard. But you can't trust them. I was lucky. He had bullets for his gun. Some of them sell their bullets. Their guns are empty!"

Luc looked at me and shrugged. "It's true," he said.

Gabriel said he had heard stories of security guards turning on their employers. He had heard of people—he didn't say who—being tied up by their own guards, watching helplessly as the guards robbed them. Then he nodded at his new house, at the maid working in the kitchen. He didn't trust her. He was sure she was stealing from him.

"You can't trust these people," he said, with his usual tone of derision for the working poor. He was worried that the maid would tell people about his house, that she would let a gang inside and that the gang would kill him and take everything.

Later that afternoon, I thought about how Gabriel had so gleefully called for the coup. I thought about his house in Martissant, empty and burnt, and about his new house in the hills. He was right to be worried, but I couldn't muster much sympathy for him. Gabriel thought violence was something that happened to other people. He never thought it might happen to him.

Violence is strange. When wielded by those in power it has the stamp of legitimacy; we call it law. When wielded by those who later take power, as in a revolution, it morphs—shifting from warfare to a founding violence that gives birth to new nations, new orders, new governments. And when used in ritual practice, violence, like fire, is a transformative element. It cleans and purifies, it turns death into sacrifice. It makes and remakes the world.[22]

What is it, then, this force we call violence? Perhaps it is better to ask how it feels. For violence is not an event, it is not something that just happens. There is always the possibility of violence, lurking in the world, contained by systems of order, captured by those institutions and actors who claim the sovereign right to wield it. Yet, if there is the possibility of violence, there is also the possibility of nonviolence, of it not happening. In the middle lies anticipation. When violence does strike, when it is actualized, it is with a sense of both shock and knowing, suddenness and expectation. And then there is the way that violence takes shape not in blows and wounds, but in stories, in everyday encounters as people work to make sense of the world around them.[23] As I listened to people narrate these everyday forms of violence, I came to see that everyone, across the great social, political, and economic schisms of the country, was touched by it in some way.

But not everyone was touched in the same way.

THE BLACKOUT

I had been waiting for the call all morning. When it finally came, I jumped.

"Vincent? How are you?"

"Not good," he said. "Not good."

His voice was thin, his breathing shallow. When he spoke, nearly every sentence was interrupted by a violent cough. It was summer 2006. The city was burning.

I hadn't seen Vincent in over a year. He had fled Martissant and gone into hiding after the coup. A few weeks ago, I had sent a message through Roland, a mutual friend who knew where Vincent was living. Two days ago, Roland had brought me a phone number. I called it dozens of times, but the line was always dead. Yesterday morning, it finally worked. Vincent's godson Laurent answered. He said Vincent was sleeping. He said he was sick. He had been sick for a while. We made a plan for Vincent to call me later. I spent the rest of the morning anxiously drinking coffee and trying to read. Watching the phone. Waiting for it to ring.

We talked only for a few minutes. His coughing grew worse as we spoke. He was clearly tired. I was worried. I told him I wanted to see him, that I had a *ti kado* (small gift) for him. He wanted to see me too. Laurent got on the line and we made arrangements to meet later that afternoon.

When I first met Vincent, years ago at Habitation Leclerc, I had been struck by his persistent joyfulness, even in the face of the obvious difficulties that came with looking for life in the city. Back then, he had spent his days maintaining his small medicinal garden and working to become an herbalist. He had also worked with Maxo and others in the SCPE to establish good relations with the squatter community in the forest. But Maxo had grown increasingly suspicious of Vincent after his role in the cleansing rite in 2004. In the intervening years, Vincent had lost any kind of stable position with the SCPE or with the squatters. The situation had turned increasingly violent when a new gang took over the area, a gang that cared little about the fragile network of alliances Vincent and others had built between residents and the squatters. Amid a wave of violence, the SCPE had retreated from Martissant and were petitioning the UN and the police to clear the forest. Vincent and Laurent left the area, moving to a different part of the city. After they were gone, someone set fire to a block of houses. Vincent's house was completely destroyed.

Now they were living in Laurent's aunt's house. Being in hiding, being displaced was hard on them, especially Vincent. He had lived in Martissant all of his life, just like his father had before him. He had had a deep relationship with the forest too, and with Katherine Dunham, whom he referred to as his godmother. When I told him that Dunham had passed away, I could see sadness fill his eyes. I told him there had been a beautiful service in her honor in Washington, D.C., that many people had come from around the world to pay their respects. He seemed please to know she had had the

Vincent's garden in Martissant. Photo by author.

funeral she deserved. But I couldn't help feeling that he was realizing that his whole world was slowly fading away. He told me about his house, how it had been burned down by one of the gangs in Martissant. He said that even if he could go back there without being killed, he had nowhere to go, nowhere to live.

We spoke only briefly before his coughing grew worse and he asked me to leave. I was even more worried now that I had seen him in person. He was clearly very sick. His normally slender torso was skinny and frail. I urged him to see a doctor. My little gift included enough money to cover a visit and some medication, as well as other living expenses. He said he would go, but I doubted that he would. He drank herbal tea as we spoke, and it seemed to ease the worst of his coughing fits. Vincent was then in his mid-fifties and, given his physical condition and his illness, was beginning to wonder how much longer he could go on. He told me how the violence and disorder were making it hard for him to live.

"I had to leave Martissant," he said. "I had to leave my garden. I don't have any medicine. I don't have any money to buy medicine. To buy food. To buy anything. Life is expensive in Haiti. You understand? But my life, it's not worth much. I can't eat. I can't live. We are all hungry now." He paused. Another coughing fit.

"I am sick," he said.

I nodded.

"I feel weak all over. I can't do anything. When there is a blackout in the city, you can't do anything. For me, now, for us, we are living in a blackout *[blakawout]*. This is the worst time. Things in Haiti are very bad. We cannot live." Hunger, illness, poverty, misery, insecurity, and violence. They were everyday occurrences for Vincent and Laurent, as for so many others in the city. This is how crisis felt. Intimate. Like something that was happening to you. It felt like not being able to live.

I didn't stay long. He needed to rest, and I needed to get back across the city before the sun set. Laurent walked with me back downtown. As we walked, he told me that after the coup there had been violence every day, that everyone was in a state of constant shock. It made you tense, he said. He said that that was what Vincent had meant when he said they were living in a blackout. You knew it was coming but you never knew when it was coming. I listened as Laurent described his childhood in Martissant, before the coup. His father had once paid a man to hook up their house to the electrical grid. Such connections were illegal and dangerous. The people you paid to do it were experts, they knew what they were doing. Laurent said a neighbor, balking at the price for a connection, had tried to do it himself and had been shocked and badly injured.

Electrical shocks *(chòk)* are not the same as other kinds of shocks, the ones called *sezisman* or *kriz* (crisis). The latter are brought on by extreme emotional states, like grief or trauma. Such shocks touch you directly, they make you dizzy and weak, they make you collapse. They might make your whole body seize up. You might go rigid and then lose all energy and collapse. You might black out.

The anthropologist Paul Brodwin, in his discussion of illness categories in Haiti, says that sezisman and kriz are "unmediated bodily responses to loss" that leave your body weakened and prone to illness or even to sudden death.[24] But they aren't quite unmediated, even if they feel immediate and direct. Bodily responses to shock are mediated by culture and experience. In Haiti, a person is composed of different parts. There is the body, of course, but it is only a temporary home for the soul. The soul itself has three parts: the *ti bon anj* (little good angel), which is the seat of conscience and morality; the *mèt tèt* (master of the head), which is a guardian lwa inherited from the family line of spirits; and the *gwo bon anj* (big good angel), which is a manifestation of Bondye or God and serves as "the invisible force that generates action in a person's body."[25] After death, the gwo bon anj goes to Ginen, where it joins the ancestors and, over time, becomes a lwa. During life, when the gwo bon anj is weakened, the animating forces that make a person capable of acting in the world are reduced. Their blood goes bad or slows down. They grow sick and lose power.[26]

Perhaps Vincent had all of this in mind when he spoke of the blackout. He was, after all, quite sick himself. And he was trained as an herbalist or leaf doctor; he had an intimate knowledge of health and illness, of the underlying theories of the body and the self. Whether he was conscious of it or not, his account of living in a blackout made it seem like the blackout was a kind of illness—a generalized lack of power caused by an inability to act autonomously in the world.

As I dwelt on his comment, I came to understand Vincent's use of the image of the blackout as a phenomenology of political crisis, one that grounds the experience of the collapse of the state, the coup and the violence, and the everyday disruptions of ensekirite in the bodily sensation of a loss of power and a loss of consciousness. For Vincent and others like him, the violence after the coup came suddenly but certainly, and it created a shared sense of expectation and experience that shaped people's lives in intimate and immediate ways. You couldn't escape it because it was in your body, in your sense of self. Living in a blackout wasn't just living with the lights off—it was living with the constant possibility of your own death.

LOSING POWER

"Here in the city we have lots of blackouts, you understand?" Jean said.

We were sitting with Toto and Wilfred, in the shade of a tree, on the lawn of a hotel where Jean and Toto sometimes worked. The lawn had a secluded feel to it. We were far enough from the hotel lobby to be out of earshot of the staff and the guests (all journalists and aid workers), and we were ensconced behind a low stone wall beyond which we could dimly hear the sounds of the city streets. I had asked them about the term *blakawout*. It was an English word, borrowed into Kreyòl. It meant power outages, of course. But it meant much more than that, as I had come to learn. When I asked them about the word, they all nodded thoughtfully. I told them a friend had said Haitians were "living in a blackout" and they readily agreed. Now they were explaining what the word meant to them.

"When there is a blackout in the city, you can't do anything," Jean said. "Today, for us, we are in a blackout. If I don't have rice and beans, I can't do anything." He shook his hands in the air, palms facing me, making a "no" gesture. "Without money, I can't live. A blackout is like that. We don't have power [*pouvwa*]."

Jean was describing the blackout as a loss of personal power. Vincent had used it to name a debilitating physical condition. In these phrases, both of them extended the meaning of *blakawout*, broadening it from a temporary loss of electrical power to an individual and collective experience of a loss of agency. In Kreyòl the most common terms for electrical power are energy *(kouray)*, electricity *(kouran)*, and light *(limyè)*. These are the words people typically use to talk about blackouts. When the lights shut off, you might say that there is no kouray. I was surprised, then, when Jean described the blackout as a loss of *pouvwa*—a word that can mean electricity but is much more commonly used to name the capacity for doing work, as in labor power, and the control or influence one has over others, as in political power.[27] The potency of the metaphor of the blackout came, then, from its ability to bring all of these meanings to mind at once. The blackout was a kind of "thick ethical concept," one that was deeply embedded in the concrete experiences of daily life.[28]

What, then, does the blackout bring to mind? There is the sudden loss of electrical power, which is a reminder of the state's lack of capacity, the government's inability to provide basic services to citizens. There is the memory of the army's use of blackouts, when they would cut power to neighborhoods before beginning their assaults, a tactic used often in Martissant and other slums during the de facto period. Blackouts are also potent reminders of the problem of the informal city, where the only way to get access to services like electricity is to take the dangerous path of illegal hookups. Blackouts can be felt intimately, by individuals and their families, but they are also generalized social phenomena—you can literally see their effects across a neighborhood, or even across the city itself. In the midst of a blackout, the absence of civic infrastructure becomes all the more visible.[29]

The blackout means even more than this. It also brings to mind power in a general sense, the power to control one's body, to do things in the world, to make value, to make things happen. For men like Vincent or Jean, men who were constantly looking for life, the blackout was a way of talking about their inability to find it.[30] Of course, Vincent was quite sick, and as his health deteriorated, his ability to work declined. But the loss of his home and his own displacement in the city were also part of what it meant to be living in a blackout. It was a kind of uncanny—in the sense of unhomely—condition, in which you couldn't do much of anything anymore. This lack of capacity for action had a social sense as well. After the coup, talk of blackouts was also a coded way of talking about the loss of *political* power that had come with the removal of Aristide. The blackout was a concrete image that brought all of these things together at once. In Haitian oratorical practice, the blackout was a *pwen* (literally, "point")—a mode of public commentary that, as Karen Brown describes it, "captures the essence or pith of a complex situation."[31]

Talk of blackouts is partly talk of the lack of something—a lack of services, of a responsible government, or of the wealth to power one's own private generators. To live in a blackout, though, was something more than a lack; it was an existential condition, a way of being in the world. And in this sense, talk of blackouts was always a way of commenting on matters of life and death, on the experience of a life shrouded in the possibility of its opposite, on the ever-present fact of darkness. The blackout is how crisis feels when it happens to you. It is concrete and abstract, acute and chronic, anticipated and sudden. It is an individual and a shared experience. Like ensekirite, the blakawout is both a disruption *in* routine and a disruption that *has become* routine. It is a kind of ontological insecurity in which people lose autonomy and control over the practices that anchor social life. And like ensekirite, people feel this loss of autonomy as a kind of sickness—a shock to their sense of self and to their emotional, physical, and bodily integrity.

Jean had described the blackout at some length. Later, after the conversation had moved on to other topics, he returned to the issue of power. He lamented the removal of Aristide and the losses that his Lavalas movement had suffered, losses that included scores of deaths, arrests, and prosecutions, and, most recently, the marginalization of Aristide's political party. "Before," he said, "with Aristide, we didn't have all this ensekirite." He gestured to the wall, to the city behind it. "We didn't have kidnappings. We didn't have gangs. We weren't starving. With Aristide, if you were hungry you could tell him and he would listen. Now, no one hears you if you are hungry." Wilfred and Toto were quick to agree. They said that with Aristide gone, the people had lost all power. They said the elite and the international community were killing the people, that the UN mission was a "third U.S. occupation." They said that the world didn't want Haiti to be free.

As they spoke, I thought of how the loss of national sovereignty shaped their own sense of a loss of autonomy and control over their bodies and their lives. A collective loss of sovereignty. The blackout meant that too.

A GHOSTLY STATE

Years ago, before the coup, Alexis said the problem with Aristide was that he had not been strong *(fò)* enough, that he should have taken a stronger stance against the opposition. Not killing the protesters—just strong enough to make sure they couldn't make disorder, couldn't make a coup. It was a common feeling at that time, at least for Aristide's supporters. Many of them had wanted him to do more to prevent the opposition from destabilizing the country. I had even heard some people say, in hushed tones in private spaces, that they hoped Aristide would call on the gangs to attack the elite and the opposition. And yet, even for those who made such pronouncements, there was always a recognition of a problem—that in Haiti, a strong state has always meant a dictatorship, and no one wanted a return to those days.

Now, after the coup, people were saying the state was too weak, that it couldn't prevent the violence. Or that it was too strong, in the bad sense, and that the state was causing the violence. Both seemed equally true, and both sentiments pointed to a deeper issue, which was the role of the state in people's lives.

When Haitians talk about the state, they often talk about it as something they want to get away from, as something that threatens them or exploits them or that might kill them. *Leta*, the Kreyòl word for state, means both the government and a bully. Peasants want to be free from state agents like tax collectors or section chiefs. Those who work in the informal sector in the city, men like Wilfred and Alexis, want to get away from the police, inspectors, or government officers who might limit their activities. The promise of Aristide's Lavalas movement had been, in part, the promise of a new relationship between the state and the people, one that made the people the locus of sovereignty and the state an agent that owed something to them. In the democratic era, people said they wanted the state to be "responsible" to them, that the state had an obligation to serve them. They expected the state to provide them with access to basic services, like housing, water, and electricity. They wanted the state to stop terrorizing them and to go after the big gangs, the makout and the paramilitaries and the drug runners. They wanted the state to protect them from the worst ravages of a parasitic global economy.[32]

The coup had meant the end of Aristide's program. The end of the dream of a state that worked for the people, not against them. The provisional government had brought back the repressive state, the state that strikes you, the state that kills. The state that you fear. The state that you flee. But as the provisional period came to a close, and a newly elected government took power, people were starting to talk about the state again, about what they expected from it, wanted from it, and needed from it.

"We have a new government now," Jean said. I was with him and Wilfred at the gift shop. "But we don't have a state."

I asked him what he meant. He said it was like the state had died when the coup happened. He said the provisional government had tried to kill the people, but the people were still here. Now there had been elections again and the people had spoken.

"Haiti needs a strong [fò] state," Wilfred said. "Not strong like makout killing people. But strong." He held his arms in front of his body and flexed them, his hands in fists. "Fò," he said. "You understand? Strong enough to correct bad people." He used the English word *correct*. "To put them in jail and correct them. In the United States, you do that. It's called corrections." Again, he shifted into English as he spoke.

We were talking about the violence, about gangs and the police, about the state. It was summer 2006. Recent elections had brought an end to the provisional government. The return to a constitutional state had been much heralded by the UN mission. Never mind that Haiti was still being occupied by foreign soldiers, or that UN forces had recently announced that, now under the direction of the new government, they would step up their military campaign against the gangs. Wilfred was happy about the election, and he hoped that the violence would soon end. But he also felt that the Haitian state was unable to do what it needed to do, that it was not strong enough to be responsible for its own citizens. Wilfred thought the state was weak, but I had heard many others saying there was no state in Haiti at all, as if it had simply disappeared.[33]

The disappearance of the state had much to do with the removal of Aristide. After the coup, the provisional government was seen as little more than a mask of legitimacy for the repressive forces that wanted to destroy Aristide's base of support. The campaign of violence against the gangs was partly an attempt to kill off Aristide's armed supporters, but the specter of armed gangs was also used to criminalize the poor and to indiscriminately attack them in their own neighborhoods. When the election finally came, Aristide's Fanmi Lavalas party was excluded by the Electoral Council. There had been much turmoil in the Fanmi Lavalas anyway, as the party was organized almost exclusively around Aristide himself and there was no clear successor who had the same appeal or charisma. Instead, voters turned to a new party, Lespwa (Hope), headed by René Préval, who had been a leading figure in the popular movement for decades. Préval had served as prime minister during Aristide's first presidency and had been president after Aristide (from 1996 to 2001). Despite the new party affiliation, Préval was seen by nearly everyone in Haiti as the heir to Aristide.

While he won by a clear margin, the election was marred by controversy. Truckloads of ballots were found after the election, partially burned, in the city dump. The international community intervened and declared Préval the winner.[34] There was little doubt that he had won the election, but the way events unfolded left Préval's government vulnerable to critiques from all sides. His opponents saw it as an illegitimate government that had been "selected" or imposed by the international community; his supporters were happy he had won but wanted the government to investigate the destroyed ballots; and the international community wanted his cooperation with the peacekeeping mission. Instead of closing the political crisis by restoring a constitutional government, the election simply transformed it from a state of exception into an electoral crisis that would continue through much of Préval's term. The crisis left his government weak and unable to do much of anything. To make matters worse, Préval inherited the UN mission and the fight against the gangs, and he had no choice but to back the military raids in the red zones. It was this lack of capacity to protect the people and to govern the country that had led Wilfred to say Haiti needed a strong state. And it was this curious sense that the state was only a proxy for the occupying forces that led so many others to say there simply was no state at all.[35]

It was not only Haitians who spoke this way. I heard UN officials and aid workers say the same thing, that there was no state or that Haiti was not able to govern itself. Some said they thought the UN mission should stay in the country for at least twenty-five years. Others said one hundred years. They amounted to the same thing—an overriding sense that the crisis was permanent and, therefore, the intervention would need to be permanent too. One observer summarized this view by declaring that what Haiti needed was a "good, old fashioned trusteeship" headed by a "multilateral force with a 25-year mandate to rebuild the country year by year."[36]

Calls for a trusteeship and a permanent mission assume that Haiti is a failed state, that it cannot properly function without outside assistance. The violence of the post-coup period was all the evidence the international community needed to prove their point, that the government could not provide the basic political good of public security. Yet, as the UN mission stepped in to provide security, it also became implicated in state violence and state terror. Residents of the red zones described case after case of UN involvement in police killings. There were rumors that UN soldiers were involved in the kidnapping rings, or that they were sponsoring sex-trafficking networks. And there were many reports of collateral damage from UN raids. In the summer of 2006, I spoke with several MINUSTAH staff. They were aware of the critiques of the mission but brushed them off.

"Where would the country be if we weren't here," one of them said to me.

I waited for him to continue. He raised his eyebrows and held out his hands. "I mean, really," he said. "Where?"

"If there hadn't been a coup—"

"Come on!" He sat back in his chair and swatted a hand in the air. "Look," he said, leaning forward again. "Haiti's a mess. We all know that." He paused and looked at me. "You know that." He gestured to the restaurant around us, to the street outside. "Everyone in here knows it. Everyone out there knows it. This country is a fucking mess."

He waited, as if daring me to disagree. I mumbled some kind of response. He interrupted me. "You talk about Martissant," he said. I had told him about the forest and about my research, about my friends who lived there and the ones who had to leave. "But do you want to go there now?" He let the question hang in the air for a moment. "We're there every day. The gangs are organized. They're fighting us, they're fighting each other. If we weren't there, the gangs would be killing everybody!"

The UN had recently declared Martissant a "High Crime Threat Area." It was no longer just a red zone, a zone of indiscriminate danger and insecurity. It was now an unlawful zone, a place full of crime and criminals. The new designation came with new patrols. The first few years of the UN mission had been framed as peacekeeping. Now, with the Préval government in place and constitutional order restored to the country, the mission had shifted its focus from peacekeeping to policing.

When I asked UN staff about this shift, they said it was how such missions worked. They told me that peacekeeping missions often began as military missions, then moved into policing and state-building efforts. Policing, they said, was the first step in transitioning from a military to a civilian mission. One staffer was explicit about the need for policing in Haiti, saying that the national police force was too weak and too corrupt to provide adequate security.

"Look at Bel Air and the airport road," he said. "We've got things under control there now. The police, they couldn't do anything without us."

The airport road had been secured, which in turn had made it easier for people to get in and out of the city. The UN had also claimed a major victory in Bel Air, a central slum in the city's downtown core. It was still officially a red zone, but it was safe to go in and out of the neighborhood now. One day, I had asked some friends at the gift shop about the operations in Bel Air. They knew the area well and knew many people who lived there.

"Yes, it's true," Wilfred said. "They have security now."

"It's safe," Alexis added, "but it's empty."

I asked him what he meant.

"Empty," Alexis said again, smacking his hands together. "All the people are gone."

Later that day, while driving with Alexis, I asked about Bel Air again. "I'll show you," he said. He drove downtown, past the National Palace and the government buildings, then up a wide street toward Bel Air. It was empty. He had been right. The street was usually full of market stalls and crowds, of people out in public, working, walking, joking, talking. We continued, turning onto narrower streets. A few people sat in doorsteps, but for the most part these were empty too. I remember thinking how eerie it was to see the wide boulevards without people, how the emptiness seemed to fill the street with a kind of negative space.

We drove through another street. In the coming weeks, I would return to Bel Air repeatedly, as Alexis and others took me around. They introduced me to friends of theirs who were still in the neighborhood, and we would talk about the raids. They told me how the UN and the police had set up roadblocks all around the neighborhood. How the security forces had checked everyone who went in and out of the area. How the police and the UN had announced that they would start patrolling, that they would treat anyone who was out in the streets as if they were a gang member, a criminal, a thug. They told me how the police would drive into Bel Air and shoot anyone they saw. They would shoot at houses. At stores. "They shot everything," one resident said. "So, the people left." He said anyone who could get out did so.

The criminalization of the urban poor is a global phenomenon. It turns economic poverty, political marginalization, and social exclusion into a general state of being and it treats slums and other poor areas as if they are, by their very nature, disorderly environments. As Jean and John Comaroff have suggested, this idea of a natural disorder has come hand-in-hand with a new mode of governing that reduces politics to policing. But after the coup, acts of policing revealed a strange fact about the political situation: the dual features of the police—force and law, or violence and legitimacy— where dispersed across two different organizations. On one hand, the national police, as agents of the Haitian government, had the legal authority to use lethal force against citizens. On the other hand, the police did not have the logistical capacity or the firepower to fend off the counter-violence of the gangs and other armed actors. The solution was a kind of hybrid force, a chimera, a monstrous violence that combined the military power of MINUSTAH with the sanctifying force of the police.[37]

One day, as Alexis and I were driving to Bel Air, a UN vehicle stopped traffic in front of us. Several Haitian police officers opened the UN truck and escorted four young men, all in handcuffs, across the street. We watched as the UN soldiers held the traffic at bay, guns at the ready, and as the police brought their prisoners into a government building. Alexis shook his head and made a disapproving sound. I asked him was going on.

"They are taking them to be judged," he said. "They like to stop us, so we can all see. They always show us the little gangs *[ti gang]*." He pointed out the window at the four men. "They never show us the big gangs *[gwo gang]*. We have lots of those in Haiti too. Everyone knows, but no one says anything. They are big politicians. Big government. Big police."

We waited as the police went inside the building. The UN truck, gleaming white in the sun, remained parked in the middle of the street. Traffic backed up, the heat of the engines adding to the heat of the day. I wished for a breeze to blow through the car window. A young boy ran over to the car, selling small sachets of water. I bought two, and Alexis and I each tore a corner off the little plastic bags, spit the plastic out the window, and drank the warm water. Eventually, the police returned to their vehicle and left, followed by the UN truck, and then the rest of the traffic began to move again. We drove on, and as we did I thought about how the spectacle of policing was being played out every day in these recurring rituals of armed patrols, checkpoints, and raids. The repetition was no doubt meant to bolster the claim that the state had returned, that it did, in fact, have the capacity to provide security. But it was hard to believe that it had that capacity. The raids were too violent to feel legitimate. And the arrests, the public performance of policing and security, all felt like an empty gesture, as empty as the streets of Bel Air had been.

THE POWER TO KILL

"The Haitian state has no moral authority to kill people," Georges said. We had just finished dinner and were moving on to drinks. It was a hot night in August 2006. A fan moved slowly above our heads, the gentle breeze a small comfort.

We were talking about the new government, the violence, and the UN mission. I told Georges about a press conference I had gone to that morning, where a group of lawyers called the Comité des Avocats pour le Respect des Libertés Individuelles (CARLI) had denounced what they characterized as unchecked gang violence and had called on the Haitian government to reestablish the death penalty. The press conference had been at a downtown hotel once frequented by guides like Manuel and Richard. Now it was full of UN staff and foreign aid workers. The guides and taxi drivers had been replaced by private security guards and hired chauffeurs.

The press conference came at the end of a difficult week. At least six people had been shot in Martissant in the days before the conference, and while kidnappings and shootings had declined in August, compared to the previous month, there had still been dozens of reported incidents. There had even been shootings outside of the city, most recently in Fonds-Parisien near the Malpasse border crossing. The Dominican Republic had responded by closing the border. In the capital, everyone was saying that the border violence was because of drug gangs, which seemed likely given that the police had recently busted a large cocaine-smuggling operation in the town of Croix-des-Bouquets.

There didn't seem to be much public support for CARLI's proposal. The death penalty had been abolished in Haiti decades earlier, and it had only ever been used by dictatorships to kill "enemies of the state," often in grisly public spectacles. I wondered, though, who the audience for the proposal really was, given its location? It certainly seemed to give general support to a kind of de facto death penalty that had been enacted recently. Two weeks earlier, the government had issued an ultimatum to the gangs, telling them in no uncertain terms that they must surrender their weapons to MINUSTAH's Demobilization, Disarmament, and Reinsertion (DDR) campaign. As the prime minister, Jacques Édouard Alexis, had put it, "It is clear. You surrender your weapons and enter the DDR program. If you refuse, you will be killed."[38] Some gang leaders had issued a public response to the government, rejecting the terms of the DDR and arguing that they could not disarm when the police and MINUSTAH were conducting regular raids on their neighborhoods and killing people. The gangs needed their guns, their leaders insisted, to defend themselves. And in response to the gangs, the UN officials issued their own public statement, saying they were renewing their antigang program. The day before CARLI's press conference, the head of MINUSTAH, Edmond Mulet, said that the government of Haiti had granted the UN mission the authority to respond to the security situation and that the UN would now be engaged in its own policing and pacification campaigns as part of its effort to reinforce the "presence" of the state.[39]

Georges thought that CARLI's proposal was absurd, and he assured me that the government and the courts would never restore the death penalty. Too many people remembered how the dictatorship had killed people. Too many people had lost loved ones or had been tortured by past regimes.

Many of them, including Georges, still had the scars to remind them. But he was much more concerned with the government's announcement that the gangs must disarm or die, and he was livid at the continued presence of the UN mission.

"The only solution to insecurity is to restore the Haitian army," he told me.

I wasn't so sure. The Haitian army had only ever been used to attack Haitians or to make coups. Georges brushed aside my concerns. He held up a finger in the air, shaking it slightly. "No, Grégoire," he said. "The Haitian army, the *real* Haitian army, always refused to seize political control of the state. It is true that in the 1980s and the 1990s a few military leaders were pressured by the U.S. and the elite to make a coup. But the real army is the only national institution that can defend the country. It is the only solution to the political crisis and to the insecurity we see all around us today." He gestured to the edge of the veranda, to the city beyond it, as if the city itself was a symbol of crisis and insecurity.

But hadn't the army attacked the people? Hadn't they killed thousands? Georges agreed that they had done so, but he said the coups in the '80s and '90s were just further proof of the need for a robust and independent military. He said the violence during that period had been the result of politicians capturing the military. If the military had been stronger, it would have been able to keep the state in check, to limit the power of the presidency and of the political class. It would have *defended* the people against violence and insecurity.[40]

"The army is called for by the Haitian constitution. Our country was founded by an army—by Dessalines's army. The army was there before the state. No one else can defend us."

What about the UN, I asked?

"How can an international group police us? What right do they have? And what happens when they leave? Who will prevent a warlord from attacking the National Palace and proclaiming himself president?"

I was already quite familiar with Georges's stance on the UN mission. Georges was a devout nationalist, and we had had many conversations about the first UN mission in the '90s, the one that brought Aristide back from exile. He associated that mission with Bill Clinton, a man whom he despised immensely. Georges's animosity for Americans ran deep, as did his sense that Haiti needed to constantly defend itself from foreign incursions. When he spoke about the return of the army, he was careful to distinguish what he called the "real" army from the proxy one established by the United States during the occupation. (It was the latter, he noted, that had become involved in politics and coups.) The real army had given "birth" to the country. That army had been founded on the "principles of honor" that precluded it from entering into politics. The U.S. occupation of 1915–34 had replaced the Haitian army with a new force, one trained to protect the interests of its "foreign master." He said, "When we restore the army, we will restore the *Haitian* army, not the American one!"[41]

He paused as I took notes. Our conversations often had this rhythm, as if he were giving a lecture. He took a drink before continuing. "Aristide got rid of the army, but this was not constitutional. And it was a fatal mistake for him. If there had been an army, they would have *prevented* the [2004] coup." I said I wasn't so sure of that, especially since many former army officers had been leaders of the so-called rebels. I reminded Georges that René Préval had been the only president to fulfill a term in office since the end of the Duvalier regime, and that many people attributed that fact to the abolition of the army. "No," he said. "It was because of the UN."

Georges had been calling for the return of the army ever since it had been disbanded. He was glad, though, that Aristide had abolished the army, since it afforded a rare opportunity to think about the form and function of the military in Haiti. It accomplished, in his mind, the abolition of the proxy American army and made it possible to think about restoring a properly Haitian force. Georges also felt that Aristide's move against the army "shows for history the true face of the Lavalas people. It tells us they do not respect law, constitutionality, and so forth. This single act discredits Lavalas politically forever!" He was visibly excited as he said it. I recalled his visceral anger at Aristide and his certainty that the coup was coming, that Aristide would be killed and his dead body paraded in the streets. He took another drink and continued.

"Nothing is heavier than military tradition. It is as hard as concrete, as hard as steel." He brought a hand down on the table, hard. I steadied my glass as I recalled the Kreyòl proverb "Konstitisyon se papye, bayonèt se fè"—constitutions are made of paper, but bayonets are made of iron. The glorification of the military, like the glorification of the revolution, was an enduring theme among Haitian nationalists, many of whom were more committed to a strong state than they were to the democratic process. Indeed, some nationalists, including Georges, claimed that the "Haitian mentality" was more suited to a benign dictator than it was to democracy.

Georges could tell I was skeptical of his position. He looked at me over the top of his glasses, which had started to slide down his nose. He asked me what I thought. I said I didn't think Haiti needed another army. He smiled slightly. "If we don't need an army in Haiti, why is there a military component to the UN mission? Why not just have UN police here? Or engineers?" He let the questions hang in the air for a moment. Then he continued. "If the army is reinstated, we will have peace and we can return to reconstruction. If not, we will go into a downward spiral and soon have another foreign invasion to stop a likely civil war. If this is not enough, we will go through another transition, another cycle of armed violence, and another foreign invasion. And so on and so on. Forever." He leaned back in his chair and finished his drink.

Georges was not alone in calling for the return of the army. He had, in fact, been appointed by the provisional government to a committee tasked with producing a report on the history of the army in Haiti and on the legal and political case for restoring it. But the committee had been left in limbo, underfunded and with little support, and Georges had found out later that the provisional government had also commissioned a counter-report, from a U.S. consulting firm, outlining the case *against* restoration of the military.[42] It mattered little now, since the Préval government was not going to entertain the possibility of a return of the army. I asked Georges why he thought the provisional government, which had been backed by ex-army officers and soldiers, had sidelined the committee. He said the provisional government had been too weak and that they were too deferential to their "master," by which he meant the United States. "They didn't want us to produce a report," he said. Then he sat up and raised a finger in the air. "But we did our civic duty. We worked from the day we were appointed to the last day." Georges was quiet for a moment, then he continued. "We have started a national debate about the army in Haiti."

There was a national debate taking place, but it was only partially about the return of the army. The deeper issue was the power to kill and the right over life and death. It was, in essence, a debate about sovereignty.[43] The lawyers in CARLI were arguing for the state to reclaim its right to decide about life and death, to reclaim its sovereign power by restoring the death penalty, the most obvious example in modern politics of the state's claim that it can legally kill its own citizens.[44] But even without the death penalty in place, the state was already killing people, and declaring those killings legitimate and legal. After the coup, the provisional government attacked whole sectors of the population under the guise of security operations. After the election, the Préval government gave the UN the authority to police the population and publicly declared those who did not disarm to be killable.

Modern states are defined by their monopoly over the means of violence.[45] When states act violently, their violence is said to be in service of the law—to uphold it, to enact it, to restore it. Legitimate violence is essential to politics because it is the means through which state power is enacted. States demonstrate and reproduce their sovereignty by wielding power over the life and death of their citizens.[46] The Préval government's declaration that gangs must "disarm or die" was thus a political gesture in which the Haitian state sought to reclaim its sovereignty. And yet the statement was anemic, because the state itself was too weak. It could not enact its sovereign power to kill without the support of UN forces. In the end, the power over life and death was held by a hybrid agent, a sovereign force comprised of the national police and UN soldiers. On the ground, in red zones, markets, and homes, sovereign power was played out in a series of policing operations—raids and patrols, checkpoints and searches, shootings and arrests. Policing, in turn, became a public spectacle in which this hybrid sovereign was able to let some people live and make others die.[47]

BAD PEOPLE

Summer 2006. "These people are terrorists! That's what everyone is saying now," Denis said. We were at his house, sitting in the garden with Robert and two other men, whom I had just met.

"Terrorists?" I asked. It seemed a bit of an overstatement.

"Yes!" Denis said. The others agreed. They said the gangs in the slums were just like al-Qaeda. One of the men even claimed there was a mosque in Cité Soleil that was the base of operations for the gangs. When I looked dubious he became insistent, telling me that one of the hijackers who flew into the Twin Towers had come from Haiti. It wasn't true, but it was good branding, casting the street gangs in the role of global bad guy.

"I don't know about mosques," Robert said, pulling the conversation back from the conspiratorial brink.

"They're terrorists!" the man said again, waving a hand in the air.

"Warlords," the second man said. "Like in Somalia."

Robert shook his head. "Haiti is not fucking Somalia! The gangs are just people who've gone crazy. They're all fucking crazy. Have you ever seen someone on crack? They have really short-term goals. They have guns and money and drugs and that's it. They know they have no future and they're just crazy!"

Everyone seemed to accept Robert's assessment, and the conversation moved on to considerations of the best strategies for getting rid of the gangs. One of the men said that the only way to do it would be a military operation. "The police can't do it," he said. The UN would have to cordon off the slums and go street by street, door to door, with tanks and guns. "That is the only way," he said. In a matter of months, the UN would do exactly that. I leaned back in my chair and drank my coffee as I listened to them debate strategies, weapons, and approaches, discuss the most important neighborhoods to secure first and why. I listened as they talked about who should be killed and how, as if killing were the only solution on the table, as if killing were the only interaction they would ever have with "these people."

"It is true," Alexis said. "The gangs have gone crazy." I was sitting with Alexis and Wilfred. I had told them about the conversation with Denis and Robert and the other men.

"We call that *moun fou*," Alexis said. But he said there were lots of people who were crazy *(fou)* who were not violent, not in gangs, who did not kill people. He said that some of the gangs, the big gangs, were really just makout or other bad people who did what people paid them to do.

"The gangs are all bad people," Wilfred said.

I asked him what he meant.

Bad people *(move moun)* were thieves. Killers. Gangs. Sometimes bad people did magic. They served evil spirits or devils. Or they had bad blood *(move san)*, which meant that they were bad on the inside, as if their badness were an incurable condition, a substance inside them that could never be changed.[48] Wilfred said some of the gangs were orphans—they didn't have parents, so they were not raised properly. They had been raised on the street, and that had made them into bad people. Others, he said, were criminals from the United States, drug dealers who had been deported and sent back to Haiti. "They come back here and they have no family so they join gangs."

I asked what the government should do about the gangs. They both thought that the government would have to arrest them, or maybe kill them. But they were concerned that the government had gone too far. They said the provisional government had deemed everyone a criminal, as an excuse to kill anyone they wanted to kill.

There is a long history in Haiti of the state killing people. The Duvalier dictatorship had declared anyone opposed to the regime an enemy of the state. They had called them *kamoken* (rebels) or *kominis* (communists).[49] Just being called one of those names in public was enough to get you arrested, exiled, or killed. After the dictatorship fell, there had been a wave of popular violence against the makout. Former agents of the state were caught by angry crowds and "necklaced"—killed by having burning tires placed around their necks. And then there had been the first coup, and the army and paramilitary groups had killed anyone they suspected of being "with Aristide." People hid pictures of Aristide (photographs of his inauguration had been a common household item among his supporters) and anything else that might expose them as being with Lavalas. The first UN mission and the abolition of the army were supposed to bring an end to the violence. But most of the soldiers and officers from the former military had ended up joining the ranks of the newly created national police, the change from green to blue uniforms doing little to conceal the underlying continuities.[50] For men like Wilfred and Alexis, there was little point in trying to make distinctions between the army, the police, and the gangs. They were all, in a sense, bad people. Any of them might kill you.

Once, years ago, I sat in the forest with Laurent on a warm spring day. We were talking about his family, about growing up in the neighborhood, about life in the city, when Laurent asked if I had heard what happened to Félix. I knew parts of the story. I knew Félix had disappeared the previous year and that no one had seen or heard from him since. I knew his car had been found abandoned and partially burned in Titanyen, an infamous dumping ground for bodies on the outskirts of the city. People told me Félix was the leader of a powerful gang in Gran' Ravine, that he had been responsible for a massacre in the Fort Mercredi neighborhood, and that Aristide had brokered a truce between Félix's gang and a rival gang. And I knew that, until his disappearance, Félix had been the director of the Port-au-Prince cemetery, a fact that many took to be evidence of his close connection to Aristide.[51] The cemetery job was a lucrative one, as it put Félix at the center of the official and unofficial economies of death in the city. Tombs cost money, and those who ran the cemetery took a cut from the sales. But tombs were also sold and resold to multiple families, or even rented for brief periods of time. Salaries, sales, and kickbacks were augmented by the thriving trade in tomb raiding and the selling of bodies and body parts. At least that's what people said.

I also knew that Félix had been a chimè and that his death had brought much speculation that Aristide was finally turning on the gangs. The year before his disappearance, Aristide had made several public declarations against the gangs, as his government came under pressure from the international community to curb gang violence. On June 20, 2001, Aristide gave a speech at the Haitian National Police headquarters announcing a new zero-tolerance policy. Referring to *zinglendo*, a term used to name criminal gangs often associated with the drug trade, Aristide said:

If it's a zenglendo *[sic]*, zero-tolerance. If a zenglendo stops a car in the street, puts his hand on the key to make the driver get out so he can take the car, he is guilty, because the car is not his. You do not need to lead him to the court to have him judged because the car is not his . . . he is guilty. If a criminal grabs someone in the street by the collar and puts him on the ground to beat him or shoot him, [the police] do not need to wait to go to court with him to prevent him from doing that.[52]

The recent disappearance of high-profile gang leaders like Félix seemed to suggest that the zero-tolerance policy was in force and being directed against the chimè.

"Yes, but do you know *why* he was killed?" Laurent asked. I said I thought Aristide was trying to reign in the gangs.

"No, no," said Laurent, shaking his head. He told me Aristide personally ordered Félix's death because Félix saw something he wasn't supposed to see. Laurent told me that Félix witnessed the ritual sacrifice of a *kabrit san kòn*, a goat without horns. It was a phrase often used as a veiled reference to child sacrifice. Human sacrifice has never been part of Vodou, but accusations of such practices are a potent way of talking about how others use magic for the illicit and immoral accumulation of wealth and power. Laurent said Aristide had sacrificed a newborn baby stolen from the public hospital and that Félix was killed because he had witnessed it. Félix had seen the source of Aristide's power, so he had to be killed—and thus he too became a kind of sacrifice in a public display of the occult power of the state.[53]

When Laurent first told me the story, I thought it was just a rumor, one of many that seemed to cast Aristide as a mad dictator. Years later, as the government and the UN set about killing gangs, as people talked about the gangs as terrorists, as orphans, as people who had gone crazy, as bad people, I came to see Laurent's story in a different light. In retrospect, it seemed like a perfect story about the central place of death in all politics. There was the gang leader who killed people but was never arrested. There was the city cemetery, where death became the currency of power and profit. And then there was Félix's disappearance and (presumed) death at the hands of the state. It was mythic—poetic even—in its thematic cohesion, and it was an elegant theory, in its own right, of the relationship between violence, death, and sovereign power.

And now Préval had announced his own version of a zero-tolerance policy, as his government boldly declared that the gangs must disarm or die. This time, there were no rumors of secret rituals, no talk of sacrificial death, no reports of Préval's personal involvement in the killings. The gangs were simply bad people, and if you were killed during the policing operations it meant you were a bad person too. There was no sense that your death was part of a ritual in which power was remade. There was just the overwhelming fact of your death. The killing of bad people became the basis of politics. It gave rise to the fiction of power—the sovereign power to kill.[54]

WHAT BECOMES OF HOPE

Fall 2006. "Préval is the man," Robert said as he lit a cigarette. He inhaled and then breathed out smoke. "We're in a new phase now."

I asked him what he meant.

"Haiti," he said. He said it as if it would clarify things.

We were sitting at a table, drinking beer. A few months ago, under the direction of the Préval government, the UN mission had launched a new, more aggressive campaign against the gangs. I drank my beer, hoping the silence would encourage him to elaborate. Robert looked me in the eyes, his head making a slight bobbing movement. He took another drag from his cigarette, blew the smoke out, held the cigarette as he spread his arms wide. "Can't you feel it?"

I didn't know how to respond.

"It's a new time for Haiti!" He leaned forward in his chair, his whole body humming with excitement. I asked if he thought Préval would be able to stop the violence and bring an end to the insecurity.

"That's done, man!" he said, still excited. The UN had everything confined to a few red zones. Soon, he said, they will have everything under control.

"It's going to be a new phase," he said again. "A new two hundred years of history for Haiti." Did he really think so? He leaned back, the cigarette between his lips, and nodded slowly. "Yeah, man."

He said the crisis was over and Haiti was on the road to recovery. He saw it as a new moment that would be just as significant as the revolution. (It didn't seem to matter to him that the country was occupied by a foreign military.) "I know. I know," he said, as if anticipating what I might say. "We still have kidnappings and all that shit. But we've got it contained to a few areas. You go anywhere else in the country and people are busy planting their gardens. Working. Once we get things calmed down in the city, the diaspora will come back. They'll go back to their hometowns. People will invest. You'll see," he said, smiling. He tilted his head back and closed his eyes, perhaps picturing the scene he had just described.

There was a reason Préval had called his new party Lespwa. He wanted people like Robert to be able to see a possible future again, to be able to feel again the possibility of change, of a new Haiti. But Préval's version of hope was modest at best. In his political speeches, he spoke at length about building roads across the country, as if to lower expectations, to warn people in advance that the problems facing Haiti were so great, the best he could do was to peck away at them one road at a time. He said people should not expect much from him, that he only had five years as president and it would take much longer to fix Haiti. This kind of hope was a stark contrast to Aristide's millenarian dreams, which had promised a total transformation of the country, an end to the suffering of the people, a new world of liberty and justice for all Haitians. If Aristide was a prophet, Préval was a pragmatist. He was also a reluctant politician. Trained as an agronomist, he had spent the last few years in the north of the country, working with peasants to expand agricultural yields and experimenting with bamboo and other fast-growing wood crops. "Préval doesn't want to be president," Robert said. "We had to convince him to do it. That's what will make him so good at it. He's not corrupt. He knows how to do projects. He wants to bring back the peasantry, the countryside. That's what we need."

I wanted to share Robert's vision of a restored peasantry, of a country reborn. It was the same dream that had first drawn me in to the botanic garden project, the same dream that had animated so many people's hopes for decades. But Préval was saying it would take decades to fix Haiti, just as the UN and foreign aid workers and the international community were saying it would take ten, fifteen, twenty-five, or one hundred years. Who could wait that long?

Summer 2007.   After a year-long campaign against the gangs, the city was finally easing into a quiet calm. It seemed the violence was ending. Reflecting on the success of the UN policing operations, head of mission Edmond Mulet declared that Haiti was "living a very special moment in its history." He continued: "I think that it is an exceptional moment. We have the right ingredients. . . . I think that Haiti has an enormous potential." Mulet conceded that the first years of the mission had been hampered by the fact that the provisional government lacked a "legitimate voice." But things had changed. Under the Préval government, the UN mission had the authority to tackle the security situation on its own terms, to take on the work of the state and govern the ungovernable spaces, arrest and kill the bad people, police the country. One year into the policing campaign, Mulet proudly declared that the UN mission had brought peace and stability to the country and set Haiti on a new path.[55] It was a remarkably candid statement, one that seemed to publicly acknowledge the strange legal and political framework that now governed the country. But it was also a surprisingly utopian statement, casting the future of Haiti as radically open.

Even as he said it, few people seemed to believe it. There were exceptions, of course. Robert and others, mostly from the elite, could begin to see a future for the country. People opened their factories again. It was business as usual. For most people, though, business as usual meant a return to the ordinary crises they lived with all the time. It meant a return to such ordinary things as poverty, misery, and hunger. To all those other forms of violence that had always been there. The ones you couldn't police. The ones that never seemed to go away.

"It would be better if they weren't here," Wilfred said. We were at the gift shop again. He said that the UN did nothing, they didn't help anyone.

"It would be better if the U.S. was here," Jean said. He often called the UN mission the "third U.S. occupation." He said everyone thought Haitians would like the UN mission better because the soldiers came from Brazil. "But the master just sent his dogs!" Jean wished the master had come directly—at least the situation would be clear for all to see.

"These guys are no better than the gangs," Toto said. "They're looking to eat too!" He meant that the UN soldiers were all here to make money, and not always in legal ways. There were rumors and reports of UN soldiers involved in drug and sex trafficking. People joked that the UN soldiers were just like tourists—they were here to go to the beach and drink beer and have sex. But they didn't do anything to help the country.

"I think one day we will be fighting them," Jean said. He didn't think the occupation would ever leave without being forced out of the country, and he didn't think they would ever deliver on their promises to rebuild the economy, to help develop Haiti.

Whatever dreams people had of development and progress were soon dashed, as global food prices skyrocketed at the end of 2007 and throughout the following year. In Haiti, the already unaffordable cost of living jumped yet again. There were fuel shortages and food riots. Then there was a series of devastating hurricanes in 2008 that flooded Gonaïves and the surrounding area, causing mass displacements. People complained that the government and the UN mission were not doing anything to stop the violence caused by a ravaged economy and a destroyed environment. As one friend put it, "If it was the gangs doing this they would do something about it. But with ensekirite, they say this is just how things are in Haiti."

"Things must change or we will all be in the ocean," Jean said. We were sitting at the gift shop with Wilfred and Toto. They were telling me how they were struggling, looking for life but not making it. For years now they had been living on borrowed time, borrowed money. Living on the strength of their networks in the city, on their good relations. How long can you live on credit? As Jean's comment suggests, he felt people would have only one option: leaving the country, risking the sharks and the sea and the uncertainty of an undocumented life elsewhere.

I knew, though, that the men who gathered at the gift shop would never leave. To go *lòt bò*, over there, to look for life overseas, was expensive and risky. It was a younger person's game. The more likely scenario for people like Jean was that he would send some of his children overseas, or make renewed appeals to those already working outside of Haiti to send more money back.

"The country too. Haiti is sinking," Wilfred said, adding another layer of meaning to Jean's comment. It wasn't just migrants who were in the ocean, swimming for a distant shore. The whole country was caught up in a situation that couldn't last—like a sinking stone, like a drowning swimmer. Everything was going down, going under.

I tried to think of something to say. Eventually I offered a platitude, an old slogan from the first years of the democratic transition. *Fòk sa chanje.* "Things must change," I said.

Wilfred looked at me, his head nodding slightly. "Yes," he said, without much enthusiasm. "Things must change. But I don't have much hope."

Jean held his hands out in the air. "Ah," he said. "In Haiti, today we have Hope [Lespwa], but we don't have hope."

The others nodded in agreement. Toto even laughed. It took me a moment to understand the joke. Jean was playing on the double meaning of the word *lespwa*, which meant hope but which was also the name of Préval's new political party. He was saying that even though the Hope party was in power, he did not have much hope that things would be different. Préval himself had offered little in the way of hope to those who had voted for him. During the election, when voters complained to him of the high cost of living, complained that they were hungry, that they were living with misery, Préval had responded by saying that everyone had to *naje pou sòti*—swim to get out. A generous interpretation would be that he was saying we all need to move forward, to get out of the current mess. But most people heard him saying it was everyone for themselves and that the only future for most Haitians was to go somewhere else.

"It's always the same," Wilfred said. "This president or that president is coming up. They tell you 'I am going to make change.' But nothing changes. Nothing."

I listened as Jean and Wilfred talked politics. Toto was his usual taciturn self, nodding along but saying little. These men had been active supporters of Aristide and Préval. They had been waiting for two decades for the changes that had been promised them. For how much longer could they wait? After all, hope doesn't buy food.

At the gift shop again. The new campaign against the gangs was in full swing. The UN had stepped up its policing efforts throughout the city, and the Préval government had declared that all gangs must disarm or die. The summer was over, but it was still hot.

Wilfred was telling me about the golden years, when the city was full of tourists. "You could walk through the city at any time, day or night," he said. "We used to dance through the streets, from downtown to Carrefour in the middle of the night. No problem." He said that back then he knew everyone, and not just in Haiti. Many of the tourists who came to Port-au-Prince would return frequently, and they would always come back to see him. "But my friends haven't been back in twenty years," he said, his voice deepening. He used to stay in touch with them. They would send letters, and sometimes money, from Canada, the United States, or elsewhere. But they didn't write him anymore, and he couldn't write to them because his wallet, where he had kept their addresses, had been stolen years ago. He shrugged, as if shaking off the memories. Then he gestured to the street in front of us and said, "We didn't have all this insecurity."

The next day, I was back at the gift shop. This time, we didn't talk about the past, about the good days. This time, we talked about the political crisis, about ensekirite, about living in a blackout. Wilfred's tone was harsher as he spoke.

"In Haiti today," he said, "we can't live. All the things you need to live are too expensive. To live, you have to buy rice, beans, cooking oil, charcoal, and water. I don't have pipes in my house, you see. I send someone to get water. But you need many buckets. To drink, to wash, to cook. I need at least four buckets of water each day. But now, I can't work, I can't eat. I can't live."

Things had been expensive for years. The Haitian gourde was losing value, and prices were going up more and more each year. With less and less work, Wilfred was stuck trying to look for life without much success. He told me, again, about how he had once been offered a job on a cruise ship. He had turned it down after his wife became sick. He told me that he knew he would have more money if he had gone, but that he had needed to stay to help his wife recover and to help raise his four kids. His kids were now all in their twenties. Two of them were looking for life overseas, two were still in the city. "If I didn't return," Wilfred said, "I would have criminals for kids." It was a common refrain in Haiti that the gangs were made up of orphans who had turned to a life of crime because they had not been raised properly. Wilfred looked away.

I asked how his kids were doing. He looked back at me. "They're looking for life too. But they don't find it." He paused for a moment. "Maybe one day I will come home with money and they will kill me."

THE FLAME THAT DOESN'T BURN

Summer 2006.   I was driving through the city with Alexis. Traffic was sparse, the streets almost empty. I looked out the window, watching houses drift by. The late summer sun filled the air, reflecting off the white concrete surfaces. Everything was in sharp contrast, all light and shadow. The streets looked like photographs of a bygone era, a ghost town.

We drove through the popular quarters, or at least the ones where it was safe to go, stopping to check on friends, hear the latest reports. People said UN tanks were firing at houses. They said dozens of people had been killed in recent raids. They showed us bullet holes in the walls of their homes. The official reports from MINUSTAH denied any civilian casualties, but, unlike the police, UN soldiers are not required to investigate where their bullets go.[56]

Later we drove downtown and stopped to eat. Then Alexis took me to see the Marron Inconnu or Nèg Mawon (the Maroon Man), a statue of a runaway slave blowing into a conch shell, calling others to rise up and rebel against slavery. The statue was built by the architect and artist Albert Mangonès in 1967. Two decades later, the UN put a picture of it on a stamp commemorating Article Four of the Universal Declaration of Human Rights, which states that "no one shall be held in slavery or servitude; slavery and the slave trade shall be prohibited in all their forms."[57] During the uprising after the fall of the Duvalier regime, angry crowds had tried to raze the monument. The statue withstood the attacks, but an eternal flame that once burned at its base was extinguished. Alexis pointed to the place where the flame had been and told me a gas line ran underground, from the statue to the National Palace across the road. As if it were the state itself that made the flame burn.

"This isn't it," Alexis said, pointing at the statue. I ran a hand along the base of the monument, touched the foot of the runaway slave. Maybe I needed to confirm it was there. I asked Alexis what he meant. He said the

An unfinished monument. Photo by author.

original was much larger, but it had been taken away and replaced with a small replica. He said the provisional government sold the original to France. "They want to buy all of our monuments."

It wasn't true. The monument we were looking at, the one that I was touching, was the same one Mangonès had built in 1967, that people had attacked in 1986, that UNESCO had relit in August 2004 as part of its year-long global commemoration of the abolition of the slave trade. Yet Alexis was not alone in believing this one to be a fake, a diminished version of one of the most important public testaments to freedom in the country. As we stood by the statue, several passersby approached, all of them saying that the real one had been taken away. It was a pervasive belief—and it seemed to me that it was true, actually. That the stories of the disappearance of the Maroon Man, of his sale to the French, were accurate, even if their truth was different than the obvious materiality of the statue itself. The stories of the disappearance of the Nèg Mawon captured the sense of a diminished freedom, of the recolonization of Haiti, of the theft of the people's power by the provisional government. The extinguishing of the revolutionary flame.

Elsewhere in the city, there is another monument. It towers above the street, a multistory pyramid made of thick slabs of concrete and iron scaffolding. I remember watching as it was being built, years ago, before the coup. At the time, no one seemed to know what it was going to be, although everyone knew that Aristide had commissioned it. He had been building new monuments around the city in anticipation of the upcoming bicentennial. This one, though, was never finished. The construction was halted after the coup. It was meant to be an Eternal Flame, a monument to Haiti's bicentennial and to the country's enduring freedom. But it was never lit. It became a ruin, never completed. A monumental reminder of a future that never was, of dreams that now seem impossible. A flame that will never burn.

5.   Aftermath

There is, in the end, the problem of displacement. Things move and shift, something new comes to occupy the space where you once were. The world that was there is replaced with a different one, like in a dream where everything is a substitute for something else.[1] The new world, the dream world, feels strange and unhomely. You move through it with a sense of uneasy familiarity, since you both recognize it and recognize that things are no longer how they once were. You feel it as a dream, a dream from which you are trying to wake up, or maybe a dream dreamt by someone else, in which you are stuck waiting as the story unfolds around you. What has really happened, you wonder? And you wonder if things can ever be put back the way they were.

You've come here, to a conference held at this prestigious place, to talk about Haiti, to talk about disaster and about what came after. There are other people here talking about other places, other disasters. Before you, on the same panel, there is a psychologist who describes the effects of trauma on children in Gaza.[2] There is a slideshow behind him as he speaks. There are photographs, documents of rubble and ruin. Houses razed by bulldozers and bombs. Concrete buildings reduced to angular sculptures that no one can live in now. The architecture of ruin. There are experts who investigate such ruins, who conduct forensic analyses that move backward in time, from effect to cause, from after to before, so that we can know what happened.[3] As you listen to the psychologist talk about life amid the rubble, as you look at the collapsed houses in Gaza, you are transported back to Haiti, where the houses looked the same. You wonder if rubble looks the same everywhere—all around the world are there the same shards, the same ruins, the same monuments to disaster?

The effect is uncanny. You look at the slideshow, at the aftermath of destruction, at the jagged lines of metal rebar sticking out of gray concrete slabs, at walls tilted and collapsed, roofs where floors once were. You think about how strange it is—houses look so different around the world, people dwelling in such different spaces, and yet ruined houses always look the same. They look like the absence of dwelling, the absence of home. Then you return to the present and remember where you are, you remember these are not photographs of Haiti, these are pictures of the aftermath of war, remnants of deliberate actions. Somebody made those ruins. Somebody destroyed those homes. Wasn't it different in Port-au-Prince? Wasn't the disaster just something that happened, not something that was done? Some called it a natural disaster; some called it an act of God. Maybe it was just bad luck. If that's the case, then why, you wonder, should war and disaster look so much alike? You remember what the city looked like after the earthquake. The crushed houses and the rubble in the streets; the bodies and the bones; the camps for displaced persons; the lines for food and the people who didn't have any. And you begin to think that maybe there was a war there too.

THE WORLD IN FRAGMENTS

I was at home when it happened, in my apartment in Chicago. I don't remember what I was doing, but shortly after it happened, I received a message from a friend. "A big earthquake in Haiti," it said. I checked the news. Tried the telephone. Sent emails. I spent the rest of the night waiting to find out what had happened.

There has been a big earthquake.

It hit Port-au-Prince.

It's bad.

I couldn't reach anyone. The phones and the Internet weren't working. But soon there would be more information. Soon I would see photographs, and then there would be foreign correspondents broadcasting from the city with their own mobile communication systems. I watched as talking heads talked over images of a city turned to dust. Some began to call it the worst disaster in modern history.[4] They said these things as they showed piles of bodies being scooped up in bulldozers, dropped into dump trucks, and taken away to mass graves. They said it as if it were just a news story, something tragic that had happened in a faraway place, a place all too familiar with tragedy, a place where you could come in with your cameras and take pictures of dead bodies and not even ask who they were or what had happened to their families. A place where the dead were just a number, a number that told you, in its cold, calculating way, how bad the disaster was. A number that let you compare it to other disasters. A number that told you how much it would cost to rebuild. A number that told you how sad to feel, so that you could call or text the other numbers, at the bottom of the screen, to send money to help in the rescue and relief efforts.[5]

I sent money. I cried as I watched those bodies being dumped in trucks, my body shaking with grief as my wife held me. Mostly I was in shock, numb as I tried to find any information I could, to find out who was alive and who was not. The silence from Port-au-Prince, the inability to reach people there, was filled by an explosion of possible information as news agencies and survivors uploaded thousands of images to public sites online. Someone made an app that let you scroll through the images and tag them, so you could identify a location or a person. It was a kind of crowdsourced long-distance emergency response. I sat at my computer, looking at pictures. Was that her? Could that be him in the background? I was stuck to my screen, to the pictures and the news sites, to my email and my phone. Slowly, information trickled in about friends and colleagues. It was easiest to confirm things when someone was alive, because you could talk to them, or talk to someone who had talked to them, seen them, touched them. Proof of life. And so, the shock and sadness was punctuated by moments of great joy. Later the news was worse, and you knew people were gone and that you would never see them again.

I arrived in Port-au-Prince two months after the earthquake. The airport was damaged but operational, and commercial flights had been restored. The search-and-rescue phase was over. The international aid apparatus was moving on to relief operations, setting up short-term medical aid, temporary housing, and food and water delivery systems. There were over a thousand official camps set up around the city, sheltering a million and a half internally displaced persons (IDPs). A sea of tents, blue and white tarps flapping in the hot wind.[6]

I met Flore at the airport, after getting my bag. She was a friend's cousin. We had never met, but my friend wanted to make sure I had someone to meet me at the airport. I followed her to her car, a new-model SUV.

"This is Geslin," Flore said, pointing to a young man who stood beside the car. "He's my driver. The best driver in all of Haiti!" Geslin smiled.

We climbed into the car and left. Traffic was thick. There were a lot of people coming to Haiti these days. Journalists, aid workers, doctors, nurses. Maybe even a few tourists. Geslin pulled into a line of SUVs, each with a different logo and acronym on it, each carrying someone who worked on water, sanitation, housing, or some other post-disaster project. "We've got the whole alphabet here," Flore said, laughing.

Flore had been living in the United States for years, but after the earthquake she flew into the neighboring Dominican Republic and came over to Port-au-Prince by land, driving through the mountains. She planned on staying in Haiti for good now. She bought a house in the southern coastal town of Jacmel and found a job with an NGO in Port-au-Prince. "There's so much work," she said. "They're all throwing money around, and they all want to hire Haitians who can speak English and who have gone to university." She laughed—she had left Haiti because there had been no jobs and she couldn't see a future for her here. The quake had changed all that. She thought the disaster would change everything. The reconstruction would revive the economy. Things would be different.

Flore tapped Geslin on the arm. "Wait. Stop here."

Geslin pulled the car to the side of the road.

"Hey!" Flore shouted out the window. A man in a well-pressed suit stood up. He had been sitting on a small wooden box drinking a beer and talking to the women who ran food stalls along the airport road. He walked over to the car, still carrying his bottle, a broad smile on his face.

"Flore!" he said, waving.

"What are you doing here?" she asked. The man leaned through the window and gave her a kiss on the cheek.

"You know me," he said. "I just got back."

"You don't have a car?" Flore asked.

The man said he did, but he had sent the car and his driver out on an errand. "I was going to walk into town," he said. "I like to be with the people!" He gestured behind him to the market women. He drank from his beer and looked at me.

"Get in," Flore said. The man got into the backseat with me.

"I'm Lyonel," he said. We shook hands and I told him my name. Geslin pulled the car back into the street, cutting into the line of traffic.

Lyonel and Flore were old friends. They had grown up together. While she had left to go to school abroad, he had stayed in Haiti to run his family's business. His family owned several garment factories and he had just returned from a trip to Montreal, where he had been brokering a deal with a textile firm. Lyonel seemed excited. I listened as he talked about the earthquake as a great business opportunity. Behind him, I saw slums and shantytowns out the window. Clusters of tents. Places where houses used to be.

We dropped Lyonel off at one of his factories and then drove downtown. I was staying at the Plaza Hotel for a few days. I didn't want to burden anyone by asking them to host me in their house, if they still had one. As we drove through the metal doors, past the armed guards, and into the parking lot behind the hotel, I thought about how the Plaza had come back from the brink of obscurity. Now it was full of guests, all of them paying large sums in U.S. currency. Across the street from the hotel was the central public plaza, where one of the largest camps for IDPs was now located. And behind the tent city there was the National Palace, which had collapsed in on itself.

I invited Flore and Geslin to eat with me. We sat at a table on a patio and talked about the earthquake and the reconstruction. Geslin had been lucky; his house was still standing, although it had been damaged. He had tried to get work with an NGO, but he had been unable to find a job. His aunt had once worked as a cook for Flore's mother, and when he was younger he had worked as a caretaker in her garden. He had stopped only to go to school, but he had not been able to finish his university degree. After she returned, Flore hired him to drive for the family and he was hoping he could parlay the gig into a permanent job as a driver for an NGO.

After they left, I tried to sleep but couldn't. Every time I closed my eyes I saw the city, framed by the car window—a city I had once known but no longer recognized. I saw the city moving, and it seemed to me that it wasn't the car that was moving anymore, that the car was standing still and the city was moving around me, rearranging itself into a jumble of smashed concrete, pancaked houses, and canvas tents. Then the city stopped moving and I felt a great sadness, a great emptiness. I felt like someone had punched a hole in the world. I felt as if I were standing in the place where the world had once been.

In the morning, after breakfast, I went out into the road. Buildings were still standing here, in this part of the city, although many of them were cracked and damaged. Some were leaning in on themselves, others hung over the street. I walked through hard angles and strange shapes. The street was like a puzzle. I could recognize each piece on its own but couldn't make sense of the whole. Nothing was where it was supposed to be.

A large concrete slab dangled over the sidewalk. There had been an advertisement painted on it, perhaps for beer or a cell phone provider. Here and there, bright swatches of red and yellow stuck out, but mostly the slab was gray, the outer surface of the concrete cracked and chipped away, revealing its powdery interior. The wall was slowly becoming limestone again, as small clouds blew off in the wind, covering everything in a fine layer of chalky dust. I bent down to walk under the slab, then thought better of it and stepped into the street. A man was inside the building, chipping away at it, pulling out the rebar that had been in the wall.

I remembered a conversation I'd had a few weeks earlier with an engineer. He was a Haitian American who had been hired by an international firm to head a team sent to assess structural damage. Many buildings had been completely destroyed, but many others had only been damaged, and the task now was to determine which of those could be salvaged and which had to be torn down. He told me his team had three colors of spray paint. They went house by house, building by building, making determinations about the structural integrity of the remains. Any structure that was critically unsafe was marked with red. Buildings that were significantly damaged but potentially repairable were marked with yellow, warning people not to go inside until they were repaired. Buildings that were structurally sound were marked with green. I had met the engineer in New York, at a conference about emergency and disaster response. He said they had already checked a lot of buildings. "People were already back inside them, living in them and working in them. So, we marked them yellow or green. But really, they should probably all be red. If we were doing this in the U.S., they would all be marked red." He shrugged. "Most of the buildings in Port-au-Prince don't meet international safety standards anyway. That was before the earthquake. So how do you assess their safety after it?" I knew what he was saying. In the world of disaster relief, international standards and best practices are often revised downward, to fit the local context.[7]

I continued walking, trying to make sense of the street. A friend had told me that the Artist Gift Shop was still standing, and I wanted to see it for myself. The same friend had said Wilfred was alive, but I had not been able to reach him, and I had heard nothing about the other men who gathered at the shop. I stopped at a corner and stood for a moment beside a photocopier. It had slid into the sidewalk. Once there had been a small shop here that made copies for people. There was a small niche market for documents in the city, and there had been several kiosks on this street that catered to those who needed papers printed or copied, or maybe even forged. Now the outer walls of the shop were gone, leaving the copier, a desk, and a chair exposed. Somehow the upper floors had not fallen down and crushed the shop. They had simply disappeared. Shaken into dust.

A man came around the corner. When he saw me looking at the copier, he said the shop wasn't open today, they didn't have electricity. But he said to come back to see him if I needed copies. He would be open again soon. A motorbike drove down the road, the driver weaving around a pile of rocks in the middle of the street. His passenger was holding a cake box steady on his lap. The bike turned down a side street. I watched it drive through the rubble, past a house that had fallen on a car.

I walked on. The street was starting to look more familiar, but that was strange too. I passed a two-story wooden building that seemed unscathed. In the midst of all this destruction, how could something still be standing, unharmed? Perhaps the wood had been flexible enough to bend but not break. Perhaps there was hidden damage somewhere. I saw a green circle painted on the building, beside the front door. A team had declared it safe.

A hand touched my arm. I turned to see a young man beside me. "*Gade deyò,*" he said, pointing above us. Look out.

I looked up. There was a nest in the sky above our heads. I couldn't understand what it was. I tried to follow the lines of the thing, to figure out its shape. How did it get so tangled? The nest was hanging from a thick black line. A metal box in the center glinted in the sun. More lines radiated outward from it.

"What is it?" I asked.

"*Liy kouran,*" the young man said, gesturing for me to move. Power lines.

He pointed again, this time not at the nest above us but at two lines dangling down, almost touching my shoulder as they swayed in the wind. I stepped back, now understanding what he was telling me. The man with the photocopier had said there was no power, but I imagined these two lines full of electricity, I imagined them gently moving toward each other, coming together in an explosion of sparks above my head, sending a shock through my body, the power coursing through me and then out through the bottom of my feet and into the ground.

I took another step away from the dangling lines. The young man had left before I could thank him. He was already far down the street. I watched as he turned into a square concrete building. The front wall was gone and the roof hung out at an odd angle. Through the missing wall I watched him climb the stairs to the second floor. Then he moved deeper into the building and disappeared from view.

I continued. It wasn't much farther now. Soon I could see the gift shop up ahead. My friend had been right, it was still there. It looked fine. No damage. My pace quickened. And then I was there.

"Hello," I called, looking inside. The same paintings still hung on the walls, the same crafts still sat on the floor and the shelves. But there seemed to be no one there.

"Eh, eh!" a voice called.

I turned and saw Wilfred coming toward me, smiling. "Are you looking for me?" he said. And then I saw that Alexis was with him. I ran over to them. "Alexis! Wilfred! You're alive!"

"Yes," Alexis said. "We're here."

THE ROAD TO MAPOU

Fall 2006.   Dany drove slowly over the rocks. The front left side of the car lifted off the ground and came back down gently. Then the back tire did the same. Now the right side went up and over, down and up again. It was a good car, and Dany was an excellent driver, but I was still bouncing around in the backseat, trying to find something to hold on to. I winced each time we went over a rock, expecting to hear a crunch or scrape or the sound of metal being pierced, the sound of the underside of the car being torn away by the rocks below, by the rocks that were really boulders, by the rocks that had come rolling down the side of the mountain and settled into the middle of the road. The road that had once been a river.

The four of us—Dany, Suzanne, Paul, and I—were traveling through a gorge left by a river that had run dry. The other road, or rather the thing that had once been a road, was impassable, gutted and rutted and torn up from trucks and rainstorms and mudslides. Now all the traffic in the area went through the old riverbed and the gorge, which also meant it went through the remains of a small village. The village had been next to the river, and it was easy to imagine an idyllic past, some pastoral scene of peasant life in which a few tightly knit families once lived here, in houses beside a rushing river. They had water to drink and water for their fields. They farmed on land that they owned and they grew their own food, lived their own lives here, far from the city. Sometimes, when they had more than they needed, the women from the village would walk over the mountain pass and sell food or small handicrafts at the weekly markets there.

That village was gone, if it had ever existed. As we drove over the riverbed, I could see what remained. A few houses still stood, but no one was in them and they were leaning to the side, waiting to fall over. There had been a cemetery near the riverbank, with big, brightly painted tombs built to house the dead, to honor the ancestors who had founded the village and who had gone under the water and crossed over to Ginen to join the lwa. The tombs had collapsed as the ground beneath them gave way to erosion and runoff. Portions of them stuck up in the air, the stone and paint now faded by the sun and worn by the wind.

Dany stopped the car and we all looked out the windows. We sat quietly for a moment, then started again. The car went up and over the rocks as Dany eased us through the riverbed. Eventually the gorge opened onto a flat rocky plain and we picked up speed. Later there was a road, a real road, with a small town running alongside it. Beyond the road were mountains. Beyond the mountains were more mountains.[8]

It was an accidental expedition. The week before, I'd had a strange dream: I was in the high mountains of Haiti, living in a wooden house painted blue and green. I opened the shutters and looked out on a valley below. Birds flew by in the distance and I could hear the sounds of animals on farms, people in their fields. The sounds of life. Then I jumped out the window and flew in the air, over a hill covered in pine trees. I flew until the clouds came in and settled around me. Then I woke up.

The next day, I told Georges about my dream. He grew quiet. He held my arm, and in a serious voice he told me it was an important message. "You must go to the mountains," he said. "There are invisible forces that guide us," he said. He likened dreams to the experience of searching in an archive and unexpectedly finding something you didn't know you were looking for. I thought of such experiences in terms of the unconscious, but Georges said the lwa worked in this way. They came in dreams and told you what to do.

I didn't make much of it until later that day, when I got a phone call from Suzanne. She was planning a trip to the Forêt des Pins (Pine Forest), a national protected area on the top of a mountain chain in the southeast of the country, near the border with the Dominican Republic. Suzanne was going on a scouting mission, to see if it would be possible to offer tourist packages out to the pine forest to UN staff and their families. She asked if I wanted to come with her. Dany would drive, and my friend Paul, an agronomist, would come too. We spent the next few days planning the trip. We were all eager to get out of the city for a while—especially Suzanne, who still had a cast on her arm after an attempted carjacking the month before. Suzanne wanted to check out a guest house in Thiotte and a waterfall along the southern road to the Pine Forest. She thought they would both be good additions to a package tour. Paul and I wanted to see the forest and talk to any local rangers who might still be working there about logging, charcoal production, and deforestation. We also wanted to see the villages of Mapou and Fond Verettes, which were just beyond the Pine Forest; they had been flooded two years earlier by a tropical storm. After several days of planning, we packed Suzanne's car and headed out of the city.

It was a long drive even though it was a short distance. We had decided to approach the forest from the south because the roads were in better condition, but still there were points that seemed impassable. Dany's skills were immediately apparent. He would downshift to avoid the worst of the ruts, and he would skirt the edge of the road to allow the large, overloaded trucks to pass us. He took it slow and steady, although steady became a relative word. As we made our way into the mountains, I recalled my first trip into the countryside, when my wife and I had taken a bus from Port-au-Prince to the northern city of Cap-Haïtien. A major national highway runs between the two cities, which are only about 240 kilometers apart, but still the trip had taken over twelve hours. The bus kicked up gravel and dust as we drove through small towns. When we passed through Gonaïves, a few small boys leaped up on the side of the bus and held on to the open windows. They made quick deals with the passengers, selling small sachets of water. Later we stopped when the bus blew a tire. All the passengers got off. Some of them bought food at market stalls on the side of the road. We were high in the mountains and the air was cool. Small clouds drifted by, so low you could touch them. The tire was fixed and we returned to the bus, but coming down the mountain the engine caught fire. We pulled over for quick repairs and then hit the road again. Now running very late, the driver took to speeding and it seemed as if we would launch off the side of the road into the valley below.

Driving through the southern mountains now, remembering that ride to the north, I thought of René Préval's recent campaign promise. He had told his supporters that he would build roads in the country, that he would be the president who built roads. It had seemed like such an anemic campaign promise in a country that needed so much, and yet, driving to the Pine Forest, it was easier to understand what a road might mean.

We stopped at Cascade Pichon, one of the locations Suzanne wanted to scout. Decades ago, Jean-Claude Duvalier had declared it one of the country's premier tourist destinations, back when there were tourists. It was beautiful, even if it had taken us the better part of the day to get there. A freshwater spring inside the mountain burst out of the cliff-side, sending dozens of small waterfalls cascading down the rock face. At the bottom was a large lake, filled with clear blue water. A few men were bathing at the shore, and a group of women stood farther into the lake, washing clothes near several large rocks. Suzanne took pictures of the waterfall, and we chatted briefly with some women sitting in the shade of a tall tree. They seemed surprised we had traveled so far from the city. I tried to imagine

Suzanne bringing a group of tourists here. They would no doubt appreciate the beautiful landscape, but it took so long to get here, and there was no infrastructure nearby to service them—no hotels, bad roads, no places to go other than the falls. What would they do? Would they swim in the lake as the men and women from the nearby villages did their washing? For the people who lived here, the water was part of a domestic world of work, not a place for leisure and recreation.

We ate a snack under a tree, then returned to the car and continued up the mountain. Along the way, we saw a farm with a couple of large tents on it. We pulled off the road and took a dirt path toward the center of the farm, which was quite big, much bigger than any peasant farms I had seen in the area. A man, who turned out to be the property owner, came to greet us as we got out of the car. It was a strawberry farm, and the tents were to protect the soft berries from the harsh sun. He showed us around and let us pick fresh, juicy berries. We ate them as he told us about his business. His family had owned the land for years but had mostly paid peasants to farm it. Recently they had expanded into a few niche crops, supplying local restaurants in the city. The strawberries were a new venture that had proved quite lucrative. He could make more money selling them than he ever had before with coffee, the main cash crop in the southern mountains.

We chatted a bit longer, thanked him for the strawberries, then left, the strawberry fields receding into the distance behind us. It had been a little oasis and a nice break from the bumpy road and the heat of the car. Once we were back on the road, though, Paul started to tell us how all the big farms in Haiti were taking the best agricultural land away from peasants.

"All this land," he said, pointing outside the car windows. "It should be used to grow food!"

Paul was upset. For him, the only viable future for Haiti was one in which there was a concerted effort to restore the peasantry, to invest in agriculture, and to make the country self-sufficient. Most peasants grow export crops like coffee. Having so much land set aside for exports or niche products that only catered to the urban elite was, for Paul, an irrational and ultimately destructive use of the land. Haiti imports the vast majority of its food, and the dependence on imported food—or, increasingly, on food aid— leaves many Haitians defenseless against fluctuations in the global price of foodstuffs. To make things worse, growing export crops like coffee leaves peasant families doubly dependent on the vagaries of the global market.[9]

I recalled previous conversations with Paul, when we had talked about the crisis in the countryside, about the steep decline in food production, and about the problem of land ownership and land use in Haiti. Once, when

I had just returned from a trip to the north, I remarked to him that I was surprised to see so many peasant farms. I had expected to see more large estates, with fewer people on them. Paul nodded at me and smiled. "Yes," he said, holding a slender finger in the air. "It is true. Everywhere you look you see a peasant. On every piece of land there is a peasant." He paused, smiling again. "But that does not mean that every peasant has a piece of land."[10]

We arrived in Thiotte a few hours before sundown. The guesthouse we were staying in was near the center of town. It was a surprisingly large complex, with a house for the family, a house and kitchen for guests, and another large concrete building used for group meetings. Marie Solange, the woman who owned the compound, welcomed us and showed us to our rooms. The guesthouse was full. Marie Solange told us she had a few guests most nights, but weekends were always busy. Most of the guests were truck drivers who brought overloaded trucks full of goods from the mountain villages and markets down to the city. Sometimes, though, there were groups of missionaries or, occasionally, aid workers.

After we unpacked, I decided to take a walk through the town. Paul and Suzanne joined me, and as we left the compound a few young boys approached us. They led us on a tour of sorts, showing us a new school that had recently been built by the government. It was a low concrete building with two rooms and a tin roof. After it was finished, the boys said, the government had promised to send a teacher but a teacher never came, so the school was still empty. We passed the center of town, where there was a government administrative building, its walls covered in peeling paint. A few yards away, there was an old army vehicle stuck in a muddy ditch at the side of the road. A small thicket had grown up around it. I joked that it looked old enough to be from the U.S. occupation, but Paul said it looked like it was from the Duvalier era. The hood was propped up with a stick, and most of the engine and much of the rest of the mechanical systems were gone, leaving just a fading green metal husk.

From the point of view of the capital, Thiotte is a remote commune far from the hub of social, economic, and political life. But it is well situated between the coastal town of Belle-Anse and the mountain villages of the South-East and West departments. Coffee is king in these mountains, but there seemed to be a thriving trade in other agricultural goods, as well as in charcoal, lumber, and a wide assortment of food and other commodities coming over the nearby border. Later that night, back at the guesthouse, we learned more about the town from Marie Solange. She had lived there her whole life, and she said the town had grown significantly over the past few decades, as peasants sold or lost their land and moved to town to open shops. Some families lived in the town but worked elsewhere. She said there were many men who worked in Belle-Anse or even in Port-au-Prince. They commuted on trucks, packed in alongside bags of coffee or charcoal, traveling up and down the mountains each week. So many trucks now passed through the town that it had become a kind of economic center for the region, as people set up businesses to cater to the truck drivers and migrants. There were bars, hotels, restaurants, and auto repair shops. There were several new churches, all Protestant. And there were markets at which traders bought goods that they packed into large sacks to send elsewhere on the trucks. Or they bought large sacks of goods—cooking oil or food or charcoal—and broke them down into smaller units to sell to the women who came from surrounding villages to buy household necessities.

On our tour, the boys had described Marie Solange as the wealthiest person in town. It was easy to believe them. The guesthouse had electrical power from a generator, and as we chatted, Marie Solange's teenage children watched a movie on a VCR and television set in the corner. The bedroom floors were covered in wall-to-wall carpet, something I had never seen in Haiti. Marie Solange told me that her husband, who worked in a factory in New Jersey, would return several times each year with money and various goods. Last year he had brought the carpet, telling her that every floor of every house in New Jersey was covered in it. It was strange to walk on carpet here, where the humid but cool air made it feel spongy and wet. I could only imagine, though, the pride that she and her husband felt each time he returned with something—a roll of carpet, another television set (they had two already), or a VCR. These were unheard-of luxury items in the countryside, items that people associated with the city or with the bigger cities "over there," in the United States and Canada. Marie Solange told us that she and her husband were Christian, by which she meant they were not Catholic and they did not serve the Vodou lwa. They had converted to Protestantism decades ago. Her husband had joined a church abroad that was full of other Haitian migrants, and she had converted a few years later, joining a church in town.[11]

We went to bed early, tired from the long drive. The next morning, I awoke to the sound of chickens in the yard and to the smell of coffee brewing over a charcoal fire. I washed up in a tiled bathroom stall. The guesthouse had plumbing, further proof that the boys had been right, that Marie Solange was the wealthiest woman in town. I filled a bucket with cold water from a pipe in the wall, then washed with the bucket and a cloth. We ate spaghetti for breakfast, with fresh bread and coffee. Then we all got back in the car and left, driving out of town and heading north, toward the forest.

I could already smell the pine trees. The smell reminded me of my home in Canada. So, too, did the cool morning air, although we were high enough in the mountains now that the air would remain cool all day, and many of the men we passed on the road, men on their way to check on their goats or their fields, wore wool caps and long sleeves. After about an hour we arrived. We pulled into the national park, and Dany found a shady spot to park the car. There was no one around, no rangers or park officials, so we wandered about aimlessly. Suzanne and Paul had both been here before, but not for several years. Paul immediately started looking at the trees, examining the size of the trunks and the spacing between the pines, bending down to examine the other foliage that was growing amid the needles that covered the forest floor. Suzanne and I walked off into the forest, leaving Paul to his survey. Dany opted to stay with the car.

"The cabins are over here," Suzanne said, pointing through the trees. I had heard there were wooden guesthouses up here, that families used to vacation in the forest during the hottest weeks of the summer. Georges had once described the place to me as being like Switzerland, which turned out to be an apt description, since the cabins, when we found them, looked like Swiss chalets. There were several of them scattered in a clearing in the middle of the forest. We walked up to them but they were all empty and shuttered, with locks and chains on the doors. Suzanne was disappointed. She had hoped they would be operational and that she would be able to bring tourists here to stay the night. It was too long a trip to do in a day.

We walked quietly among the trees. I was taken aback. I had rarely seen such forest coverage in Haiti. I thought of the forest in Martissant and of the deforested and eroded hillsides throughout the country.

"There are supposed to be rangers here," Suzanne said as we walked.

Paul approached us. "They've been cutting the trees," he said, pointing to a stand of trees behind him. He waved for us to follow him. He said the trees were too thin, they must be from a reforestation campaign.

"The trees should be bigger," he said. "Thicker. These are new trees, young trees. And look here." He crouched down and pointed to the base of several trees. The bark was black from the ground to about a foot high on the trunk. I ran a hand over the blackened bark. It was dry and brittle, and the ground around the tree was ashy.

"Someone's been burning the trees," Paul said. It was a common practice on state land. If you lit a small fire at the base of a tree, it would burn the outside. Over time, the burnt base would kill the entire tree. Once it was dead, you could legally harvest it, since the laws against cutting trees applied only to living ones. Paul pointed to the adjacent stands of trees. They were all blackened around the base, dozens of dying trees. It was a concerted effort, a well-funded operation. Someone had planned this. They had probably hired local peasants to build the fires and paid off the rangers, wherever they were. Someone was logging the forest.[12]

Paul stood up and looked around. He shook his head slowly in dismay. We had spoken several times about the problems of logging and charcoal production. The cities were hungry for wood for building materials and fuel. And peasants were in desperate need of cash. It was a vicious cycle. Paul had hoped there would be rangers and guards in the forest, and other signs of government protection. He had told me repeatedly that the state needed to develop the infrastructure that would allow it to manage and protect the national parks, including better roads so that government officials could travel to remote areas. He had even dreamed, once, that tourism might help protect the environment, on the assumption that if people came here to enjoy the trees, to be in the natural world, they would become politically invested in responding to the environmental crisis. Now, as we walked back to the car, he said, perhaps only to himself, "This is only going to get worse."

I asked him what he meant.

"When they fix the roads," he said. "Think of how many trees they can take when Préval builds the roads."

When we left the forest, we went north and west, driving for about an hour until we found the village of Mapou. Or, rather, until we found the place where Mapou used to be.

Mapou was once nestled in a small valley between the mountains. The valley had good land for growing crops, and the surrounding mountainsides were ideal for herding goats and growing coffee. The slopes around the village were gentle enough that rainfall provided irrigation to the fields without inundating them. Or, at least, that was the case until two years ago, when the village had been hit by a series of deadly storms.

In May 2004 it rained for weeks. The village was flooded. Houses, animals, and people washed away in the rain. So, too, did the already terrible roads, making much of the remote area inaccessible. The U.S. military, which was in the country responding to the fallout of the coup, had used helicopters to airdrop food and other supplies. Across the southern mountains, aid workers estimated that at least two thousand people had been killed by the storms in Haiti and the neighboring Dominican Republic.

Thousands of homes were destroyed and over eleven thousand people were displaced. At the time, people called it "one of the worst natural disasters in Caribbean history."[13] It was a designation that wouldn't hold true for long.

When the rains came, the fertile valley became a bowl that filled with water as high as the trees. Now, two years later, the water was gone, but little remained of the valley. The few trees still standing were dead, headless palms waiting to fall to the ground. In the aftermath of the flood, the village had been moved to higher ground. Two years after the storms, the survivors were still displaced, living in torn tents in a small relief camp, although most of the aid workers were long gone. Most families were still struggling to recover. People had lost their homes and their animals, not to mention their loved ones. They had lost their crops, and the land had remained flooded and wet for so long that many farmers had been unable to replant anything. Some were planning on moving back, while others were thinking of moving on, moving to a nearby town, or to the capital, or maybe trying their luck in the Dominican Republic. A double displacement.

As we left, I read the wooden signs that stood at the entrance to the camp. They were like advertisements, proudly announcing the many international organizations that had provided building materials and food to the villagers. At the edge of the camp was a single-story concrete building. I thought it might be an administrative center, but as we got closer I saw it was a bakery. An enterprising family had set up shop. A symbol that the temporary encampment was becoming permanent.

We took the inland road back to the city. In terms of distance it was much shorter than the way we had come, but the roads were much worse and it took us the rest of the day to make it home. We were quiet on the way back, partly so that Dany could concentrate on the task at hand, partly, perhaps, out of fear of a crash. Partly, too, because we had been saddened by the trip. Dany took the car through the mountains with a calmness that seemed to me out of proportion with the dangers ahead. He drove deftly across the single-lane switchbacks. He found room at the side of the road when the overloaded trucks came barreling at us at high speeds, sometimes hugging the inside of the lane, so close it seemed we could touch the mountainside from the car windows, sometimes skirting the gravelly edges where there were no guardrails, only the empty space between the cliff and the valley below.

ORDINARY DISASTERS

On the way back from Mapou, we came out of the mountains and down to a flat rocky plain. Looking back at the mountains, we could see the green tree canopies on the top give way to brown slopes with fewer trees and thinner soil, and then, closer to the ground, the mountains were a gleaming white where the dirt had been carved away to reveal the limestone underneath. These white spots were the mountains' bones *(zo)*, the skeletal insides that had once been covered by tissues of soil and trees.

"Look at the erosion," I said, pointing at the bones.

"It's not erosion," Paul said. "Those are mines."

I looked again through the back window. Paul continued: "They mine the rocks, the limestone, and they use it to make concrete. They are slowly picking the mountains apart."

We drove on in silence. I thought about all the squatter settlements in Martissant, the ones that hung on the slopes of Morne l'Hôpital so that the mountain above the city was no longer covered in soil and trees but was now covered in houses upon houses, houses made of concrete, made of concrete that had once been a mountain. Houses made of bones.

The mountains and the mines faded into the distance. On the way to the city, we drove through Croix-des-Bouquets, with its goat markets and artisan workshops. Alongside the road, we passed a large area where men were making concrete blocks for construction. The same blocks that were sold in the city, that people used to build their houses. A few men worked with shovels to mix the concrete in piles on the ground. Others poured it into molds. We drove past row after row of blocks drying in the late afternoon sun. The mountain's bones, pressed into new shapes.

A few days after we returned to Port-au-Prince, a tropical storm hit the city and it rained for twelve hours. I spent the day in a leaky house, anxiously watching as the storm blew trees and signs down. The rain and wind seemed to come from all directions. Water poured through the city streets, rushing down to the canals and to the bay below. I watched as a lone van drove down a sloped road, skidding and sliding on top of the gushing water. I watched until the van disappeared at the end of the street, hoping that it would not crash or flip over.

The storm had been expected. It was, after all, the rainy season, the time of year when the rains bring much-needed water to the land and the trees, to the farms and the rivers. But sometimes there is too much rain. Sometimes the storms are too strong and the ground cannot hold the water. It comes running down the mountains furiously, taking people and animals and houses with it. These are the lavalas, the floods. They are so common now that the rainy season regularly brings disaster. Just as people have come to expect blackouts, they also expect mudslides and floods in the rainy season and drought and hunger in the dry season. The oscillation between drought and flood, between dearth and superfluity, marks out the rhythm of daily life. Underneath it all, the ever-present anticipation of disaster.

After the floods that destroyed Mapou, the United Nations Development Programme (UNDP) launched a flash appeal for funding to provide relief to the village and to the surrounding area. In their appeal, they described Haiti as "one of the Caribbean's most disaster-prone countries."[14] Unless the underlying problems of environmental degradation and poverty were addressed, the UNDP warned, there would be more and worse disasters in the future. And, of course, there were. In September 2004, just months after the flooding of Mapou, Tropical Storm Jeanne struck Gonaïves. It killed thousands of residents, destroyed tens of thousands of homes, and displaced hundreds of thousands of people. The city was underwater for weeks and the damage was extensive. Farms and fields were flooded, crops were lost, and most of the city's infrastructure was damaged or destroyed. Meteorologists have since classified Tropical Storm Jeanne as one of the deadliest Atlantic hurricanes.[15]

The flooding of Gonaïves was devastating, but it was hardly a unique event. The scale of the damage was much larger than the flooding of Mapou, but the underlying facts were the same. Both cases were examples of what Mike Davis calls "ordinary disaster," by which he means the "explosive mixture of natural hazards and social contradictions."[16] In the academic field of disaster studies, it is commonplace to say that there is no such thing as a natural disaster, that there is nothing natural or given about disaster. But just because disasters are not natural—they emerge out of the mixture of natural hazards like hurricanes or earthquakes and the artificial fault lines of inequality—does not mean they are not normal. Many disasters are, as Charles Perrow put it, "normal accidents," the tragic results of social systems that, because of their scale and complexity, are bound to fail. What defines disaster, for most people, is not the event or even the cause, but rather the effect, the "social calculus" according to which some people live and others die.[17]

When Tropical Storm Jeanne hit, there was little anyone could do. The Civil Protection Directorate (Direction de la Protection Civile, DPC) that had been set up to respond to such disasters was itself chronically unprepared. Worse, the DPC offices in Gonaïves had been sacked during the coup. After the floods, the few police stations that remained in the area were also attacked and looted.[18] The provisional government declared a state of emergency and appealed for international support. The Red Cross tried to reach the city, but their trucks were stopped at the city limits by angry crowds who stole the food and supplies. The city had no electricity or water, and hospitals and government buildings were damaged or destroyed. The flood-water was as high as ten feet in many areas. There were no shelters for the displaced and no plan for how to deal with the dead bodies.

The UN mission eventually mobilized in response, although I heard many people complain they had waited too long. They used helicopters to bring food and water and medical supplies to the city, and they authorized mass graves for the bodies amid public fears of the health risks posed by the sheer number of corpses. Bodies were buried without being identified, which only added to the uncertainty and trauma of the disaster, because family members and the government were both unable to determine who was dead and who was missing. Almost a week after the storm, the World Food Programme began sending trucks to the city, but armed gangs attacked the trucks and the distribution centers, stealing food and threatening aid workers.[19] Four years later, in September 2008, the same scenario played out again as four tropical storms hit Gonaïves in less than a month. The city, still recovering from Jeanne, was ruined again. Yet again, the roads to the city were impassable and it was difficult to deliver aid to the survivors. Yet again, houses and other buildings were damaged and thousands of people were displaced. The fertile agricultural zones around the city were hit, too, and about 70 percent of local crops were destroyed. That same year, a global spike in food prices caused riots around the country.[20] And that, too, was an ordinary disaster.

THE THING

Far under the ground, beneath the town of Léogâne, two sections of the earth's crust moved. They had been locked in a slow grind for centuries, moving over and under each other, causing tension to build in the land above them. In geological time, this oblique collision happened slowly. But in human terms it was very fast. At 4:53 P.M. on January 12, 2010, the col-lision shook the world above for less than a minute. The ground made a loud noise. And then everything started to collapse. Later the shaking would repeat, again and again, in a series of strong aftershocks that lasted for months.[21]

"I was at work when it happened," Georges said. We were sitting outside drinking beer. It was a pleasantly cool evening in March, two months after the earthquake. Georges was telling me about how he had survived.

"I was on the top floor of the building. I don't know what happened, but I felt something." He looked at me, to see if I understood. "Before the building started to shake I felt something," he said. "And in that moment, I knew that I had to get out. Everyone started to run. Three flights of stairs. I ran down the stairs and then down the hall and finally out the door. And just like that," he said, smacking his hands together, "the building collapsed behind me."

He looked at me over the top of his glasses. I didn't say anything. Finally, he spoke again. "If I had been a second slower I would be dead."

Everyone had similar stories, at least those who were still alive to tell stories. There was always the suddenness of the quake, the quickness of the collapse. Some were stuck inside but survived, living under walls and ceilings for hours or days. Some were covered in dust and debris, some were untouched when the city imploded. Like so many others, Georges helped those he could, those who were stuck in the rubble of their offices. Later he would make his way through the shattered streets to his home, which was still standing, and to his wife and children, who were still alive.

Later that night, looking over my notes, I thought of Georges again and of the others like him who had survived. As he told it, he sensed but did not know what was happening. He felt it, and in feeling it, he acted quickly enough to outrun a possible death. It happened so fast that it was only after it was over, after the world stopped shaking, at least momentarily, that people began to understand what had happened to them. And it was even later, as no help arrived, as they tried in vain to reach family and friends, as they moved about the city and saw the extent of the damage, that a larger picture of the event began to take shape. How do you make sense of something so vast, so unthinkable? In the aftermath, there were many names for the quake. It would be called *douz* (twelve), in honor of the date; it would be called *goudougoudou*, an onomatopoeic expression that captures the sound the earth made when it shook; it would be called a *tranbleman tè*, an earthquake; the experts would call it a temblor. Georges called it *bagay la*. The thing.[22]

The thing. In English it sounds ominous, like a living abstraction, but in Kreyòl it is quite specific, quite concrete. You just have to know what it means. *Bagay* is one of the most common words in Kreyòl. It means "thing," but it can mean just about anything. People use the word to point out objects around them, even if those objects have names. They also use it to talk about events or happenings. In linguistic terms, this is a kind of context-specific mode of indexical reference, a way of designating things and actions in the world that relies on a shared sense of spatial and temporal reference points. You have to be there during the conversation to understand the meaning of an utterance like "Give me that thing." And you have to know who is speaking and what the broader terms of reference are to understand someone when they tell you a story about "when that thing happened." When Georges called the quake a thing, he wasn't making it into an object or an abstraction. He was giving a name to a situation, to a happening. What went unspoken was all the rest—the thing that happened *to me*, the thing that happened *to us*. It was as if he were talking about the very process of objectification itself, about how the disaster had obliterated not only the material stuff of everyday life but the very possibility of being an active and willing subject in the world.

In the first days and weeks after the quake, there was a rush not only to intervene to help people, but also to explain the meaning of the quake, its significance. It was called the worst disaster in modern history, and it eclipsed by far all those other "worst disasters" like the floods in Mapou and Gonaïves. There were comparisons to other earthquakes, including a much stronger one in Chile later that same year, where only a fraction of the number of people died. There were endless details, as if the list of the number of buildings destroyed or the number of people killed would some-how capture the meaning of what had happened. As if you could list all the schools and hospitals, all the government buildings and churches, all the roads and bridges, all the dwellings and buildings that were now gone and, in the act of listing them, have some account of the event. The accounting was, of course, important, since it bore directly on how much aid might be sent to the country. But the most easily measurable things are not always the most important.[23]

When I returned to Haiti after the quake, I was surprised that anyone was still alive. I was surprised to find Wilfred and Alexis where they always were, sitting and waiting, looking for life. I was surprised to see Georges, even though we had spoken over the phone. Surprised, too, that Robert was alive and well, despite having been badly injured. He had been lucky enough to be sent to a medical tent far from the city, where he was spared what so many others had to endure—the amputation of a crushed limb. A friend was living in his car because his house had collapsed. Another friend showed me the ruins of his house. He had rented it, along with another family. Two families in one house, taking turns living in it, as if living were a shift you took, with one family using the house during the day and the other at night. He had not been home, but the other family had been. They were gone, along with the house, and he was living in a tent with his wife and children. I walked down a street in Martissant, past the empty space where a school had once stood. Incredibly, amid the rock and rubble, someone had set a small potted plant on a flat chunk of concrete, its green leaves the only thing that wasn't gray.

I wrote down the names of the dead and missing. The stories of survival. People told me about those first nights, about the fear that the quake might trigger a tsunami, about how everyone had helped one another, how they had spent the night with strangers, with the other survivors. About how, all through the darkened city, people were singing, their voices a beacon rising up in the night. They told me how much it had meant to know that others were out there too, that others had survived. But the thing that surprised me the most was that everyone, myself included, had so much hope. Hope that finally, after all this, things would change.[24]

Maybe I shouldn't have been surprised. As Rebecca Solnit has noted, hope and disaster often go together, as the shared experience of a terrible event gives rise to a sense of solidarity.[25] There was already a strong tradition of mutual assistance in Haiti before the quake. That is, after all, how most people live. They build relations, they have obligations, they help others just as, one day, they too are helped. They share money and food, they share stories. After the quake, these practices of *youn ede lòt*, helping one another, were extended beyond kin and friends to strangers. Survival was a collective effort.[26]

The thing happened, but it didn't just happen. Like everything else in life, disasters are complex. They have a history and an afterlife. We feel them sometimes as a moment out of time, as something extraordinary, as a thing set apart. And yet they are deeply embedded in the contours of social life. Even an earthquake, which geologists will tell you is beyond the realm of human action, is a kind of social thing. If the ground shakes and there is no one there to feel it, does it still happen? Better to ask, does it still matter?

The anthropologist Anthony Oliver-Smith has suggested we think of disasters as processes, not events.[27] As multidimensional occurrences that take shape at the intersection of social life and the physical world. Perhaps the most important aspect in the making of a disaster is what he and others call *vulnerability*. Vulnerability could be a shoddily constructed house. It could be watered-down concrete. It could be a bare mountainside underneath a hurricane. It could be crushing poverty that forces some people to live in harm's way, to live with the risk of possible or even certain death. In Haiti, vulnerability means that sometimes when you look for life, you die. In Port-au-Prince, vulnerability was built into the very foundations of social life.

Vulnerability is only one way of explaining why some things become disastrous. Another way to think about disaster is to think about its effects, not just the material ones of crushed homes and broken bones, but the psychological and social ones. Seen in this way, disaster is not the blow but the wound it leaves behind. It is the outcome of what happened that matters, the way it lingers in the landscape, or the way it scuttles our sense of trust in the institutions that govern our lives. To come through such disasters, disasters that the sociologist Kai Erikson calls "a new species of trouble," is to suffer a profound experience that alters one's sense of self, that alters the prevailing social relations, that alters the world itself.[28]

A PORTRAIT OF THE CITY

March 2010. There was a line of dump trucks, fourteen of them, on one side of the street. On the other side was rubble, and amid the rubble were young men and women wearing brightly colored shirts. A work crew clearing the street. Some pushed the rubble aside while others scooped chunks of concrete and stone with shovels, then lifted the shovels above their heads, throwing the debris into the trucks. Others held pickaxes and sledgehammers and swung them in a slow rhythm, piercing the irregular shapes and splintering them. Sometimes the tools stopped abruptly and made a high-pitched metallic sound as they hit the twisted lines of metal rebar inside the concrete. There were similar crews all over the city. It was the first phase of the reconstruction—rubble removal. It would take years before they finished.[29]

We drove past the line of trucks. Alexis had the car in a low gear as we moved slowly around the debris. Wilfred sat with him in the front. We were heading out of the city, to the lookout at Boutilliers. When I first arrived in the city after the quake, I saw so many cars crushed by the walls of nearby buildings that I felt certain Alexis's car would be gone too, smashed or buried somewhere. But it had made it through unscathed. It was just one of those small miracles of survival.

We stopped in some heavy traffic. Up ahead, several shipping containers blocked the road. A woman sat at a desk inside one of the containers, and in front of her stretched a long line of people.

"What are they doing?" I asked.

"They're looking for jobs," Alexis said. I looked at the line. Most of the people in it were young, maybe in their twenties. They were dressed professionally, in slacks or skirts with pressed dress shirts tucked into them. The men had their shoes shined. They were all holding stacks of papers. Résumés and documents. Just like the work crews clearing the streets, this was part of what the international community called the "Haitian-led recovery."

They would hire as many Haitians as possible for the reconstruction. Haitians to carry the rocks. Haitians to shovel the dust. Haitians to break apart the crushed houses, to sit at desks, to drive cars. Even in the reconstruction you could see the inequalities of the global economy at work. How much were those workers in the street being paid? How many of these people standing in line all day would be hired, and to do what? And how many foreigners were coming or were already here, working in air-conditioned offices, earning first-world salaries as they decided who got food and shelter and who didn't?

Still the traffic didn't move. Throughout the city, the usual patterns of movement and flow had been rearranged by the quake, as roads were filled with the remnants of houses, or with trucks and shipping containers. The rubble and the reconstruction had taken over the city, but in the small gaps, everyday life resumed. Near the car, a woman was selling little cakes from a stall. We waved her over and bought some. I gave her too much money and she thanked us and left. As we ate the cakes a group of young boys approached the car, begging, their arms outstretched and reaching through the windows. We gave them the cakes. The oldest boy took them from us and broke them up into equal parts before handing them out to the rest. In front of us, the traffic cleared and we drove on.

Soon we were climbing the slopes and looking down at the city. It was breezy. Outside the window, I watched as people walked up and down the mountain. We passed a few stores, still standing, still open for business. Then we arrived at Boutilliers. Alexis parked the car near the side of the road and we got out. There was a group of artisans sitting on the ground, in front of blankets covered with carved wooden handicrafts. A few men stood near racks with paintings hanging on them. One of these was Wilson, the painter with whom Wilfred sometimes worked. He waved at us and we went over to talk to him. After a brief round of pleasantries, Wilson and Wilfred started to talk business. I quietly excused myself and walked down some stone steps to the observatory—a concrete platform hanging off the side of the mountain, jutting out over the city.

On the platform, a man was standing next to an easel, painting. I introduced myself. His name was Berthony. He was twenty-five, born in the city just as the Duvalier regime fell. He was apprenticing to be a painter. As we talked, he continued to work on his painting. I thought about what it must have been like, how he had lived through the aftermath of the dictatorship and through the democratic transition, through the first free elections and then the coup, through the de facto period when the army killed so many of Aristide's supporters, through the UN mission in the 1990s, and, later, through the second coup and another provisional government and another intervention. And now this. In his classic ethnography of HIV/AIDS in Haiti, Paul Farmer noted that people in the village where he worked talked about the period after the dictatorship as *evènman sou evènman,* event after event.[30] They talked about the aftermath of the dictatorship as if it had been a series of crises, thing after thing, one disaster after another. I thought about the 2004 coup and how everyone said the violence that followed it had been the worst, worse even than the de facto period, worse than the dictatorship. But nothing could compare to the quake.

Berthony's house was gone. Before, he had been living in a small rented house near downtown with his family, but it had been completely destroyed. Some of his family had died in the house. A younger sister had been killed at her school when the roof came down on the classroom. I listened to his story but I didn't know what to say, except that I was sorry for his loss. He shrugged and said that it was "God's will," that sometimes God works in mysterious ways. Then he gestured to the city below us.

"I live there," he said, pointing to an area near the National Palace. He was lucky enough to have a spot in a tent in a large camp for displaced persons.

We looked out over the city, both of us quiet for a moment. I realized he was painting a picture of the city, a portrait of Port-au-Prince. He told me he'd had a dream the night before the quake, in which a spirit told him to paint the city. Now that so much of the city was gone, he had to paint it from memory. I looked more closely at the canvas. He was painting the city as it had been, as it had been before. His own private reconstruction.

We stayed at the lookout for the afternoon, none of us eager to return to the city below. Up here, things were calm. Things felt normal, or like what normal used to be. As the afternoon wore on, the conversation became livelier. The men told jokes and laughed. No one talked about the earthquake. No one talked about the reconstruction or the tents and the camps. As we joked, one of the men brought out a container of kleren. He handed out small plastic cups and poured two fingers of the homemade rum in each. The others finished their rum quickly and more was poured. I sipped mine, wincing as each swallow burned my throat.

A pickup truck came down the road, slowing as it neared us. The driver stopped in front of us and jumped out, an excited smile on his face. He walked quickly over to the group, but he looked only at me. When he was close enough, he held out a hand for me to shake. He asked what we were doing. Suspicious, I didn't say much, only that we were enjoying the lookout.

"You like rum?" he asked, looking down at the cup in my hand. I nodded.

"I'm Rohan," he said, touching a hand to his chest. "I can get you a good price on Indian whiskey."

Rohan was a businessman from Delhi who had moved to Haiti just months before the earthquake. He ran an import-export business in the capital, and he told me that he was bringing in cheap whiskey and iron from India. He said if I didn't want whiskey he could give me a good deal on scrap metal. When I told him that I wasn't in the market, he gave me his card, got back in his truck, which he had left running, and drove off down the road. With billions of dollars pledged to the reconstruction, Haiti was open for business.[31]

"The thing about the quake is that it touched everyone," Flore said as she steered the car around a dog that was sleeping in the street. "Markets, businesses, stores, houses. Everything was damaged. Every neighborhood. It was a great leveler."

Flore shifted gears and drove up a hill, accelerating to pass a minibus. We were on our way to Pétion-Ville to see Lyonel, who had invited us both for breakfast. I looked out the window at a supermarket that had collapsed. Flore was right—this might be the first disaster that was truly national in scale and scope, the first disaster that hit the elite right where they lived, the first time their wealth and privilege had not mattered, had not been able to insulate them from loss or protect them from harm. The earthquake had been a great leveler indeed, leveling so much of the city. But just because it touched everyone in some way doesn't mean it touched everyone in the same way.

Flore turned into the central plaza, where the public park had been turned into a camp for displaced persons. Around the camp were the storefronts and restaurants of downtown Pétion-Ville. Flore drove past the tents, down a side street, and parked in a short alley. We got out and walked to a café. Across the street, a woman sat in front of a tent, bathing a child. The child stood in a bucket as the woman scrubbed his body and splashed water on him. We turned and entered the café.

Inside, the walls were painted a warm hue. There were potted plants along the edges of the tiled floor, and paintings hung on the walls. The room was empty except for Lyonel, who was already sitting at a table waiting for us. He stood up when he saw us enter and held an arm out wide. "Welcome, welcome," he said. "Come, sit down. Have you eaten yet?" Before either of us could answer, he added, "I've ordered breakfast for us."

We sat and I listened as Flore and Lyonel slipped into the kind of talk shared by childhood friends, conversations that relied on insider knowledge, talk that was intimate, that evoked shared experiences, a shared life. I had been surprised when Flore told me Lyonel had invited us both to meet him. I wasn't sure what I was doing there.

Breakfast came: cups of coffee and plates filled with eggs, fresh bread, and fruit. We ate and they talked some more. I asked Lyonel how his family was doing. He said his aunt had lost her house but that everyone was still alive and that was what mattered. He seemed excited, exuberant. He told us about all the ways Haiti was going to change now, after the quake.

"Yes!" Flore said. "Yes, it's like people finally get it now!" She was excited too.

"You'll see," he said, looking at me. "The diaspora will come back. No more of this bullshit," he said. "The world is watching. We're going to build the country right this time." He was already planning for the future. His family owned several factories near the airport and he was imagining expanding them. I drank my coffee.

Later the conversation shifted as Flore and Lyonel asked about mutual friends. Flore laughed and said she had met one of their childhood friends the night before. She had gone dancing at a newly reopened club, she had needed to blow off steam. The club had thrown a celebration for all those who were still alive. "Everyone was there," she said as she lit a cigarette. "It was crazy!" She told us there had been a line of cars but nowhere to park them. People were lined up on the sidewalk to get into the club. Inside, people drank and danced all night. Outside, the homeless slept on sidewalks, the lucky ones slept in tents.

Luc drove down the street and came to an intersection. I braced myself, remembering the large hole in the middle of the road, but then relaxed when I saw the hole was gone, replaced by a new road, one that was solid and firm. I had not been back to Martissant in over a year, and as we passed through the neighborhood I was struck by the discrepancy between the new roads and standpipes and the cracked and crushed homes. Luc still had his house in Martissant. He had been unable to sell it during the violence after the coup. It had been damaged but not destroyed by the quake, and he was going to check on the repairs.

The front gate had buckled and a fence had fallen down. Inside the house there were cracks in the walls, but Luc assured me the damage was not structural. We walked through the kitchen and he handed me a bottle of soda and a glass with ice. He led me through the house, telling me about the repairs he still needed to do, and then we stepped outside into the garden. A mason was there, repairing cracks in a wall that ringed the yard. We sat at a small table in the garden. The warm soda was already melting the ice in my glass.

Years ago, Luc had told me that the city had exploded. He was referring to the slums and squatters, to the anarchic urbanism that had taken shape in the capital, first under the dictatorship and later during the democratic transition.[32] Luc had spent decades advocating for urban planning by the state and by non-governmental institutions. But little had been done to stem the tide of urban migration, of ad hoc construction, of settlements and shoddy building materials. The city had grown more and more each year, and each year it had grown more and more vulnerable, precarious, and dangerous. Now it seemed as though the city had imploded—collapsed into itself.

"They shouldn't rebuild the city," Luc said finally. "They should move it."

I had heard others say similar things, that the government should build a new capital somewhere else or even build two new, smaller cities, one for administration and one for industry. Luc said there was no way to protect Port-au-Prince from future catastrophes, because it was located atop a major fault line (not the same one that had caused the quake) and because the increasingly bare mountains above the city brought annual floods and mudslides. The only way to reduce the risk of disaster was to relocate the capital altogether. He envisioned a planned city with a new and expanded port, with adequate and functional infrastructure, with houses that followed the zoning laws and building codes. Listening to Luc, I could almost see his vision. With all the aid money being raised for Haiti, I had a vision too—I thought of it as a "Marshall Plan" for Haiti. The comparison was a common one in the months after the quake.[33] I had suggested the idea at a conference in February 2010. Someone in the audience asked if it was really possible in a place like Haiti. "Why not?" I had said. "After all, they rebuilt Europe in four years after the war." Now that I was back in Haiti, I was less sure.

I said to Luc, "It will be a moral indictment of us all if we spend billions of dollars to rebuild Haiti as the poorest country in the hemisphere."

Luc turned to look at me, his eyes wide and his head nodding slightly.

"It will be criminal," he said.

We sat in silence, watching the garden, drinking our drinks. I thought about the problem of the informal city, about slums and squatters, about concrete and vulnerability. If there was a crime here, who was the criminal? Who was responsible?

Sometimes those questions are easy to answer. Fourteen months before the earthquake, a large three-story building collapsed in Pétion-Ville. It was a privately run school that had been built on the steep slope of a mountain, overlooking a ravine below. When it collapsed, the ceiling of the first floor buckled and gave way and the upper floors came crashing down. At least ninety-four children died, and hundreds more were injured. Everyone knew the school was dangerous. It had partially collapsed several years earlier and had been repaired, but there had been complaints about the quality of the building materials and the location of the building. After it fell, people blamed the lack of building codes and zoning laws, the lack of planning. President Préval, who went to the disaster site many times, reminded people that the zoning regulations and building codes did, in fact, exist. But they had not been followed or enforced. After the disaster, the owner of the school was charged with involuntary manslaughter. He later admitted they had not used enough steel rebar to adequately reinforce the concrete blocks. Yet Préval's comments seemed to suggest that beyond the criminal charges was a deeper problem—the lack of the state. Who was responsible for the state's inability to provide the material infrastructure for security and survival?[34]

The line for breakfast at the Plaza Hotel was long. They were serving what they advertised as an American buffet. News spread quickly from the front of the line that they were already out of bacon. When it was my turn, I got some coffee and eggs and toast, then went to sit at a table with a group of doctors and nurses who were in Haiti for a two-week medical humanitarian mission. Brian and Scott were surgeons from Chicago, Deborah was a nurse from New York, and Astrid was a nurse from Denmark. Brian, Deborah, and Astrid had finished their missions and were leaving that afternoon. Scott had just arrived and was heading out of the city later that day to work at a field site near the Dominican border. It was easier to bring supplies through the land border there, since the airport and the port had both been damaged by the quake.

I asked Brian and Deborah about the conditions at the border. They shook their heads and launched into complaints about the lack of adequate supplies and the terrible logistics.

"It's just so difficult," Deborah said. "The need is so great, and we're here and want to help but there's only so much we can do."

"It's like a war zone," Astrid said. It was her second mission since the quake. She had worked all over the world, mostly in Africa, but she said the situation in Haiti was one of the worst she had ever seen. Part of the problem was the complexity of the disaster, which had damaged or destroyed most of the infrastructure and institutions needed to respond to emergencies. We all knew that the ports and roads had been damaged, as well as government buildings and hospitals. Doctors were doing emergency surgeries in open fields or amid the rubble. Astrid shook her head and quietly said, "And all those nurses." She was referring to the nursing school that had collapsed during the quake, killing more than 150 students.

Scott looked nervous. He asked if it was really that bad.

"It's worse than you think it'll be," Brian said. He was visibly angry. "This is the first time most of these people have ever been to a doctor! I had patients showing up who were sick with cancer. A mother brought her son to the clinic, he had encephalitis. We had to turn them all away." He waved a hand in the air like he was making a "no" gesture. "We had to tell them we can't help them, we're only here to fix bones, to deal with the injuries from the quake." He looked away for a moment, then continued. "If I was back in the U.S. I could save them, I could help them. It's not hard, goddammit. We just need the medicine, the supplies. All we did was treat broken bones. All we did was cut off limbs." He paused. "We cut off a lot of fucking limbs."

We all sat in silence, looking down at the table. Someone dove into the pool, making a small splash. They began to swim laps, back and forth, back and forth. I looked up and watched a woman jogging around the dining room and hotel lobby. She was running in circles.

I drove with Flore and Geslin to the edge of the city. There was an American military camp out there and we wanted to see it. The Haitian government asked the U.S. military to take over the airport after the quake, since the UN mission was hampered by its own losses when their main office collapsed. It was the largest loss of life for UN personnel outside of a conflict zone.[35]

We found the sprawling camp outside the city, in a large dirt field. There were U.S. military vehicles everywhere, and tents with air-conditioning units humming away. We pulled to the side of the road. Flore smoked a few cigarettes and just looked at the camp. Eventually she stood up and said, "I can't believe they're fucking here again!" She had lived in the United States, traveled there repeatedly, she had no problem with Americans, but she could not stand to see their military occupying her country again. "All of this," she said, pointing to the tents and trucks, "all of it has to go! Just leave us the fuck alone."

Years ago, when I first came to Haiti, Manuel once asked me what the United States wanted with his country. I didn't know what to say. He asked again, telling me he had heard that George W. Bush, who was president at the time, had a file on his desk about Haiti. I told Manuel that the United States wanted to remove Aristide. He agreed and said everyone knew that, but he thought there was something deeper, he thought that the United States hated Haiti because of the revolution and wanted to ensure that the Haitian people would never be free. Now, after the quake, people were saying similar things. A friend told me that the U.S. government had caused the quake so that they could take over the country. Another said the quake had been caused by an American company drilling for oil beneath the sea. "We have lots of oil and gas," he told me. "They want to take it." Others told me that American companies were buying up land for gold mines or for new factories. "Haiti is just a labor camp, one big labor camp," a friend said.

After a while, Flore wiped her face and crushed the butt of her cigarette into the ground. We got in the car to head back into the city. The traffic in front of us was heavy and slow. Later, as we finally inched down the road, we saw what had caused the backup. A large military vehicle had tried to make the sharp turn into the U.S. encampment but had flipped on its side instead. Its hulking frame blocked both lanes. Soldiers directed traffic into the ditch by the side of the road. Geslin eased the car into the ditch, up onto a dry patch of land, and then, eventually, back to the paved road. He shifted into a higher gear and drove off, leaving the camp and the crash behind us, barely visible now through the cloud of dust made by our tires.

In the city, there are two kinds of camps. There are the camps for those who have been displaced, for those made homeless by the quakes. And then there are the humanitarian enclaves, the "spaces of aid" in which foreign aid workers live and move about.[36] The office buildings and SUVs, the hotels and military camps, the medical facilities and supply chains—these all make up part of a global network of humanitarian aid through which move foreign aid workers, humanitarian supplies, and billions of dollars in bilateral aid and international donations. After the quake, it was like an army of aid organizations and NGOs descending on Port-au-Prince. There were white cars everywhere with slogans and logos and acronyms on them, with Haitian drivers and foreign passengers. Each organization had a project. Some worked on water. Some on housing. Few of them were regulated or officially listed with the Haitian government. Years before the quake, critics had noted the prevalence of NGOs, calling Haiti a "Republic of NGOs." In the months after the quake it would become commonplace to hear people say that Haiti had the second highest number of NGOs per capita in the world (just below India). Even Bill Clinton, UN special envoy to Haiti, said there were ten thousand NGOs in the country, an unverifiable number that, even if false, sounded true.[37]

Everyone wants to help Haiti. A telethon after the quake raised over $60 million and drew an audience of over eighty million. People texted their support and donations daily. At an international donors' conference, the global community pledged over $5 billion for relief and reconstruction.[38] And that was just the money. People sent all kinds of goods, too. In the first days after the disaster, there were people who chartered planes and flew into the country. Some flew into the Dominican Republic and brought goods over by land. Some sent boats. One American businessman sent an entire shipping container full of boxes of energy drinks.

I heard about the container of energy drinks from Beth, a human rights lawyer who was in the country on a fact-finding mission, monitoring the distribution of aid. The airport had been partially damaged during the quake and had limited capacity to receive large shipments. The U.S. military had taken over logistics and were prioritizing military supplies over medical relief. They had turned away a plane chartered by Doctors Without Borders. "The airport is a mess," Beth said. "All of this stuff is coming in and it needs to be dealt with. People sent everything. There were planes and containers full of cardboard boxes filled with everything from expired medicine to teddy bears. There were a lot of teddy bears."[39]

The supply chain into Haiti was only part of the problem. The bigger issue was how to get food and aid to everyone who needed it. The international aid mission was distributing aid to local authorities that had been established in the camps, but there were rumors the system was being abused.[40] Aid workers were making critical decisions about who received aid and who did not. It was a difficult position to be in, Beth said. She told me that some organizations were worried about what they called "ghost camps"—camps set up by Haitians who had not been directly harmed by the quake but who wanted access to food and other supplies. "Because in Haiti," she said, "you don't have to be an earthquake victim to need food."[41]

THE END OF A WORLD

March 2010.   I drove to Bel Air with Alexis and Wilfred on a sunny morning in March to meet with a few men and women who led a grassroots community organization in the neighborhood. They had been working for years to get development projects to come to Bel Air. In the aftermath of the 2004 coup and the police and gang violence that came with it, they had called for the government and the international community to invest in schools and

Camp in Bel Air. Photo by Luke Mattar.

sanitation, in water and electrical services, and in road repair and jobs. Now they were once again petitioning the international community and the NGO system for aid and assistance, only this time they were all homeless.

Bel Air was one of the hardest-hit areas of the city, but there was little evidence of a sustained aid effort there two months after the quake. I listened to residents as they told me about the quake and about what happened after it. In the days following the thing, they had not waited for help, they had helped each other. They searched for survivors, and later, when there were no more survivors, they disposed of the bodies. They took a census and conducted their own needs-assessment survey. They took on the task of distributing aid to residents, planning and managing an unofficial camp, locating building supplies and food, and appealing to international aid organizations for assistance. About a month before my visit, a European NGO had come to the area to build several public showers and latrines, but they left only a half-finished structure. When it was clear they were not coming back, camp residents took apart the structure to use the wood to secure their new, temporary homes.[42]

After I had listened to their stories of survival, they led me through their camp. We met families doing perfectly ordinary things. A woman was hanging clothes to dry in the sun. Two small boys were playing with cars they had made from plastic soda bottles. Some men slapped dominoes down emphatically on a small wooden table, the table tilting on the uneven ground with each play they made. Some of the camp residents were happy to talk. Others wanted privacy, and I tried to give it to them. A woman told me there had been others to see the camp, a few aid workers and some journalists. She said they came and took pictures but they didn't do anything. I felt doubt spread through me. What was I doing here? How could I help? Was I just a tourist taking notes and pictures, documenting a shattered world?

We left the camp and walked across a street that was partially cleared, the debris gathered to one side so people and cars could travel on the road. We walked past a school, its roof caved in but the walls otherwise intact. Daphne, one of the leaders of the community organization, was worried about what the children would do all day without school. She feared they would run away and join gangs, that Bel Air would be engulfed in violence again, as it had been after the coup. She and a few other residents had started to gather the children in the mornings for lessons, but they needed school supplies, they needed books and paper and pencils.

We continued walking. Daphne told me about the history of the neighborhood. She had lived there all her life. Bel Air is one of the oldest neighborhoods in the city, and the people who live there have deep ties to the area, unlike those who live in the more recent squatter settlements of Martissant or the sprawling slum of Cité Soleil.[43] Bel Air residents are known throughout the capital for their tight networks of kinship and affiliation.

"Here," she said. Daphne stopped walking and pointed to a large empty space on the side of the road. The ground was covered in debris. She led me into the rubble. We stepped carefully over and around it. Then, when we couldn't get around it, we walked on top of the jagged pieces of concrete. She gestured to some large sections of a broken wall, which we climbed. From this vantage point I could see just how far the rubble went, just how much was gone. Daphne pointed to a particular area of rubble. It was where

Aftermath of the earthquake. Photo by Luke Mattar.

her house had been. She said she was lucky to be alive and she praised God that her family had survived. I tried to picture the houses as they were before, to imagine how many houses had filled this space and how many people had lived in each one. Daphne stood beside me and gave names to the empty spaces. She told me who had lived where, pointing each time to a portion of rubble, to a place where a house had been.

A family had lived in a one-room house there.

There, two families had rented houses.

There was the place where her aunt had lived.

There was the place where her neighbor had died, crushed by a wall.

And there, in a small cave made by fallen walls, was where they had brought the bodies when no one came to collect them. It was there that they burned the remains, as they had not been able to bury the dead.

In Bel Air again. In the camps. Timo, another community leader, took me on a walk through the camp and then through another set of destroyed homes. Below us, we watched a work crew breaking concrete with sledgehammers and shoveling the debris into trucks. At the end of the walk, Timo sat down on a pile of rubble and gestured to the surrounding debris.

"I lost my house," he said. "We all lost our houses. We lost everything. Family. Friends. But now, the real problem is aid. All of these foreigners—

why are they here? They come and go. They wave food all around. We sniff at it but we don't get it." He rubbed his fingers together under his nose. He said, "They treat us like animals. Haitians are dogs now."

Haitians are dogs now. The phrase struck me, struck me as much as Manuel's comment that Haiti was dead had. I didn't know what to make of Timo's comment, but I felt he might be right. He seemed to be saying that international aid had turned Haitians into powerless beings who were now dependent on others for their very survival. People were living in the streets, just like dogs, scrounging for their next meal, hoping to get by on the beneficence of others. In the years after the quake, others would tell me the same thing, over and over again. Some said they were being treated like animals, others said they were being treated worse than animals. Most drew on the figure of the street dog, a ubiquitous animal in the city, to name this feeling. To name their dehumanization.[44]

When foreigners come to Port-au-Prince, they always comment on the number of "stray" dogs roaming the streets. But they are not strays. Most of them are attached to a house or family in ways not always easily seen. These street dogs are like the millions of village dogs around the world—they are guard dogs. They are left to run free, scavenging for food and receiving the occasional handout, but they always return to a household. Street dogs are not, however, treated like pets or companion animals, which is why foreigners always seem to think they have been abandoned. Pets are invited into homes, they become part of the family. Street dogs are marginal figures. They cross the symbolic boundaries of house and road, domesticated and wild life, inclusion and exclusion. They live among people and in the midst of social life, but they do not participate fully in that life. They are liminal animals, living on the edges of a world inhabited by people.[45]

The comparison to dogs was ready at hand after the quake, as people found themselves living in conditions that were degrading and dehumanizing. But the weight of Timo's comment comes from the deeper history of dogs in Haiti, a history filled with violence.[46] Dogs were first brought to the Americas by the Spanish, who used them to hunt and kill indigenous people and runaway slaves. This "canine warfare" was used in the French colony of Saint Domingue, too, where slaves were sometimes fed to dogs trained to eat black flesh.[47] In the final years of the Haitian Revolution, when the remaining French planters and soldiers were holed up in the northern port of Le Cap, former slaves and revolutionaries were thrown into pits to be eaten by dogs in public spectacles of torture. For many Haitians, dogs are strongly associated with the legacies of colonial violence and racism. Dogs are not trusted or well liked and are often associated with sorcery. To be turned into a dog is a terrible fate, in part because dogs are a visceral reminder of what it is like to be unmade as a person, to be torn asunder.

When I asked people about Timo's comment, some of them brought up this history. They told me that blan trained dogs to "eat people" *(manje nèg)*. The deep history of the colonial relationship was easily applicable to the present situation, where humanitarians were once again a foreign group that held almost total power over the life and death of so many people. Alexis reminded me that some dogs were treated much better than Haitians, that the elite let their dogs live inside their houses and fed them imported food. He said that those dogs got to eat every day, which was more than many Haitians could say. And Paul reminded me that the Kreyòl words for disaster *(dezas)* and disorder *(dezòd)* had as their synonym the expression *chen manje chen*, dog eat dog. The statement "Haitians are dogs now" meant lots of things to lots of people. It drew on a shared set of experiences and a shared history of violence and exploitation. Yet, for Timo, the comparison was rather simple—the people living in the camps were now wholly dependent on others for food and shelter, just like dogs.

In Haiti, relations of care and dependency are talked about in terms of feeding and eating. The Kreyòl word *manje* means both "to eat" and "to feed," and it is one of the most important terms for talking about moral relationships. As Alta Mae Stevens has shown, *manje* carries both positive and negative connotations. In its positive sense, it "connotes *abundance, friendship, sex,* and—above all—*power,*" while in its negative usage it stands for "powerlessness, impotence, zombification, destruction of the self through witchcraft or cannibalism, either real or symbolic."[48] Family members have an obligation to share food with each other, just as they are obliged to provide food to the spirits during ritual services. Sharing food is a way of reproducing and expressing the good relations that one has with others. Food also symbolizes obligations in general, and people often say they must "feed" the lwa when they talk about ritual service. To feed and be fed is central to what it means to be a moral person, and those who are higher in the social hierarchy bear greater responsibility to feed those below them. Those who eschew such obligations, who do not share food and other resources, are thieves *(volè)* or big eaters *(gran manjè)*, and those who use magic or other nefarious means to cause misfortune are said to eat people *(manje moun)*.[49] Those who fulfill their obligations to feed people gain respect *(respè)*.

Before the quake, Timo worked as a community organizer. He made a living by cultivating relationships both in the neighborhood and across the city. Like the men who gathered at the gift shop, he was able to turn those relationships into durable forms of value like money, credit, and, most importantly, respect and social prestige. Timo, who was in his late forties, had worked hard to negotiate with NGOs, raise funds for neighborhood projects, and mediate and settle disputes among local residents. Many others in Bel Air, especially younger residents in their teens and twenties, had been less successful at making a living. The chronic lack of jobs meant that many men found themselves idle in public spaces for much of the day. Some turned to criminalized entrepreneurial work, joining gangs that controlled rent and housing, water and electricity, security and policing, and drugs and prostitution in the expanding black markets of the city's slums.[50]

Looking for life and earning respect was hard for men like Timo before the quake. Things became immeasurably harder afterward, when foreign NGOs controlled almost all access to resources like water, shelter, food, and cash. The only way to get food was in the form of aid from the international disaster response or in the form of work programs run by the UN and international NGOs. Being dependent on foreigners for aid and assistance was only part of the problem. The deeper issue was the way in which the international community approached food distribution and service provision. Post-quake systems of aid completely changed what it meant to feed other people. International aid transformed relations of exchange and, in the process, changed the very meaning of personhood.

Bel Air was one of the first sites for the United Nations Cash for Work program after the quake. These programs paid people up to 150 gourdes (about U.S. $3.50) per day for short periods, typically no more than a week or two. The name was a misnomer, as crews were more often paid in food than in cash. The UN contracted with NGOs to run the program, which focused on rubble removal. The foreign NGOs that implemented the Cash for Work program preferred to hire women and young men, which meant that older men—people like Timo who had previously been leaders in their community and had commanded a great deal of respect—were unable to get food or earn cash. That, in turn, meant that older residents were unable to fulfill their obligations to feed and take care of those who were dependent on them. Instead, younger dependents became the primary economic agents in the new shelter households, a shift that reversed traditional roles of gender and age. By hiring young men for rubble removal, the Cash for Work program changed the very conditions of possibility of respè. With no available work, older men like Timo had to rely on the younger generation for support or turn to systems of credit. In either case, the result was the same: older men became indebted to younger men and were unable to give or get the kind of respè they felt they deserved. For men like Timo, the most important virtue anchoring social life and one's relation to the world was experienced predominantly through its negation—as disrespect.

The situation was not much better for younger men, who gained immediate access to food and cash but who soon lost their jobs as NGOs moved to other areas of the city or replaced workers with new crews in an effort to employ as many people as possible.[51] This highlighted one of the most difficult aspects of the new relations of feeding in Haiti—NGOs and the international community sought to develop short-term relations of exchange that worked like contracts. These short-term contracts were quite different from the embedded relations of reciprocal obligation and responsibility that formed the basis of social life in the city. In the latter type of relationships, dependents can always call on those with more prestige or power to act responsibly and to fulfill their obligations to others (to feed them, for example). But the new relations of exchange brought by the aid apparatus made people dependent on others for their survival and it made them powerless to shape the terms of the exchange. All they could do was wait and hope that someone would graciously give them what they needed. They were left, like a dog, begging for their next meal. For men like Timo, becoming a dog felt like the end of a whole way of life. It felt like the end of a world.

AFTER DISASTER, MORE DISASTER

There is a common saying in Haiti: *Dèyè mòn, gen mòn.* After the mountains, more mountains. It is an apt description of the countryside, where much of the landscape is indeed rough and rugged terrain. Like any good proverb, this one makes a simple fact of geography stand for the experience of striving to move forward, to move toward a future you can't yet see, to come over and through adversity. The meaning, of course, is that after this, there will be something else. This is the case not only for mountains, but also for political upheavals, crises, and disasters. Whatever else the future might hold, one can be sure there will be more challenges ahead. Yet disasters are not quite like mountains. They are not a matter of geography. Disasters are made.

Driving through the city after the quake, Alexis tells me that "disaster is big business," that it is the same as dezòd, that it is just like a coup. The elite and the international community use it to make money. "They make lots of money," he says. "They eat. We suffer."

After the quake, I bring a little packet of money, a ti kado, to a friend. We hug and I tell him I am happy he is alive. I had not been able to reach him since the thing happened. We sit down and he takes the envelop, thanks me. But he is weary, his body is hunched over. I wonder if he is hurt and ask if he has seen a doctor. He says no, he's not hurt. He tells me that he is already dead.

Daphne points to where her house once was. I look at the rubble in silence. Among the rocks and debris are bones, a spinal column still intact but charred from a fire. Later she shows me her shelter, a small single room made of wood and corrugated tin and cardboard. It is not big enough for me to stand up inside, so I stoop. She tells me the earthquake was an act of God. The real disaster, she says, gesturing to her shelter and to the camp around us, is what has come after.

A joint report on disaster and risk, prepared in 2014 by the Haitian government and the UNDP, says that Haiti is one of the most vulnerable, most disaster-prone countries in the world. Haiti holds many such titles. They say it is the poorest country in the Western Hemisphere. That it is the most water-poor country in the world. When you look at the numbers, on ranking after ranking, Haiti is always near the bottom. On the human suffering index, Haiti routinely ranks among countries that are in the midst of protracted civil wars. The report on disaster says there have been over forty major disasters—meaning disasters that affected ten thousand people or more—in the country since 1963. Since the report was written, there have been even more. The most curious thing is that the report fails to mention the cholera epidemic.[52]

In October 2010, a contingent of Nepalese soldiers arrived in Haiti as part of the UN mission. Some of them carried a strain of the bacterium *Vibrio cholerae* inside their bodies. Days after their arrival, sewage from their UN camp was dumped into a local stream and flowed from there into the Artibonite River. Cholera cases were soon reported in regional hospitals and clinics. The disease, which is spread through contaminated water, causes diarrhea and vomiting and, if untreated, can quickly kill those it infects. It is easy to treat, if patients have access to clinics where they can be given fluids and antibiotics. There is even an oral vaccine available. In Haiti, after the quake, it has been difficult to treat and prevent the disease. Within just a few months after the first reported cases, the Haitian cholera epidemic was ranked the worst in the world.[53]

More than ten thousand Haitians have died from cholera since the outbreak began. At first the United Nations refused to acknowledge its role in the epidemic, but after years of protests and independent investigations, the UN finally conceded that it brought the disease to Haiti. In December 2016, UN Secretary General Ban Ki-moon issued an apology and said the UN had a "moral responsibility" to respond to the epidemic. (The UN has continued to deny any legal responsibility.) He promised that the UN would create a $400 million fund for treatment and prevention of the disease, but a year after his apology they had only secured a tenth of that amount.[54]

After the quake, the international community embraced a simple slogan: Build Back Better. It fit well with the prevailing sense that Port-au-Prince would have to be almost entirely rebuilt. Yet the slogan was an old one. Bill Clinton had used it after the 2004 South Asian Tsunami. Clinton, who was UN Special Envoy for Tsunami Relief, was charged with raising money for the post-disaster reconstruction. He praised the Indonesian government's reconstruction agency as a successful model of its type and later urged a similar approach in New Orleans after Hurricane Katrina. In 2009, Clinton was appointed UN Special Envoy to Haiti, where he took on the task of encouraging development. Again, he used the slogan "Build Back Better," although his vision seemed to be limited to developing the tourist sector and building factories. After the earthquake, Clinton spearheaded an international donors' conference where he secured billions in pledged reconstruction funds. But donors were not willing to give those funds to the Haitian government directly (as they had done in Indonesia). Instead, Clinton helped set up a trusteeship that would oversee the funds.[55]

And so, after the quake the international community set out to rebuild Haiti using a script that was decades old. The goal was to create jobs, and according to the economist Paul Collier, who had served as a UN special advisor to Haiti in 2008, the only jobs worth creating in Haiti were low-paying factory jobs in export-producing zones. He marveled at the opportunity, noting that "the garments industry has the scope to provide several hundred thousand jobs to Haitians."[56] Collier added that labor costs in Haiti were so low that they were competitive with China. It was the same plan for economic development that had been implemented in the 1970s, during Jean-Claude Duvalier's "economic revolution." It was the same plan that had brought hundreds of thousands of people to the slums of Port-au-Prince in the first place. And it was the same plan that had kept wages so low in the factories that workers could barely afford to live on them. The same plan that had required violence and terror to enforce it, that had gone hand-in-hand with the suppression of democracy in the country. It was the same plan that had made the disaster in the first place.[57]

Watching the reconstruction take shape, I felt like I was on the road to Mapou again, that I was watching a disaster unfold in slow motion, spreading out in time and space in front of me and behind me, moving along the fault lines of inequality. On the road to Mapou, I had seen cut trees and charcoal, bare mountains and mines, and concrete blocks that would become houses in the expanding slums of the city. It was like a map of displacement, the displacement not just of trees and dirt but also of people. Now everyone was being moved again, pushed and pulled this way and that. I thought about how disaster can feel very fast and very slow at the same time, how you could expect the shock and still be surprised by it. I thought about the repeated declarations that each new disaster was somehow "the worst" and about how they still all felt, each one of them, oddly ordinary. I thought about the aftermath of disaster, about the people still living in tents years after their village flooded in Mapou, and as I write this, I think about the people in Port-au-Prince who are still living in tents now, almost a decade after the earthquake. After disaster, more disaster.

Years after the quake, the plan is slowly taking shape. There are new factories, although not as many as some may have imagined. There are new hotels too, expensive hotels, and more and more foreigners in the country all the time. Yet men like Alexis and Wilfred, who were once widely regarded as pillars of the tourist sector in the city, have seen little of the new business. The promise of money and jobs hangs in the air, like the smell of food in the camps. Everything remains just out of reach. Years after the quake, the IDP camps are mostly gone, but that doesn't mean that those displaced people now have a home. Many of them, too many of them by far, remain displaced. One day, a friend tells me that Port-au-Prince is filling up again, that new people are arriving each day to look for jobs or money, to look for life.

And that, too, feels like a disaster. A disaster without end, as the city fills up with displaced people again.

Postscript

On the southwestern edge of Port-au-Prince there is a small forest, nestled into the bottom of a mountain. Inside the forest is a memorial for those who died in the earthquake. A monument to a lost world. A testament to what is gone and to what remains.[1] Where better to hold on to the memory of that world than in the forest, the forest that has been there so long, the forest that bears the traces of what came before. The forest that remains, despite all that has happened. The forest that tells so many stories.

The memorial in the forest marks an absence. It is not itself a gravesite; there are no bodies buried there. After the quake, the bodies went to mass graves outside the city. Tens of thousands of them were dumped in a place called Titanyen. It is a place everyone in Haiti knows, a place made famous by the Duvalier dictatorship and by the military and paramilitary regimes that followed it. Each successive regime has dumped its bodies in Titanyen. Repetition reveals a structure.

The mass graves are a perverse kind of national cemetery. A place full of ghosts. Years ago, there were ghosts living in the forest, too. In the 1950s, Katherine Dunham, who owned the forest at the time, asked a powerful mambo from the north of Haiti to divine the source of the haunting. The mambo, a woman named Kam, spent days living in the forest, communicating with the spirits. They were the ghosts of former slaves killed by the French during a military campaign meant to end the Haitian Revolution and restore slavery to the colony. The ghosts of the revolution, the ghosts of national independence. Kam performed a ceremony to help the ghosts find their way to their final resting place in Ginen. She helped them find their way home.[2] Once again, the forest plays this role.

Repetition reveals a structure.

The forest is a place where the living remember and care for the dead. Caring for the dead in Haiti, as in so many other places, means separating the soul from the body. It means, too, separating the soul from this world, so that it is free to move on to the next world, the world of the dead and the ancestors and the lwa. The ritual of separation is a rite of passage—a transformative act that moves a person from one place to another, from life to afterlife.

I remember once getting lost with Manuel. We were on our way to collect an old drum used in Vodou rituals to communicate with the lwa. Manuel was excited; he was about to make a big sale. We squeezed our bodies through a crowded market. It was hot inside. Of course it was hot; the market was built of iron, the famous Iron Market. They say it was originally meant to be a train station in Egypt, but that after a business deal fell through it ended up here, in downtown Port-au-Prince. Years later, it was destroyed by a fire and then rebuilt. It had been destroyed again in the quake and again rebuilt. The new market was heralded as a centerpiece of post-quake reconstruction. Bill Clinton cut the ribbon at its reopening. Then, in February 2018, there was another fire and it was once again destroyed, along with the goods and livelihoods of so many traders.

But we didn't know any of that then. At the time, the market was one of the few places where Manuel could still make big deals selling art objects to foreign collectors. I had tried to keep up with him as he weaved through the stalls, but I soon lost sight of him. The tables around me were full of sweet-smelling spices, piles of rice, and baskets of fruits and vegetables. I stood on my toes to see over the crowd. There was Manuel, several stalls away. He was jumping up and down and waving an arm in the air. He was smiling. I waved back and moved through the crowd again. When I caught up to him, we were both sweaty and giddy with excitement. There it was on the ground, the *tanbou assoto*, the big drum.[3]

It was over six feet tall, a tree trunk really, just hollowed out and covered on one end with a skin. Manuel and a friend picked it up and hoisted it onto their shoulders. People smiled and murmured as we walked with it, and the crowd, which had seemed so thick before, now parted to let us through. I heard someone say they hadn't seen a tanbou assoto in years. It was probably true; they had become rare in Haiti. This one had been bought by an international art collector, who, in buying it, was saving it from the dust and heat and inevitable destruction of the back rooms of the Iron Market. But it would never be played again, it would never again beat out the rhythms that call the lwa down from Ginen. It would no longer play a vital role in the ritual communication between the living and the dead.

And yet Manuel had been happy that day, the day he sold the drum, the day he carried it, sweaty and smiling, through the crowds. Later we drank beer and talked about the past. He remembered when the hotels were open, when there were tourists. How they had stayed up all night, dancing in the streets. How there had been money and jobs, how he had been able to make a good living.

Sometimes I still see Manuel's face. I see him jumping up over the crowd, waving to me. I remember his eyes, his presence, his determination to live a life he thought worth living. I remember Manuel that way. And I am reminded that everything has an ending, and nothing is ever really finished.

I'm writing this postscript while perusing the UN's Humanitarian Response Plan for Haiti for the coming year. Reading the report about what they call the "humanitarian situation" is like being buried under an avalanche of facts and figures. The report says that Haiti is ranked 159th out of 160 countries on the Logistics Performance Index, which means it is one of the most difficult places in the world for humanitarian operations. The report says that almost the entire population of the country is "living constantly" under the threat of natural hazards. It says there are still thirty-seven thousand people living in camps after being displaced by the earthquake eight years ago. To these are added about half a million displaced persons along the border, the so-called "returnees" from the Dominican Republic. These returnees were, until recently, Dominican citizens of Haitian descent, but they have now been denationalized and deported. Another act of displacement. The report also says that one million people are still in need of humanitarian assistance after Hurricane Matthew, which struck the southern peninsula of Haiti in 2016. Cholera and widespread food insecurity continue to threaten the population.[4]

Reading the report, I am reminded again of the distinction between the situation and the story. As Vivian Gornick puts it, "The situation is the context or circumstance, sometimes the plot; the story is the emotional experience that preoccupies the writer: the insight, the wisdom, the thing one has come to say."[5]

The thing one has come to say. What I have come to realize is this: While the facts and figures matter, there is no way to understand crisis without first thinking of it as something that happens to people. When I think about Manuel saying Haiti is dead, I think of him as trying to tell us something profound. I think of him telling us about how crisis feels. But he is not talking about the same kind of thing as the situation report. The situation report normalizes crisis, treats it as an objective fact in the world and then tries to locate it in space and time, so that experts can intervene with development projects, humanitarian relief efforts, and all the other ways people have devised to manage such crises. Manuel was talking about something else, something far less easy to put on a map. He was telling us that the version of Haiti he knew and loved was gone. That he felt as if he now lived in a different world, a present separated from a desired past to which he could no longer return.

It is easy to mistake his comment that Haiti is dead as fatalistic resignation. Yet, when I think of Manuel, when I remember his smile, remember running through the market with him, remember all the other things he said and did, the things he hoped for and dreamed about, I hear him saying something terribly sad and yet also profoundly hopeful. I hear him trying to come to terms with the fact that the future is radically open, that even if it is full of crisis, it is also full of possibility—full of all the things that have not yet been and that might yet be. Over the years, I have found myself replaying that conversation with him, turning it over in my mind, amending it. I imagine him saying it over and over again. Haiti is dead. Haiti is dead. There is no more Haiti.

And then I imagine him saying something he didn't say.

Haiti is dead. Long live Haiti.

In the midst of crisis, it can seem that the future is impossible. It can seem like crisis will last forever, that we are stuck in it. To be sure, there will be more crises in the future. It is part of the human condition that we are vulnerable beings, and thus always open to the risk and possibility of crisis. It is equally true that we live in a world full of oppressive forces, and that those forces are not going to go away easily or any time soon. And yet it remains possible to imagine—to hope for—a future without crisis, a future in which we can live. The paths to those futures are all around us. They are in the gardens in the valleys, where peasants live. They are in the terraces on the mountains, where they grow food. They are in the forest and in the city, in the networks and relationships that bind people together. In the ways people look for life. In the stories of people helping people, in the stories of survival, the stories of the aftermath of disaster. The paths to those futures dwell in the stories we tell, the stories we share so that we can know what has happened, so that we can give those happenings a name and a form. The stories we weave together so they become an immense collection of shared thoughts and feelings.

The thing one has come to say is this.

Stories matter. *These* stories matter. They matter because *these* people—Manuel, Alexis, Wilfred, and all the others—*matter*. Their lives and their deaths matter. They lived ordinary lives, suffered ordinary crises, and some of them died ordinary deaths. Yet beyond all this ordinariness lies something else: an account of what it is like to feel powerless in the face of oppressive forces. To feel powerless and yet to keep going.

Notes

1. Trouillot (1995).
2. Trouillot (1990b:5). See also Trouillot (1990a, 1995). For extended discussions of the significance of Trouillot's work, see Beckett (2013d), Bonilla (2014), and Scott (2012).
3. See Das (2007) for a related account of the ordinary.
4. Herskovits (1937, 1938, 1966). For a more theoretically sophisticated account of the process of world making among slaves on Caribbean plantations, see Mintz and Price (1992).
5. Dunham (1994) recounts her experiences in the field in Haiti and her decision to undergo initiation into Vodou in her memoir, *Island Possessed*. Her research on dance in Vodou was published in Dunham (1983). The letters between Herskovits and Dunham are in the Melville J. Herskovits Papers at the Northwestern University Archives in Evanston, Illinois. For more on Dunham, see Aschenbrenner (2002), Beckford (1979), Clark (1994), Dayan (2001), and Glover (2016). For a discussion of Dunham and Herskovits and the "politics of dance anthropology," see Ramsey (2000).
6. Manuel said it in English at the time, but over the years, I heard him and others use English, Kreyòl, and French phrases to express the same idea. In Kreyòl, people would say either *Ayiti mouri* (Haiti is dead) or *Ayiti fini* (Haiti is finished). Mark Schuller (2008) reports that the latter phrase was especially popular in Cité Soleil around this same time.
7. The women I worked with made similar comments, although in general they were more likely to say they were holding strong in the face of present and future crises. There was thus a clearly gendered dimension to such sentiments. Fatalistic-sounding statements, like Manuel's comment, tended to be used more often by urban men who had found themselves in positions in which they were no longer able to generate social forms of value like money or prestige. See chapter 2 for a fuller discussion.

8. Desmangles (1992). For more on death and funerary rites in Vodou, see Deren (1953), Herskovits (1937), and Métraux (1972).

9. See Jackson (1996:2), Geertz (1973), and Desjarlais and Throop (2011:92). For an excellent overview of phenomenological and existential approaches in anthropology, see Desjarlais and Throop (2011). For classic works in phenomenology, see Husserl (1962), Merleau-Ponty (1962), and Schutz (1967). While there is a wide variety of phenomenological approaches in anthropology, the ones that have most influenced the analysis here bring together a focus on subjectivity, moral experience, temporality, and action. See, for example, Biehl (2013), Biehl et al. (2007), Csordas (1994), Das (2007), Desjarlais (2016), Jackson (2005, 2012), Kleinman (1999, 2006), Mattingly (2010a, 2010b), Munn (1986, 1990), Throop (2003, 2010), Turner and Bruner (1986), Willen (2014), and Zigon (2007).

10. Behar (1996). On thick description, see Geertz (1973). On intimacy and ordinary affect, see Berlant (2000) and Stewart (2007).

11. My approach is influenced by feminist anthropological responses to discussions about ethnographic representation, notably the refusal, as Ruth Behar (1995:7) puts it, to "separate creative writing from critical writing."

12. Williams (1977:132). See also Jackson (2013), who argues that storytelling is the primary way in which people mediate between their personal experiences and the public, shared world of meanings and values.

13. Beckett (2014). For a classic discussion of the relation between the city and the country, see Williams (1973). The best accounts of the political crisis in Haiti are Trouillot (1990a) and, more recently, Fatton (2002, 2017).

14. For an excellent ethnography of democratic and popular movements in the 1990s, see Smith (2001). Erica James (2010) offers a rich and nuanced account of the terror and violence that followed the first election of Aristide and the military junta that held power from 1991 to 1994. Paul Farmer famously refers to many of the deaths in Haiti as "stupid deaths" in his work (see Farmer 2005). See also Farmer (2006) for an account of HIV/AIDS alongside the fall of the Duvalier dictatorship. Aristide has published his own views on the democratic transition (Aristide 1990, 1996), and he infamously described the international community's focus on trade liberalization as giving Haitians "a choice between death and death" (Aristide 2000:9).

15. Elsewhere, I have critiqued these various approaches to crisis in Haiti. See Beckett (2013c). See also Farmer (2003, 2006) and Polyné (2013). For critiques of the narratives used in writing about Haiti, see Trouillot (1990b) and Ulysse (2015).

16. Habermas (1975:1). For an overview of the concept of crisis and its application in Haiti, see Beckett (2013c). For related accounts of crisis in Haiti, see Hector (2006) and Trouillot (1990b). For critical histories of the concept of crisis, see Bidney (1946), Goldstone and Obarrio (2016), Koselleck (1988, 2002), Lomnitz (2003), Mbembe and Roitman (1996), Roitman (2014), Starn (1971), and Vigh (2008).

17. Critical phenomenology has done much to show that people are not powerless, even in the most damaging and oppressive of circumstances. For an

overview of critical phenomenology, see Desjarlais and Throop (2011). For extended cases that reclaim subjectivity in the face of terrible situations, see Garcia (2010), Jackson (2012), and Willen (2007, 2014). For accounts of how moments of breakdown and rupture can lead to transformation, see Lear (2006) and Zigon (2007).

18. Richman (2005:266–267).

19. Narayan (2012:13).

20. Jackson (2013:14, 23); see also Behar (1996). See also Joan Didion's (1990:11) famous suggestion that "we tell ourselves stories in order to live."

21. Ochs and Capps (2001:7).

22. In a few cases, I used different pseudonyms in previous publications. Here, I have changed the pseudonyms to better indicate people's social class, region, and background while still concealing their identities.

CHAPTER ONE. THE FOREST AND THE CITY

1. Pogue Harrison (1992:1).

2. Dunham (1994) recounts stories of people searching for buried treasure on the property.

3. For a comprehensive account of the pastoral and the idea of arcadia, see Schama (1995).

4. Marx (2000:21).

5. See Williams (1973) for a detailed account of the relation between the country and the city.

6. CRESDIP (1991). For a long durée account of environmental transformation in the region, see Richardson (1992).

7. Maxo was speaking of the tropical almond tree *(Terminalia catappa)*.

8. CRESDIP (1991:17).

9. For general accounts of political ecology and political economy in anthropology, see Biersack (2006) and Wolf (1972). For related discussion of political ecology in geography, see Robbins (2012). In Haiti, conservationists have argued that the environmental crisis is deeply connected to economic and political issues. CRESDIP (1991) provides the best overview of political ecology in Haiti. See also Catanese (1991). Development experts have long focused on the problem of deforestation (although they have tended to treat the environmental crisis as separate from the broader political and economic crises). The development literature on Haiti is vast, but see the work of Gerald Murray (1979, 1980, 1984, 1990) and Glenn Smucker (1981, 1983, 1988), as well as Murray and Bannister (2004), Smucker and Timyan (1995), Street (1989), Timyan (1984, 1996), and Zimmerman (1986). See Escobar (1996) for a discussion of the relation between liberation theology and political ecology. For a related discussion that links environmental crises to critiques of capitalism, see Peet and Watts (1996).

10. On popular organizations in Haiti, see Smarth (1998) and Smith (2001).

11. See Corvington (1991), Mangonès (2001), and Manigat (1997). For a related discussion of middle-class and elite concerns about urban crime and safety in Brazil, see Caldeira (2000).

12. For a detailed account of the urban crisis, see Beckett (2014). See also Fass (1978a, 1978b), Locher (1978), Mangonès (2001), and Manigat (1997). For ethnographic accounts of neighborhoods in Port-au-Prince, see Kivland (2012a, 2014), Kovats-Bernat (2006b), Lageurre (1982), and Maternowska (2006).

13. Richman (2005).

14. On rural to urban migration in Haiti in the twentieth century, see Farmer (2006), Fass (1978a), Laguerre (1982), Locher (1978), Manigat (1997), and Richman (2005). See Portes et al. (1997) and Potter (2000) for extended discussions of urbanization in the Caribbean region. For a comprehensive history of Port-au-Prince, see Corvington (1975a, 1975b, 1977a, 1977b, 1984, 1987, 1991).

15. The idea that the city has been invaded by "the people" is a potent one among urban elites and the fledgling urban middle class. For a discussion of middle-class fears of the masses in public space, see McAlister (2002:177–181).

16. Wargny (1996:18).

17. For more on Dunham, see Aschenbrenner (2002), Beckford (1979), Clark (1994), Dayan (2001), and Glover (2016). See Dunham (1994) for her own account of her time in Haiti and her relationship to Habitation Leclerc.

18. Pogue Harrison (1992:1).

19. Pogue Harrison (1992:2–3).

20. See Schama (1995) for an excellent account of mythic nature in the Western imaginary. For related discussions of the idea of nature, see also Glacken (1967), Pogue Harrison (1992), Merchant (1980, 2003), A. Schmidt (1971), and Williams (1973).

21. Grove (1995:474).

22. Merchant (2003). See also Glacken (1967) and Grove (1995).

23. Mintz (1966, 1989, 2010) and Trouillot (1992, 2003).

24. Richardson (1992). See also Crosby (1972) and Glissant (1989).

25. Murray (1990:2).

26. CRESDIP (1991). For a discussion of the environmental crisis in Haiti and the differences between Haiti and the Dominican Republic, see Diamond (2005:329–357). While deforestation has been extensive in Haiti, Alex Bellande (2015) has recently shown that the rates of vegetation coverage in the country are higher than previously estimated.

27. McClintock (n.d.) and Murray and Bannister (2004).

28. Haiti did have a botanic garden when it was a French colony. In the eighteenth century, France had the largest and most active network of gardens and botanical research stations in the world. In Saint Domingue, there were at least four colonial gardens built or planned between 1777 and 1804. One of these, the Jardin Botanique du Roi, was located at the Military Hospital in Port-au-Prince and was irrigated by a canal that brought water from the springs at Habitation Leclerc. A new and expanded version of the Jardin Botanique was

proposed in 1789 but was never built. See Corvington (1975a) and McClellan (1992).

29. "Development Plan," September 21, 1993, prepared by E. Forero, P. S. Wyse-Jackson, and T. A. Zanoni, 17–18. Katherine Dunham Botanic Garden Foundation Archives, Martissant, Haiti.

30. "Development Plan," 6.

31. Diamond (2005:329).

32. See Collie (2003), CRESDIP (1991), and Regan (2004).

33. Talk of the death of the lakou in Haiti is now almost a century old. The size of peasant homesteads decreased significantly during the twentieth century, and there has been a general shift away from large, extended cooperative labor organizations and toward individual farming and wage labor. See Smith (2001:89–90) for a brief overview of this literature. See also Bastien (1961, 1985), Conway (1989), Courlander (1960), Herskovits (1937), Lundahl (1979, 1983), Métraux (1951), and Moral (2002). Scholars have tended to focus on both the spatial disintegration of the lakou (smaller plots and the breaking up of peasant households) as well as the withering away of the social relationships associated with such compounds. Nevertheless, the idea of the lakou is a potent one in Haiti, both in the countryside and in the city. As Leslie Desmangles (1992:65) notes, "despite the fact that the lakou has almost disappeared in Haiti recently, the spirit of community in Haitian life has persevered in the face of drastic socioeconomic changes. . . . The spirit of the lakou has not been erased from the Haitian mind, where it continues to survive in ideology rather than in reality." Laguerre (1982) argues that the lakou has survived as a spatial and social form in the cities, where it shapes residence patterns in the slums and popular quarters.

34. The literature on rural life in Haiti is vast, but see, for example, Anglade (1974), Bastien (1961, 1985), Casimir (1982), Comhaire-Sylvain (1961), Courlander (1960), Herskovits (1937), Lahav (1975), Leyburn (1941), Lundahl (1979), Métraux (1951), Mintz (1959, 1961, 1989), Richman (2005), Simpson (1941), Smith (2001), Smucker (1983), Wingfield and Parenton (1965), and Woodson (1990).

35. For excellent discussions of the lakou and family land, see Bastien (1961), Comhaire-Sylvain (1961), Larose (1978), Mintz (1989), and Woodson (1990).

36. Patterson (1982).

37. Mintz (1989:236). See also Mintz and Price (1992).

38. Mintz (1989:155). See also Besson (2002) and Woodson (1990).

39. Woodson (1990:197).

40. "Situation Report," March 2002. Katherine Dunham Botanic Garden Foundation Archives, Martissant, Haiti.

41. Kivland (2012a, 2012b, 2014, 2017, n.d.). For a related discussion of garrison constituencies, see Bogues (2006), Henry-Lee (2005), and Roitman (1998). On the withdrawal of the state from urban life in Port-au-Prince, see Beckett (2014).

42. For a classic account of water markets and water access in Port-au-Prince, see Fass (1982).

43. Chatterjee (2004).

44. Beckett (2014).

45. At the same time, Evans Paul noted that members of the elite had seized land from national parks during the coup period. See Rohter (1995).

46. On the politics of hope, see Appadurai (2007). On disenchantment and Caribbean politics, see Bonilla (2015). On the sense of stuckness and tragedy in Caribbean politics, see Beckett (2017b) and Scott (2014).

47. For a discussion of Celeste and her role in the dispute, see Beckett (2004).

48. "Incident Report for Haitian Government Minister of Foreign Affairs Jean Phillipe Antonio," April 2003. KDBGF Archives, Port-au-Prince, Haiti.

49. On thin simplification and top-down views, see Scott (1998).

50. Dawdy (2016) uses the concept of patina to discuss the archaeology of ruins.

CHAPTER TWO. LOOKING FOR LIFE

1. See Marx (1976), who shows how the wage-labor economy began when peasants were "freed" from the land (that is, dispossessed) and thus unable to live by any means other than selling their labor-power. For a related discussion of migration, see Berger and Mohr's (2010) excellent study of the experience of migrants to Europe in the 1970s.

2. See Simone's (2004) discussion of networks and "people as infrastructure" in South Africa.

3. Farmer (2006).

4. See Maternowska (2006) for a related discussion of "looking for life."

5. Rodman (1988) provides an excellent account of various styles and periods in Haitian art.

6. See Marx's (1976) discussion of primitive accumulation; for an updated account, see Denning's (2010) discussion of what he calls "wageless life." On labor migration in Haiti, see Locher (1978) and Richman (2005). On the development of the industrial, artisanal, and tourist sectors in Port-au-Prince, see Dupuy (1997), Farmer (1988b, 2003), Grunwald et al. (1984), Moral (1959), and Trouillot (1990a).

7. Laguerre (1982). For a general history of urban development in Haiti, see Corvington (1975a, 1975b, 1977a, 1977b, 1984, 1987, 1991).

8. On the issue of planning and the city, see Beckett (2014), Mangonès (2001), and Manigat (1997). On Caribbean cities in general, see Portes et al. (1997) and Potter (2000). For an overview of anthropological approaches to the study of cities and urban life, see Hannerz (1980) and Low (1996).

9. On the history of this spatial and social division, see Anglade (1974), Girault (1981), Moral (2002), and Trouillot (1990a). In Haiti, ideas of color and class are intimately bound up with spatial and social divisions. See Leyburn (1941), Nicholls (1971, 1979a), Trouillot (1990a), and see also Price-Mars (1919)

for a critical discussion of the Haitian elite. For a comparative discussion, see Holston's (2008) rich ethnographic account of social divisions in Brazil, where he suggests that the primary social cleavage is between "insurgent" and "entrenched" citizens.

10. This is very different from the situation of overseas migrants, most of whom do send remittances back to their families and one day hope to return home. For some migrants, though, the demands are heavy. As Richman (2005) argues, some migrants opt out of the demands for remittances by strategically converting to Christianity. The men discussed here are not Evangelical or Protestant Christians, but they have "converted" in a social sense, reorienting their attachments and sense of personhood to the city and the informal economy. For a related discussion of Haitian migration, see Glick Schiller and Fouron (2001); for an overview of the importance of remittances from overseas migrants to the Haitian economy, see Fagen (2006).

11. The men at the shop often used two different Kreyòl terms for talking about work and related activities. When they spoke of wage labor or work that they found to be exploitative, they called it *travay* (laboring). When they spoke of the kinds of artisanal and social activities they engaged in (and which they hoped would earn them money), they called it *fè* (making). In general terms, the distinction was between work done for someone else or under someone else's direction (travay) and work done for oneself (fè). The activity of making also earned money and could be seen as a kind of displaced sale of labor power, but it held a special importance for these men because it included a sense of autonomy over one's activity. For an insightful discussion of these two terms in Haiti, see Conway (1979). For a related discussion of the stigma of wage labor in Haiti and of the importance of individual and collective control over activity and forms of value, see Richman (2005). See also Arendt's (1958) classic discussion of labor and activity.

12. Simone (2004:408). Larkin (2013) provides an excellent overview of anthropological accounts of infrastructure, including of the kinds of social networks discussed here.

13. Mintz (2010). For more on the importance of markets in Haiti, see Girault (1981), Lundahl (1979, 1983), Mintz (1959, 1989), and Woodson (1990).

14. Trouillot (1990a).

15. Mintz (1961:4).

16. Mintz (1961:3); Moral (1959:70). For a classic anthropological discussion of relations of reciprocal exchange and obligation, see Mauss (2000).

17. Mintz (1959, 1961). There are other kinds of networks and relations of reciprocal exchange that also form the foundation of social life in rural Haiti, such as cooperative work groups and peasant groups and associations. See Herskovits (1937), Smith (2001), and Woodson (1990:140).

18. Simone (2004). See also Larkin (2013).

19. Larkin (2013:331).

20. For an excellent account of personhood in Haiti, see Woodson (1990).

21. For a discussion of such networks among street children in Port-au-Prince, see Kovats-Bernat (2006b).

22. On good conduct and character, see Woodson (1990). On responsibility, see Glick Schiller and Fouron (2001).

23. Glick Schiller and Fouron (2001) and Richman (2005).

24. Haiti is a transshipment point for drugs coming into the United States. Drug trafficking began in earnest in the 1980s, amid chronic political instability. The drug trade was originally controlled by the Haitian army and by members of the Duvalier dictatorship. After the fall of the regime and the disbanding of the army, there has been competition among various groups to control the trade.

25. Trouillot (1990a) shows how the transition from the Duvalier dictatorship allowed for much continuity. See also Barthelemy (1992).

26. I have written elsewhere about respè (Beckett 2017a). See also Glick Schiller and Fouron (2001), Kivland (2014), and Smith (2001). Sennett (2003) provides an interesting account of respect as a social value and an ethical disposition. For a related ethnographic account of the place of respect in social relations, see Bourgois (2003).

27. Beckett (2017a). On respect, gender, and class in the Caribbean more broadly, see Wilson (1973).

28. On everyday ethics and interaction, see Lambek (2010).

29. For related discussions of the breakdown of social worlds, see Erikson (1994) and Lear (2006).

30. Schuller (2012:29) discusses the issue of inflation during the 2004–6 provisional period. Protests over the high cost of living have a deep history in Haiti. See Hector (2006) and Nicholls (1979b) for discussions of rural and urban protests over wages, prices, and related costs of living. The high cost of living has become a flashpoint of contemporary politics throughout the Caribbean. See Bonilla (2015:148–173) for a related discussion of such political protests in Guadeloupe.

31. McGuigan (2006). See also Dupuy (1997).

32. See Neiburg (2016) for a discussion of the Haitian dollar. For historical accounts of U.S. dollar diplomacy in Haiti and the Caribbean, see Plummer (1988) and H. Schmidt (1971).

33. At the time of this writing, the current rate is about 70 HTG to 1 USD.

34. For related anthropological accounts of value, see Appadurai (1986), Blunt (2016), Graeber (2001), Marx (1976), Munn (1986), and Turner (2008, 2012).

35. Denning (2010).

36. Informality and precarity are the prevailing conditions for most of the world's population. See Davis (2006), Muehlebach (2013), and Standing (2011). For an excellent ethnographic analysis of precarity, see Allison (2013).

37. See Minn (2016) for an insightful discussion of moral economies in Haiti.

38. Hannah Arendt (1958) provides an excellent philosophical discussion of the relation between action and the world. For detailed accounts of the collapse

of social worlds, see Erikson (1994) and Lear (2006). For an overview of phenomenological approaches to action in the world, see Desjarlais and Throop
(2011) and Jackson (1996, 2005, 2012).

39. On shock as a medical condition, see Brodwin (1996) and James (2004, 2008, 2010).

CHAPTER THREE. MAKING DISORDER

1. I give an overview of these representations of Haiti in Beckett (2013c). See also Trouillot (1990b) and Ulysse (2015). In 2018, President Trump referred to Haiti as a "shithole country."

2. The state telecommunications company was privatized in 2010.

3. See Nicholls (1978, 1979a), Pressoir et al. (1953), and Trouillot (1999). The first great Haitian historians provided the template for the relationship between historiography and the political claims of various social groups and political parties. See Ardouin (1958) and Madiou (1989).

4. Trouillot (1990a) argues that Duvalierism was a kind of totalitarianism. For more on the relationship between color and politics in Haiti, see Duvalier (1968), Leyburn (1941), Nicholls (1979a), and Price-Mars (1951, 1983).

5. For an excellent discussion of Aristide's oratory, see Meehan (1999). For examples of Aristide's mode of speaking and writing, see Aristide (1990, 1996, 2000).

6. For an insightful discussion of the use of such "culture heroes" by politi-cians, see Dunham (1994:161–165). See also Lhérisson (1954).

7. See Aristide (2008) and Nesbitt (2008). Aristide's attempt to "complete" the revolution of Toussaint Louverture was not well received. His claim for reparations was roundly rejected by France, and the Haitian elite cast Aristide as an authoritarian leader who was politicizing history. See Beckett (2013a), Chomsky et al. (2004), and Hallward (2007).

8. Laferrière et al. (2005). Dessalines is framed as a monster by foreigners in part because, after declaring independence, he ordered the killing of most of the white planters who remained in the former colony.

9. Beckett (2013a) and Dubois (2012).

10. Beckett (2013a) and Dubois (2012, 2013).

11. Trouillot (1995).

12. For more on cleansing rites in Haiti, see Beckett (2004).

13. For an extended discussion of the ceremony, see Beckett (2004). See also Courlander (1960) and Métraux (1972) for detailed accounts of Vodou. For a related discussion of Earth-Mother spirits in Afro-Caribbean religions, see Herskovits (1966). On the relationships between family and land in Vodou, see Larose (1978).

14. This is quite similar to how Dunham (1994) says she was "told" to live at Habitation Leclerc by her patron lwa.

15. Tidjo was drawing on Aristide's populist discourse, which casts the elite as "big eaters" *(gran manjè)* who take everything and leave nothing for the

people. One of Aristide's main metaphors for democracy was that everyone would be able to sit at the same table and eat together. See Aristide (1990, 1996) and Meehan (1999).

16. See Laguerre (1982), Lahav (1975), Nicholls (1979a), and Trouillot (1990a).

17. For more on the chimè, see Fatton (2002).

18. On color and class in Haiti, see Nicholls (1979a) and Trouillot (1990a).

19. Beckett (2004).

20. Throop (2014:80). For a related discussion of the ethical aspects of emotions, see Fassin (2013).

21. Aristide was elected in 1990—and removed by a coup just seven months after he took office. He was in exile for three years and returned to Haiti only after a U.S.-led military intervention in 1994. The international community called for new elections at the end of his five-year term, despite protests from his supporters that he had not been able to govern during most of his appointed term in office. The U.S.-led mission and the UN-led civilian mission that followed it are often referred to in Haiti as the second U.S. occupation (the first being the U.S. military occupation of 1915–34).

22. The best account of the violence of the de facto period is in James (2010).

23. Herzfeld (1997:3).

24. Luc was drawing on a range of class signifiers. He said that in the early years, those associated with Lavalas really were "of the people"—that is, they were black and from poor neighborhoods or rural areas. For Luc, this was key to their success during the elections, but it also meant they were not competent leaders because they lacked the training, skills, and expertise that members of the elite possessed.

25. During this period, some members of the opposition revived an old slogan from the mulatto elite that called for power to go to the most competent (rather than to the most representative, as black political leaders often claimed). For a historical account of black and mulatto party politics in the nineteenth century, see Nicholls (1971, 1974, 1978, 1979a, 1979b) and Trouillot (1990a).

26. For more on this period, see Dupuy (2005a, 2007). On the relation between the state, civil society, and NGOs, see Fatton (2002), Glick Schiller and Fouron (2001), and Schuller (2007, 2008, 2012).

27. There were reported irregularities with several seats won in legislative elections in 2000, but the opposition also denounced the presidential elections the following year, despite the international community's declaration that the presidential elections had been free and fair. The Organization of American States tried to broker a solution to the political crisis that followed the elections. The opposition rejected the results and tried to form their own government. Later they rejected all power-sharing solutions and proclaimed that only the removal of Aristide himself would solve the crisis. See Dupuy (2005a, 2007) and Fatton (2002).

28. For discussions of how terror infiltrates everyday life, see Das (2007) and Taussig (1992).

29. See Das (2007) on the problem of sharing the experience of pain and the representation of violence and terror.

30. People would also say *m pa nan politik,* I'm not in politics.

31. James (2010) offers a detailed account of insecurity and terror during and after the 1991–94 de facto period in Haiti. For a related discussion of terror and insecurity, see Taussig (1992).

32. Laguerre (1982) shows how, during the Duvalier dictatorship, the makout controlled many neighborhoods in the city. In the ensuing decades, various armed groups, generally now called gangs (although there have been different names for different groups over the years), have taken control of many urban areas. These zones are similar to the infamous garrison communities of Kingston, Jamaica, which have been an entrenched part of that country's political system for over fifty years. Garrison communities in Kingston are typically poor, underserved, low-cost urban areas that are under the de facto control of gangs linked to the country's various political parties. Anthony Bogues (2006:23) argues that in such communities, violence "links itself to the operation of power in small geographical spaces—lanes, streets or other divisions of small communities. This violence is not an incipient form of insurgency, but rather a way of constructing rule in local communities, a form of disorder deployed to produce or create order." For more on the Jamaican case, see Henry-Lee (2005) and Thomas (2011, 2016). See also Barker (2006), Comaroff and Comaroff (2006), and Roitman (1998). For an excellent ethnographic account of contemporary gangs in Haiti, see Kivland (2012b, 2014, 2017). James (2010) offers a detailed account of how paramilitary and military groups exerted a different kind of violence on urban communities. In Port-au-Prince, it is widely suspected that many former military and paramilitary personnel are the leading figures of the newer gangs.

33. Taussig (1992).

34. Comaroff and Comaroff (2004). See also Aretxaga (2005) for an innovative theoretical approach that shows how violence and terror are essential elements of political order.

35. Groupe des 184's platform was solidly neoliberal; they wanted to reduce the role of the state and liberalize trade. The group's founders were heavily invested in the export business and, not surprisingly, their overall economic plan favored using public money to expand the private sector. They described themselves as a civil society movement and as a popular middle-class movement, although members and supporters were mainly from the country's most elite families. For a general discussion of the concept of civil society and its various political uses, see Comaroff and Comaroff (1999).

36. In the negotiations during the political crisis, France and other members of the international community sided with the Groupe des 184 and the Democratic Convergence and urged Aristide to step down. Withholding foreign aid was one of the key tactics used by the international community to weaken the Aristide government and prevent it from effectively governing. See Dupuy (2005a, 2005b).

37. Many people with HIV/AIDS die from opportunistic infections, and in Haiti tuberculosis is a common cause of such deaths. Haiti has historically had one of the highest rates of HIV infection in the Caribbean, although the rate has gone down in recent years. In the 1980s, Haiti was falsely accused of being the origin-point of the spread of HIV/AIDS into North America. In part because of this history of blame, there remains much stigma associated with the illness in Haiti. See Farmer (2006).

38. Bloch and Adorno (1988:9). See also Bloch (1986).

39. Aristide added to the quote after his own kidnapping, saying, "I declare in overthrowing me they have uprooted the trunk of the tree of peace, but it will grow back because the roots are Louverturian." See Dubois (2007).

40. For critical assessments of the 2004 coup, see Arthur (2004), Beckett (2010), Blumenthal (2004), Chomsky et al. (2004), Dupuy (2005a, 2007), Hallward (2007), and Sprague (2012).

41. For more on Chamblain and his role in paramilitary violence and human rights violations, see Farmer (2003), Grann (2001), Human Rights Watch (1994), and Sprague (2012).

42. Trouillot (1990a:224–225, italics in original). See also Beckett (2010), Blumenthal (2004), Chomsky et al. (2004), Hallward (2007), and Sprague (2012). For a critical overview of how the foreign press covered the 2004 coup, see Soderlund (2006).

43. Lévi-Strauss (1963) argued that repetition reveals the underlying structure of a myth.

CHAPTER FOUR. BETWEEN LIFE AND DEATH

1. This is a commonly told joke in Port-au-Prince.

2. This account of Haitian concepts of death and funerary rites is taken from interviews and from the ethnographic literature on Haiti. See, especially, Desmangles (1992:68–72) for a thorough overview. See also Deren (1953), Herskovits (1937), and Métraux (1972).

3. Accounts of civil war were common in Port-au-Prince, among all social classes, although it was not a very accurate description. What was really happening was a systematic campaign of political violence and repression meant to break the back of the popular movement. Nevertheless, it was also the case that criminal and political gangs were fighting for their territories and their lives, as internecine warfare broke out between rival gangs and between the gangs, the police, and the UN. For an account of this period that examines it as a civil war, see Kovats-Bernat (2006a, 2006b). For a criticism of the framing of this period as a civil war, see Sprague (2012). I have elsewhere (Beckett 2010) argued that the 2004 coup is perhaps better understood through the concept of a state of exception, although as Giorgio Agamben (2015) has suggested (writing of a different context), civil war is the flip side of the state of exception.

4. This account is based on telephone interviews and personal communication, as well as interviews conducted after I returned to Haiti in 2006.

5. The information here is based on human rights reports, investigative reports, and also interviews during and after this period. In some cases, I omit identifying names and descriptions to protect sources. For more on this period, see Chomsky et al. (2004), Delva (2006a), Griffin (2004), Kolbe and Hutson (2006), Kovats-Bernat (2006a, 2006b), Lindsay (2006), Schuller (2008, 2012), and Sprague (2012).

6. Griffin (2004).

7. These stories and images were circulated online, in email listservs, and in other venues. In 2006, *The Lancet* published an article that confirmed many of these stories, although some of the details of the article were later challenged by MINUSTAH. See Kolbe and Hutson (2006).

8. There is still much debate about the origins and intended meaning of "Operation Baghdad." Some gangs adopted the term to describe their insurgency. From my own experience, the term was most often used by the provisional government and its supporters to portray the gangs as terrorists. It was meant to appeal to a global audience and to call to mind the War on Terror launched by the United States. For a discussion of Operation Baghdad from the point of view of the Bel Air neighborhood, see Kivland (2012a, 2012b, 2014, 2017).

9. Scarry (1985). As Bahrani (2008) notes, the body is central to war and violence, but so too are rituals, monuments, and the space of the city itself, all of which are often reconfigured in dramatic ways by the violence of sovereign power.

10. René Girard (1977) offers a powerful way to think about how violence spreads contagiously through mimicry and reciprocal exchanges of violent acts. For ethnographic accounts that build on Girard's work, see Aretxaga (2005, 2008) and Feldman (1991).

11. See Caldeira (2000) for a related account of how the threat and fear of violence circulates through rumor, public speech, and what she calls "crime talk."

12. James (2008:135; cf. James 2010).

13. James (2004, 2008, 2010) provides the best account of ensekirite in Haiti.

14. Quoted in James (2010; see also James 2004, 2008). James's fieldwork was also based in Martissant, and her work provides a rich ethnographic account of the experience of terror in Martissant during the 1990s, as well as the equally disastrous experience of the aid apparatus in the aftermath of the de facto regime.

15. Giddens (1984:61). Giddens's discussion of ontological security and insecurity is based on Bruno Bettelheim's account of his experience in a Nazi concentration camp. For a related discussion of the importance of the concentration camp to contemporary experiences of political instability and insecurity, see Giorgio Agamben (1998, 1999).

16. See Kai Erikson (1994) for his discussion of how violent disasters destroy the context for meaning and action in social life.

17. Trouillot (1990a) argues that the Duvalier dictatorship changed the established rules of the game and made new groups possible targets of political violence (notably women). James (2010) shows how the military and paramili-

tary violence after the fall of the dictatorship opened up even more possibilities for violence and terror. In the period after the 2004 coup, criminal violence from gangs was felt by many urban residents to be a new phenomenon, in part because it meant that social class or political affiliation were no longer enough to protect people from violence. Despite the widespread experience of violence during this period, Haiti has had historically low levels of violent crime, especially when compared with other countries in the Caribbean and the Americas (see Thomas 2011).

18. Das (2007) and Thomas (2011).

19. On the spread of violence and reciprocal violence in the midst of crisis, see Girard (1977). For compelling theoretical and ethnographic accounts of exceptional and ordinary violence and on the relationship between violence, time, space, experience, and subjectivity, see Das (2007), Das et al. (1997), Feldman (1991), and Thomas (2011, 2016).

20. See Das and Kleinman (1997:12) for a discussion of the "survivor's tale" and the "sufferer's lament" as key ways in which those who have suffered violence try to restore a sense of ordered temporality to their experience. Mattingly (2010a, 2010b) explores the role of narrative and "moral willing" in making it through difficult life events and charting a possible future. Ochs and Capps (2001:6–7) argue that conversation is the primary mode people use to work through "unresolved life events" and make sense of what has happened to them. Talking about violence after the coup was thus both a way of making sense of events that threatened to destroy meaning and context and, at the same time, a way of refashioning people's sense of self and subjectivity in the face of alienating and objectifying forces.

21. Anthropologists Gerald Murray and Glenn Smucker have long been proponents of similar ideas and have argued for the importance of development projects that focus on trees as cash crops (rather than on conversation projects). They have both written extensively on the topic, but see especially Murray (1979, 1980, 1984), Murray and Bannister (2004), Smucker (1981, 1983, 1988), and Smucker and Timyan (1995).

22. See Girard (1977) for more on how violence operates in ritual contexts to reproduce social order. See also Aretxaga (2005), Bahrani (2008), Benjamin (1978), Derrida (1991), and Scarry (1985).

23. See Das (2007), Das and Kleinman (1997), and Das et al. (1997). For a detailed account of how violence obliterates but also shapes social life in Haiti, see James (2008, 2010).

24. Brodwin (1996:101, 210, n. 17). For more on Haitian concepts of the body and illness, see Farmer (1988a), James (2004, 2008, 2010), and Philippe and Romain (1979). Brown (2001) provides an excellent account of the relationship between Vodou and healing in Haiti.

25. Desmangles (1992:67). See also Brodwin (1996), Deren (1953), and Métraux (1972). This was how people in Port-au-Prince talked about the relation between the soul and the body, but this cosmological model is not used everywhere in Haiti.

26. Desmangles (1992:67–68).

27. In Kreyòl there are two related ways of talking about actions that accomplish things in the world. *Pouvwa* (power) is more closely related to labor or labor-power and is used to name the ability to get work done. *Fòs* (force) also names the ability to act in the world but typically means strength or a more general ability to do things. It also has a political sense, as in its use in the national slogan, from the revolutionary era, that "union makes strength" *(l'union fait la force).* For a nuanced account of pouvwa and fòs in contemporary Haiti, see Kivland (2012b). See also Arendt's (1958) philosophical account of action.

28. The philosopher Bernard Williams (1985) drew a distinction between thin ethical concepts (abstract ideas such as the right or the good) and thick ethical concepts (culturally embedded values like gratitude, shame, or respect). Williams was likely influenced by Gilbert Ryle's phrase "thick description," which was famously used by Clifford Geertz (1973) to describe a rich and nuanced ethnographic account of other people's lives. For related accounts that situate morality and ethics in a kind of thick phenomenology, see Desjarlais (2016), Garcia (2010), Throop (2010, 2014), and Willen (2007, 2014).

29. The state-run electrical company, Electricité d'Haïti (EdH) is widely regarded to be both corrupt and inefficient and is known to cut service to those unwilling to pay extortion schemes (like double or triple billing, extra fees for no additional service, etc.). Blackouts and brownouts are regular occurrences in the city, and there are many areas of the country with no access to the power grid. Elite families and private businesses use generators to insulate themselves from blackouts, converting their wealth and privilege into privatized sources of power when the public grid fails. For related discussions of electrical services, see Martínez (2007) and Schnitzler (2013).

30. It was not just Vincent and Jean who spoke of blackouts in this way. It became a prominent way of speaking about crisis after the 2004 coup.

31. Brown (1987:151–152); Richman (2005:15–16).

32. Trouillot (1990a) provides an excellent overview of the Haitian state and shows how most Haitians see the state as oppressive and as something from which they want to escape. Supporters of the democratic transition imagined a transformation of the relationship between state and society, and the promise of the Lavalas movement was that the state would finally become "responsible" for (and to) citizens. On the idea of the responsible state in Haiti, see Glick Schiller and Fouron (2001). On the possibilities and problems of the democratic era, see Dupuy (2007) and Fatton (2002). For an excellent discussion of the "unmaking of the state" in Haiti, see Kivland (2012b). For a detailed account of how foreign aid and the presence of NGOs has undermined the ability of the Haitian state to govern, see Schuller (2007, 2008, 2012).

33. Glick Schiller and Fouron (2001) refer to "the apparent state" to capture the idea that the state is not present or actively governing. Kivland (2012b) describes it as the "unmaking" of the state. During this period, it was common to hear people in Port-au-Prince say that "there is no state" or "we don't have a state."

34. Dupuy (2007:194–203).
35. See Kivland (2012b) for a related discussion.
36. Soderlund (2006:95). See also Greenburg (2013).
37. Kivland (2012b:257).
38. Delva (2006b).
39. Mulet, on *Radio Metropole*, August 24, 2006. The initial mandate for MINUSTAH required it to operate under the direction of the Haitian National Police. Beginning in August 2006, the Préval government granted the UN the power to carry out its own operations without the police.
40. For more on the history of the armed forces in Haiti, see Dumas (1988), Laguerre (1993), and Trouillot (1990a).
41. See Trouillot (1990a:104–108) on the creation of an American-trained army during the U.S. occupation of 1915–34. For a discussion of the uses of "political armies" as American proxies, see Beckett (2010).
42. The restoration of the Haitian armed forces remains a charged issue. President Martelly (2011–16) promised to restore the army, although he was unable to do so during his term. In 2017, after the UN announced plans to withdraw its troops at the end of the year, the Haitian government formally reinstated the armed forces.
43. It was no accident that the crisis of sovereignty generated talk of the death penalty and of the military. As many scholars have noted, sovereignty is intimately bound up with the power over life and death. See Benjamin (1978) for a famous account of sovereign power and violence. See also Agamben (1998, 2005) and Foucault (1986). For an excellent overview of the literature on sovereignty, see Hansen and Stepputat (2006); and for ethnographic studies of sovereignty, see Hansen and Stepputat (2005). See also James's (2010) detailed account of the politics of death in Haiti.
44. Derrida (2014).
45. This was Max Weber's famous definition of the state. See Giddens (1987) on the relation between the state and violence.
46. Foucault (1986, 2003).
47. On policing, violence, and sovereign power, see Agamben (2000:103–107). See Denyer Willis (2015) for an ethnographic account of police violence in Brazil.
48. See Marcelin (2012:259) for a similar discussion of *move san* and *move moun*. See Farmer (1988a) on *move san* as an illness that can be treated.
49. Marcelin (2012:259).
50. The Haitian National Police (HNP) was created in 1994 to replace the armed forces, which had been disbanded that same year by Aristide. The creation of the HNP was contentious, with various groups vying for control over what would become the only legitimate armed force in the country. See Podur (2012:22–24) for more on the creation of the HNP and the prevalence of former military and paramilitary personnel in the new force. For a general theoretical discussion of the relation between military and police forces, see Jauregui (2010).

51. Félix's connections to municipal and state officials were well known throughout the neighborhood. His arrest was widely reported in local media, although the HNP later denied that he had been arrested and that he was in police custody.

52. Deibert (2005:144); Kovats-Bernat (2006a:132). Some saw the zero-tolerance policy as a cover for Aristide to politicize the HNP and direct them against his political opponents. Aristide's supporters saw it as a necessary corrective to the continued presence of other armed groups in the country. For more on zinglendo and chimè, see Fatton (2002). For a detailed assessment of the role of paramilitaries in Haiti, see Sprague (2012).

53. For more on the links between sorcery, sacrifice, and magic on one hand and moral discourses about power and authority on the other, see Brown (2001), Hurbon (1987), Larose (1978), and Richman (2005). Stephan Palmié (2002) provides a rich theoretical discussion of magic and power in the Caribbean region more widely.

54. Agamben (1998).

55. Lulu Garcia-Navarro, 2007, "Violence-Plagued Haiti Sees More Peaceful Days," NPR, August 1. http://www.npr.org/templates/story/story.php?storyId = 12424369.

56. Podur (2012:129).

57. See Frédérick Mangonès, 2014, "Le Marron Inconnu d'Albert Mangonès," *Le Nouvelliste,* July 8. http://lenouvelliste.com/lenouvelliste/article/132915/Le-Marron-Inconnu-dAlbert-Mangones (accessed August 15, 2017).

CHAPTER FIVE. AFTERMATH

1. In psychoanalytic terms, displacement is a part of the distortion and censorship of the dream-work and is a process by which the mechanisms of repression conceal or transform the meaning of unconscious desires. In international law, displaced persons are those who have been forced to leave their home because of a violent conflict or a disaster. In this chapter, I am interested in how displacement feels and how, over time, it comes to provide a set of new spatial and social coordinates as temporary emergency responses become permanent fixtures of daily life. See Georgina Ramsay (2017) for a related discussion of what she calls "displaced lives" and the violence of refugee resettlement. For an evocative account of migration and displacement, see Berger and Mohr (2010).

2. Erikson (1976, 1994) suggests that we should redefine disasters by their effects, notably by how such events cause individual and collective trauma.

3. Eyal Weizman (2011, 2017) has pioneered the field of forensic architecture.

4. For example, soon after the earthquake, the Inter-American Development Bank (2010) described it as "the most destructive natural disaster in modern times." That designation was based both on the loss of life and on the estimated costs of recovery and reconstruction. For general accounts of the earthquake

and its aftermath, see Bell (2013), Farmer (2011), Greenburg (2013), Katz (2013), Kivland (2012a), Klarreich and Polman (2012), Laferrière (2011), Munro (2010), Orner and Lyon (2017), Schuller (2012, 2013, 2015, 2016), Schuller and Morales (2012), Titus (2012), and Ulysse (2015).

5. For more on the coverage of the earthquake and on international aid, see McAlister (2012), Munro (2010), and Ulysse (2015).

6. There were just over 1,300 camps officially registered with the International Organization of Migration, but there were hundreds of unofficial or "ghost" camps that were unregistered and thus cut off from the formal channels of aid delivery. See Mark Schuller's excellent ethnographic work on the camps in Haiti (Schuller 2012, 2013, 2015, 2016; Schuller and Morales 2012). See also Bell (2013), Kivland (2012a), Orner and Lyon (2017), and Titus (2012).

7. See Satterthwaite (2011) and Satterthwaite and Moses (2012) for critical discussions of how indicators are used by humanitarian agencies.

8. "Beyond the mountains, more mountains" *(Dèyè mòn, gen mòn)* is a famous proverb in Haiti.

9. See McGuigan (2006) for a classic account of the effects of trade liberalization on food production and on food prices in Haiti. For historical accounts of the collapse of the agricultural sector, see Farmer (2003), Lundahl (1979, 1983), Trouillot (1990a), and Woodson (1997).

10. Land ownership is a key issue in Haiti. After independence, former slaves opted to become cultivators, and they exerted enormous effort to acquire their own land through purchases, land grants, or squatting. Since that time, the problems of population pressure and land degradation have been further exacerbated by forceful dispossession, as peasants have been moved off their land. While there is still a sizable peasantry in Haiti, many rural farmers now work on land they do not own, either as wage laborers or as sharecroppers. See Richman (2005) for a detailed account of the expropriation of land in and around Léogâne. For more on land tenure in Haiti, see Lacerte (1975, 1978, 1981), Lahav (1975), Larose (1978), Lundahl (1983), Métraux (1951), Moral (2002), Murray (1980), Trouillot (1990a), Woodson (1990), and Zuvekas (1979).

11. Karen Richman (2005) suggests that conversion to Protestantism is sometimes a strategic move that allows people to opt out of the demanding ties of responsibility and obligation to family, ancestors, and the Vodou lwa. Protestant churches disavow Vodou rites and the relations of mutual support that go with them, and Protestantism encourages an ethic of individual accumulation that is quite different from the ethic of reciprocal exchange commonly found in Haitian Vodou. Many Protestants in Haiti, however, see their conversion as part of a spiritual calling.

12. See Catanese (1991), CRESDIP (1991), Pierre-Louis (1986), Pierre-Louis (1989), Smucker (1981), Street (1989), and Voltaire (1979) for more on deforestation, logging, and charcoal production in Haiti.

13. See Weiner (2004) and Weiner and Polgreen (2004).

14. UNDP (2004:3). In the late 1990s, the UNDP had been tasked with creating a National Plan for Disaster and Risk Management in Haiti. As part of

their plan, they had paid for the development of Haiti's Civil Protection Directorate (Direction de la Protection Civile, DPC), an organization that was charged with assessing and managing risks and responding to disasters. But the DPC was chronically underfunded and was unable to adequately prepare for or respond to disasters.

15. See the Weather Underground's list of the deadliest Atlantic hurricanes. https://www.wunderground.com/hurricane/deadly.asp.

16. Davis (1998:54). See also Beckett (2013b) and Calhoun (2004) on emergencies. For more on the relation between natural hazards and social disasters, see Hoffman and Oliver-Smith (2002), Oliver-Smith (1996, 2002, 2006), and Perrow (1999, 2007). For an expansive account of disaster as a social event, see Erikson (1994).

17. On normal accidents and technological disasters, see Perrow (1999). On the social calculus of disaster, see Smith (2006).

18. Arthur (2004) and Pina (2004).

19. See Arthur (2004), Danticat (2004), Gubbels and Brakenridge (2004), Pina (2004), and UNDP (2004).

20. See Marc Lacey, 2008, "Meager Living of Haitians Is Wiped Out by Storms," *New York Times*, September 10. http://www.nytimes.com/2008/09/11/world/americas/11haiti.html.

21. On the geology of the quake, see Mercier de Lépinay et al. (2011). The temblor added tension to a major fault line, and some warned that the 2010 earthquake might be a triggering event for another, equally strong temblor in the near future. See also "Six Years after Devastating Haiti Quake, Risks Still High," *Jamaica Observer*, January 12, 2016. http://www.jamaicaobserver.com/news/Six-years-after-devastating-Haiti-quake—risks-still-high.

22. For more on how people talked about the earthquake, see Bell (2013), Farmer (2011), Laferrière (2011), Munro (2010, 2015), and Titus (2012).

23. Of course, the counting did matter, although there was much debate that surrounded it. In the first weeks after the earthquake, the Haitian government estimated that 316,000 people had been killed. Some disputed that number, suggesting that the death toll was somewhere between 65,000 and 111,000. Most aid workers and researchers have accepted the higher numbers. The death toll, along with other measures such as the destruction of property and infrastructure, are key ways that donors estimate the amount of aid needed for reconstruction. See Lundahl (2012:202–209) for an overview of the controversy surrounding the counting of the dead. For an insightful theoretical discussion of the "social life of numbers" in the aftermath of genocide and disaster, see Nelson (2015).

24. In the immediate aftermath of the earthquake, there were many stories of hope and survival, of people helping people. See Bell (2013), Farmer (2011), Kivland (2012a), Laferrière (2011), McAlister (2012), Munro (2010), Schuller (2016), Titus (2012), and Wagner (2015).

25. Solnit (2009); see also Erikson (1994:235).

26. For detailed ethnographic accounts of helping others, especially in the camps, see Schuller (2012, 2016).

27. Oliver-Smith (2002). See also Hoffman and Oliver-Smith (2002).

28. Erikson (1994:240–241).

29. It took about four years to clear all the rubble. Much of it was dumped in unofficial sites outside the city.

30. Farmer (2006:255).

31. Katz (2013) and Farmer (2011).

32. Beckett (2014) and Mangonès (2001).

33. Farmer (2011) also invoked the idea of a "Marshall Plan for Haiti."

34. Katz (2013:5–12) discusses the collapse of the school. On the question of the lack of the state, see Beckett (2014:49–50), Kivland (2012b), Glick Schiller and Fouron (2001), and Schuller (2007, 2012).

35. On the UN losses in the quake and on the American military presence in Haiti, see Farmer (2011).

36. Smirl (2015). For an excellent discussion of the aid apparatus in Haiti, see James (2010) and Schuller (2012, 2016).

37. Klarreich and Polman (2012).

38. Klarreich and Polman (2012) and McAlister (2012).

39. See Malkki (2015) for a related account of teddy bears and humanitarian giving.

40. On the camp authorities and aid in the camps, see Schuller (2013, 2016) and Schuller and Morales (2012).

41. On the problem of "victim" as a category in aid work, see James (2010).

42. Beckett (2014, 2017a). For more on Bel Air after the quake, see Kivland (2012a). For a related account of Cité Soleil after the earthquake, see Marcelin (2015).

43. On the history of Bel Air, see Kivland (2014, 2017) and Laguerre (1982). For comparable histories of Cité Soleil, see Marcelin (2015), Maternowska (2006), and Schuller (2008, 2012). For a general history of Port-au-Prince, see Beckett (2014), Corvington (1975a, 1975b, 1977a, 1977b, 1984, 1987, 1991), and Mangonès (2001).

44. I explore the meaning of Timo's comment in greater detail elsewhere (Beckett 2017a).

45. See Coppinger and Coppinger (2001), Franco (2014), Ingold (1994), and Tuan (1984).

46. See Beckett (2017a) for an extended discussion of the meaning of dogs in Haiti.

47. On canine warfare, see Johnson (2009).

48. Stevens (1995:75, emphasis in original).

49. Beckett (2017a). See also Glick Schiller and Fouron (2001), Kovats-Bernat (2006b), Smith (2001), and Stevens (1995).

50. For an expanded discussion of Bel Air and gangs, see Kivland (2012b, 2014, 2017).

51. Women also played a key role in the delivery of food and other aid in the camps. See Schuller (2013, 2015, 2016).

52. Government of Haiti (2014). On Haiti's rank as a water-poor country, see Lawrence et al. (2002). Farmer (2005:30) notes how Haiti's rankings on human security are consistently on par with countries in the midst of protracted civil war. On cholera in Haiti, see Frerichs (2016). For critical accounts of the humanitarian response to the earthquake, see Katz (2013) and Schuller (2016).

53. For an overview of the epidemic, see Frerichs (2016).

54. Esquivel et al. (2017) and Lederer (2017).

55. Katz (2013:135–154). Fatton (2017) argues that Haiti has become a trusteeship. For more on the crisis of sovereignty in Haiti after the quake, see Maguire and Freeman (2017).

56. Collier, cited in Katz (2013:139).

57. For general accounts of these economic development plans, see Dupuy (1997, 2005a), Farmer (2003, 2006), and Trouillot (1990a).

POSTSCRIPT

1. The memorial was created in January 2012 and is located at Habitation Leclerc, which is now a national park. Following the death of Katherine Dunham in 2006, ownership and control of Habitation Leclerc passed from the KDBGF to a new organization called FOKAL (Fondasyon Konesans ak Libète), a Haitian civil society group that works with local communities, the Haitian government, and international NGOs on urban renewal projects. Under FOKAL's direction, Habitation Leclerc was renamed Parc de Martissant. They have since built a library and a cultural center on the property, in addition to the memorial for the victims of the earthquake. See http://fokal.org.

2. Dunham (1994).

3. On the tanbou assoto, see Roumain (2007).

4. United Nations, 2018, "Revised Humanitarian Response Plan, January–December 2018." https://reliefweb.int/sites/reliefweb.int/files/resources/2018_haiti_revised_hrp_2.pdf.

5. Quoted in Narayan (2012:13).

References

Agamben, Giorgio. 1998. *Homo Sacer: Sovereign Power and Bare Life*. Translated by Daniel Heller-Roazen. Stanford, CA: Stanford University Press.

———. 1999. *Remnants of Auschwitz: The Witness and the Archive*. Translated by Daniel Heller-Roazen. New York: Zone Books.

———. 2000. *Means without End: Notes on Politics*. Translated by Vincenzo Binetti and Cesare Casarino. Minneapolis: University of Minnesota Press.

———. 2005. *State of Exception*. Translated by Kevin Attell. Chicago: University of Chicago Press.

———. 2015. *Statis: Civil War as a Political Paradigm*. Translated by Nicholas Heron. Stanford, CA: Stanford University Press.

Allison, Anne. 2013. *Precarious Japan*. Durham, NC: Duke University Press.

Anglade, Georges. 1974. *L'Espace Haïtien*. Montréal: Les Presses de l'Université du Québec.

Appadurai, Arjun, ed. 1986. *The Social Life of Things: Commodities in Cultural Perspective*. Cambridge, UK: Cambridge University Press.

———. 2007. "Hope and Democracy." *Public Culture* 19(1): 29–34.

Ardouin, Beaubrun. 1958. *Études sur l'Histoire d'Haïti* (11 volumes). Port-au-Prince: François Dalencour.

Arendt, Hannah. 1958. *The Human Condition*, 2nd edition. Chicago: University of Chicago Press.

Aretxaga, Begoña. 2005. *States of Terror: Begoña Aretxaga's Essays*. Edited by Joseba Zulaika. Reno: Center for Basque Studies, University of Nevada.

———. 2008. "Madness and the Politically Real: Reflections on Violence in Postdictatorial Spain." In *Postcolonial Disorders*, edited by Mary-Jo DelVecchio Good, Sandra Teresa Hyde, Sarah Pinto, and Bryan J. Good, 43–61. Berkeley: University of California Press.

Aristide, Jean-Bertrand. 1990. *In the Parish of the Poor: Writings from Haiti*. Edited and translated by Amy Wilentz. Maryknoll, NY: Orbis Books.

———. 1996. *Dignity*. Charlottesville: University of North Carolina Press.

———. 2000. *Eyes of the Heart: Seeking a Path for the Poor in the Age of Globalization*. Edited by Laura Flynn. Monroe, ME: Common Courage Press.

———. 2008. "Introduction." In *Toussaint L'Ouverture: The Haitian Revolution*, edited by Nick Nesbitt, vii–xxxvi. London: Verso.

Arthur, Charles. 2004. "Squalid Excuses." *The Guardian*, September 29, 2004.

Aschenbrenner, Joyce. 2002. *Katherine Dunham: Dancing a Life*. Urbana: University of Illinois Press.

Bahrani, Zainab. 2008. *Rituals of War: The Body and Violence in Mesopotamia*. New York: Zone Books.

Barker, Joshua. 2006. "Vigilantes and the State." *Social Analysis* 50(1): 203–207.

Barthelemy, Gérard. 1992. *Les Duvaliéristes après Duvalier*. Paris: Editions L'Harmattan.

Bastien, Rémy. 1961. "Haitian Rural Family Organization." *Social and Economic Studies* 10(4): 478–510.

———. 1985. *Le Paysan Haïtien et sa Famille*. Paris: Éditions KARTHALA.

Beckett, Greg. 2004. "Master of the Wood: Moral Authority and Political Imaginaries in Haiti." *PoLAR: The Political and Legal Anthropology Review* 27(2): 1–19.

———. 2010. "Phantom Power: Notes on Provisionality in Haiti." In *Anthropology and Global Counterinsurgency*, edited by John D. Kelly, Beatrice Jauregui, Sean T. Mitchell, and Jeremy Walton, 39–51. Chicago: University of Chicago Press.

———. 2013a. "The Ontology of Freedom: The Unthinkable Miracle of Haiti." *Journal of Haitian Studies* 19(2): 54–74.

———. 2013b. "The Politics of Emergency." *Reviews in Anthropology* 42(2): 85–101.

———. 2013c. "Rethinking the Haitian Crisis." In *The Idea of Haiti: History, Development and the Creation of New Narratives*, edited by Millery Polyné, 27–49. Minneapolis: University of Minnesota Press.

———. 2013d. "Thinking with Others: Savage Thoughts about Anthropology and the West." *Small Axe* 42:166–181.

———. 2014. "The Art of Not Governing Port-au-Prince." *Social and Economic Studies* 63(2): 31–57.

———. 2017a. "A Dog's Life: Reflections on the Humanitarian Situation in Haiti." *American Anthropologist* 119(1): 35–45.

———. 2017b. "The Politics of Disjuncture, or Freedom from a Caribbean Point of View." *Small Axe* 21(2): 184–192.

Beckford, Ruth. 1979. *Katherine Dunham: A Biography*. New York: Marcel Dekker.

Behar, Ruth. 1995. "Introduction: Out of Exile." In *Women Writing Culture*, edited by Ruth Behar and Deborah A. Gordon, 1–29. Berkeley: University of California Press.

———. 1996. *The Vulnerable Observer: Anthropology That Breaks Your Heart*. Boston: Beacon Press.

Bell, Beverly. 2001. "Introduction: The Women of Millet Mountain." In *Walking on Fire*, 1–22. Ithaca, NY: Cornell University Press.

———. 2013. *Fault Lines: Views across Haiti's Divide*. Ithaca, NY: Cornell University Press.

Bellande, Alex. 2015. *Haïti Déforestée, Paysages Remodelés*. Montréal: Les Éditions du CIDIHCA.

Benjamin, Walter. 1978. "Critique of Violence." In *Reflections: Essays, Aphorisms, Autobiographical Writings*, edited by Peter Demetz, 277–300. New York: Schocken Books.

Berger, John, and Jean Mohr. 2010. *A Seventh Man*. London: Verso.

Berlant, Lauren, ed. 2000. *Intimacy*. Chicago: University of Chicago Press.

Besson, Jean. 2002. *Martha Brae's Two Histories: European Expansion and Caribbean Culture-Building in Jamaica*. Chapel Hill: University of North Carolina Press.

Bidney, David. 1946. "The Concept of Cultural Crisis." *American Anthropologist* 48(4): 534–552.

Biehl, João. 2013. *Vita: Life in a Zone of Social Abandonment*, new edition. Berkeley: University of California Press.

Biehl, João, Byron Good, and Arthur Kleinman, eds. 2007. *Subjectivity: Ethnographic Investigations*. Berkeley: University of California Press.

Biersack, Aletta. 2006. "Reimagining Political Ecology: Culture/Power/History /Nature." In *Reimagining Political Ecology*, edited by Aletta Biersack and James B. Greenberg, 3–40. Durham, NC: Duke University Press.

Bloch, Ersnt. 1986. *The Principle of Hope* (3 volumes). Translated by Neville Plaice, Stephen Plaice, and Paul Knight. Cambridge, MA: MIT Press.

Bloch, Ernst, and Theodor W. Adorno. 1988. "Something's Missing: A Discussion between Ernst Bloch and Theodor W. Adorno on the Contradictions of Utopian Longing." In *The Utopian Function of Art and Literature: Selected Essays*, by Ernst Bloch, translated by Jack Zipes and Frank Mecklenburg, 1–17. Cambridge, MA: MIT Press.

Blumenthal, Max. 2004. "The Other Regime Change: Did the Bush Administration Allow a Network of Right-Wing Republicans to Foment a Violent Coup in Haiti?" *Salon*, July 16. http://www.salon.com/news /faeture/2004/07/16/haiti_coup.

Blunt, Robert. 2016. "Old Age and Money: The General Numismatics of Kenya." *Suomen Anthropologi* 41(1): 37–44.

Bogues, Anthony. 2006. "Power, Violence and the Jamaican 'Shotta Don.'" *NACLA Report on the Americas, Our Caribbean: Between Paralysis and Upheaval* 39(6): 21–26.

Bonilla, Yarimar. 2014. "Remembering the Songwriter: The Life and Legacies of Michel-Rolph Trouillot." *Cultural Dynamics* 26(2): 163–172.

———. 2015. *Non-Sovereign Futures: French Caribbean Politics in the Wake of Disenchantment*. Chicago: University of Chicago Press.

Bourgois, Philippe. 2003. *In Search of Respect: Selling Crack in El Barrio*. New York: Cambridge University Press.

Brodwin, Paul. 1996. *Medicine and Morality in Haiti: The Context for Healing Power.* Cambridge, UK: Cambridge University Press.

Brown, Karen M. 1987. "Alourdes: A Case Study in Moral Leadership in Haitian Vodou." In *Saints and Virtues,* edited by J. Hawley, 144–167. Berkeley: University of California Press.

———. 2001. *Mama Lola: A Vodou Priestess in Brooklyn,* updated edition. Berkeley: University of California Press.

Caldeira, Teresa P. R. 2000. *City of Walls: Crime, Segregation, and Citizenship in São Paulo.* Berkeley: University of California Press.

Calhoun, Craig. 2004. "A World of Emergencies: Fear, Intervention, and the Limits of the Cosmopolitan Order." *Canadian Review of Sociology and Anthropology* 41(4): 373–395.

Casimir, Jean. 1982. "Two Cultures and Two Classes in Contemporary Haiti." In *Contemporary Caribbean: A Sociological Reader,* vol. 2, edited by Susan Craig, 181–210. Trinidad and Tobago: The College Press.

Catanese, Anthony V. 1991. *Rural Poverty and Environmental Degradation in Haiti.* Occasional Paper no. 5, Series on Environment and Development. Indiana Center on Global Change and World Peace. Bloomington: Indiana University.

Chatterjee, Partha. 2004. *The Politics of the Governed: Reflections on Popular Politics in Most of the World.* New York: Columbia University Press.

Chomsky, Noam, Paul Farmer, and Amy Goodman. 2004. *Getting Haiti Right This Time: The U.S. Military and the Coup.* Monroe, ME: Common Courage Press.

Clark, Vévé. 1994. "Performing the Memory of Difference in Afro-Caribbean Dance: Katherine Dunham's Choreography, 1938–87." In *History and Memory in African-American Culture,* edited by Geneviève Fabre and Robert O'Meally, 188–204. New York: Oxford University Press.

Collie, Tim. 2003. "The Eroding Nation." *Sun Sentinel,* December 7. http://www.sun-sentinel.com/news/caribbean/sfl-haiti,0,5762688.storygallery.

Comaroff, Jean, and John L. Comaroff. 2004. "Criminal Obsessions, after Foucault: Postcoloniality, Policing, and the Metaphysics of Disorder." *Critical Inquiry* 30(4): 800–824.

———. 2006. "Law and Disorder in the Postcolony: An Introduction." In *Law and Disorder in the Postcolony,* edited by Jean Comaroff and John L. Comaroff, 1–56. Chicago: University of Chicago Press.

Comaroff, John L., and Jean Comaroff. 1999. "Introduction." In *Civil Society and the Political Imagination in Africa: Critical Perspectives,* edited by John L. Comaroff and Jean Comaroff, 1–43. Chicago: University of Chicago Press.

Comhaire-Sylvain, S. 1961. "The Household at Kenscoff, Haiti." *Social and Economic Studies* 10(2): 192–222.

Conway, Frederick J. 1979. *A Study of the Fuelwood Situation in Haiti.* USAID Mission to Haiti.

———. 1989. "Haiti: The Society and Its Environment." In *Dominican Republic and Haiti: Country Studies,* edited by R. A. Haggerty, 239–278. Washington, DC: Library of Congress Federal Research Division.

Coppinger, Raymond, and Lorna Coppinger. 2001. *Dogs: A New Understanding of Canine Origin, Behavior and Evolution*. Chicago: University of Chicago Press.

Corvington, Georges. 1975a. *Port-au-Prince Au Cours des Ans, vol. 1: La Ville Coloniale, 1743–1789*. Deuxième Édition. Port-au-Prince: Imprimerie Henri Deschamps.

———. 1975b. *Port-au-Prince Au Cours des Ans, vol. 2: Sous les Assauts de la Révolution, 1789–1804*. Deuxième Édition. Port-au-Prince: Imprimerie Henri Deschamps.

———. 1977a. *Port-au-Prince Au Cours des Ans, vol. 3: La Métropole Haïtienne de XIXe siècle, 1804–1888*. Port-au-Prince: Imprimerie Henri Deschamps.

———. 1977b. *Port-au-Prince Au Cours des Ans, vol. 4: La Métropole Haïtienne de XIXe siècle, 1888–1915*, 2nd edition. Port-au-Prince: Imprimerie Henri Deschamps.

———. 1984. *Port-au-Prince Au Cours des Ans, vol. 5: La Capitale d'Haïti sous l'Occupation, 1915–1922*, 2nd edition. Port-au-Prince: Imprimerie Henri Deschamps.

———. 1987. *Port-au-Prince Au Cours des Ans, vol. 6: La Capitale d'Haïti sous l'Occupation, 1922–1934*, 2nd edition. Port-au-Prince: Imprimerie Henri Deschamps.

———. 1991. *Port-au-Prince Au Cours des Ans, vol. 7: La Ville Contemporaine, 1934–1950*. Port-au-Prince: Imprimerie Henri Deschamps.

Courlander, Harold. 1960. *The Drum and the Hoe: Life and Lore of the Haitian People*. Berkeley: University of California Press.

CRESDIP. 1991. *Haiti, Terre Délabrée: Écologie et Dictature, Deuxieme Édition*. Pétion-Ville, Haiti: Centre de Recherches et de Diffusion Populaire.

Crosby, Alfred. 1972. *The Columbian Exchange: Biological and Cultural Consequences of 1492*. Westport, CT: Greenwood.

Csordas, Thomas J., ed. 1994. *Embodiment and Experience: The Existential Ground of Culture and Self*. Cambridge, UK: Cambridge University Press.

Danticat, Edwidge. 2004. "A Very Haitian Story." *New York Times*, November 24.

Das, Veena. 2007. *Life and Words: Violence and the Descent into the Ordinary*. Berkeley: University of California Press.

Das, Veena, and Arthur Kleinman. 1997. "Introduction." In *Violence and Subjectivity*, edited by Veena Das, Arthur Kleinman, Mamphela Ramphele, and Pamela Reynolds, 1–18. Berkeley: University of California Press.

Das, Veena, Arthur Kleinman, Mamphela Ramphele, and Pamela Reynolds, eds. 1997. *Violence and Subjectivity*. Berkeley: University of California Press.

Dash, J. Michael. 1997. *Haiti and the United States: National Stereotypes and the Literary Imagination*, 2nd edition. New York: St. Martin's Press.

Davis, Mike. 1998. *Ecology of Fear: Los Angeles and the Imagination of Disaster*. New York: Vintage Books.

———. 2006. *Planet of Slums*. London: Verso.

Dawdy, Shannon L. 2016. *Patina: A Profane Archaeology*. Chicago: University of Chicago Press.

Dayan, Joan. 2001. "Haiti's Unquiet Past: Katherine Dunham, Modern Dancer, and Her Enchanted Island." In *Women at Sea: Travel Writing and the Margins of Caribbean Discourse,* edited by Lizabeth Paravisini-Gebert and Ivette Romero-Cesareo, 281–291. New York: Palgrave.

Deibert, Michael. 2005. *Notes from the Last Testament: The Struggle for Haiti.* New York: Seven Stories Press.

Delva, Joseph G. 2006a. "Haiti Blames Kidnappings on Colombians, Politics." *Reuters,* January 6.

———. 2006b. "Haiti Tells Gangs to Disarm or Face Death." *Reuters,* August 10.

Denning, Michael. 2010. "Wageless Life." *New Left Review* 66:79–97.

Denyer Willis, Graham. 2015. *The Killing Consensus: Police, Organized Crime, and the Regulation of Life and Death in Urban Brazil.* Berkeley: University of California Press.

Deren, Maya. 1953. *Divine Horsemen: The Living Gods of Haiti.* New York: McPherson.

Derrida, Jacques. 1991. "Force of Law: The Mystical Foundations of Authority." *Cardoza Law Review* 11:920–1045.

———. 2014. *The Death Penalty,* vol. 1. Translated by Peggy Kamuf. Chicago: University of Chicago Press.

Desjarlais, Robert. 2016. *Subject to Death: Life and Loss in a Buddhist World.* Chicago: University of Chicago Press.

Desjarlais, Robert, and C. Jason Throop. 2011. "Phenomenological Approaches in Anthropology." *Annual Review of Anthropology* 40:87–102.

Desmangles, Leslie. 1992. *Faces of the Gods: Vodou and Roman Catholicism.* Chapel Hill: University of North Carolina Press.

Diamond, Jared. 2005. *Collapse: How Societies Choose to Fail or Succeed.* New York: Viking.

Didion, Joan. 1990. *The White Album: Essays.* New York: Farrar, Straus, and Giroux.

Dubois, Laurent. 2007. "A Free Man." *The Nation,* March 29. https://www.thenation.com/article/free-man/.

———. 2012. *Haiti: The Aftershocks of History.* New York: Picador.

———. 2013. "Confronting the Legacies of Slavery." *New York Times,* October 28.

Dumas, Pierre-Raymond. 1988. "Legitimizing Politics." In *Haiti's Future: Views of Twelve Haitian Leaders,* edited by Richard A. Morse, 13–20. Washington, DC: Wilson Center Press.

Dunham, Katherine. 1983. *Dances of Haiti.* Los Angeles: University of California Press.

———. 1994. *Island Possessed.* Chicago: University of Chicago Press.

Dupuy, Alex. 1997. *Haiti in the New World Order: The Limits of the Democratic Revolution.* Boulder, CO: Westview Press.

———. 2005a. "From Jean-Bertrand Aristide to Gérard Latortue: The Unending Crisis of Democratization in Haiti." *Journal of Latin American Anthropology* 10(1): 186–205.

———. 2005b. "Globalization, the World Bank, and the Haitian Economy." In *Contemporary Caribbean Cultures and Societies in a Global Context*, edited by Franklin W. Knight and Teresita Martinez-Vergne, 43–70. Chapel Hill: University of North Carolina Press.

———. 2007. *The Prophet and the Power: Jean-Bertrand Aristide, the International Community, and Haiti*. Lanham, MD: Rowman & Littlefield.

Duvalier, François. 1968. *Oeuvres Essentielles*, vols. 1 and 2, 3rd edition. Port-au-Prince: Presses Nationales d'Haïti.

Erikson, Kai. 1976. *Everything in Its Path: Destruction of Community in the Buffalo Creek Flood*. New York: Simon & Schuster.

———. 1994. *A New Species of Trouble: The Human Experience of Modern Disasters*. New York: W.W. Norton.

Escobar, Arturo. 1996. "Constructing Nature: Elements for a Post-Structural Political Ecology." In *Liberation Ecologies, Environmental Development, Social Movements*, edited by R. Peet and M. Watts, 46–68. London: Routledge.

Esquivel, Adolfo Pérez, Jody Williams, Shirin Ebadi, Rigoberta Menchú Tum, and Betty Williams. 2017. "The UN Owes Haiti Relief from Cholera Epidemic It Introduced." *Miami Herald*, June 21. http://www.miamiherald.com/opinion/op-ed/article157499959.html?utm_content = buffer6b732&utm_medium = social&utm_source = facebook.com&utm_campaign = buffer.

Fagen, Patricia. 2006. *Remittances in Crises: A Haiti Case Study*. Humanitarian Policy Group. London: Overseas Development Institute.

Farmer, Paul. 1988a. "Bad Blood, Spoiled Milk: Bodily Fluids as Moral Barometers in Rural Haiti." *American Ethnologist* 15(1): 62–83.

———. 1988b. "Blood, Sweat, and Baseballs: Haiti in the West Atlantic System." *Dialectical Anthropology* 13:83–99.

———. 2003. *The Uses of Haiti*. Monroe, ME: Common Courage Press.

———. 2005. *Pathologies of Power: Health, Human Rights, and the New War on the Poor*. Berkeley: University of California Press.

———. 2006. *Aids and Accusation: Haiti and the Geography of Blame*, new edition. Berkeley: University of California Press.

———. 2011. *Haiti after the Earthquake*. Edited by Abbey Gardner and Cassia Van Der Hoof Holstein. New York: Public Affairs.

Fass, Simon. 1978a. "Families in Port-au-Prince: A Study of the Economics of Survival." PhD diss., University of California, Los Angeles.

———. 1978b. "Port-au-Prince: Awakening to the Urban Crisis." In *Latin American Urban Research*, edited by Wayne Cornelius and Robert Kemper, 115–180. Beverley Hills, CA: Sage.

———. 1982. "Water and Politics: The Process of Meeting a Basic Need in Haiti." *Development and Change* 13:347–364.

Fassin, Didier. 2013. "On Resentment and Ressentiment: The Politics and Ethics of Moral Emotions." *Current Anthropology* 54(3): 249–267.

Fatton, Robert, Jr. 2002. *Haiti's Predatory Republic: The Unending Transition to Democracy*. Boulder, CO: Lynne Rienner.

———. 2017. "Haiti and the Limits of Sovereignty: Trapped in the Outer Periphery." In *Who Owns Haiti? People, Power, and Sovereignty,* edited by Robert Maguire and Scott Freeman, 29–49. Gainesville: University Press of Florida.

Feldman, Allen. 1991. *Formations of Violence: The Narrative of the Body and Political Terror in Northern Ireland.* Chicago: University of Chicago Press.

Foucault, Michel. 1986. *History of Sexuality,* vol. 1. Translated by Robert Hurley. New York: Vintage Books.

———. 2003. *Society Must Be Defended.* Lectures at the Collège de France 1975–1976. Translated by David Macey. New York: Picador.

Franco, Cristiana. 2014. *Shameless: The Canine and the Feminine in Ancient Greece.* Translated by Matthew Fox. Berkeley: University of California Press.

Frerichs, Ralph R. 2016. *Deadly River: Cholera and the Cover-Up in Post-Earthquake Haiti.* Ithaca, NY: Cornell University Press.

Garcia, Angela. 2010. *The Pastoral Clinic: Addiction and Dispossession along the Rio Grande.* Berkeley: University of California Press.

Geertz, Clifford. 1973. *The Interpretation of Cultures: Selected Essays.* New York: Basic Books.

Giddens, Anthony. 1984. *The Constitution of Society.* Berkeley: University of California Press.

———. 1987. *The Nation-State and Violence.* Berkeley: University of California Press.

Girard, René. 1977. *Violence and the Sacred.* Translated by Patrick Gregory. Baltimore, MD: Johns Hopkins University Press.

Girault, Christian A. 1981. *Le Commerce du Café en Haïti: Habitants, Spéculateurs et Exportateurs.* Paris: CNRS.

Glacken, Clarence J. 1967. *Traces on the Rhodian Shore: Nature and Culture in Western Thought from Ancient Times to the End of the Eighteenth Century.* Berkeley: University of California Press.

Glick Schiller, Nina, and Georges E. Fouron. 2001. *Georges Woke Up Laughing: Long-Distance Nationalism and the Search for Home.* Durham, NC: Duke University Press.

Glissant, Edouard. 1989. *Caribbean Discourse.* Translated by J. Michael Dash. Charlottesville: University of Virginia Press.

Glover, Kaiama L. 2016. "'Written with Love': Intimacy and Relation in Katherine Dunham's *Island Possessed.*" In *The Haiti Exception: Anthropology and the Predicament of Narrative,* edited by Alessandra Benedicty-Kokken, Kaiama L. Glover, Mark Schuller, and Jhon Picard Byron, 93–109. Liverpool, UK: Liverpool University Press.

Goldstone, Brian, and Juan Obarrio, eds. 2016. *African Futures: Essays on Crisis, Emergence, and Possibility.* Chicago: University of Chicago Press.

Government of Haiti. 2014. "Haiti: Facing Risks Together: Achievements in Disaster Risk Management since 2010." http://www.ht.undp.org/content/dam/haiti/docs/Prevention%20des%20crises/UNDP-HT-GRD-Haiti_facing_risks-en_20150305.pdf (accessed July 17, 2017).

Graeber, David. 2001. *Toward an Anthropological Theory of Value: The False Coin of Our Own Dreams.* New York: Palgrave.

Grann, David. 2001. "Giving 'The Devil' His Due." *Atlantic Monthly* 287(6): 54–75.

Greenburg, Jennifer. 2013. "The 'Strong Arm' and the 'Friendly Hand': Military Humanitarianism in Post-Earthquake Haiti." *Journal of Haitian Studies* 19(1): 60–87.

Griffin, Thomas M. 2004. *Haiti Human Rights Investigation: November 11–21, 2004.* Miami: Center for the Study of Human Rights, University of Miami School of Law.

Grove, Richard. 1995. *Green Imperialism: Colonial Expansion, Tropical Island Edens and the Origins of Environmentalism.* New York: Cambridge University Press.

Grunwald, Joseph, Leslie Delatour, and Karl Voltaire. 1984. "Offshore Assembly in Haiti." In *Haiti, Today and Tomorrow: An Interdisciplinary Study,* edited by Charles R. Foster and Albert Valdman, 231–52. Lanham, MD: University Press of America.

Gubbels, Timothy, and Robert Brakenridge. 2004. "Flood Disaster Hits Hispaniola." *Earth Observatory.* http://earthobservatory.nasa.gov/Study/Haiti2004/.

Habermas, Jürgen. 1975. *Legitimation Crisis.* Boston: Beacon Press.

Hallward, Peter. 2007. *Damning the Flood: Haiti, Aristide, and the Politics of Containment.* London: Verso.

Hannerz, Ulf. 1980. *Exploring the City: Inquiries toward an Urban Anthropology.* New York: Columbia University Press.

Hansen, Thomas Blom, and Finn Stepputat, eds. 2005. *Sovereign Bodies: Citizens, Migrants, and States in the Postcolonial World.* Princeton, NJ: Princeton University Press.

———. 2006. "Sovereignty Revisited." *Annual Review of Anthropology* 35:295–315.

Hector, Michel. 2006. *Crises et Mouvements Populaires en Haïti,* 2nd edition. Port-au-Prince: Presses Nationales d'Haiti.

Henry-Lee, Aldrie. 2005. "The Nature of Poverty in the Garrison Constituencies in Jamaica." *Environment and Urbanization Journal* 17(2): 83–99.

Herskovits, Melville J. 1937. *Life in a Haitian Valley.* New York: Alfred A. Knopf.

———. 1938. *Acculturation: The Study of Culture Contact.* New York: J.J. Augustin.

———. 1966. "Problem, Method and Theory in Afroamerican Studies." In *The New World Negro: Selected Papers in Afroamerican Studies,* edited by Frances Herskovits, 43–61. Bloomington: Indiana University Press.

Herzfeld, Michael. 1997. *Cultural Intimacy: Social Poetics in the Nation-State.* New York: Routledge.

Hoffman, Susanna, and Anthony Oliver-Smith, eds. 2002. *Catastrophe and Culture: The Anthropology of Disaster.* Santa Fe, NM: SAR Press.

Holston, James. 2008. *Insurgent Citizenship: Disjunctions of Democracy and Modernity in Brazil.* Princeton, NJ: Princeton University Press.

Human Rights Watch/Americas and National Coalition for Haitian Refugees. 1994. *Terror Prevails in Haiti: Human Rights Violations and Failed Diplomacy*, vol. 6, no. 5 (April).

Hurbon, Laënnec. 1987. *Le Barbare Imaginaire*. Port-au-Prince: Éditions Henri Deschamps.

Husserl, Edmund. 1962. *Ideas: General Introduction to Pure Phenomenology*. New York: Collier.

Ingold, Tim. 1994. "Humanity and Animality." In *A Companion Encyclopedia of Anthropology*, edited by Tim Ingold, 14–32. London: Routledge.

Inter-American Development Bank. 2010. "Haiti Reconstruction Cost May Near $14 Billion, IDB Study Shows." http://www.iadb.org/en/news/webstories /2010–02–16/haiti-earthquake-reconstruction-could-hit-14-billion-idb,6528.html.

Jackson, Michael, ed. 1996. *Things as They Are: New Directions in Phenomenological Anthropology*. Bloomington: Indiana University Press.

———. 2005. *Existential Anthropology: Events, Exigencies, and Effects*. New York: Berghahn Books.

———. 2012. *Lifeworlds: Essays in Existential Anthropology*. Chicago: University of Chicago Press.

———. 2013. *The Politics of Storytelling: Variations on a Theme by Hannah Arendt*. Copenhagen: Museum Tusculanum Press.

James, Erica C. 2004. "The Political Economy of 'Trauma' in Haiti in the Democratic Era of Insecurity." *Culture, Medicine and Psychiatry* 28(2): 127–149.

———. 2008. "Haunting Ghosts: Madness, Gender, and Ensekirite in Haiti in the Democratic Era." In *Postcolonial Disorders*, edited by Mary-Jo DelVecchio Good, Sandra Teresa Hyde, Sarah Pinto, and Bryan J. Good, 132–156. Berkeley: University of California Press.

———. 2010. *Democratic Insecurities: Violence, Trauma, and Intervention in Haiti*. Berkeley: University of California Press.

Jauregui, Beatrice. 2010. "Bluing Green in the Maldives: Countering Citizen Insurgency by 'Civil'-izing National Security." In *Anthropology and Global Counter Insurgency*, edited by John D. Kelly, Beatrice Jauregui, Sean T. Mitchell, and Jeremy Walton, 23–38. Chicago: University of Chicago Press.

Johnson, Sara E. 2009. "'You Should Give Them Blacks to Eat': Waging Inter-American Wars of Torture and Terror." *American Quarterly* 61(1): 65–92.

Katz, Jonathan. 2013. *The Big Truck That Went By: How the World Came to Save Haiti and Left Behind a Disaster*. New York: Palgrave.

Kivland, Chelsey. 2012a. "To Defend or Develop? On the Politics of Engagement among Local Organizations, before and after the Earthquake." *Journal of Haitian Studies* 18(1): 75–99.

———. 2012b. "Unmaking the State in 'Occupied' Haiti." *PoLAR: Political and Legal Anthropology Review* 35(2): 248–270.

———. 2014. "Becoming a Force in the Zone: Hedonopolitics, Masculinity, and the Quest for Respect in Haiti's Streets." *Cultural Anthropology* 29(4): 672–698.

————. 2017. "Street Sovereignty: Power, Violence, and Respect among Haitian Baz." In *Who Owns Haiti? People, Power, and Sovereignty*, edited by Robert Maguire Robert and Scott Freeman, 140–165. Gainesville: University Press of Florida.

————. n.d. *Street Sovereigns: Young Men in Search of the State in Urban Haiti.* Manuscript.

Klarreich, Kathie, and Linda Polman. 2012. "The NGO Republic of Haiti: How the International Relief Effort after the 2010 Earthquake Excluded Haitians from Their Own Recovery." *The Nation*, October 31.

Kleinman, Arthur. 1999. "Experience and Its Moral Modes: Culture, Human Conditions, and Disorder." In *The Tanner Lectures on Human Values*, vol. 20, edited by G. B. Peterson, 357–420. Salt Lake City: University of Utah Press.

————. 2006. *What Really Matters: Living a Moral Life amidst Uncertainty and Danger.* Oxford, UK: Oxford University Press.

Kolbe, Athena, and Royce A. Hutson. 2006. "Human Rights Abuse and Other Criminal Violations in Port-au-Prince, Haiti: A Random Survey of Households." *Lancet* 368: 864–873.

Koselleck, Reinhart. 1988. *Critique and Crisis: Enlightenment and the Pathogenesis of Modern Society.* Cambridge, MA: MIT Press.

————. 2002. *The Practice of Conceptual History: Timing History, Spacing Concepts.* Translated by Todd Samuel Presner et al. Stanford, CA: Stanford University Press.

Kovats-Bernat, J. Christopher. 2006a. "Factional Terror, Paramilitarism and Civil War in Haiti: The View from Port-au-Prince, 1994–2004." *Anthropologica* 48: 117–39.

————. 2006b. *Sleeping Rough in Port-au-Prince: An Ethnography of Street Children and Violence in Haiti.* Gainesville: University Press of Florida.

Lacerte, Robert K. 1975. "The First Land Reform in Latin America: The Reforms of Alexander Pétion, 1809–1814." *Inter-American Economic Affairs* 28(4): 77–85.

————. 1978. "The Evolution of Land and Labor in the Haitian revolution, 1791–1820." *The Americas* 34(4): 449–459.

————. 1981. "Xenophobia and Economic Decline: The Haitian Case, 1820–1843." *The Americas* 37(4): 499–515.

Laferrière, Dany. 2011. *The World Is Moving Around Me: A Memoir of the Haiti Earthquake.* Vancouver, BC: Arsenal Pulp Press.

Laferrière, Dany, Louis-Philippe Dalembert, Edwidge Danticat, and Évelyne Trouillot. 2005. "Roundtable: Writing, History, and Revolution." J. Michael Dash, moderator. *Small Axe* 9(2): 189–201.

Laguerre, Michel. 1982. *Urban Life in the Caribbean: A Study of a Haitian Urban Community.* Cambridge, MA: Schenkman.

————. 1993. *The Military and Society in Haiti.* Knoxville: University of Tennessee Press.

Lahav, Pnina. 1975. "The Chef de Section: Structure and Functions of Haiti's Basic Administrative Institution." In *Working Papers in Haitian Society and Culture*, edited by Sidney W. Mintz, 51–83. New Haven, CT: Yale University Press.

Lambek, Michael, ed. 2010. *Ordinary Ethics: Anthropology, Language, and Action*. New York: Fordham University Press.

Larkin, Brian. 2013. "The Politics and Poetics of Infrastructure." *Annual Review of Anthropology* 42:327–343.

Larose, Serge. 1978. "The Haitian Lakou: Land, Family and Ritual." In *Family and Kinship in Middle America and the Caribbean*, edited by Arnaud Marks and René Römer, 482–512. Willemstad: Institute of Higher Studies in Curaçao.

Lawless, Robert. 1992. *Haiti's Bad Press*. Rochester, VT: Schenkman Books.

Lawrence, Peter, Jeremy Meigh, and Caroline Sullivan. 2002. *The Water Poverty Index: An International Comparison*. Keele, UK: Keele University. http://www.keele.ac.uk/depts/ec/wpapers/kerp0219.pdf.

Lear, Jonathan. 2006. *Radical Hope: Ethics in the Face of Cultural Devastation*. Cambridge, MA: Harvard University Press.

Lederer, Edith M. 2017. "UN Assembly Backs $40.5 Million for Haiti Cholera Victims." *ABC News*, July 13. http://abcnews.go.com/US/wireStory/assembly-backs-405-million-haiti-cholera-victims-48626038.

Lévi-Strauss, Claude. 1963. *Structural Anthropology*. Translated by Claire Jacobson and Brooke Grundfest Schoepf. New York: Basic Books.

Leyburn, James G. 1941. *The Haitian People*. New Haven, CT: Yale University Press.

Lhérisson, Lélia J. 1954. *Les héros de l'Indépendance dans l'Histoire d'Haïti*. Port-au-Prince: Collection du Centcinquantenaire de l'Indépendance d'Haïti.

Lindsay, Reed. 2006. "Peace despite the Peacekeepers in Haiti." *NACLA Report on the Americas* 39(6): 31–36.

Locher, Huldrych C. 1978. "The Fate of Migrants to Urban Haiti: A Survey of Three Port-au-Prince Neighbourhoods." PhD diss., Yale University.

Lomnitz, Claudio. 2003. "Times of Crisis: Historicity, Sacrifice, and the Spectacle of Debacle in Mexico City." *Public Culture* 15(1): 127–147.

Low, Setha M. 1996. "The Anthropology of Cities: Imagining and Theorizing the City." *Annual Review of Anthropology* 25:383–409.

Lundahl, Mats. 1979. *Peasants and Poverty: A Study of Haiti*. New York: St. Martin's Press.

———. 1983. *The Haitian Economy: Man, Land, and Markets*. New York: St. Martin's Press.

———. 2012. *The Political Economy of Disaster: Destitution, Plunder, and Earthquake in Haiti*. London: Routledge.

Madiou, Thomas. 1989. *Histoire d'Haïti* (8 volumes). Port-au-Prince: Impr. E. Chenet.

Maguire, Robert, and Scott Freeman, eds. 2017. *Who Owns Haiti? People, Power, and Sovereignty*. Gainesville: University Press of Florida.

Malkki, Liisa. 2015. *The Need to Help: The Domestic Arts of International Humanitarianism*. Durham, NC: Duke University Press.

Mangonès, Albert. 2001. *En Toute Urbanité*. Port-au-Prince: Éditions Mémoire.

Manigat, Sabine. 1997. "Haiti: The Popular Sectors and the Crisis in Port-au-Prince." In *The Urban Caribbean: Transition to the New Global Economy*, edited by Alejandro Portes, Carlos Dore-Cabral, and Patricia Landolt, 87–123. Baltimore, MD: Johns Hopkins University Press.

Marcelin, Louis H. 2012. "In the Name of the Nation: Ritual, Blood, and the Political Habitus of Violence in Haiti." *American Anthropologist* 114(2): 253–266.

———. 2015. "Violence, Human Insecurity, and the Challenge of Rebuilding Haiti: A Study of a Shantytown in Port-au-Prince." *Current Anthropology* 56(2): 230–255.

Martínez, Samuel. 2007. *Decency and Excess: Global Aspirations and Material Deprivation on a Caribbean Sugar Plantation*. Boulder, CO: Paradigm.

Marx, Karl. 1976. *Capital: A Critique of Political Economy*, vol 1. Translated by Ben Fowkes. London: Penguin Books.

Marx, Leo. 2000. *The Machine in the Garden: Technology and the Pastoral Ideal in America*. New York: Oxford University Press.

Maternowska, M. Catherine. 2006. *Reproducing Inequities: Poverty and the Politics of Population in Haiti*. New Brunswick, NJ: Rutgers University Press.

Mattingly, Cheryl. 2010a. "Moral Willing as Narrative Re-envisioning. In *Toward an Anthropology of the Will*, edited by Keith M. Murphy and C. Jason Throop, 50–67. Stanford, CA: Stanford University Press.

———. 2010b. *The Paradox of Hope: Journeys through a Clinical Borderland*. Berkeley: University of California Press.

Mauss, Marcel. 2000. *The Gift: The Form and Reason of Exchange in Archaic Societies*. Translated by W. D. Halls. New York: W.W. Norton.

Mbembe, Achille, and Janet Roitman. 1996. "Figures of the Subject in Times of Crisis." In *The Geography of Identity*, edited by Patricia Yaeger, 153–186. Ann Arbor: University of Michigan Press.

McAlister, Elizabeth. 2002. *Rara! Vodou, Power, and Performance in Haiti and Its Diaspora*. Berkeley: University of California Press.

———. 2012. "Soundscapes of Disaster and Humanitarianism: Survival Singing, Relief Telethons, and the Haitian Earthquake." *Small Axe* 16(3): 22–38.

McClellan, James E., III. 1992. *Colonialism and Science: Saint Domingue in the Old Regime*. Baltimore, MD: Johns Hopkins University Press.

McClintock, Nathan C. n.d. "Agroforestry and Sustainable Resource Conservation in Haiti: A Case Study." http://www.piphaiti.org/overview_of_haiti2.html (accessed January 4, 2007).

McGuigan, Claire. 2006. *Agricultural Liberalisation in Haiti*. London: Christian Aid.

Meehan, Kevin. 1999. "'Titid ak pèp la se marasa': Jean-Bertrand Aristide and the New National Romance in Haiti." In *Caribbean Romances: The Politics of Regional Representation*, edited by Belinda J. Edmundson, 105–122. Charlottesville: University Press of Virginia.

Merchant, Carolyn. 1980. *The Death of Nature: Women, Ecology, and the Scientific Revolution.* San Francisco: Harper & Row.

———. 2003. *Reinventing Eden: The Gate of Nature in Western Culture.* New York: Routledge.

Mercier de Lépinay, B., et al. 2011. "The 2010 Haiti Earthquake: A Complex Fault Pattern Constrained by Seismologic and Tectonic Observations." *Geophysical Research Letters* 38, L22305, doi:10.1029/2011GL049799.

Merleau-Ponty, Maurice. 1962. *Phenomenology of Perception.* London: Routledge & Kegan Paul.

Métraux, Alfred. 1951. *Making a Living in Marbial Valley (Haiti).* Occasional Papers in Education. Paris: UNESCO.

———. 1972. *Voodoo in Haiti.* Translated by Hugo Charteris. New York: Schocken Books.

Minn, Pierre. 2016. "Components of a Moral Economy: Interest, Credit, and Debt in Haiti's Transnational Health Care System." *American Anthropologist* 118(1): 78–90.

Mintz, Sidney W. 1959. "Internal Market Systems as Mechanisms of Social Articulation." *Proceedings of the 1959 Annual Spring Meetings of the American Ethnological Society.* Seattle: University of Washington Press.

———. 1961. "Pratik: Haitian personal economic relations." *Proceedings of the 1961 Annual Spring Meetings of the American Ethnological Society.* Seattle: University of Washington Press.

———. 1966. "The Caribbean as a Sociocultural Area." *Cahiers d'histoire mondiale* 10(4): 912–937.

———. 1989. *Caribbean Transformations.* New York: Columbia University Press.

———. 2010. *Three Ancient Colonies: Caribbean Themes and Variations.* Cambridge, MA: Harvard University Press.

Mintz, Sidney W., and Richard Price. 1992. *The Birth of African-American Culture: An Anthropological Perspective.* Boston: Beacon Press.

Moral, Paul. 1959. *L'Economie Haitienne.* Port-au-Prince: Imprimerie de l'État.

———. 2002. *La Paysan Haitienne.* Port-au-Prince: Les Editions Fardin.

Muehlebach, Andrea. 2013. "On Precariousness and the Ethical Imagination: The Year 2012 in Sociocultural Anthropology." *American Anthropologist* 115(2): 297–311.

Munn, Nancy D. 1986. *The Fame of Gawa: A Symbolic Study of Value Transformation in a Massim Society.* Durham, NC: Duke University Press.

———. 1990. "Constructing Regional Worlds in Experience: Kula Exchange, Witchcraft and Gawan Local Events." *Man* 25: 1–17.

Munro, Martin, ed. 2010. *Haiti Rising: Haitian History, Culture and the Earthquake of 2010.* Liverpool, UK: Liverpool University Press.

———. 2015. *Tropical Apocalypse: Haiti and the Caribbean End Times.* Charlottesville: University of Virginia Press.

Murray, Gerald F. 1979. "Terraces, Trees, and the Haitian Peasant: An Assessment of 25 Years of Erosion Control in Rural Haiti." Port-au-Prince: USAID.

———. 1980. "Population Pressure, Land Tenure, and Voodoo: The Economics of Haitian Peasant Ritual." In *Beyond Myths of Culture: Essays in Cultural Materialism*, edited by Eric B. Ross, 295–321. New York: Academic Press.

———. 1984. "The Wood Tree as a Peasant Cash Crop: An Anthropological Strategy for the Domestication of Energy." In *Haiti: Today and Tomorrow*, edited by C.R. Foster and A Valdman, 141–160. Lanham, MD: University Press of America.

———. 1990. "The Protection of Wood or the Production of Wood: Comments on the World Bank's Staff Appraisal Report of the Haitian Forestry and Environment Project." Typescript.

Murray, Gerald F., and M.E. Bannister. 2004. "Peasants, Agroforesters, and Anthropologists: A 20-Year Venture in Income-Generating Trees and Hedgerows in Haiti." *Agroforestry Systems* 61: 383–397.

Narayan, Kirin. 2012. *Alive in the Writing: Crafting Ethnography in the Company of Chekhov*. Chicago: University of Chicago Press.

Neiburg, Federico. 2016. "A True Coin of Their Dreams: Imaginary Monies in Haiti." *Hau: Journal of Ethnographic Theory* 6(1): 75–93.

Nelson, Diane. 2015. *Who Counts? The Mathematics of Death and Life After Genocide*. Durham, NC: Duke University Press.

Nesbitt, Nick. 2008. *Toussaint L'Ouverture: The Haitian Revolution*. London: Verso.

Nicholls, David. 1971. "Biology and Politics in Haiti." *Race* 13(2): 203–214.

———. 1974. "A Work of Combat: Mulatto Historians and the Haitian Past, 1847–1867." *Journal of Interamerican Studies and World Affairs* 16(1): 15–38.

———. 1978. "The Wisdom of Salomon: Myth or Reality?" *Journal of Interamerican Studies and World Affairs* 20(4): 377–392.

———. 1979a. *From Dessalines to Duvalier: Race, Colour and National Independence in Haiti*. Cambridge, UK: Cambridge University Press.

———. 1979b. "Rural Protest and Peasant Revolt in Haiti (1804–1869)." In *Peasants, Plantations and Rural Communities in the Caribbean*, edited by Malcolm Cross and Arnaud Marks, 29–53. Guildford, UK: Department of Sociology, University of Surrey.

Ochs, Elinor, and Lisa Capps. 2001. *Living Narrative: Creating Lives in Everyday Storytelling*. Cambridge, MA: Harvard University Press.

Oliver-Smith, Anthony. 1996. "Anthropological Research on Hazards and Disasters." *Annual Review of Anthropology* 25: 302–328.

———. 2002. "Theorizing Disasters: Nature, Power, and Culture." In *Catastrophe and Culture: The Anthropology of Disaster*, edited by Susanna M. Hoffman and Anthony Oliver-Smith, 23–47. Santa Fe, NM: SAR Press.

———. 2006. "Disaster and Forced Migration in the 21st Century." *Understanding Katrina: Perspectives from the Social Sciences*. Social Science Research Council. http://understandingkatrina.ssrc.org.

Orner, Peter, and Evan Lyon, eds. 2017. *Lavil: Life, Love, and Death in Port-au-Prince*. New York: Verso.

Palmié, Stephan. 2002. *Wizards and Scientists: Explorations in Afro-Cuban Modernity and Tradition.* Durham, NC: Duke University Press.

Patterson, Orlando. 1982. *Slavery and Social Death: A Comparative Study.* Cambridge, MA: Harvard University Press.

Peet, Richard, and Michael Watts, eds. 1996. *Liberation Ecologies: Environment, Development, Social Movements.* New York: Routledge.

Perrow, Charles. 1999. *Normal Accidents: Living with High-Risk Technologies.* Princeton, NJ: Princeton University Press.

————. 2007. *The Next Catastrophe: Reducing our Vulnerabilities to Natural, Industrial, and Terrorist Disasters.* Princeton, NJ: Princeton University Press.

Philippe, Jeanne, and Jean B. Romain. 1979. "Indisposition in Haiti." *Social Science and Medicine* 13B: 129–133.

Pierre-Louis, Claude. 1986. *Haïti 2000: Bois et Reboisement.* Port-au-Prince: Imprimerie Express.

Pierre-Louis, Raoul. 1989. "Forest Policy and Deforestation in Haiti, the Case of the Forêt des Pins (1915–1955)." Master's thesis, University of Port-au-Prince.

Pina, Kevin. 2004. "Victims of the Storms over Haiti." *San Diego Union-Tribune,* September 28.

Plummer, Brenda G. 1988. *Haiti and the Great Powers, 1902–1915.* Baton Rouge: Louisiana State University Press.

Podur, Justin. 2012. *Haiti's New Dictatorship: The Coup, the Earthquake and the UN Occupation.* London: Pluto Press.

Pogue Harrison, Robert. 1992. *Forests: The Shadow of Civilization.* Chicago: University of Chicago Press.

Polyné, Millery, ed. 2013. *The Idea of Haiti: Rethinking Crisis and Development.* Minneapolis: University of Minnesota Press.

Portes, Alejandro, et al., eds. 1997. *The Urban Caribbean: Transition to the New Global Economy.* Baltimore, MD: Johns Hopkins University Press.

Potter, Robert B. 2000. *The Urban Caribbean in an Era of Global Change.* Burlington, VT: Ashgate.

Pressoir, Catts, Ernst Trouillot, and Henock Trouillot. 1953. *Historiographie d'Haïti.* Mexico: Instituto Panamericano de Geografia e Historia.

Price-Mars, Jean. 1919. *La Vocation de l'Élite.* Port-au-Prince: Imprimerie Edmond Chenet.

————. 1951. *Folklore et Patriotisme.* Port-au-Prince: Les Presses Libres.

————. 1983. *So Spoke the Uncle.* Translated by Magdaline Shannon. Washington, DC: Three Continents Press.

Ramsay, Georgina. 2017. "Incommensurable Futures and Displaced Lives: Sovereignty as Control over Time." *Public Culture* 29(3): 515–538.

Ramsey, Kate. 2000. "Melville Herskovits, Katherine Dunham, and the Politics of African Diasporic Dance Anthropology." In *Dancing Bodies, Living Histories: New Writings about Dance and Culture,* edited by Lisa Doolittle and Anne Flynn, 196–216. Banff, AB: Banff Centre Press.

Regan, Jane. 2004. "Treeless Forests." *Latin American Press*, July 29.

Richardson, Bonham C. 1992. *The Caribbean in the Wider World, 1491–1992*. Cambridge, UK: Cambridge University Press.

Richman, Karen E. 2005. *Migration and Vodou*. Gainesville: University Press of Florida.

Robbins, Paul. 2012. *Political Ecology: A Critical Introduction*, 2nd edition. New York: Wiley-Blackwell.

Rodman, Selden. 1988. *Where Art Is Joy: The First Forty Years*. New York: Ruggles de Latour.

Rohter, Larry. 1995. "Among Haiti's Poor, A Land Rush Without Rules." *New York Times*, February 19.

Roitman, Janet. 1998. "The Garrison-Entrepôt." *Cahiers d'études africaines* 150–152, XXXVIII (2–4): 297–329.

———. 2014. *Anti-Crisis*. Durham, NC: Duke University Press.

Roumain, Jacques. 2007. *Le Sacrifice du Tambour-Assôtô(r)*. Port-au-Prince: Presses Nationales d'Haïti.

Satterthwaite, Margaret L. 2011. "Indicators in Crisis: Rights-Based Humanitarian Indicators in Post-earthquake Haiti." *International Law and Politics* 43: 865–964.

Satterthwaite, Margaret L., and P. Scott Moses. 2012. "Unintended Consequences: The Technology of Indicators in Post-Earthquake Haiti." *Journal of Haitian Studies* 18(1): 14–49.

Scarry, Elaine. 1985. *The Body in Pain: The Making and Unmaking of the World*. New York: Oxford University Press.

Schama, Simon. 1995. *Landscape and Memory*. New York: Alfred A. Knopf.

Schmidt, Alfred. 1971. *The Concept of Nature in Marx*. Translated by Ben Fowkes. London: NLB.

Schmidt, Hans. 1971. *The United States Occupation of Haiti, 1915–1934*. New Brunswick, NJ: Rutgers University Press.

Schnitzler, Anita von. 2013. "Traveling Technologies: Infrastructure, Ethical Regimes, and the Materiality of Politics in South Africa." *Cultural Anthropology* 28(4): 670–693.

Schuller, Mark. 2007. "Seeing Like a 'Failed' NGO: Globalization's Impacts on State and Civil Society in Haiti." *PoLAR: Political and Legal Anthropology Review* 30(1): 67–89.

———. 2008. "'Haiti Is Finished!' Haiti's End of History Meets the Ends of Capitalism." In *Capitalizing on Catastrophe: Neoliberal Strategies in Disaster Reconstruction*, edited by Nandini Gunewardena and Mark Schuller, 191–214. Lanham, MD: AltaMira Press.

———. 2012. *Killing with Kindness: Haiti, International Aid, and NGOs*. New Brunswick, NJ: Rutgers University Press.

———. 2013. "Cholera and the Camps." In *The Idea of Haiti: Rethinking Crisis and Development*, edited by Millery Polyné, 181–201. Minneapolis: University of Minnesota Press.

———. 2015. "'Pa Manyen Fanm Nan Konsa': Intersectionality, Structural Violence, and Vulnerability before and after Haiti's Earthquake." *Feminist Studies* 41(1): 184–210.

———. 2016. *Humanitarian Aftershocks in Haiti.* New Brunswick, NJ: Rutgers University Press.

Schuller, Mark, and P. Morales, eds. 2012. *Tectonic Shifts: Haiti since the Earthquake.* Sterling, VA: Kumarian Press.

Schutz, Alfred. 1967. *The Phenomenology of the Social World.* Translated by G. Walsh and F. Lehnert. Evanston, IL: Northwestern University Press.

Scott, David. 2012. "The Futures of Michel-Rolph Trouillot: In Memoriam." *Small Axe* 39: vii–x.

———. 2014. *Omens of Adversity: Tragedy, Time, Memory, Justice.* Durham, NC: Duke University Press.

Scott, James. 1998. *Seeing Like a State: How Certain Schemes to Improve the Human Condition Have Failed.* New Haven, CT: Yale University Press.

Sennett, Richard. 2003. *Respect in a World of Inequality.* New York: W.W. Norton.

Simone, AbdouMaliq. 2004. "People as Infrastructure: Intersecting Fragments in Johannesburg." *Public Culture* 16(3): 407–429.

Simpson, George E. 1941. Haiti's Social Structure. *American Sociological Review* 6(5): 640–649.

Smarth, Luc. 1998. *Les Organisations Populaire en Haïti: Une Étude Exploratoire de la Zone Métropolitaine de Port-au-Prince.* Port-au-Prince: CRESDIP/Bois Caiman Press.

Smirl, Lisa. 2015. *Spaces of Aid: How Cars, Compounds and Hotels Shape Humanitarianism.* London: Zed Books.

Smith, Jennie M. 2001. *When the Hands Are Many: Community Organization and Social Change in Rural Haiti.* Ithaca, NY: Cornell University Press.

Smith, Neil. 2006. "There's No Such Thing as a Natural Disaster." *Understanding Katrina: Perspectives from the Social Sciences.* Social Science Research Council. http://understandingkatrina.ssrc.org.

Smucker, Glenn R. 1981. *Trees and Charcoal in Haitian Peasant Economy: A Feasibility Study of Reforestation.* Haiti: USAID.

———. 1983. "Peasants and Development Politics: A Study in Haitian Class and Culture." PhD diss., New School for Social Research.

———. 1988. *Decision and Motivations in Peasant Tree Farming: Morne-Franck and the PADF.* Pan American Development Foundation.

Smucker, Glenn R., and Joel Timyan. 1995. *Impact of Tree Planting in Haiti: 1982–1995.* SECID/Auburn PLUS Report no. 23.

Soderlund, Walter C. 2006. "US Network Television News Framing of the February 2004 Overthrow of Haitian President Jean-Bertrand Aristide." *Journal of Haitian Studies* 12(2): 78–111.

Solnit, Rebecca. 2009. *A Paradise Built in Hell: The Extraordinary Communities That Arise in Disaster.* New York: Penguin Books.

Sprague, Jeb. 2012. *Paramilitarism and the Assault on Democracy in Haiti.* New York: Monthly Review Press.

Standing, Guy. 2011. *The Precariat: The New Dangerous Class.* London: Bloomsbury.

Starn, Randolph. 1971. "Historians and 'Crisis.'" *Past and Present* 52 (August): 3–22.

Stevens, Alta Mae. 1995. "Manje in Haitian Creole: The Symbolic Significance of Manje in Haitian Creole." *Journal of Haitian Studies* 1(1): 75–88.

Stewart, Kathleen. 2007. *Ordinary Affects.* Durham, NC: Duke University Press.

Street, D. R. 1989. *The Charcoal Market in Haiti: Northwest to Port-au-Prince.* USAID Haiti Agroforestry Research Project. South East Consortium for International Development and Auburn University.

Taussig, Michael. 1992. *The Nervous System.* New York: Routledge.

Thomas, Deborah. 2011. *Exceptional Violence: Embodied Citizenship in Transnational Jamaica.* Durham, NC: Duke University Press.

———. 2016. "Time and the Otherwise: Plantations, Garrisons and Being Human in the Caribbean." *Anthropological Theory* 16(2–3): 177–200.

Throop, C. Jason. 2003. "Articulating Experience." *Anthropological Theory* 3:219–241.

———. 2010. *Suffering and Sentiment: Exploring the Vicissitudes of Experience and Pain in Yap.* Berkeley: University of California Press.

———. 2014. "Moral Moods." *Ethos* 42(1): 65–83.

Timyan, Joel. 1984. *Production Analysis of a Three-Year Old Leucaena Leucocephala Seeding Stand in Haiti.* USAID Agroforestry Outreach Project.

———. 1996. *Bwa-yo: Important Trees of Haiti.* Washington, DC: South-East Consortium for International Development.

Titus, Nicole. 2012. *From Disaster to Hope: Interviews with Persons Affected by the 2010 Haiti Earthquake.* Xlibris.

Trouillot, Michel-Rolph. 1990a. *Haiti, State against Nation: The Origins and Legacies of Duvalierism.* New York: Monthly Review Press.

———. 1990b. "The Odd and the Ordinary: Haiti, the Caribbean, and the World." *Cimarron: New Perspectives on the Caribbean* 2(3): 3–12.

———. 1992. "The Caribbean Region: An Open Frontier in Anthropological Theory." *Annual Review of Anthropology* 21: 19–42.

———. 1995. *Silencing the Past: Power and the Production of History.* Boston: Beacon Press.

———. 1999. "Historiography of Haiti." In *General History of the Caribbean, vol. 6: Methodology and Historiography of the Caribbean,* edited by B.W. Higman, 451–477. Paris: UNESCO.

———. 2003. *Global Transformations: Anthropology and the Modern World.* New York: Palgrave.

Tuan, Yi-Fu. 1984. *Dominance and Affection: The Making of Pets.* New Haven, CT: Yale University Press.

Turner, Terence S. 2008. "Marxian Value Theory: An Anthropological Perspective." *Anthropological Theory* 8(1): 43–56.

———. 2012. "The Social Skin." *Hau: Journal of Ethnographic Theory* 2(2): 486–504.

Turner, Victor W., and Edward M. Bruner, eds. 1986. *The Anthropology of Experience.* Urbana: University of Illinois Press.

Ulysse, Gina Athena. 2015. *Why Haiti Needs New Narratives: A Post-Quake Chronicle.* Middletown, CT: Wesleyan University Press.

UNDP. 2004. "Haiti 2004: Flash Appeal." United Nations Development Programme. http://www.undp.org/cpr/disred/documents/news/oct04 /unfa_haitifloods04.pdf.

Vigh, Henrik. 2008. "Crisis and Continuity: Anthropological Perspectives on Continuous Conflict and Decline." *Ethnos* 73(1): 5–24.

Voltaire, K. 1979. *Charcoal in Haiti.* USAID, Haiti.

Wagner, Laura R. 2015. *Hold Tight, Don't Let Go: A Novel of Haiti.* New York: Abrams.

Wargny, Christophe. 1996. "Introduction." In *Dignity: Jean-Bertrand Aristide,* translated by Carrol F. Coates, 3–37. Charlottesville: University Press of Virginia.

Weiner, Tim. 2004. "A Haitian Village Gets a Barrage of Care." *New York Times,* May 31.

Weiner, Tim, and Lydia Polgreen. 2004. "Grief as Haitians and Dominicans Tally Flood Toll." *New York Times,* May 28.

Weizman Eyal. 2011. *The Least of All Possible Evils: Humanitarian Violence from Arendt to Gaza.* New York: Verso.

———. 2017. *Forensic Architecture: Violence at the Threshold of Detectability.* New York: Zone Books.

Willen, Sarah S. 2007. "Toward a Critical Phenomenology of 'Illegality': State Power, Criminalization, and Abjectivity among Undocumented Migrant Workers in Tel Aviv, Israel." *International Migration* 45:8–36.

———. 2014. "Plotting a Moral Trajectory, *Sans Papiers:* Outlaw Motherhood as Inhabitable Space of Welcome." *Ethos* 42(1): 84–100.

Williams, Bernard. 1985. *Ethics and the Limits of Philosophy.* Cambridge, MA: Harvard University Press.

Williams, Raymond. 1973. *The Country and the City.* New York: Oxford University Press.

———. 1977. *Marxism and Literature.* New York: Oxford University Press.

Wilson, Peter J. 1973. *Crab Antics: The Social Anthropology of English Speaking Negro Societies of the Caribbean.* New Haven, CT: Yale University Press.

Wingfield, Roland, and Vernon J. Parenton. 1965. "Class Structures and Class Conflict in Haitian Society." *Social Forces* 43(3): 338–347.

Wolf, Eric. 1972. "Ownership and Political Ecology." *Anthropological Quarterly* 45:201–205.

Woodson, Drexel. 1990. "Tout Moun Se Moun Men tout Moun Pa Menm: Microlevel Sociocultural Aspects of Land Tenure in a Northern Haitian Locality." PhD diss., University of Chicago.

————. 1997. "Lanmanjay, Food Security, Sécurité Alimentaire: A Lesson in Communication from BARA's Mixed-Methods Approach to Baseline Research in Haiti, 1994–1996." *Culture & Agriculture* 19(3):108–122.

Zigon, Jarrett. 2007. "Moral Breakdown and Ethical Demand." *Anthropological Theory* 7:131–150.

Zimmerman, T. 1986. "Agroforestry: A Last Hope for Conservation in Haiti?" *Agroforestry Systems* 4: 255–268.

Zuvekas, C. 1979. "Land Tenure in Haiti and Its Policy Implications: A Survey of the Literature." *Social and Economic Studies* 28:1–30.

Index

displacement *(continued)*
224–227, 229–230, 234, 237, 258n6; of peasantry class, 246n1; from storms, 207–208, 210–211. *See also* natural disasters
Doctors Without Borders, 224
dogs, 85, 228–229
Dominican Republic: border, 43, 177, 201, 221; botanical project and, 41, 42; displaced Haitians in, 208, 237; military training in, 76, 131, 145; natural disasters in, 207
dreams, 201
drug trade, 87–89, 91, 177, 183, 187, 248n24
Dunham, Katherine: affiliations and relationships of, 3–4, 37–38; on Aristide, 129; death of, 165, 261n1; forest estate of, 33–38, 235, 249n14; *Island Possessed*, 241n5; on treasure hunting, 243n2; Vodou and, 3–4, 116–117, 241n5. *See also* Habitation Leclerc
DuPres, Abel, 54–55, 60–62, 155
Duvalier, François, 67, 91, 109, 150
Duvalier, Jean-Claude: on Cascade Pichon, 202; economic policies of, 72, 233; environmental policies of, 24, 51; makout of, 90–91; totalitarian regime of, 120, 249n4, 253n17

Earth-Mother spirits, 116–117
earthquake (2010): death statistics of, 194–195, 259n23; displacement from, 193–194, 217, 218, 224–227, 229–230; economic opportunities from, 196, 215–216, 218, 231–232; event descriptions of, 194–195, 211–212; Inter-American Development Bank on, 257n4; monument for, 235; physical damage from, 193–194, 197–199, 213–214, 227fig.; relief operations after, 195–196, 223–224, 230; rubble removal from, 215, 230, 260n29; terms for, 212–213
economic development, 39–40, 72, 233

economy, informal and formal: charcoal business, 23, 24, 36, 37, 41, 66, 201, 204; coffee industry, 1, 110, 203, 204, 207; drug trade, 87–89, 91, 177, 183, 187, 248n24; garment factories, 6, 67, 75, 196, 233; inflation and, 101–104, 248n30; logging industry, 40, 201, 204, 206–207; shift to wage-labor, 5–6, 52, 65–66, 245n33, 246n1; terms for, 247n10, 247n11; tourism, 67–72, 97, 161–162, 189, 202–203; wages in, 103–104. *See also* social networks and relations; work opportunities
ecotourism, 44
electrical shocks, 167, 199
Electricité d'Haïti (EdH), 255n29
electricity. *See* blackouts *(blakawout)*
ensekirite (term), 79, 156–157. *See also* terror and insecurity
environmental crisis: deforestation, 24, 43–44, 201, 243n9, 244n26; development methods for, 39–41; Duvalier's policies and, 24; erosion, 1, 21, 24, 31, 36, 160, 200; flooding-drought cycles, 209–210; Luc on, 20–21, 23–25, 28; political ecology, 23–24, 30, 243n9. *See also* forest; natural disasters
Erikson, Kai, 215
erosion, 1, 21, 24, 31, 36, 160, 200. *See also* deforestation; environmental crisis
Eternal Flame monument, 191fig., 192. *See also* Nèg Mawon statue
ethnography, 10–11, 74. *See also* anthropology; storytelling

family obligations, 67, 84, 247n10, 258n11. *See also* social networks and relations
Fanmi Lavalas party, 52, 134, 172. *See also* Aristide, Jean-Bertrand; Lavalas movement
Farmer, Paul, 217, 242n14
Félix, 183–184, 257n51
fè pratik, 80–85, 97–98, 231. *See also* social networks and relations